# A LIFE OF

# Matthew G. Lewis

# A LIFE OF
# Matthew G. Lewis

BY

LOUIS F. PECK

HARVARD UNIVERSITY PRESS

Cambridge, Massachusetts

1 9 6 1

PR
4888
P4

Distributed in Great Britain by Oxford University Press, London

Publication of this book has been aided by a grant from the Ford Foundation

Library of Congress Catalog Card Number 61–11027

Printed in the United States of America

# PREFACE

BY HIS notorious Gothic romance *The Monk*, written when he was nineteen, Matthew Gregory Lewis—"Monk" Lewis—has won himself a place in nearly every history of English literature. Biographical notices of him usually record also that he was a friend of Walter Scott, published a collection of ballads called *Tales of Wonder*, wrote the absurd and highly successful melodrama *The Castle Spectre*, translated parts of Goethe's *Faust* to Lord Byron, told ghost stories to the Shelleys at Diodati, visited the West Indies to improve the condition of his slaves, and died at sea on the way home. These often-repeated facts are perhaps sufficient to satisfy the curiosity a general reader may feel concerning the author of *The Monk*, and for a long time they satisfied scholarship too. In recent years, however, Lewis has received increasing attention from students of the Romantic movement, who recognize him as an important figure not only among the Gothic writers of the period but in the realm of comparative literature as well. Yet the only full-length biography of this author, which appeared twenty-one years after his death, was considered inadequate even in its own day, and scholars have frequently pointed out the need for a more reliable account of Lewis and his writings. The present book attempts to supply that need.

The original biography, the two-volume *Life and Correspondence of M. G. Lewis, Author of "The Monk," "The Castle Spectre," &c. with Many Pieces in Prose and Verse, Never Before Published* (London, 1839), appeared anonymously, but the author, Mrs. Cornwall Baron-Wilson, named the work as hers on the title page of a later publication (*Our Actresses; or, Glances at Stage Favourites, Past and Present*, London, 1844). A biography of Lewis, who had died in 1818, had long been needed to dispel his early reputation as an immoral and blasphemous author. In 1839, moreover, it was still not too late to preserve anecdotes and biographical details which otherwise inevitably would have been lost, and his letters presented him in a new and favorable light. All this may be said in grateful acknowledgment to the author of the *Life*.

At the same time, criticism has often been directed against the biography. What could have been written in one volume was padded out to fill two, and in the effort to restore Lewis to the esteem of mankind the author went perhaps too far in presenting her subject as an altogether lovable figure. Concerning his writings, many of which she seems not to have read, there are numerous errors of fact, whatever one may think of the critical judgments in the book. The greatest value of the *Life* has always been that it reproduced some eighty letters by Lewis; but here again there are grounds for dissatisfaction, since present-day editorial standards permit considerably less freedom in transcribing manuscripts than Lewis' biographer enjoyed. Scholars have complained that the dates of some of the letters must certainly be wrong and have questioned the reliability of the texts—indeed, it could have been pointed out that the work presents its own certification of inaccuracy by quoting a letter at one point and again later with differences in wording. These suspicions are amply confirmed by a comparison of the originals of about sixty of the letters with their published texts. The dates of some are overlooked, suppressed, or arbitrarily altered in the biography; one letter is divided and presented as two written in different years; two others are combined into one; and numerous passages are deleted, sometimes with, more often without, any indication of omission. In reproducing one text from a mutilated manuscript, the biographer silently filled in the lacunae with plausible readings for half a page, then through weariness or caprice abandoned the effort and brought the letter to a sudden close. There are also, of course, small verbal changes in the interests of decorum in both the letters and the fragments of Lewis' writings included in the *Life*: for instance, "sensual" is softened to "shameful"; "vices," "bed-gown," and "petticoats" become, respectively, "disagreeables," "dressing-gown," and "dress." While it must be said that none of the verbal alterations, inadvertent or deliberate, are of great consequence, it is still true that hardly a sentence in the manuscripts available for the present study is reproduced in the *Life* exactly as it was written.

Since the publication of the biography, sources of information concerning Lewis have accumulated which were not available in 1839. Many diaries, memoirs, and volumes of correspondence of his contemporaries published over the last hundred and twenty years contain references to him; newly discovered letters by Lewis himself have from time to time found their way into print; and a number of specialized studies concerned with one or several of his works have appeared. Meanwhile, the *Life* has remained the basis of all later accounts. Three of these may be mentioned here as being more substantial than the usual notices in literary histories. That they are, in order of publication, some ten, twenty, and forty thousand words in length suggests roughly the rate at which interest in Lewis has grown. In 1906 a biographical sketch, anonymous but attributed to Francis Reginald Statham, served as the introduction to an edition of Lewis' romance *The Monk* (Gibbings and Co., London). This sympathetic, if often inaccurate, account turned to several sources of information in addition to the *Life* and has been republished more than once. In 1927 there appeared Eino Railo's *The Haunted Castle* (London), a book in which the author originally intended to treat Lewis as the central figure. Railo's interest admittedly became diverted to wider aspects of the Romantic period, however, and Lewis was relegated to a single chapter. Valuable as the book is in its analysis of certain aspects of Romanticism, the broad scope of the study precluded a detailed examination of Lewis' works, and the writer's contempt for their author sometimes led to errors which give a false impression of Lewis as an individual. In Montague Summers' *The Gothic Quest* (London, 1938), Lewis was again granted a chapter to himself, a chapter which on literary matters is often useful, sometimes bewildering, in its compilation of details. For biographical information it relies, as usual, largely upon Mrs. Baron-Wilson, though frequent speculations are added with such assurance that they are difficult to separate from facts.

In view of shortcomings in the original biography, the accumulation of new material, and the growing interest in Lewis, a new account of this author seems justified. Since his writings are for the most part important not in themselves but for their influence upon later writers or as indications of literary tendencies, the facts of composition, publication, and even content have under-

standably been slighted in treatments of Lewis. The present study
eschews broad literary considerations in favor of an account of
the output of one man, who remains the focal point throughout.
It assumes that most readers have at some time read Lewis' *The
Monk* but have not read and will not read many of his other
writings. On the biographical side, it attempts to present a more
objective and accurate account of Lewis than is found in the
*Life*. Perhaps it violates a principle of much modern biography
in having been undertaken with no preconceived interpretation of
its subject and in failing to discover him to be infinitely more
important and exciting than he has been supposed; but, having
no talent for fiction, I have tried to tell only what Lewis did and
what his contemporaries thought of him. If he emerges from
these pages looking, on the whole, rather well, he may thank
himself.

For my part, I must thank several institutions and individuals
for help with this book. Harvard University granted me a Dexter
Scholarship for research in England; and from the Pennsylvania
State University I received three grants from the Central Research
Fund and, in 1959, an appointment as Research Scholar in the
College of Liberal Arts. A principal source of pleasure, always, in
pursuing work of this sort is the opportunity and necessity of
working at great libraries and accepting the help of the intelligent
people who staff them. In this respect my heaviest debts are to
the Harvard College Library, the British Museum Library, the
Victoria and Albert Museum in South Kensington, the Henry
E. Huntington Library, and the Yale University Library. For per-
mission to publish manuscript material, elsewhere specified, I
thank the following: the British Museum, the Goethe- und
Schiller-Archiv in Weimar, the Harvard College Library, the
Henry E. Huntington Library, the Institute of Jamaica in
Kingston, B. W. I., the University of Kansas Library, the National
Library of Scotland, the National Library of Wales, Dean Julian
Park of the University of Buffalo, the Pierpont Morgan Library,
the Victoria and Albert Museum, and the Yale University Library.
I am grateful to the following officials for having photostats made
and sent: Miss Mary A. Brebner (Institute of Jamaica), Mr. Her-
bert Cahoon (Pierpont Morgan Library), Mr. James S. Ritchie
(National Library of Scotland), Mr. Joseph Rubinstein (Uni-

versity of Kansas Library), and Mr. Arthur Wheen (Victoria and Albert Museum). To four of my colleagues at the Pennsylvania State University I owe thanks for helpful suggestions: Professors Arthur O. Lewis, Jr., Robert R. Reed, Jr., and Philip A. Shelley, each of whom read portions of this work in manuscript, and Professor Henry W. Sams, who read the whole. The book has profited inestimably, in the course of copyediting, from the critical comments of Mrs. Joyce Lebowitz of Harvard University Press. Other debts are acknowledged in the notes.

My curiosity concerning Lewis was awakened many years ago when I listened to lectures on the English Romantic poets by the late Professor John Livingston Lowes of Harvard University, who gave me generous advice and encouragement in the early stages of my research. It was appropriate that his lectures should stimulate my interest in a Gothic author: they were often akin to Gothic thunderstorms—less for the thunder, however, than for the flashes of sudden light.

November 1960

L. F. P.

# CONTENTS

# ILLUSTRATIONS

# A LIFE OF
# Matthew G. Lewis

# 1 ✍

## EARLY YEARS

The sentimental portrait of Matthew Gregory Lewis' mother presented in the *Life and Correspondence*, though it carefully avoids some details, is justifiably full, because there was a close sympathy between Matthew and his mother and because it was from her that he derived his imaginative, artistic traits. Of Lewis' other parent little is said, but a prominent side of Matthew's character—his respect for principle, his good judgment, his ability always to distinguish what was frivolous from what was important—reflects his father's influence. For these reasons a few additional facts concerning the elder Lewis will aid in an understanding of Matthew.

Matthew Lewis, the father of Matthew Gregory Lewis, was born in Jamaica in 1750, the son of William Lewis of Jamaica and Jane Gregory, eldest daughter of Dr. Matthew Gregory. Matthew Lewis had three sisters and a brother; one sister married Lieutenant-General Whitelock, another Sir Robert Brownrigg who later became a general, and the third a West India planter named Blake. The brother, John Lewis, served as Chief Justice of Jamaica. There are records also of the family's earlier connections with Jamaica.[1] Matthew Lewis attended Westminster School and Christ Church, Oxford, where he took his bachelor's degree in 1769 and his master's in 1772.[2] In the same month, on the recommendation of William Wildman, second Viscount Barrington, the Secretary at War, he was appointed Chief Clerk in the War Office with authority over three principal and five subordinate clerks.[3] When in December 1775 he took over as well the office of Deputy-Secretary at War, again by Lord Barrington's appointment, he became with one exception the first person ever to hold both offices at once.[4] Although his two salaries were fixed, the work was remunerative in fees, a source of income which greatly increased during war years. His total income for the first ten years averaged £1,955 a year; for the next fifteen, from 1782 to 1796, it averaged £5,393; in 1796 he received £18,238.[5] The fees paid in to the War Office became a subject of public controversy in 1797 and were abolished. At the same time Mr. Lewis' two salaries were increased, quite justly, it seems, since the positions for which he received them were by no means sinecures. In a report to his superiors in 1797 he points out that the sums he has received are "the Pay of double Duty, of double responsibility, and of far more unremitting personal attend-ance than if the Offices had continued in separate hands." He states that between November 1792 and the end of July 1796, nearly four years, he never missed a day's attendance at the War Office except for reasons of serious illness, nor had he dined or slept outside London more than three times in any one of those years.[6]

His son's biographer says of the elder Lewis: "At a very early age he entered the War Office, and by his great talents, and almost unexampled assiduity, he rose at length to the honourable post of Deputy-Secretary at War" and asserts that his first rise in the world was entirely the result of his own exertions, a circumstance which, "no doubt, much contributed to steel, as it were, his character, and to add a degree of sternness to its natural inflexibil-ity."[7] We may grant that twenty-two is a very early age at which to assume a responsible government position, and there is no doubt that he worked hard and faithfully, but the phrase "great talents" seems an amiable exaggeration. If by his first rise in the world is meant his War Office appointments, they were handed to him by Lord Barrington; during his remaining twenty-eight years at the Office he received no official advancement, and the increase in his income was fortuitous. One gains the impression from Mr. Lewis' letters that he was reserved and formal in manner but kindhearted and not entirely without humor. His son Matthew in later years described him as "one of the most humane and generous persons that ever existed."[8] He was a dependable and judicious deputy under seven Secretaries at War, and by at least one of them—Charles Jenkinson, who became first Earl of Liverpool and was said to enjoy immense influence at court—was cherished as a friend.

Mr. Lewis owned considerable property in Jamaica, the principal estate lying within four miles of Savanna la Mer, in the Parish of Westmorland, the works on which had been finished about 1765 at a cost of over £25,000. Such West India investments were hazardous. After a hurricane and earthquake which shook Jamaica in 1779, when the sea burst over Savanna la Mer and flowed inland half a mile to the perpendicular depth of ten feet, Mr. Lewis' loss was estimated at £20,000. "All our Buildings of every kind," he wrote, "are demolished—the only Walls left in the Parish of Westmorland are *our Cellars*, in which a *young* Sister of mine & her two Infants, who were thrown out of the Window of their own House, in the moment of it's Demolition, were glad to take Shelter for four days & Nights. We have, notwithstanding, suffered less upon the whole than our Neighbours—have lost only eight Negroes, while others have lost the whole." A similar though less costly disaster occurred the following year.[9]

About a year after entering the War Office, Mr. Lewis married Frances Maria Sewell, third daughter of Sir Thomas Sewell, Master of the Rolls from 1764 to 1784. The Lewis and Sewell properties adjoined, and, like the Lewis family, the Sewells were associated with Jamaica. Frances Maria's mother was buried in Spanish Town and her brother Robert was Attorney General of Jamaica at his death.[10] One of eight children of Sir Thomas' first marriage, Frances Maria spent her childhood at Ottershaw, her father's estate, where, as the *Life* exquisitely puts it, "she grew up as blooming and artless as the simplest wild rose that smiled beneath the forest shade of the domain."[11] According to that authority, she was a handsome girl, talented musically, and for her graceful dancing became immediately popular when introduced at court. She married young, and, as it proved, was not temperamentally suited to be the wife of Matthew Lewis.

Four children were born, Matthew Gregory, the oldest, on July 9, 1775; Maria, Barrington, and Sophia Elizabeth followed in that order.[12] Matthew's early letters give occasional glimpses of their childhood. At the age of sixteen he wrote to his mother, then in France: "My Sisters are perfectly well. Sophy is wonderfully pretty, but very little. She is so childish, so heedless, so inattentive, that she provokes every body; and when any body talks to her, she will cry vehemently and play with the Cat's tail all the while. She dances very prettily, has a very good ear for musick, and a charming voice. in short She may do very well if She will. Maria improves every day; She is a charming and interesting Girl. She plays really finely, and her understanding is infinitely superior to Girls of her age. She is very tall, and has a very fine figure. She has quite outgrown me, I promise to be a remarkably little personage."[13]

Mrs. Lewis was fond of surrounding herself with gay company, and her soirées became well known to musical, theatrical, and literary people. At an early age her son Matthew acquired his appetite for such entertainment. She herself had literary inclinations, though from Matthew's letters her tastes appear to have been more miscellaneous than promising: "I have just read the Excursion," Matthew writes to her, naming a now forgotten novel by Mrs. Frances (Moore) Brooke, "and could not help fancying it was just the kind of Book you would have writte[n,] the style was so like your common language" (F 8). Recommending his own translation of Schiller's *Kabale und Liebe*, he says "I am sure you will like it, for both the Characters, incidents and style of the whole play seems exactly adapted to your Taste" (F 20); and again, "Have you read Cowper's 'Task'? . . . If not, read it; It will suit your taste exactly . . ." (F 38). Joseph Glanvil's book on witchcraft, we are told, was a favorite work "among the subjects of her more serious attention."[14] Mrs. Lewis collaborated with Matthew in his early literary attempts and once wrote a novel which only his eloquent dissuasion saved from publication.

Anecdotes of his childhood present Matthew as affectionate, precocious, and spoiled, inclined to imitate the gravity and sophistication of his elders, always ready with opinions on matters literary or musical, and given to moods of deep detachment. He delighted to dress himself in whatever of his mother's jewelry and gaudy clothing he could find and parade before her mirror, a foreshadowing, perhaps, of the lavish display of costume in some of his melodramas. From the first he had a lively interest in drama. Upon returning from the theater one evening, he surprised his mother by repeating nearly the whole of Mrs. Bellamy's celebrated scene in *Cleone*, imitating the actress' shriek with "thrilling accuracy," and later, as a schoolboy home for the holidays, he often entertained his mother's guests with dramatic recitations.

Some of his childhood was spent at Stanstead Hall, the nearby home of relatives on his mother's side. Writing to Walter Scott the year following Matthew's death, his sister Sophia described it as "a fine *old* Mansion" and said, "I have heard my Brother say that when a child he imbibed his first taste for Romance, from the terrible stories of an old Nurse who used to gain much of his attention" when he was visiting Stanstead.[15] One room of the mansion was said to be haunted, a circumstance which later impressed itself upon his writings: "In maturer years, Lewis has frequently been heard to declare, that at night, when he was conducted past that gloomy chamber, on the way to his dormitory, he would cast a glance of terror over his shoulder, expecting to see the huge and strangely-carved folding-doors fly open, and disclose some of those fearful shapes that afterwards resolved themselves into the ghastly machinery of his works. To such juvenile feelings he ascribed some of the most striking scenes in 'The Castle Spectre.' "[16] Indeed, in the stage directions of three or four of his melodramas there are folding doors or large painted windows which can—and they all do —burst open to reveal some frightful apparition, and the large hall at Stanstead was, according to Sophia, exactly described in *The Monk* under the name of the "Hall in Lindenberg Castle."[17]

Matthew's formal education began at Marylebone Seminary, a preparatory school of the Reverend Dr. John Fountain, Dean of York, a friend of the Lewis and Sewell families. The students were largely of the nobility and gentry. George Colman the younger, who attended Marylebone a few years before Lewis matriculated, described it as a fashionable steppingstone to Westminster and other public schools of the first order. The curriculum included Latin, Greek, French, writing, arithmetic, drawing, dancing, and fencing; the boys were allowed to converse only in French throughout the day. Dr. Fountain, a "worthy good-natured *Domine*, in a bush wig," was an indulgent master whose pupils, according to Colman, were not obliged to learn anything.[18] From the seminary Matthew at the age of eight proceeded inevitably to Westminster School, which his father had attended.[19] Of his life there we know only that he particularly distinguished himself as an actor in the Town Boys' Play, taking the part of Falconbridge in *King John* and of My Lord Duke in *High Life Below Stairs*.[20]

While Matthew was still at Westminster his parents separated. The biography, no doubt wisely, glosses over the matter with these words: "That the tempers of Mr. and Mrs. Lewis were incompat-

ible with their mutual happiness, there can be no doubt. The one
was all gentleness and complacency, even to a fault, and was greatly
admired and sought after; the other, on the contrary, although firm
in his friendships, was yet stern in his purposes, and implacable in
his resentments. Misunderstandings and jealousies, therefore,
arose."[21] Toward the end of volume one, however, we read of
Matthew's mother that the "history of her former errors was almost
unknown, or at least fast becoming forgotten,"[22] and the son's published letters, though they give no details of the affair except to say
that at the time of the separation Mr. Lewis' anxiety was "perfect
phrenzy," nevertheless contain two passages which point in the
direction of that "gentleness and complacency, even to a fault"
conceded by the biography: "I conceive your heart to be so good,
your mind so enlightened that I am astonished that you could be
led into those errors, when the strength of your understanding must
have shown to you the calamities you were bringing upon yourself"
(F 26), and again, "those who alone know you by report, can only
know that you formerly took a step in defiance of the declared
principles of society" (F 42).

If the truth is preferable to a lingering, half-veiled scandal, a brief
account of the facts may be given here, though they are unpleasant
and rather pathetic. The Lewises were said to have lived together
happily at first, but about July 1781 differences arose between them
and Mrs. Lewis left her husband on July 23. Matthew, the oldest
child, was then six, his sister Sophia, the youngest, less than a year
and a half. Mrs. Lewis took a lover—a music master named Harrison[23]—and frequently changed her address in order to avoid her
husband. In July 1782 she was lodging in Brompton, Yorkshire.
From here she sent a servant to Arundel, West Sussex, to receive
letters from Mr. Lewis, who supposed her to be there, and to send
her answers from the same town so that the postmark would conceal her true address. She lived at Brompton under the pseudonym
of Langley, and, having engaged a doctor other than the one who
had formerly attended her, gave birth to a child on July 3, 1782.
Mr. Lewis, having discovered the truth, dramatically arrived at
Brompton on the same day. A servant went down on her knees and
dissuaded him from entering Mrs. Lewis' room, but he insisted
upon having his wife's letters and papers. These included a letter
which Mrs. Lewis had written to her husband, to be delivered in

case of her death, and which she now instructed to be given to him anyway.[24]

Mr. Lewis' superior at the War Office wrote to his deputy on July 27 of this year: "I am sorry to hear of the disagreeable Scenes in which you have for some time been engaged; I hope however that you will soon get rid of a Connection which has long been a Torment to you."[25] Mr. Lewis took steps to do so. On February 27, 1783, he obtained in the Consistory Court of the Bishop of London a judgment against his wife for adultery and on April 4 petitioned the House of Lords for permission to bring in a bill of divorce. Permission was granted on that date and the bill was read for the first time. A copy was served Mrs. Lewis on April 10. Apparently she did not see fit to oppose it, because at the second reading, scheduled for April 28 but put off until May 6, no counsel to present her case appeared before the House of Lords. Mr. Lewis' counsel produced ten witnesses who testified to the details summarized above. He also offered as evidence the already mentioned letter by Mrs. Lewis; but the Lords, after debate, voted not to hear it. The bill of divorce was then voted upon. It was rejected, and Mr. and Mrs. Lewis remained officially married for life.

The sex of the illegitimate child is not given in the record— merely the fact that one witness saw it a fortnight after birth.[26] While there is no proof, it seems reasonable to conclude that this child is to be identified with the "Miss Lacey" mentioned frequently in Matthew's and his mother's letters, whom Mrs. Lewis was so solicitous to establish in life and to whom in her will she left everything she owned.

The family circle was permanently broken. Mrs. Lewis, obliged to withdraw from society, retreated for a time to France, then took various lodgings in London and later lived in retirement in a cottage at Leatherhead. Mr. Lewis bought a house in Devonshire Place, where he remained ever after. Here the daughters probably lived until they married, as did Barrington until his death in 1800. When Matthew left Oxford, it became his home until he leased a cottage in Barnes, whence he moved to quarters in the Albany in Piccadilly.

This family affair placed Matthew for years in the awkward position, which he assumed with great tact and common sense, of intermediary between his parents, both of whom he loved. Some ten years after the separation, when Mrs. Lewis entertained the idea of reuniting with her husband, a move which Matthew was obliged to oppose as harmful to his unmarried sisters, he exclaims: "You have put me into the most distressing and embarrassing situation in the world; you have made me almost an umpire between my Parents; I know not how to extricate myself from the difficulty; I can only believe neither of you to be in the wrong, but I am not to determine which is in the right" (F 26). From certain of Matthew's letters Mrs. Lewis emerges as a person easily wounded and lacking in judgment. Though she received an allowance—by all accounts a generous one—from her husband, she was often in need of money, a want Matthew relieved as best he could: "the little presents I have occasionally made you have been merely what I have either spared from my pocket money or by fortunate success at play (which however I use but seldom) and have been enabled to dispose of in the manner which was most agreable to me" (F 7). Despite sincere if sometimes effusively expressed affection for Mrs. Lewis, he never spoke unjustly of his father, whom he felt to be in the right. He even gently reproaches his mother in the tone of an aggrieved parent: "I cannot help recollecting the pain and anxiety you have occasioned to my dear my worthy Father, and that it is owing to your conduct that my Sisters are deprived of maternal care and attention, and, of receiving the benefits of those little instructions and observations, so necessary to make young Women accomplished, and which are in the power of a Mother alone to point out to them with success" (F 25). Permanent too was the fear of reawakening the family scandal. "As to what you say about my calling myself your Nephew, do about it as you think proper. . . . When I do not say that I have a Mother living I do it to give the shortest answer and save myself from an explanation which must be very unpleasant to me" (F 60).

With Westminster behind him, Matthew, still following his father's example, entered Christ Church on April 27, 1790, aged fifteen,[27] equipped with a smattering of polite studies and a better-than-average foundation in Greek and Latin. Colman notes that at Oxford "much courtesy is shown, in the ceremony of matriculation, to the boys who come from Eton and Westminster; insomuch, that they are never examined in respect to their knowledge of the School Classicks;—their competency is consider'd as a matter of course."[28] Of Matthew's life at Christ Church, then under the deanery of the

Reverend Cyril Jackson, long a friend of the Lewis family,[29] there is little information, except that he read verses of his own at the Oxford Encaenia and took his degree in the usual four years.[30] Although an inquisitive reader all his life, he was never a scholar. His published letters from Oxford offer only one fleeting reference to studies: "here have I run on to you, whilst I ought to have been crossing the Hellespont with Xerxes, or attending to the pleadings of Cicero" (F 1). His attendance at the university, interspersed with visits to London and Chatham, was appropriately casual, and before graduating he had been to the Continent twice.

The summer vacation of 1791 he spent in Paris. Since his one surviving letter from Paris tells nothing of his experiences there, one can only speculate to what extent his sentiments are reflected in those he later assigned to Don Raymond in *The Monk*:

Paris was my first station. For some time I was enchanted with it, as indeed must be every man who is young, rich, and fond of pleasure. Yet, among all its gaieties, I felt that something was wanting to my heart: I grew sick of dissipation: I discovered that the people among whom I lived, and whose exterior was so polished and seducing, were at bottom frivolous, unfeeling, and insincere. I turned from the inhabitants of Paris with disgust, and quitted that theatre of luxury without heaving one sigh of regret.[31]

Matthew familiarized himself with the French drama of the day and probably with German *Sturm und Drang* productions, many of which had been translated into French. His chief concern in Paris was writing, in which he showed remarkable industry. By the beginning of September he had completed and sent his mother a farce called *The Epistolary Intrigue*, intended for Drury Lane, the principal role being designed for Mrs. Jordan. It was refused at both Drury Lane and Covent Garden and appears to be lost. He also sent his mother songs he had composed for a dramatic piece that she was writing, and reported the composition of two volumes of a novel which he expected to complete before leaving Paris. A fragment of this work was reproduced in the *Life* with numerous small changes by the editor.[32] *The Effusions of Sensibility; or Letters from Lady Honorina Harrow-heart to Miss Sophonisba Simper—a Pathetic Novel in the Modern Taste. Being the First Literary Attempt of a Young Lady of Tender Feelings* is a burlesque in epistolary form of the cult of sensibility. Although precociously shrewd in its appreciation of feminine vanity and social foible, it relies for humor principally upon extravagant periphrases and crude comic incident. A reader will not regret that only thirty pages of the manuscript survive.

Returning to Oxford, he continued literary activities, now with the added incentive of supplying his mother with funds. His letters of this period bristle with projects. He is not discouraged by the refusal of the farce. In March 1792 he is finishing a translation of *Felix*, a French opera, for his mother to offer Drury Lane and mentions "two or three other things for you to try your fortune with" (F 6). He knows "at least twenty French Operas which if Translated would undoubtedly succeed" (F 6). It is worth noting that he expresses surprise at Kemble's refusing "the most interesting production of that kind," *Blue Beard*, and to recollect that this piece was exceedingly popular at Drury Lane a few years later. He refers to Benoît Joseph Marsollier's *Camille ou Le Souterrain* and Jacques Marie Boutet de Monvel's *Les Victimes Cloîtrées* as promising pieces for translation but says "I shall not throw away any more time till I have got one of the things I have already finished upon the Stage" (F 6).[33] In a later letter we read, "I have begun something which I hope and am inde[ed] certain will hereafter produce you a little money though it will be some time before it is compleated from the length of it and the frequent interruption and necessity of concealment I am obliged to use in writing it. It is a Roma[nce] in the style of the Castle of Otranto" (F 8). Of this reference his biographer wrote, "The romance here spoken of was, like the novel formerly alluded to, never published; but he subsequently founded upon it his popular drama of 'The Castle Spectre.' "[34] This statement has been accepted as final but will bear further discussion in connection with the writing of *The Monk*.

By 1792 Lewis had also completed his comedy, *The East Indian*, performed at Drury Lane seven years afterward. Though composed largely from the work of others, it is a remarkable accomplishment for a sixteen-year-old author. A careful reading of his letters will show that it is not, as has sometimes been thought,[35] a reworking of the earlier *Epistolary Intrigue*. The composition of *Village Virtues, a Dramatic Satire*, published in 1796, probably belongs to this period also. Ghosts, robbers, and theatrical wonders were presently to lure him from an early ambition to be the witty censor of society into Gothic realms where he excelled as he never could have in the field of satire.

Since his father wished him to take up a diplomatic career, Lewis was sent in the summer of 1792 to Germany to learn the language. After a passage, memorable only for seasickness, from Harwich to Helvoet, he reached Weimar on July 27, 1792, in high good humor to judge from his first letter: "As I know my dear Mother, you must be anxious to hear that I have escaped all sorts of perils and dangers, both by land and by water, women labouring with Child, all sick Persons and young Children, I take the very earliest opportunity of letting you be ascertained that I arrived safe at Weimer three days ago" (F 11). The capital of Saxe-Weimar-Eisenach under the Duke Karl August was then in its golden age, a center for the drama, music, and art of Germany. At the time of Lewis' visit, however, the spirit of the town was somewhat dampened by impending war with the French revolutionists. Austria, Prussia, and Russia had formed an alliance the year before, and the Duchy of Weimar was subject to a levy of troops and to the expense of sustaining Prussian battalions.[36] Many of the socially promient had withdrawn to country houses or were at Coblenz with the Duke, who had left Weimar for military duty shortly before Lewis arrived.

The quarters Matthew engaged at Weimar were haunted, or so, it is reported, he explained to Byron in later years. He was awakened every morning by the rustling of papers in a closet adjoining his room but never found anyone there. The servant of the house explained that this phenomenon was occasioned by the ghost of the former owner, a mother who every day at the hour of her death had continued to search frantically the closet filled with foreign newspapers for news of her only son, who had been lost at sea.[37]

Matthew, to whom languages came easily, attacked his new task with enthusiasm: "I am knocking my brains against German as hard as ever I can: I take a lesson every morning; and as I apply very seriously, am flattered with the promises that I shall soon speak very fluently in my throat, and that I already distort my mouth with extremely tolerable facility" (F 11). He boarded at the house of Karl August Böttiger, then rector of the gymnasium at Weimar and a friend of Andrew Dalzel, professor of Greek at the University of Edinburgh. In a letter of July 24, 1793, Böttiger remarked to Dalzel that German is not hard to master: "A striking instance of this assertion has been the young gentleman by whom you have had my last letter, Mr. Lewis of London, who has boarded in my house, and, by dint of but an indifferent application to our language, within a few months has brought himself up to understand the most difficult poets, and has begun a translation of 'Wieland's Oberon,' in stanzas, which I suppose he will soon publish in his country."[38]

Social diversions vied with linguistic and literary interests. In Weimar, where Lewis could enjoy the excitement of associating with nobility, one sees his developing taste for élite society: "I must tell you that my situation is very pleasant here. Nothing can be more polite than the people belonging to the Court; the two Duchesses are extremely affable, and condescending; and we have nothing but balls, suppers and Concerts" (F 14). In some ways life was less civilized than he could wish: "for instance the Knives and Forks are never changed, even at the Duke's table, and the Ladies hawk and spit about the rooms, in a manner the most disgusting: but as . . . everybody is extremely obliging, I put up with everything else, and upon the whole amuse myself tolerably well" (F 16). On a short visit to Berlin he was "perfectly astonished at the crowds of Princes, and Princesses, Dukes, and Duchesses, which were poured upon me from every quarter. It put me in mind of Foote's observation upon France, that 'every mangy Dog he met, was either Duke, or Marquis.' I was at one Court or other to Supper every night, that I passed in Berlin; and I verily believe it would be possible to stay a year in that Town, and sup with a new Highness at least six days out of every seven" (F 16).

Among those he met at Weimar was Goethe, or as he says, "Mr. de Goethe, the celebrated author of Werter: so that you must not be surprized if I should shoot myself one of these fine Mornings" (F 12). Goethe, who had come to Weimar the year Lewis was born, had been appointed, in the year previous to the latter's visit, director of the ducal theater. To Lewis, the Englishman, he was "the celebrated author of Werter," though Goethe had long since turned from Werterism. They could have had little association, for the German poet left Weimar to join the Duke a few days after Lewis' arrival. Nevertheless, when seven years later Lewis had occasion to write a letter of introduction to him for a young countryman visiting Weimar, he recalled showing Goethe his translation of *Erl-König* and sent grateful remembrances to the Duchess Dowager: "Probably, She has forgotten me; Pray, assure her, that I never shall forget her kind protection of me, while at Weimar; and should any Persons there still honour me with their recollection, beg them to beleive, that I remember the time I past at Weimar with pleasure, & the Friends whom I left there with regret, when I think of the distance between us."[39]

A letter from Lewis to Wieland makes it clear that he met that German author also. When he told the latter that he had put a few stanzas of *Oberon* into English, Wieland asked to see them. Lewis sent him the translation on October 22, 1792, to be considered, he modestly explains, not as worthy, but merely as a mark of his respect for the author of the original.[40]

During his six months on the Continent Lewis' fever for writing still ran high, and he desired more ardently than ever to get something on the stage. He fills his letters with instructions to his mother respecting *The East Indian* and with speculations about Mrs. Jordan's plans. Though he will be satisfied merely with success, perhaps she will insist upon sharing the profits from the play, in which case, "though I should of course at first reject such an offer by a good deal of pressing I *might* be prevailed upon to accept it" (F 18). If *The East Indian* succeeds, he states, *Adelaide* will be next, and doubtless the opera *Felix*. Whatever money the comedy realizes is to be his mother's, though later ventures he hopes will supply spending money for himself—he wants to have his sister Maria's picture well drawn and to give her one of himself. In December he speaks of a little collection of songs he is making for his mother's amusement, apparently all translated from German. A month later the collection has become a volume of poems, partly original, partly translations, which he has no doubt of selling. His translations "have been applauded by the Authors themselves—which is no slight proof of their being tolerable" (F 18). Meanwhile the romance in *Otranto* style proceeds slowly: "I have got hold of an infernal dying Man who plagues my very heart out; He has talked for half a volume already, seems likely to talk for half a volume more" (F 12). Six weeks later he has nearly finished the second volume and has revised the first: "I find the style grows better as I get farther on" (F 14).

What activities he pursued beside dining out and writing remain unrecorded. How many stimulating and distinguished people he met one cannot tell. Nor can it be shown exactly what he derived from the Weimar theater, though he must certainly have learned much from it.[41] But though he may seem to have completed little during his half year in Germany, this visit was of the greatest importance to him. His Weimar experience may be said to have determined his chief role in literary history, that of purveyor of German materials to the English Romantic movement.

Early in 1793 Matthew returned to England and to Oxford. His letter from Christ Church in May mentions the possibility of going abroad again, though he is inclined to believe that he will pass his next three months' vacation in England. His chief concern at the moment is characteristic—he encloses verses which he wishes submitted to a newspaper, and will not "even scruple paying a guinea and a half but not more if the Editor will not put them in for nothing" (F 21). The stanzas are addressed "To C. J. F.— Esq^re on the mention made of the Empress of Russia in the House of Commons by M^r Sheridan on Thursday April the 25^th (F 22). On that date Richard Brinsley Sheridan had pointed out to the House as "proof of the virtuous conduct of Crowned Heads" that the Empress of Russia had been "graciously pleased to annex for ever to the Russian empire, several districts of Poland" and that "the great, the generous, and pious Empress, had stolen a territory, with three millions of inhabitants."[42] In the ensuing debate Charles James Fox rose to characterize the Russian policy toward Poland as "marked with duplicity, falsehood, and robbery."[43] Lewis' squib professes indignation at these slurs—"Would none defend the Spoiler's cause,/And give her lawless deeds applause?"—and abuses Fox with youthful poor taste, ending with the suggestion that both he and Sheridan show genuine patriotism by hanging themselves. Three years later Matthew was to be graciously recognized by Fox in the House of Commons and to become his admirer, and, though throughout his life he felt unfriendliness for Sheridan, at the time he wrote these verses he had probably met neither man. He merely wanted to see something of his own in print. The biography tells us that at this period he frequently sent little *jeux d'esprit* to the daily papers.

In 1793 there occurred one of Matthew's frequent visits with the Scottish nobility. He writes from Bothwell Castle: "I have been passing my time very agreably in Scotland; I like every individual of the family in which I am living. Lady Douglas in particular is the most sensible and entertaining Woman, that I almost ever met with" (F 20). He has met the Duke of Argyll's family and will stay overnight at Dalkeith, a seat of the Duke of Buccleuch. The same letter informs his mother that he has "translated part of the German Tragedy, which you have heard me extoll so highly, and have already made some progress in the fourth Act. So that I have some hopes of being able to finish it" (F 20). The tragedy is Schiller's *Kabale und Liebe*; Lewis' translation was published four years later but waited ten years for stage production.

In the spring of the following year Matthew received his bachelor's degree at Oxford and, still intent upon authorship, accepted with cheerful indifference his father's plan to have him enter diplomatic service. Such a life would at least involve foreign travel and entertaining company. His interest in diplomacy may be measured by the following remark: "It is not decided whether I shall go abroad this summer or not[.] Much will depend upon who is to fill the Embassy which Lord Auckland ha[s] quitted or is on the point of quitting at the Hague. I once thought of Brussells but Lord Elgin is by all accounts a cold unpleasant Man and by no means likely to make the place agreable to me" (F 21). In 1794 his father's influence obtained him a position in the British embassy to Holland. After bidding tearful adieu to his sister Maria, he set out for The Hague, where he arrived on May 15 and was to remain until December.

Matthew's life in Holland is pictured in four letters to his mother, in which he volubly describes his social activities. He brought with him high hopes of entertainment: "I have not as yet been presented at court, but shall be on Monday; After which as I understand, I am to send about my cards to all the principal People in the place, and I shall have immediately as much (if not more), society as I can wish for" (F 32). But the Dutch assemblies proved insufferable, and after two months he was "certain that the Devil Ennui has made The Hague his favourite abode. I have not as yet found a single soul whom I ever wish to see again" (F 35). Moreover, The Hague was expensive, as he explains in a passage deleted in the biography: "My Father allows me £400 a year, and out of this I am actually obliged to Keep House; I stare sometimes to see in the Bills what an immense sum is run up every week for trifles, such as Oil, vinegar, & c, and find it very difficult to live within my income" (F 34).[44] Later, he found congenial company at the salon of Madame de Matignon, daughter of the Baron de Breteuil, where he amused himself in a circle of French aristocracy driven from home by the revolution. "With my pen, my pencil, my Book, my fire, and above all my Dog who is beautiful, I am never weary of solitude: It is only when I go into Dutch company that I am bored. However, with this French cotérie I am never in want of society" (F 37). Of his official duties as attaché to the embassy he has nothing to say, though they apparently included excursions to towns on the edge of the war zone, during one of which a French cannonball brought a shower of tiles about his ears.

His mother continued to act as his literary agent. She arranged for a poem of his to appear piecemeal in magazines, a method of publication which he repudiated: "This is the sure way of not having it taken notice of, and it would steal out of the world in as shabby a manner as it stole in" (F 34). He considered publishing it himself in book form, "if the expense should not be very exorbitant, and if I thought the poem likely to be *read* (for that is at present my only aim)" (F 34). During this time he completed *The Twins,* a farce designed for Bannister's acting, performed five years later at Drury Lane. His most important accomplishment at The Hague—the completion of *The Monk*—shall be reserved for the next chapter.

Lewis returned to London at the end of 1794.[45] In the following year he must have been partly occupied with his two forthcoming publications, *The Monk* and the dramatic satire, *Village Virtues;* the composition of *Adelmorn,* a drama produced in 1801, may also be assigned to 1795.[46] That his plans for the future were not settled becomes clear from his father's letter of this year to William Windham, the Secretary at War:

Dear Sir,

May I, without offense, take the liberty of asking whether it would be agreeable to you to introduce my Son into the War Office in a respectable situation, when it may be done without Charge to the Public, and (if I am not much mistaken as to the sentiments of my fellow Labourers) without creating dissatisfaction among the Clerks. It would be giving me a very useful assistant, particularly in the French Branch of Business; and placing my Son in a lucrative appointment—My pretensions to such a Favour rest solely on the consideration which you may think due to a service of 23 years in a laborious Department, and to which I seem doomed to confine my views for the remainder of my Life.

Your answer, that you would rather not have the proposition brought before you, will be enough to prevent all further trouble, without creating much disappointment; indeed I am not decided that, with your consent, I shall proceed in the Business; thinking as I do, that it may be possible, by addressing Mr Pitt, to get my Son placed in some situation better suited to his ambition than the one I allude to—

I am, Dear Sir,
Your most faithful
humble Servant
M  Lewis.[47]

Lewis' seat in Parliament, obtained in 1796, was in all likelihood the result of the appeal to Pitt which his father here considers.

Up to this point, Matthew's life had been impeccably appropriate to the son of a well-to-do government official. He had been fashionably educated at Marylebone Seminary, Westminster School, and Oxford, had spent a summer in Paris, another in Weimar, and after graduating from the university had received through his father's influence a post in a British embassy. Meanwhile the direction of his interests had become fixed. In his correspondence reflecting these early years, one theme stands out— his determination, even passion, to be a professional writer. The letters are packed with literary projects in every stage of progress— dramas, verses, translations, a romance—and apparently give only a partial glimpse of how much he actually wrote. From the ages of fourteen to twenty-one, as he later explains, he passed his time "scribbling Novels and Plays" and thus had the power "to deluge the town with such an inundation of Ghosts and Magicians, as would satisfy the thirst of the most insatiable swallower of wonders."[48] In 1795, however, he still lived in carefree obscurity, a confident, impatient, and unsuccessful author.

Shortly before Lewis entered the House of Commons, an event occurred which was to have fateful consequences and to be of far greater importance to him than the mere privilege of sharing in the government of the realm. This event was the publication of *The Monk*.

# 2

# THE MONK

On September 23, 1794, Lewis wrote to his mother from The Hague, "What do you think of my having written, in the space of ten weeks, a romance of between three and four hundred pages octavo? I have even written out half of it fair. It is called 'The Monk,' and I am myself so pleased with it, that, if the Booksellers will not buy it, I shall publish it myself."[1] Thus triumphantly he announced the completion of the work destined to win him public notoriety, an enduring nickname, and a minor claim on the memory of posterity.

The same enthusiasm sparkles in his prefatory verses, imitative of Horace's *Epistle 20* and dated 1794 from The Hague. He chides his romance for desiring publication and delivers an affectionate admonition:

> Go then, and pass that dangerous bourn
> Whence never book can back return:
> And when you find, condemned, despised,
> Neglected, blamed, and criticised,
> Abuse from all who read you fall,
> (If haply you be read at all)
> Sorely will you your folly sigh at,
> And wish for me, and home, and quiet.

One senses the excitement and anticipation with which the youthful author gave his book to the world with the final blessing:

> Now then your venturous course pursue:
> Go, my delight! Dear book, adieu!

Four years later, in a rueful footnote in the fourth edition, he was to comment: "Neglected it has not been, but criticised enough of all conscience."

To challenge Lewis' statement that *The Monk* was written in ten weeks may be unkind. Speed of composition adds a kind of extrinsic value to literary work, and possibly a Gothic novel needs all the support it can get. The tendency of a legend to improve with age has even reduced the period in which *The Monk* was written to ten days.[2] Passages in Lewis' letters, however, seem to deny this book the lustre of being a sudden inspiration. Over two years before arriving at The Hague, Lewis wrote from Oxford that he had begun a romance in the style of *The Castle of Otranto* which would not be completed soon. As if unwilling to detract from his later achievement, the biography states that this romance formed no part of *The Monk* but became the basis of *The Castle Spectre*,[3] though there is no reason why it could not have done both. Nine months later Lewis is struggling with what is apparently the same work. It goes slowly; he has "got hold of an infernal dying man who has talked for half a volume already and seems likely to talk for half a volume more." After six weeks he writes: "I have nearly finished my second volume; but I found such faults upon faults, that I have actually almost made it all over again. But I find the style grows better as I get farther on." Then three days after arriving at The Hague: "I have again taken up my Romance, and perhaps by this time Ten years I may make shift to finish it fit for throwing into the fire. I was induced to go on with it by reading 'the Mysteries of Udolpho,' which is in my opinion one of the most interesting Books that ever have been published" (F 12, 14, 33, 37). The "again" seems to link this statement with the Otranto-like story. Four months later comes the announcement that *The Monk* has been written in ten weeks. While he may have begun an entirely new book during those four months, these references to earlier work suggest a portfolio bulging with material, a good deal of which found its way into *The Monk*.

In the prefatory advertisement to his romance, Lewis casually mentions the probability that his readers will find many plagiarisms of which he is unaware. This tantalizing remark, together with a general suspicion that *The Monk* was too remarkable an achievement for a nineteen-year-old author, encouraged the belief that Lewis was deliberately concealing literary debts. Within a year of the first appearance of the book, contemporary reviewers with disagreeable assurance named so many works as victims of Lewis' pilfering that in his fourth edition the author called attention to several trifling borrowings and denied others imputed to him. But he has suffered from our lack of a definition of plagiarism. Unacknowledged indebtedness in a great author somehow does him credit: it shows resourcefulness, displays the magic touch; in a writer less esteemed the same phenomenon becomes theft. Lewis' reputation as a shameless plagiarist became established quickly and has survived to this day.

Early in the twentieth century, interest in tracing the sources of *The Monk* revived and studies of Gothic literature have noted the possibility of many additional borrowings, most of which are insignificant or too nebulous to be convincing.[4] To name works Lewis may have read is easy—he read a great many; it is quite another matter to point out a scene or episode in *The Monk* which in detail corresponds to one in another work and which was not the common property of popular writers of the day. Hunting through Gothic literature for a single source is frustrating because, in finding it, one finds also a dozen others. Of the more than fifty works and authors that have from time to time been named as Lewis' creditors, some surely did and some almost as surely did not contribute to *The Monk*. There is no reason either to doubt or to attach much importance to the author's statement in his advertisement that the first idea of the romance was suggested by the story of the Santon Barsisa related in *The Guardian* (No. 148). Lewis' Ambrosio, like the Santon, is a holy man led by the devil into seduction and murder and tricked at the point of death into forfeiting his soul. There is no further similarity. Of course Lewis could have found this widespread story elsewhere, but the suggestion that he named *The Guardian* in order to defend the indecency of his book, "ingeniously intimating that plagiarized immorality is less reprehensible than original material,"[5] is trenchant but illogical. When he wrote his advertisement, Lewis probably did not consider his book indecent and certainly did not anticipate the storm it would raise.

One work frequently named as a source is Jacques Cazotte's fantastic story, *Le Diable Amoureux* (Naples and Paris, 1772). Evidence which appeared to confirm the debt to Cazotte, however, has been proved false,[6] and there seems no reason to reject Lewis' published statement that he had not seen the French story until

*The Monk* had been published.[7] Whether he found the theme of the Bleeding Nun in Musäus' "Die Entführung," another theory widely held, is less easy to decide. In his advertisement Lewis says, "The *Bleeding Nun* is a tradition still credited in many parts of Germany; and I have been told, that the ruins of the castle of *Lauenstein,* which she is supposed to haunt, may yet be seen upon the borders of *Thuringia";* elsewhere he refers to it as the "story which was related to me."[8] Thus, while not explicitly denying knowledge of a written version, he implies that, when he wrote *The Monk,* he knew the story by word of mouth only. That this was true receives some support from a letter he addressed to Walter Scott in 1807 in which he mentions, eleven years after the publication of *The Monk,* having just read Musäus and finding, he says, "the same tradition employed under the name of 'Die Entführung' which furnished me with the Bleeding Nun. . . ."[9] This seems a natural and ingenuous observation rather than a belated attempt to deceive his friend.[10] The inevitable search for borrowings by Lewis from the work of Ann Radcliffe, the other leading Gothic novelist, has not been very fruitful. The numerous similarities are not individually striking, though they suggest a pervasive influence.

On the other hand, it is quite certain that the conclusion of *The Monk* as it originally appeared was inspired by Veit Weber's (Leonhard Wächter's) *Teufelsbeschwörung* in his *Sagen der Vorzeit.*[11] Both Francesco in the German story and Ambrosio fall from a great height upon desolate rocks and suffer exactly the same agonies before they are washed away by stormy waters. Lewis later omitted this passage, possibly because the borrowing was promptly pointed out in one of the reviews.[12] Another reasonably sure source is the anticlerical drama of the French revolutionary theater. This genre developed an eminently dramatic situation, that of a young woman condemned by parental tyranny and cupidity to miserable imprisonment in a cloister. The dramas upon which Lewis may easily have drawn are Fiévée's *Les Rigueurs du Cloître* (1790), de Gouges' *Le Convent, ou les voeux forcés* (1790), M. J. Chénier's *Fénelon, ou les Religieuses de Cambrai* (1793) Charles Pougens' *Julie, ou la Religieuse de Nismes* (before 1796). He may also have known Baculard d'Arnaud's *Euphémie, ou le triomphe de la religion* (1768), and he did know Boutet de Monvel's *Les Victimes Cloîtrées* (1791), since he mentioned it to his mother in 1792 as a drama which would undoubtedly succeed and translated it for the English stage as *Venoni*. It is clear that from some of these dramas he drew details for Agnes' story in *The Monk*, such as her unwilling entrance into religious life, the letters and visits of her lover, who, disguised as a gardener, gains access to the convent, the rescue attempts, her incarceration, her rescue.[13] Similarities such as these demonstrate no more than what Lewis himself implies in the advertisement—that he took suggestions from his wide reading. Undoubtedly other incidental borrowings will be discovered from time to time. It has never been shown, however, that his debt to one or to several works was so heavy as to discredit the originality of his romance.

Oddly enough, the date of the first appearance of *The Monk* has not even now been determined to everybody's satisfaction. Older authorities named 1795 as the year of publication, a tradition which persists. Against it, however, was the fact that a copy of the book so dated could not be found, and, when investigation showed that no contemporary references or announcements of publication in the periodicals could be discovered earlier than March 1796, opinion came to favor the latter date. Examination of the paper of the preliminary gatherings next showed that the title leaves in the known copies of the earliest issue, all dated 1796, were cancels— substitutions for title leaves which had been removed. This dis- covery led to the inference that the three-volume work originally carried title pages dated 1795, that a few such copies were circu- lated that year, and that for an unknown reason the remainder of the edition was withheld until 1796 and then published with new title leaves bearing that date.[14] This theory provides an explanation both of the canceled titles and of the 1795 tradition, but *The Monk* has such a long record as a bibliographical stumbling block that without further evidence a final statement would be rash.

Whatever the solution of this puzzle, early March 1796 may be taken as the date when Lewis' romance was first presented to the general public. From either modesty or trepidation, the author withheld his name from the title page, though he could not refrain from subscribing his initials to the preface. The early notices were favorable enough to dispel fears he may have had of a hostile re- ception. Four months after *The Monk* had appeared, the *Monthly Mirror* for June gave it a page of unqualified admiration. "We really do not remember," said the critic, "to have read a more interesting production. The stronger passions are finely delineated and exemplified in the progress of artful temptation working on self-sufficient pride, superstition, and lasciviousness. . . . The whole is very skilfully managed, and reflects the highest credit on the judgment and imagination of the writer."[15] The critic also praised the verses sprinkled throughout *The Monk*; they were in fact the one detail of the book which later met with anything like unanimous approval. In October an equally friendly writer in the *Analytical Review* commended as "very happily imagined" those scenes (subsequently execrated) which mark the progress of Ambrosio's passion. This writer recklessly added that "the whole temptation is so artfully contrived, that a man, it should seem, were he made as other men are, would deserve to be d––ned who could resist even devilish spells, conducted with such address,"[16] a remark which even his use of dashes did not exempt from later censure.

The book sold well from the start, and a second edition was published in October 1796. Reassured by the reviews, Lewis affixed his name to the title page of this new edition, and, having recently taken his seat in the House of Commons, added his new title M.P., a stroke of vanity for which he was to pay dearly.

In February of the following year, as the fame of *The Monk* continued to spread, the *European Magazine* issued a warning rumble of the approaching storm: "This singular composition, which has neither *originality, morals,* nor *probability* to recommend it, has excited, and will still continue to excite, the curiosity of the public. Such is the irresistible energy of genius."[17] Plagiarism, immorality, and wild extravagance—here foreshadowed were the themes of future criticism.

In the same month a thunderclap came from the *Critical Review*. This article has special interest because Coleridge wrote it and because, as one might expect, it contains criticism as serious and penetrating as any *The Monk* has received.[18] In spite of distaste for the current popular romances of horror, Coleridge gives this one particular attention, he says, because of its unusual success—and it is, he acknowledges, "the offspring of no common genius." The subplot, though disproportionately long, is skillfully subordinated and connected with the main story. The tale of the bleeding nun is "truly terrific"; the treatment of the Wandering

Jew displays great vigor of fancy; the character of Matilda, exquisitely imagined, is the author's masterpiece. "The whole work is distinguished by the variety and impressiveness of its incidents; and the author every-where discovers an imagination rich, powerful, and fervid." But artistic faults outweigh these merits. The style is often gaudy where it should be simple, trite and colloquial where it should be solemn. A tale in which the order of nature can be changed at the author's will contains no surprises, since all events become equally probable. The punishment of Ambrosio's pride teaches no moral truth: superior to all earthly temptation, he was justified in being proud—only supernatural power could overwhelm him. Lacking moral truth, then, is *The Monk* at least pleasurable to read? It is not, for the author lacks both taste and knowledge of the human heart. The sufferings in *The Monk* are so intolerable, the abominations are described so unhurriedly and so far beyond the needs of characterization, that the reader suspects the man of a species of brutality who could find pleasure in wantonly imagining them. As for an understanding of humanity, though we may accept any wondrous situation in a romance, the characters must behave in it as our own feelings tell us they would behave. Yet Ambrosio is driven by emotions that could not possibly coexist with others which he is supposed to feel.

While these are judgments worth pondering, Coleridge's thundering peroration is less easy to take seriously. The poisonous nature of *The Monk* is "a fault for which no literary excellence can atone." It is a romance "which if a parent saw in the hands of a son or daughter, he might reasonably turn pale." Ambrosio's temptations are described with libidinous minuteness and the work leaves "the most painful impression . . . of great acquirements and splendid genius employed to furnish a *mormo* for children, a poison for youth, and a provocative for the debauchee." Coleridge then denounces Lewis' irreverent passage concerning the Bible— though he does not find it too pernicious to quote in full—and expresses the belief that "a mind may be so deeply depraved by the habit of reading lewd and voluptuous tales, as to use even the Bible in conjuring up the spirit of uncleanness." Moreover, the author is a man of rank and fortune: "Yes! the author of the Monk signs himself a *Legislator!*—We stare and tremble."

The storm now reached its height in loud and persistent blasts from *The Pursuits of Literature* by Thomas James Mathias. *The Pursuits*, a poem in the eighteenth-century satiric tradition, had first appeared in 1794 and, passing through numerous editions, accumulated strata of garrulous footnotes in which the author passed judgment on current publications. Though for the most part indiscriminate in his abuse, Mathias in an edition of July 1797 singled out *The Monk* as "one publication of the time too peculiar, and too important to be passed over in a general reprehension." He seems merely to have followed the lead of the *Critical Review*, since he dwells on exactly those objections brought forward by Coleridge. But where Coleridge had stared and trembled, Mathias bellows. As a romance *The Monk* is "disgraced by a diablerie and nonsense fitted only to frighten children in the nursery"; as pornography it is comparable to Cleland's *Memoirs of a Woman of Pleasure*. The passage concerning the Bible Mathias believes indictable under common law. To him it was inconceivable that "a legislator in our parliament, a member of the House of Commons of Great Britain, an elected guardian and defender of the laws, the religion, and the good manners of the country, has neither scrupled nor blushed to depict, and to publish to the world, the arts of lewd and systematic seduction, and to thrust upon the nation the most unqualified blasphemy against the very code and volume of our religion."[19] This violent onslaught against the little book which in manuscript had so pleased its author can only puzzle the modern reader—it must have astonished Lewis. Like Byron a few years later, but with an important difference, he awoke one morning to find himself infamous.

To account for such wrathful abuse from a writer whose scholarship in another field is remembered with gratitude, one concludes that Mathias enjoyed ranting for its own sake.[20] Yet he had other reasons too. "Literature, well or ill conducted," he believed, "is the great engine by which . . . all civilized States must ultimately be supported or overthrown."[21] Moreover, he wrote in an atmosphere charged with political and religious conservatism and for a public frightened by the French Revolution. And whether or not the desire on the part of the public for purity and virtue was sincere, a revulsion from eighteenth-century coarseness was in progress. Societies for the promotion of morality were springing up; censorship and expurgation were being carried to a point that

today seems prudishness. Public opinion and the press were particularly severe on atheism and religious defection. Despite all this
militant righteousness, however, attacks upon the Scriptures were
common: the doctrine of divine inspiration had recently been
challenged and Paine's *Age of Reason* had vilified the Bible in
terms compared with which Lewis' paragraph seems harmless
naïveté. To many it was, as Mathias put it, "an awful and a pressing
hour," and we can believe that flippancy toward the Bible may
well have heralded for him the collapse of Christian civilization.[22]

In such an atmosphere *The Monk* rapidly became a subject of
public controversy. The *Critical Review* and *The Pursuits of Literature* had pointed the way for the reviews. It was expedient either
to condemn the work out of hand or to temper praise with sancti-
monious qualifications. Thus, after halfhearted approval, the
*Monthly Review* for August 1797 warned, " A vein of obscenity,
however, pervades and deforms the whole organization of this
novel, which must ever blast, in a moral view, the *fair* fame that,
in point of ability, it would have gained for the author; and which
renders the work totally unfit for general circulation."[23] In the
same month the *Monthly Magazine* found it an invitation to
"voluptuous revelry," "a terrific and luxurious tale, more distinguished by genius than by a regard to decorum."[24] One might
suppose the *Scots Magazine*, after waiting six years before reviewing
*The Monk*, would have felt safe in relaxing a little or at least would
have had time to read the book carefully, but the same formula was
being followed in 1802: "all the faults and immoralities ascribed to
novels will be found realized in the Monk: murders, incest, and all
the horrible and aggravated crimes which it is possible to conceive,
appear in every chapter, and are dwelt on with seeming complacency."[25]

Though the reviewers played safe, some other writers who
joined the dispute took up arms for Lewis. One who signed himself
"A Friend to Genius" published an article in the *Monthly Mirror*
entitled "An Apology for the Monk," to show that the novel is not
vicious when judged by total effect rather than by isolated passages.
He courageously maintained that Lewis' comment on the Bible,
however tactlessly expressed, is essentially correct. "I have not the
pleasure of Mr. Lewis' acquaintance," he diffidently remarks, "and
I know not how this apology may be received on his part."[26] A

letter, presumably addressed to the editor of the *Monthly Mirror*, answers the questions and indicates that Lewis was taking a keen but discreet interest in the storm his book had raised:

Sir:

Should you happen to know the Author of "The Apology for the Monk," which was published in the last "Monthly Mirror," you will oblige me by letting him know (*But it must not be done through the medium of your Magazine*) that I feel myself highly indebted to him for his vindication of my Romance; and that I am proud of having acquired his approbation, since the very able manner in which that vindication is executed, convinces me, that the writer must be one, whose approbation is well worth having.

I remain<br>Your humble Servant<br>M. G. Lewis

Monday, April 22d [1797] Grosvenor St.[27]

The author of *Impartial Strictures on a Poem Called "The Pursuits of Literature" and Particularly a Vindication of the Romance of "The Monk"* devoted nearly half his essay to Lewis' defense. He argued that many works in daily circulation, such as *Peregrine Pickle, Tom Jones*, and *Ferdinand Count Fathom*, may be considered more harmful. Mathias' charge of blasphemy he believed to be unsupported by public opinion.[28] Thomas Dutton, too, in his *Literary Census: A Satirical Poem* (1798), aimed at Mathias, thought Lewis right, Mathias wrong, concerning the Bible—"But it would be an endless task to follow this frantic and sanguinary inquisitor through all his inconsistent mazes of bigot zeal, intolerance and willful misrepresentation."[29] The "beautiful episode of *Matilda*, in the first volume, furnishes an instance of the *pathetic*, perhaps never surpassed" and *The Monk* "considered in the aggregate, as a work of taste and fancy, bears the stamp and incontrovertible evidence of transcendant genius."[30] An anonymous *Epistle in Rhyme to M. G. Lewis* (1798), by Henry Francis Robert Soame, displays at least critical courage by comparing Lewis with Dante.[31]

Assurances that *The Monk* was not as dangerous as its enemies maintained failed to dampen its success with the reading public. They had been told that the book was horrible, blasphemous, and lewd, and they rushed to put their morality to the test. By 1800 five London and two Dublin editions, to say nothing of pirated versions and abridgments, were needed to supply the market.

There are innumerable references to *The Monk* in the diaries and correspondence of the time. Mrs. Piozzi jotted down what a friend had reported to her: "there is a Book in the World called the *Monk* w^ch surpasses in Horror every possible—& every Impossible Tale."[32] Anna Seward had not been able to obtain a copy by December 27, 1796, some six months after the book was first reviewed: "Of the Monk, I have been long in pursuit through the mazes of hireling circulation. Henry White, my literary huntsman, has been foiled in the track. Every mention I have heard made of that novel has excited my curiosity."[33] That a scandalous book had been published by a Member of Parliament and son of a War Office official was piquant gossip for society. William Wilberforce, to whom years later Lewis was to turn for advice regarding his West Indian slaves, recorded in his diary, "Dined Lord Chancellor's—Loughborough, Windham, Pitt, Lord Chatham, Westmoreland, &c.—talk rather loose. I fear I not guarded and grave enough. Much talk about 'The Monk,' a novel by Lewis' son."[34] Frances Lady Shelley years later recalled how when she was a girl her mother had imprudently forbidden her *The Monk*, "at that time the subject of conversation in all societies," and how one night, having received a copy from a misguided friend, she struggled long by candlelight before conquering the temptation to read it.[35]

Dramatists of the day were quick to recognize in *The Monk* material for exploitation. Henry William Grosette rifled the subplot for episodes and fashioned a two-act melodrama, *Raymond and Agnes; or the Bleeding Nun of Lindenberg* (London, 1797). In this patchwork Raymond goes forth hoping to meet adventure and by the end of two acts has no right to feel disappointed. At Madrid he falls in love with Agnes who is taking leave of a convent, and we are treated to a religious spectacle. Presently we find the hero in Baptiste's cottage in the forest, where Marguerite twice saves him from a horrid death and warns him of danger by placing a bloody pillow in his bed. Next he pursues the Bleeding Nun. He supposes her to be Agnes in disguise, but Gothic affairs are not that simple—Lewis' nun has been combined with Evelina, Agnes' murdered mother and guardian spirit, so that when Raymond attempts to embrace her she solemnly warns him to protect her child and disappears through a trap door. Her warning is not idle— robbers drag Agnes to a cavern and cast dice for her. When Raymond comes to the rescue, the nun reappears to bestow a blessing and this time ascends to Heaven in what Lewis later described as "a sort of postchaise made of paste-board."[36] *The Monk* also supplied material for a pantomime. From the Baptiste's cottage and the Bleeding Nun episodes was formed *Grand Ballet Pantomime of Action, Called Raymond and Agnes; or, The Castle of Lindenbergh*, by Charles Farley.[37] Equipped with airs and choruses by William Reeve and concluding with "a finale Spanish fandango," it proved highly serviceable to Covent Garden. The first performance was favorably noticed in March 1797; by June 1 it had been played twenty-two times.[38] In 1811 the Haymarket played *The Benighted Travellers; or, The Forest of Rosenwald*, a melodrama economically created by the mere addition of dialogue to the pantomime *Raymond and Agnes*.[39] Several standard collections of plays contain a two-act melodrama entitled *Raymond and Agnes: The Travellers Benighted; or, The Bleeding Nun of Lindenbergh* "by Matthew Gregory Lewis," for which Lewis appears to have been in no way directly responsible.[40]

In 1798 a more serious attempt to dramatize *The Monk* ran into interesting difficulties. This was James Boaden's five-act play originally to be called *Ambrosio*; in the advertisement the dramatist claimed the "generous approbation of the Author of the Romance." Lewis had remarked in a letter to Walter Scott, "Boaden has a Play, taken from 'the Monk,' in rehearsal, in which (as I am told) Ambrosio is made a very good sort of Man, and finishes by marrying Matilda! There's the very Devil's own invention for you!"[41] It was turned over to Sheridan for suggestions because Kemble, who had accepted the leading role, thought it needed additional interest. Since Lewis' monk was now reputed to be a danger to public morals, the licenser of plays objected to the title; the piece was therefore produced and later published as *Aurelio and Miranda*.[42] In adapting the romance to the stage Boaden eschewed all supernaturalism and horror and in his prologue promised entertainment at once prurient and innocuous:

> Our Author shews, to night, how love has prest,
> With subtle power to the monastick breast;
> Warming the frigid cell of cloister'd Pride
> With fires it struggled long, in vain, to hide;
> Till superstition owns, do all she can,

Woman was meant the proper bliss of Man.
    But though his Subject such, no virgin ear
  Shall startle at one loose expression here.[43]

The central situation is the monk's temptation by a woman in the monastery. Miranda, however, unlike Lewis' Matilda, is not an agent of Hell, but a virtuous if decidedly enterprising woman who has assumed the disguise of a monk in the hope of winning Aurelio for a husband. Her repudiation of illicit love preserves Aurelio's virtue. When it is revealed that he was stolen in infancy by gypsies and is the long-lost heir of the noble house of Medina— a discovery which seems automatically to dissolve his monastic vows—the couple are free to marry, and, with Raymond's rescue of Agnes and her newborn baby, none the worse for their incarceration in a dungeon, another pair of lovers unite.

Produced at Drury Lane on December 29, 1798, the play was abandoned after six nights. "Boaden's Play was so bad," Lewis wrote, "so bad! But Kemble and M<sup>rs</sup> Powell as Ambrosio & Agnes looked & acted to perfection."[44] Boaden attributed the failure to a storm of indignation "that so *immoral* a work as the Monk should be resorted to for the purposes of an exhibition, however moral in its tendency. There were not wanting an *accident* or two to help on the work of prejudice."[45] The representation of a church upon the stage was objected to, and Kemble as the monk made himself look so spiritual as to be considered sacrilegious.[46] On the other hand, "it was no sooner found out that Miranda was a virtuous woman, instead of a demon, that many in the pit and galleries evinced dissatisfaction."[47] A reader of the published version will agree that Genest hit upon the real difficulty when he wrote, "whatever may be the faults of the Romance, it is certainly interesting—the play is insipid." He relates one of the accidents referred to by Boaden: "a ludicrous circumstance took place on the first night—in the 5th act, when Mrs. Siddons took the child from Mrs. Powell, there happened to be some hissing—Mrs. Siddons, not liking this, made her exit more rapidly than usual—in her hurry she struck the wooden child so violently against the door she was going through, that the head came tumbling down on the stage—Mrs. Powell had to say immediately—'Immortal power, preserve my child.' "[48] Eleven-year-old Mary Russell Mitford was in the audience that night. More than forty years later in a letter to Elizabeth Barrett, she recalled how as a child she was taken to Drury Lane to see "a tragedy from 'The Monk,'" and that Mrs. Siddons "knocked the head of the huge wax doll she carried so violently against the wooden framework that the unlucky figure broke its neck with the force of the blow, and the waxen head came rolling along the front of the stage" to the accompaniment of laughter unrivaled since the production of *Tom Thumb*.[49] The drama to which she refers has been thought to be Sotheby's *Julia and Agnes* (1800),[50] another dramatization of *The Monk*, but either it was the performance described by Genest or Mrs. Siddons was incredibly unlucky with her dolls.

From "Alonzo the Brave," a ballad in *The Monk*, based upon the legend of the revenant who casts horror upon the wedding feast of a former lover, was formed *Alonzo and Imogine; or, The Bridal Spectre*, a ballet attributed to Thomas John Dibdin and performed at Sadler's Wells on May 8, 1797.[51] A *Grand Ballet of Alonzo the Brave and the Fair Imogine*, equipped with new scenery, machinery, dresses, and decorations, was performed at the Haymarket in 1801 and was soon billed for Kelly's benefit at Drury Lane.[52] On June 10 of the same year a "pantomimic romance" with the same title as Dibdin's ballet and attributed to the same author, appeared at Covent Garden. H. M. Milner's "legendary romantic melodrama," *Alonzo and Imogene; or, The Spectre Bride!* gives some idea of the dramatic use to which Lewis' ballad was put. Though the published text occasionally reflects the poem, the story is freely elaborated. Alonzo, not Imogine, is the faithless lover, and an entirely unrelated comic subplot is added. Inspired by Lewis' concluding stanza, Milner supplied a bridal festival among the dead in which skeletons sit about drinking blood and which the dramatic editor of one edition suggests "might be judiciously omitted."[53] The piece ends in a welter of wonders: Alonzo remorsefully kills himself; Imogene's tomb opens and she receives him dying in her arms, while half-clad skeletons look on from adjacent graves. The tomb becomes an aerial car and floats away in blue vapor.[54]

*The Monk* also supplied a brisk chapbook trade. An example among several abridgments of the novel is *The Castle of Lindenberg; or The History of Raymond & Agnes, a Romance*.[55] The title page bears Lewis' name and a preface disingenuously declares, "The ingenious author of the MONK has followed . . . the example of writers of the time in adapting his popular novel to the present rage for Romantic Fiction. In doing this, he has not only divested it of the improbabilities with which the work of his predecessors so much abound, but has also built his fabric on a permanent foundation, by making the several interesting particulars which occur in the CASTLE OF LINDENBERG appear as though they were drawn from life; and, in imitation of the immortal *Shakespeare*," and so forth. Obviously Lewis had nothing to do with the book, a mere pirating of the histories of Don Raymond and Agnes, with a few sentences added to stitch the narrative together. The redactor tried to delete all mention of Ambrosio and Antonia, but the latter escapes him at one point, where her name can only serve to mystify the reader; again, he omits the indispensable explanation that Agnes drank an opiate, not poison. Not only the whole of Ambrosio's career but all passages reflecting discredit upon the church are omitted in conformity with a guarantee in the preface that the work "may be read by the youth of both sexes without the least degree of danger." A similar abridgment ostentatiously displaying Lewis' name on the title page is *The History of Raymond & Agnes; or, The Castle of Lindenberg, a Romance*, which introduces some variety by the simple expedient of reversing the title.[56] Another is *Almagro and Claude; or, Monastic Murder; Exemplified in the Dreadful Doom of an Unfortunate Nun* (1803), in which the abridger disposes of the career of Raymond and Agnes, here renamed Almagro and Claude, in thirty-six of the forty pages; and then, finding himself still short of his quota, brings in Ambrosio, cramming into the last four pages the whole story of the monk's deterioration from a man of holiness to a condemned criminal.[57]

Lewis' name soon became so well known that other works were fathered upon him, and his publisher, Joseph Bell, on at least one occasion was obliged to give him public if ungrammatical exculpation in the *Morning Herald*, probably at Lewis' request: "Many reports having been circulated respecting the Authors of the *Progress of Satire*, and the *Sphinx's Head Broken*, two Poems, published by me, and many gentlemen have confidently asserted that they are both wrote by M. G. *Lewis*, Esq. Author of the *Monk, Castle Spectre*, &c. I take this opportunity of declaring that Mr. *Lewis* never saw either of the above Poems before they were printed, nor has he any knowledge who are the authors of them."[58]

By 1798 the scandal of *The Monk* had become decidedly embarrassing to its author, not to say alarming. It has often been stated, but is not certain, that legal action was taken to suppress the book. The source of this rumor seems to be the obituary of Lewis in the *Gentleman's Magazine* for August 1818, which says "a prosecution was talked of, and we believe commenced; but, on a pledge to recall copies, and to recast the Work in another edition, legal proceedings were stopped."[59] Twenty-one years later Lewis' biographer wrote that "the Attorney-general was actually instructed, by one of the societies for the suppression of vice, to move for an injunction to restrain its sale" and that "a rule *nisi* was obtained, and the young author did not think proper to show cause against it. The rule, however, was never made absolute, and the prosecution was dropped."[60] Later accounts gain assurance as they lose accuracy until one reads that the author was constrained "to recall almost every copy of his first edition."[61] How far this has strayed from the truth may be seen by Bell's advertisement as late as 1801 of copies of the first edition still for sale. If legal action actually was commenced, Mathias must have congratulated himself. He had buttressed his opinion that *The Monk* was indictable at common law by citing successful prosecutions against obscene and blasphemous books in a long footnote which must have made Lewis' blood run cold. In a later note Mathias suggested that the author repair his breach of public decency by suppressing the book himself or by omitting the indecent and blasphemous passages in another edition.[62]

Lewis fully complied with this last suggestion. The next edition of *The Monk*, the fourth (1798), contains nothing which could endanger the most fragile virtue. The deletions include several passages of considerable length: the mention of Ambrosio's rumored ignorance of the difference between man and woman and Leonella's accompanying comment, the monk's provocative dreams, his glimpse of Matilda's half-revealed beauty in the moonlight, the view of Antonia in the magic mirror, the love incidents between Ambrosio and Matilda. The monk's turpitude in surrendering to his temptress is lightened by "a thousand noble feelings," and the scene is stamped for disapproval by the shriek of his better angel. Of the passage concerning the Bible, of course, no trace remains. The author of *An Epistle in Rhyme* had ironically remarked that Lewis "should have recollected that we live in an age which is extremely nice in the choice of words at least; and for *that*, which he has most unwarrantably stiled *lust* (to the great offence of all well-disposed persons), every circulating library would have afforded him a thousand gentle expressions, such as *amiable weakness, exquisite sensibility*, &c. &c."[63] Whether or not Lewis read this hint, he expunged every remotely offensive word in his three volumes, with meticulous attention to *lust*. Ambrosio, formerly a *ravisher*, becomes an *intruder* or *betrayer*; his *incontinence* changes to *weakness* or *infamy*, his *lust* to *desire*, his *desires* to *emotions*. Having *indulged in excesses* for three editions, he *committed an error* in the fourth. His *avowed concubine*, if not much reformed, was at least brought up to date as his *acknowledged mistress*, and her *prostitution* became *what should be her shame*. Some of the deletions are deft—Elvira saves her sleeping daughter from the monk by entering the room *in time* instead of *just in time*. As if to make a completely new start in life, the romance even had its title changed, from *The Monk* to *Ambrosio, or The Monk*.[64] And two years later, Bell the publisher announced: "In this edition the Author had paid particular attention to some passages that have been objected to.—A few remaining copies of the original edition may be had by applying to the Publisher." By 1801 these unexpurgated copies were selling at a guinea apiece.[65]

Lewis' alterations of his romance are superficial and do not affect the narrative or the central idea of the story. Though some of the original passages display execrable lack of taste, it is hard to believe that they ever had power to do harm in the world. To class *The Monk* with deliberately pornographic literature is unjust and misleading; to call it blasphemous is irrational. At nineteen Lewis was inexperienced and overconfident and wrote without concern for the prejudices of the day, a freedom which he never again allowed himself. He bore the irresponsible attacks of the press with admirable dignity, refraining from any public comment on his romance until 1801, when, having "nearly served a seven years apprenticeship to patience, under the attacks of the most uncandid

criticism, unmitigated censure, and exaggerating misrepresentation," he published "for once, and for once only" an apologia in
the preface of another work:

> Without entering into the discussion, whether the principles inculcated
> in "The Monk" are right or wrong, or whether the *means* by which the story
> is conducted is likely to do more mischief than the *tendency* is likely to
> produce good, I solemnly declare, that when I published the work I had no
> idea that its publication *could* be prejudicial; if I was wrong, the error pro-
> ceeded from my judgment, not from my intention.
> Without entering into the merits of the advice which it proposes to
> convey, or attempting to defend (what I now condemn myself) the *lan-
> guage and manner* in which that advice was delivered, I solemnly declare,
> that in writing the passage which regards the Bible (consisting of a single
> page, and the only passage which I ever wrote on the subject) I had not
> the most distant intention to bring the sacred Writings into contempt, and
> that, had I suspected it of producing such an effect, I should not have
> written the paragraph.[66]

A fifth edition following the purified text of the fourth appeared
in 1800. By this time the sensational phase in the career of Lewis'
book was over. After its fierce early blaze, the fame of *The Monk*
rapidly subsided to a flicker, then smoldered on for years, emitting
an odor faint but somewhat disagreeable. Contemporary and later
nineteenth-century writers, aware of the scandal it had once raised,
were disappointed with the book and usually contemptuous, though
Charles Robert Maturin admired it at least for its commercial success. Writing to Walter Scott in 1813 while occupied with what
was to be the most poetic and the most powerful of all the Gothic
romances, he expressed determination to "out-Herod all the Herods
of the German school, and get the possession of the Magic lamp
with all its slaves from the Conjurer *Lewis* himself. I fear however
they will never build a palace of *Gold* for me as they did for their
Master Aladdin."[67] In the same year Byron looked at the "worst
parts" of the early text, which he had never read, "from curiosity
and recollection of the noise they made and the name they had
left to Lewis"; he called them "forced—the *philtered* ideas of a
jaded voluptuary."[68] According to Medwin, though, he considered
the romance one of the best in any language.[69] Four years later
Carlyle at twenty-two found *The Monk* "the most stupid and
villainous" novel he had read for a great while: "Considerable portions of it are grossly indecent, not to say brutish: one does not

care a straw about one of the characters—and though 'little Mat' has legions of ghosts and devils at his bidding, one views their movements with profound indifference"—an indifference, it may be noted, which kept him reading until four in the morning.[70] Lecturing in 1819 on English fiction, the year after Lewis' death, Hazlitt called some of Lewis' descriptions "chargeable with unpardonable grossness," though he placed the author second to Ann Radcliffe in the art of freezing the blood.[71] On March 9, 1869, Trollope wrote on an end leaf of his copy of *The Monk*, "This is so bad, that nothing ever could have been worse;—and yet the book had a great success! There is no feeling of poetry in it. Everything is pretended, made up, and cold. We are obliged to suppose that its charm consisted in its indecency,—which in itself would not have been much; but is enhanced by being the indecency of a monk."[72] Nineteenth-century historians of literature generally described *The Monk* as powerful but dangerous and indecent, though near the end of the century Margaret Oliphant, smug and condescending, denied it even these distinctions. To that historian Lewis is "the quaint little magician, with his trifling countenance and his mask of horror" and *The Monk* "hardly up to the mark of a 'penny dreadful,' even in point of literary merit."[73]

Over a period of more than a century and a half the general course of criticism directed at Lewis' romance has been praise, excoriation, contempt, and the patronizing interest bestowed upon a curiosity, but the world has refused to let *The Monk* die. The record of its reappearances is altogether remarkable for a Gothic romance. Aside from five London editions by the original publisher and numerous chapbook versions, some twenty British editions or reprints have been recorded in a list by no means complete.[74] *The Monk* has appeared certainly not fewer than seven times in the United States. Four German editions by 1810 have been recorded, seventeen French by 1883, and the book has been translated into Italian, Spanish, Swedish, and probably other languages.[75] Unquestionably its eroticism and early ill repute have been to a large extent responsible for this sustained and widespread popularity, though in recent years a growing interest in the minor fiction of the Romantic period on the part of students of literature has stimulated a more legitimate interest in Lewis' story. But, aside from these considerations, it remains more than a literary curiosity; in its variety, intensity, and horror *The Monk* is still a powerful book.

Lewis' narrative technique has faults, but he obviously took pains with the structure of the romance. The main story, that of Ambrosio, is well proportioned and swift—even as the monk reflects upon his impregnable virtue, Rosario, the instrument of his future destruction, knocks softly at the door. From the reader's first glimpse into the monk's arrogant heart until he sees him hurled to everlasting punishment for monstrous crimes, the theme remains the progress of Ambrosio's moral corruption. The diabolical plan revealed only at the end embraces his whole career and gives it unity and direction. This dramatic story is supplemented by an episodic subplot, the adventures of Raymond and Agnes, which as Coleridge noted is too long. Don Raymond no sooner comes upon the scene than he sits down to relate his adventures and pre-empts over one quarter of the book. There are other weaknesses. The reader's patience is sometimes tried by interpolated histories, as when Marguerite, a minor character, introduces her story with the weary formula, "I was born in Strasbourg, of respectable parents." Complex family relationships are introduced needlessly. Sudden illness automatically removes characters who are momentarily in the way: when the Baroness has outlived her usefulness to the plot she breaks a blood vessel. Having prodigally killed Antonia and exploited the pathos of her death, Lewis, bent upon a happy ending for Don Lorenzo, unreasonably requires him to fall in love all over again. Yet the two stories are on the whole skilfully handled to achieve variety and suspense and come together satisfactorily at the end.

One finds considerable variety too among the characters. They are more apt to astonish than convince, but, after all, one does not turn to Gothic novels to learn about human nature. Ambrosio is not the total villain of melodrama; he often inclines toward pity and rectitude though without sufficient strength to withstand the avalanche of disasters prepared by Satan—no character in fiction is more entitled to Parolles' complaint, "Who cannot be crush'd with a plot?" Yet, though Lewis devoted pages of analysis to Ambrosio's character in an attempt to make him credible, the story forces such bewildering psychological acrobatics upon the monk that he evokes no more sympathy than a puppet mangled in a machine. The character of Matilda, so highly praised by Cole-

ridge, is, despite her supernatural nature, much more convincing
and leaves a powerful impression. She is presented as a passionate
woman devoted to Ambrosio, at first humble, then reckless and
dominating, whose evil counsels gain ascendency over the monk's
better nature as his guilt accumulates, until at the end we are informed that she is "a subordinate but crafty spirit" sent by Hell to
ruin him. Some readers are disappointed to learn that all her love
was mere dissimulation. Byron made the interesting suggestion that
*The Monk* "only wanted one thing, as I told Lewis, to have rendered it perfect. He should have made the daemon really in love
with Ambrosio: this would have given it a human interest."[76] The
fact is, Lewis apparently by oversight did exactly that in two or
three instances—Matilda is not consistently diabolical. Once she
utters her love for Ambrosio when she thinks him asleep; later one
reads of her growing attachment to the monk and her efforts to
regain his love, and once it is told that his indifference fills her eyes
with "involuntary" tears. The suggestion has been advanced that
Lewis changed his mind in the course of the narrative, conceiving
her first as a human maiden torn with desire and later as a succu-
bus;[77] but it seems clear that the author, though he fell into inconsistencies which could easily have been removed, had determined
upon her evil nature from the start.

Don Raymond's thirteen-year-old page, Theodore, who plays a
useful part in the story as a secret messenger, is not memorable as
a character creation, yet he demands some attention here since his
author gave him so much. At several points Don Raymond inter-
rupts his narrative with intrusive panegyrics on Theodore's virtues.
Some details suggest that Lewis was describing himself as a child—
his precocious skill in music, verse, and languages, and his keenness
for authorship. Theodore "frequently composed little ballads in
Spanish." On one occasion Don Raymond surprises him in the act
of writing a poem, examines it, and points out faults Lewis may
have recognized in his own verses: "you make a terrible confusion
of metaphors; you are too apt to make the strength of your lines
consist more in the words than sense; some of the verses only seem
introduced in order to rhyme with others; and most of the best
ideas are borrowed from other poets, though possibly you are un-
conscious of the theft yourself. These faults may occasionally be
excused in a work of length; but a short poem must be correct and

perfect." When Don Raymond proceeds to lecture his page on the dangers of authorship he speaks with the tongue of prophecy for Lewis and his romance: an author is an animal whom everybody is privileged to attack; one finds the plan faulty, another the style, a third the precept which his book strives to inculcate; others stigmatize the author—"But I am conscious that all these sage observations are thrown away upon you. Authorship is a mania, to conquer which no reasons are sufficiently strong."[78]

The search for autobiography in Theodore ends abruptly when we find him described as beautiful. The nuns admire "the delicacy of his features, the beauty of his hair, and the sweetness and grace which accompanied all his actions." This fact, however, suggests another aspect of the character. He is in this respect akin to other young boys Lewis depicted: to Leolyn in the melodrama *One O'Clock* (1811), a child of "blooming beauty," and to the ten-year-old Eugene in "Mistrust," a story in *Romantic Tales* (1808), who was "singularly beautiful," whose figure might have served as a model for a Zephyr, and whose "bright and glowing hair glittered in the sun-beams like dark gold." This gloating over Eugene's "pale fair cheeks" and the "long tresses of his dark, golden hair" is vaguely disturbing, though at least it can be said for Eugene that there is nothing epicene in his susceptibility to women.

In the relationship of Elvira and her daughter, Lewis shows precocious understanding. A few scenes happily escape false sentimentality and emotional excess and bring Antonia to life as a charming, innocent girl, such as the sensitive and moving depiction of her loneliness and insecurity in Madrid after her mother's death, when she waits for her aunt who never arrived to save her. The sympathy the author occasionally succeeds in eliciting for Antonia makes it doubly difficult to forgive him the brutal misfortunes he later hurls upon her.

The other characters make little impression as individuals. One frequently gains from these figures as a whole the illusion that they are professional actors in a stock company presenting violent melodrama. When they come upon the scene, doors burst open or are thrown open; when they depart they dart, speed, or fly as if galvanized. They express their incredible emotions in soliloquy or violent physical action. Even Ambrosio, frustrated in love, does not sit moodily in his room; he howls with fury and dashes himself against the wall. "Joy! Joy!" shrieks a victim of incarceration upon being rescued. Shrieks, in fact, punctuate the whole romance. Such characteristics of popular stage entertainment, together with expository dialogue, foreshadowing, and careful timing, point to the strong probability that much of the material in *The Monk* was originally in dramatic form, that melodramas which Lewis had already written were reworked and combined to form a great part of his romance.

Lewis' early critics, though easy to ridicule today, plainly had grounds for their charges of indecency and crude horror. Though evil conduct is never condoned in *The Monk*, the description of Ambrosio's early relations with Matilda may be accused of a not very dangerous pruriency. Less easily excused than this are scenes in which Lewis determines at once to shock us and to move us to pity. The violation of Antonia amid the corpses in the catacombs is more than painful—it is revolting, and some details of Agnes' immolation with her dead infant fill the reader with shame for the author's lack of taste. Lewis never understood that some emotional appeals cannot be combined successfully, and he never learned restraint.

The charge of immorality, on the other hand, was as ironic as it was unjustified, for *The Monk* is carefully equipped with a two-fold moral lesson: pride is a sin and mercy a virtue. Coleridge missed half the point when he complained that Ambrosio's punishment teaches no moral truth. He rightly said that the monk is superior to earthly temptation and can be overcome only by a supernatural plot, but the monk's early repudiation of Agnes' plea for mercy was not ordained by Satan: it sprang from his own cruel heart. His pride, to which Coleridge felt Ambrosio had a right, entails inhumanity to others, and this is the flaw in his character. Agnes prophesies that his day of trial will come when he will solicit God's mercy and will despair of pardon; and Satan, reviewing the enormity of the monk's guilt in his last hours, exclaims, "Is pride then a virtue? Is inhumanity no fault? . . . [you] scrupled not to commit a crime, which you blamed in another with unfeeling severity." Judging perhaps that he had not sufficiently emphasized this point, Lewis in the second issue of the first edition added to the conclusion of the romance a short moralizing passage, ending "to look with mercy on the conduct of others, is a virtue no less than to look with severity on your own."

*The Monk* is good entertainment because so much happens and because we see it happen. Lewis' instinct for dramatic presentation gives him a distinct advantage over his contemporary practitioners in Gothic fiction. The action of the characters may sometimes be preposterous and their speech banal, bombastic, or frenzied, but to see and hear them directly is more effective than to read summarized narrative and conversations at second hand. The same instinct appears in his settings: caring nothing for long descriptions filled with romantic vagueness intended to evoke an atmosphere of mystery, Lewis arranges his scenes as for a stage spectacle with gaudy colors and striking contrasts of light and darkness. There is everywhere in the book a youthful boldness and confidence. If his objectives are not always worth while and not all attained, at least he always knows what they are and seizes any means to reach them. When it is time to appall or terrify, he calls upon magic and Satan himself, openly accepting the world of spirits and scorning the ingenious disappointments of the "explained supernatural." He does not tantalize us with impending disasters and squeamishly withdraw them in the nick of time: though we could sometimes dispense with the gift, he gives what he has promised. And he could rise above mere melodrama. Critical comment, perhaps following Coleridge, has singled out for praise the incident of the Bleeding Nun and the imaginative treatment of the Wandering Jew. To these may be added the mob scene in which the convent is destroyed and the Prioress meets her fate; the pathos and tension of Matilda's last visit to the wretched Ambrosio, when, radiant in the gloomy prison cell of the Inquisition, she delivers her urgent message and bids him farewell; the mounting horror of the monk's career and its smashing catastrophe. It is not hard to understand the young author's enthusiasm for his accomplishment, expressed at The Hague in the letter to his mother and in the sprightly verses of his preface to *The Monk*.

# 3 ✑

## SOCIETY

Though the public at large knew Lewis principally as the author of a notorious romance, his life during the years immediately following the publication of *The Monk* presents other facets. He now moved in the highest circles of society, met leading political and literary figures, and successfully invaded the world of the theater.

As a member of the House of Commons from 1796 to 1802, Lewis officially represented the hundred and twenty inhabitants of Hindon, Wiltshire, one of the fifty-six pocket boroughs disfranchised in the reform of 1832. Such seats were regularly controlled by a patron or sold to the highest bidder. By chance the one assigned to Lewis had recently been vacated by William Beckford, another writer remembered for an imaginative work of fiction, *The History of the Caliph Vathek.* Lewis' debut in Parliament started handsomely. According to Walter Scott, Charles James Fox "paid the unusual compliment of crossing the House of Commons that he might congratulate the young author, whose work obtained high praise from many other able men of that able time."[1] Lewis' short career in politics, however, was undistinguished and meant little to him. Perhaps its most important consequence, a sorry one, was the special censure meted out by Coleridge and Mathias to the author of an indecent book who called himself "M.P." The strenuous life of a conscientious member of the House was not to his taste and we may accept the biography's statement that his attendance soon became extremely irregular. Nevertheless, his record in Parliament is not entirely blank. He served on three select committees, each of fifteen members, appointed in November 1796 and February and March 1797, to decide on the merits of petitions submitted in protest of parliamentary election returns, routine duties which might have fallen to the lot of any member. A fourth committee, appointed in February 1797, the last on which he served, considered a petition from William Taylor, the proprietor of King's Theatre, Haymarket, for the widening of Pall Mall at the east end and the opening of a new street from the Haymarket into Charles Street, to relieve congestion on nights of performances at Taylor's theater. Possibly Lewis was selected for this committee because as a theater habitué he was well informed on the matter.[2] It is traditional that he never addressed the House, but in February 1802 a bill was introduced designed to relieve the sufferings of prisoners committed for debt. Several members commented, among whom, it is recorded, "Mr. Lewis, in support of the Bill, said, the severity with which many debtors were treated was a disgrace to civilization."[3] If this was the only occasion on which he raised his voice in the House—and there appears to have been no other—we may note at least that his sentiments were characteristically humane.

If his parliamentary career lacked glitter, his social life did not. As a young bachelor of good connections, a literary reputation, and the title of M.P., he was acceptable everywhere and even numbered royalty among his acquaintances. In particular the unhappy Princess of Wales found him a sympathetic and faithful friend. When Scott was in London, he noted that Lewis was present at all her parties.[4] He composed verses for her[5] and dedicated to her his *Monody on the Death of Sir John Moore*. His epilogue to *Adelmorn* gave her public praise in a passage beginning with tragically inapplicable verses:

> But censure must cease, while I own that we boast
> A Princess (by Hymen conferred on our coast)
> Who gilds with true glory the title of Wife,
> The friend of her consort, the balm of his life.[6]

In 1803 at the Egham Races, the Duke of Clarence, to whom he had never been presented, abruptly requested his presence at dinner to meet the Spanish deputies since he was "a man of Romance and Sentiment." Lewis commented to Lady Holland, "I am quite glad to find that Romance and Sentiment can, once in his life, get a man a dinner. I'm sure I've lost many things by them, and never got anything before."[7]

During the winter seasons he threw himself into London society. "London is mad with gaiety. There are half a dozen parties
to go to, at least, every night," he wrote to Lady Charlotte Campbell.[8] He also spent a good deal of time visiting the country estates
of English and Scottish nobility. Excerpts from one of his letters
to the poet Tom Moore give a glimpse of one such expedition:

I have been passing my time very pleasantly, though constantly upon the
move, never staying above a fortnight in the same place. I found Beaujolois
at the Duke of Athol's, whence we adjourned to Inverary; there William
Lamb, and Kinnaird, Lord Lorne, my sister, the Campbells, and numerous
other people were assembled. . . . From Inverary Count Beaujolois and myself adjourned to the Duke of Hamilton's, where we had a week's racing and
dancing. We there separated; he to pay his devoirs to Monsieur, and I to
pay mine to Lady Charlotte Campbell at her villa. . . . I am now come for
a couple of days to the Duke of Buccleuch's; I mean to pass a couple more
with Lady Charlotte, and then I shall set out for England; but as I have
some visits to make upon the road, probably I shall not travel with much
expedition.[9]

A certain ostentation in the passage substantiates Scott's comment
that Lewis was "fonder of great people than he ought to have been,
either as a man of talent or a man of fortune. He had always dukes
and duchesses in his mouth, and was particularly fond of any one
who had a title. You would have sworn he had been a *parvenu* of
yesterday, yet he had been all his life in good society."[10]

A highly civilized guest and an entertaining gossip, Lewis was
adept at devising and organizing polite frivolities, arranging amateur theatricals, dashing off impromptu verses. Thomas Raikes
recorded in his journal Lewis' turn from epigram and how at
Oatlands one evening, when Lord Erskine excited the indignation
of a lady by inveighing against marriage, saying that a wife is a tin
canister tied to a man's tail, Lewis promptly took a sheet of paper
and wrote the following reply which he presented to Her Royal
Highness:

On a late decision of an Ex-Chancellor.—M. G. Lewis. Dec[r] 26th
    Lord Erskine, at Women presuming to rail,
    Calls a Wife "a Tin Cannister tyed to one's tail;"
    And fair Lady Anne, while the subject He carries on,
    Feels hurt at his Lordship's degrading comparison.

Yet wherefore degrading?—Considered aright,
A Tin Cannister's useful, and polished, and bright;
And should Dirt its original purity hide,
That's the fault of the Puppy, to whom it was tyed.[11]

From innumerable references among the diaries and letters of his titled contemporaries he emerges at his best as talented, witty, and amusing, always talkative and always somewhat ridiculous. Caroline Fox wrote: "The little Monk is with us at present, and, having no competitor to rival him in grace and gaiety of conversation, he is in high feather and good humour, but talks so much of Lady Douglas's lapdog, *Tiney,* and other subjects equally unintelligible and uninteresting to L^d L., that I am sometimes quite distressed. . . . But he is much pleasanter in the country than I should have expected, and has one merit which few have, that is, that time does not appear to hang heavy on his hands. He is never *désoeuvré,* and never expects to be entertained in a morning."[12]

But it was easy to have too much of him. His capacity for boring his friends was enormous. Sidney Smith, comparing the various effects of ennui on different individuals, insisted that Lewis tried people as an experiment in natural philosophy; that he put Lord Donoughmore to sleep, made Lady Holland grow red and furious, and Lady B. turn pale and cry—

> She never told her grief
> But let Monk Lewis, like a worm in the leaf,
> Prey on her sinking Spirits.[13]

Not everybody was fortified by a sense of humor like Sidney Smith's. Nevertheless, the expression of unqualified aversion in the following description of Lewis is exceptional: "disliked by all man and womankind, but thrusting himself into all the best society and frequently at Kensington, a hateful little animal, with just genius enough to complete his disagreeableness, constantly talking about himself, his heart, his feelings, etc."[14]

He frequently visited, sometimes for two or three months at a time, Inveraray Castle, the seat of the fifth Duke of Argyll, whose family he had met in 1793. A letter to Moore pictures one visit: "we contrived to keep up such a continual riot, that I changed the name of Inverary to that of *Confusion Castle,* with universal ap-

probation. We had plays, music, billiards, gaming (but in modera-
tion), with a thousand other nondescript amusements; among the
most admired of which was a newspaper, giving an account of all
the domestic affairs of Inverary, and in which we all abused one
another."[15] As for dramatics at Inveraray: "Our theatricals are in
a flourishing condition: We played *The Rivals* last Monday, and
though I say it, that should not say it, it was really very well acted.
Among other dramatic schemes it was attempted to get up . . .
a *walking* ballet, and a machine was actually made in which my
Sister was to fly up into the clouds in the character of the Queen
of the Fairies. Unluckily the want of an Orchestra put a stop to this
daring attempt."[16] An incident at Inveraray which deserves mention because it illustrates, as the *Life* observes, the extraordinary
popularity a trifle from Lewis' pen was then capable of obtaining.
Walking through the woods one evening, Lewis and Lady Charlotte met a maniac girl. The encounter inspired Lewis' ballad
"Crazy Jane," which was set to music, became a hit and was responsible for the naming of the "Crazy Jane" hats then in vogue.
Drury Lane audiences heard the ballad many times, and a *Popular
Ballet of Crazy Jane* appeared at the same theater. Chapbooks were
sold giving the true history of Crazy Jane, an affecting tale of the
youngest daughter of one Mr. Arnold, a substantial farmer in
Wiltshire. The *Gentleman's Magazine* printed a Latin paraphrase
by a Rugby schoolboy "Of the well-known Song of 'Crazy Jane.' "[17]

At Inveraray Lewis became warmly attached to the daughter
of his host, Lady Charlotte Campbell, afterwards Lady Charlotte
Bury and author of several novels and the *Diary Illustrative of the
Times of George IV*. He dedicated *Romantic Tales* (1808) to her
with the following tribute:

> While stranger-eyes, whene'er her form is seen,
> Own her of captive hearts unrivalled Queen;
> While stranger-ears, catching some passing strain,
> The music of her voice through life retain;
> Admired by all, with truth she still may boast,
> The few, who know her best, admire her most.[18]

However, the *Life* seems hardly justified in romanticizing this
friendship into a "thraldom" which was "chastened in maturer
years to that sacred feeling into which unrequited love often

changes."[19] Lady Charlotte mentions a visit apparently in May 1813 from "little Matt. Lewis" who is "such a steady friend, and so amusing, that, in spite of all his *ridicules*, I like him exceedingly."[20] The fact is, he enjoyed falling in love. "By the way," wrote Sir William Gell, "Lewis also is often at Kensington. He is desperately in love comme à l'ordinaire, with Lady Sarah Bayly. It is rare fun to see him looking sentimental, as you well know."[21] William Lamb wrote of Lewis to his mother, Lady Melbourne, apparently early in 1800, "I hear he intends proposing to Emily Stratford. I think she will keep him in tolerably warm water for the rest of his life. . . . It would not be a bad speculation for her to marry him, for she may get him killed off in a duel as soon as she pleases."[22] In the same year Lady Holland wrote of Lady Georgina Dorothy Cavendish, "a most charming girl," that "Little Lewis is upon the eve of making himself a great fool about her."[23] According to the Princess, when he visited her theater box one evening, "Lewis did play de part of Cupidon, which amuse us, as you will suppose. He is grown so embonpoint, he is more droll than ever in dat character; but he tink himself charming, and look so happy when he make *les yeux doux* to the pretty ladies, dat it is cruel to tell him, 'You are in de paradise of de fools,' so me let him sigh on to My Lady Oxford, which do torment Lord Byron, who wanted to talk wid her, and never could contrive it."[24]

Lewis was prone to form enthusiastic friendships which were often punctuated by quarrels. The early letters of William Lamb, later second Viscount Melbourne, reflect such an association. Lewis was often a guest at Brocket Hall, one of the estates of the Lamb family, where William spent much of his childhood. Four years younger than Lewis, Lamb was intensely interested in literature and for a time the two were close friends. Lewis thought highly of the other's poetic abilities and introduced some verses by Lamb into his own *Love of Gain* (1799).[25] Lamb, in turn, had interesting observations to make concerning Lewis' talents. Having read William Godwin's *Caleb Williams* (1799), which he found full of blunders, he writes to his mother on January 6, 1800, "If Lewis would but give his own abilities fair play he could write a novel fifty times as good."[26] Lewis' ear for poetry, he thought, "is extremely exact, and his stanzas (not his heroic verses) have a very peculiarly beautiful glow. It must be remarked, however, that prose writing requires as correct an ear at least as poetry, for it is certainly more various. The reason that Lewis has not this in the same perfection is that he has read less prose, and has accustomed himself less to consider the cadences of periods. The same reason may be given for the mediocre rhythm of his ten-syllable verses."[27]

At the age of twenty Lamb accompanied Lewis when in 1799 the latter retired briefly "from the world and all its mockeries," as Lewis put it, to a cottage in Leatherhead expressly to study Stewart's philosophy, which he found impossible to do in the bustle of London. He explained to Walter Scott, "We are to remain here for a week, after which William goes to Brockett Hall, where I am to join him in the Easter week, that point of time being marked out for the commencement of a variety of Theatrical and other gay projects—I believe I shall have an opportunity of presenting my Friend William to you in Scotland this year, as we have nearly arranged an expedition thither in the course of next July—you will be extremely pleased with him, for in truth and without partiality He is a very superior style of young Man."[28] On January 6, 1800, Lamb, then studying in Glasgow, mentioned Lewis in a letter to his mother, Lady Melbourne, as one whose "head is always full of one vagary or another," and hopes that "you will contrive this winter to rub off a few rum ideas which he contracted in these philosophical colleges, and to divest him of rather too minute and scrupulous a morality, which is entirely unfit for this age. I suppose they did this for him a little at Edinburgh last year, but, however, I daresay some work is still left for London."[29] The two young men quarreled, it seems; or at least Lamb grew tired of his friend, for in January or February 1800 he wrote of Lewis that he "might be pleasant enough if he was not always upon the strain. I think, now that the heat of anger and dissatisfaction has passed away, I could draw a good character of him."[30] The same letter, already quoted in connection with Lewis' rumored interest in Emily Stratford, contains the curiously ambiguous comment: "She will make him shed more tears and look more doleful in assembly-rooms than ever I did."[31]

Lord Holland, nephew of C. J. Fox, was often Lewis' host at Holland House. The two had known each other at Christ Church. Lewis expressed his admiration of Fox in the dedication of the *Love of Gain* and in the "Lines Written on Returning from Fox's

Funeral" in 1806. His introduction to the brilliant circle of Holland House was presumably on November 1, 1797, when Lady Holland wrote of him in her journal, "I saw him to-day for the first time here. He is little in person, rather ugly and shortsighted; upon the whole not engaging, though better than I expected from the picture made of him to me."[32] At Holland House he sometimes paid for his entertainment as victim of Lady Holland's wit and sometimes of her anger. On one occasion when his hostess had found him particularly tiresome and provoking and high words had passed between them, he told her that common decency should prevent her using such language to Lord Holland's guests. "She replied that when people forc'd themselves into a House against the will of its owners, they must take the consequence. He said he would remain no longer: she, the sooner he went the better." Presently she relented—after all, Lewis had been invited by Lord Holland. But when she sent a peace messenger to his room, "The little man had pack'd up his night things and trudg'd to London. . . . Lady Holland absolutely condescended to ask forgiveness, and at last the little Monk yielded, and was brought back in triumph to Holland House to dinner yesterday, and will probably be driven off again before the week is out."[33]

He was quick-tempered and too easily offended. Hobhouse once observed that, despite his declared contempt of all the world, Lewis showed how much he was in the power of any man who chose to say an ill-natured thing.[34] Lady Holland records another revealing episode. Lewis sent a request to the Duke of Somerset to wait upon him the next day at one o'clock. When the duke obligingly obeyed the summons, Lewis said, "I understand . . . that you have exposed me to the contempt of being again blackballed by the New Club. I think the part you have acted by so doing unbecoming the character of a friend; thus I desire our acquaintance may drop here." He rang for the servant to open the door and so dismissed the duke. According to Lady Holland, Somerset, who was remarkably good-natured, had most certainly done what he thought Lewis would like, but "poor little man, he is very irritable and quarrelsome, and will shortly be left not only friendless, but without many acquaintances."[35] He could also be reckless of others' feelings. In later life Lady Holland used him as an example of this in an admonitory letter to her son: "My friend

Monk Lewis allowed the excellent qualities of his heart to be obscured for years, by affecting sharp sayings against all his acquaintances except just the reigning favourites." She added that he was made wretched by the insignificance into which he fell from offending so many, and that "it required all his genius, and he had a good deal, and thorough alteration of tone" to re-establish himself.[36] William Parnell-Hayes, the controversialist and friend of Tom Moore, frankly censured this habit, as well as what he considered Lewis' superficial attitude toward literature, in a note to Lewis himself:

Dear Lewis

I am very sorry I cannot dine with you as I leave town tomorrow. accept my farewell and my prayers that you may learn to value the esteem of mankind as highly as every one who has powers to acquire it, ought; and that you will forgo all your contemptuous quaintness, and your provoking short turns. You appear to possess from nature the power to write feelingly, & for no better reason than because you are familiar with it undervalue the rich gift, while you seek from art the knack of writing amazingly. If this is unkind or impertinent or anything but untrue, excuse it as the bequest of one who is going to cross Saint Georges Channel.

yours truly
W. Parnell Hayes.[37]

As Lady Holland observed, Lewis was not prepossessing in appearance. On this subject he had no illusions but described himself in the prefatory verses to *The Monk*, in imitation of Horace's *corporis exigui*, as of "graceless form and dwarfish stature." Mrs. Wyndham once asked him how, with such a comic face, he could have such a horrid imagination.[38] Scott's portrait has been often quoted: "Mat had queerish eyes; they projected like those of some insect, and were flattish in their orbit. His person was extremely small and boyish; he was, indeed, the least man I ever saw to be strictly well and neatly made."[39] In his *Journal* Scott compares him with Moore, who was

A little—very little man—less, I think, than Lewis, and somewhat like him in person—God knows, not in conversation, for Matt, though a clever fellow, was a bore of the first description. Moreover, he looked always like a schoolboy. I remember a picture of him being handed about at Dalkeith House. It was a miniature I think by Saunders, who had contrived to mufle [sic] Lewis's person in a cloak, and placed some poniard or dark-lanthorn appurtenance (I think) in his hand, so as to give the picture the cast of a Bravo. "That like Mat Lewis!" said Duke Henry, to whom it had passed in turn; "why, that is like a *man!*" Imagine the effect! Lewis was at his elbow. Now Moore has none of this insignificance; to be sure his person is much stouter than that of M. G. L.[40]

James Smith of *Rejected Addresses* recalled that Lewis had "large grey eyes, thick features, and an expressive countenance. In talking, he had a disagreeable habit of drawing the fore-finger of his right hand across his right eyelid. He affected, in conversation, a sort of dandified, drawling tone."[41] An animated description which has escaped notice occurs in "Modern Beaux. Portraits from Life," an article in *The Satirist* for 1808 by some ill-natured young lady writing under the pseudonym Susan Wilcock about "young men of supposed fashion, who favour papa with their visits *in the shooting season*":

M. G. L. (*Esquire!*) is a slim, skinny, finical fop, of modish address, with a very neatly-rounded pair of legs, and a very ugly face. His looks have nothing manly in them; but he *looks,* by his airs, as if he thought himself a little Arthur Wellesley; he seems so dapper, so jaunty, so sprack, pert, and lively. His eyes are small, and, in general, watery; but, at tea-time, (particularly if the glass has been pushed about a little by papa after dinner,) they sparkle, roll, and twinkle away most merrily, at every woman round the table. His language, then, grows rude and impudent, and he tries to be particular with any one of us who may happen to sit near him; spouting forth glibly French, Italian, Spanish, and German *fadaises,* in a lack-a-daisy kind of way, with an ill-breath; and "grinning horribly a ghastly smile," as if to shew us all his jagged and slovenly teeth. I am told he is an author, and once wrote tolerable verses for the street music-grinders to sing or say.[42]

Lewis by no means devoted all his time to society during these years. In 1797 he took a master's degree at Oxford and during the five years following the publication of *The Monk* had amply justified his early impatience and his confidence in himself as a popular writer by a remarkable record of literary production. Between the date of *The Monk* and 1801 eleven works were published or produced on the stage, to be merely named here and more fully noticed in later chapters. In 1796 he published anonymously the dramatic satire *Village Virtues,* which was scarcely noticed and immediately forgotten. *The Minister,* his translation of Schiller's *Kabale und Liebe,* completed four years before at Bothwell Castle, appeared in 1797. *The Monk* had now made him a power to be reckoned with, and the theatrical world he had tried so persistently and unsuccessfully to invade was at last opened to him. *The Castle Spectre*, performed at Drury Lane late in 1797, his first and by far his most popular drama, introduced him to theatergoers with as much éclat as *The Monk* had to the reading public. In 1799 he supplied Drury Lane with two comedies, *The Twins* and *The East Indian*, and published *Rolla*, a translation of Kotzebue's melo-drama *Die Spanier in Peru oder Rollas Tod*. *The Love of Gain*, a translation of Juvenal's thirteenth satire, also belongs to this year. In 1801 *Tales of Wonder*, a collection of ballads, was published; and *Adelmorn*, a romantic drama, was produced at Drury Lane and *Alfonso*, a blank-verse tragedy, at Covent Garden.

Probably early in 1801 Lewis found a cottage at Barnes, some four miles from Piccadilly, which became his principal dwelling until 1809. Known as Hermitage Cottage, it was on what was then Goodenough's Lane on a small common, near the church.[43] There is no trace of it today; the spot where it stood is near the head of what is now Nassau Street.[44] His only objection to the cottage was that he had to share it with the owners, who also reserved part of the garden for themselves. He leased five rooms but needed a sixth because his books crowded him.[45] Though for some time he looked upon these quarters as temporary, he retained them until his death and furnished them, the biography tells us, "in a manner in every way indicative of its sensitive occupant." Besides too many books, it contained a profusion of pictures, mirrors, seals, statues, a piano, numerous pets, and "an unusual quantity of exquisitely-finished *bijouterie*."[46] In the flower garden were statues of Cupid and For-tune. The biography describes a miniature *fête champêtre* Lewis once held here for the Duchess of York and her suite. Lewis had a customary walk on the edge of the common, where he could be seen going back and forth for a couple of hours at a time.[47]

Lewis associated with many more literary and theatrical figures of the time than can be mentioned here. He was a valuable ac-quaintance, for his prestige and connections in the literary world as well as for his generosity, to several authors, of whom the most emi-nent was Walter Scott. Lady Charlotte Campbell brought the two men together in 1798, when Lewis was visiting the Argyll family.[48] They had already corresponded on the subject of ballads Lewis was collecting. From this meeting developed what Scott called "a sort of intimacy" from which "consequences arose which altered almost all the Scottish ballad-maker's future prospects in life."[49] Lewis introduced Scott to London society, arranged with his own publisher for the printing of some of Scott's work, and used his influence in the theater to have Scott's *House of Aspen* produced.[50] But whatever debt Scott incurred he amply repaid by leaving for posterity kindly and amusing reminiscences of his friend. The voluminous literature surrounding Scott's name affords many glimpses of their intimacy, of which the most entertaining are in his own words. He thus describes one outing they took together:

We were to go up one side of the river and come down the other. In the return he was dead tired, and, like the Israelites, he murmured against his guide for leading him into the wilderness. I was then as strong as a poney, and took him on my back, dressed as he was in his shooting array of a close sky-blue jacket, and the brightest *red* pantaloons I ever saw on a human breech. He also had a kind of feather in his cap. At last I could not help laughing at the ridiculous figure we must both have made, at which my rider waxed wroth. . . . We returned to the cottage weary wights, and it cost more than one glass of Noyau, which he liked in a decent way, to get Mat's temper on its legs again.[51]

Tom Moore, making his way in London in 1801, wrote with delight to his mother, "You cannot think how much my songs are liked here. Monk Lewis was 'in the greatest agonies' the other night at Lady Donegal's, at having come in after my songs: "Pon his honour, he had come for the express purpose of hearing me.' "[52] The friendship these two formed is recorded in Moore's *Memoirs, Journal, and Correspondence.* When Moore asked Lewis' help in finding employment, Lewis offered to do all that he could, but said that "instead of ranking among your '*great friends,*' I must submit to being classed among your *little* ones in every respect. . . . All my *great friends* are merely *liaisons de société.* . . . As to Ministers, I know none of the present; and, between ourselves, have not the least inclination to know them."[53] Moore respected Lewis' knowledge of stage effect and recommended him to a friend arranging a spectacle piece: "Lewis will be of great use to you in this way; there is no man who (as they say) 'knows the *inside* of a theatre' better than Lewis."[54]

Lewis and Robert Southey were together for a time at Westminster School. Later there was a misunderstanding between them

concerning the inclusion in *Tales of Wonder* of ballads by Southey
—"a sort of Imbroglio," Lewis called it.[55] The future poet laureate
spoke more than once in disparagement of the other's verse. Of
the ballad contributed by Lewis to Scott's *Minstrelsy of the Scottish Border* he wrote, "Sir Agrethorn [sic] is flat, foolish, Matthew-
ish, Gregoryish, Lewisish. I have been obliged to coin vituperative
adjectives on purpose, the language not having terms enough of
adequate abuse."[56] But like Moore he gave Lewis credit for his
ability to please the public by stage effect, which "no dramatist
ever studied more successfully,"[57] and in this connection had occasion to be, and was, grateful. He wrote in 1805, "Matthew Lewis
has offered thro' Wynn, if I will write a play, to insure its reception
at Covent Garden and perfect secresy with regard to the author till
it shall have succeeded, if succeed it should. I cannot write a good
play, though neither Wynn nor Lewis would believe me if I said
so. . . ."[58] Two days later he addressed his friend Charles Watkin
Williams Wynn,

It is so very possible that I might by play writing get five hundred a year,
with less labour than it now costs me to get one, that I do not in conscience
think it a sufficient excuse either to others or to myself to say that I cannot
write a good play, especially when a bad one will answer the main end as
well. Lewis's offer—for which I am very much obliged to him, would remove
some very weighty objections. The fretting vexations of a green-room
negociation, and the chance of hostility from some of those persons whose
goose language is very inoffensive upon paper, but would be very mischievous
when delivered viva voce at the theatre. I will therefore thankfully accept his
offer, and seriously and resolutely set myself to work.[59]

Lewis as an author of course fell well within the range of
Byron's undiscriminating lash. When *English Bards and Scotch
Reviewers* appeared in 1809 he found himself duly pilloried as
"Apollo's sexton" who "fain would make Parnassus a churchyard!"[60] The two men apparently did not meet until four years later.
It was an awkward moment when they did. Mary Shelley records
that Lewis asked Byron earnestly, "Why did you call me Apollo's
Sexton?" and Byron "found it difficult to reply to this categorical
species of reproof."[61] Thereafter they often met in society and
supped together. Byron valued Lewis' friendship and profited from
his literary advice. His comments have a tone of affectionate ridicule, occasionally of exasperation: "It is a good and good-humoured

man, but pestilently prolix and paradoxical and *personal*. If he would but talk half, and reduce his visits to an hour, he would add to his popularity." But being *ouverte*, Lewis' vanity, Byron thought, was not offending.[62] Once Lewis had just returned from Oatlands, where Mme. de Staël had bored him with praises of himself till he sickened and as usual the two had quarreled. Byron wrote in his *Journal*, "I should like, of all things, to have heard the Amabæan eclogue between her and Lewis—both obstinate, clever, odd, garrulous, and shrill. In fact, one could have heard nothing else."[63]

There seems to be no record of a meeting between William Wordsworth and Lewis. William's brother John, however, received from Lewis an unsolicited letter of approval of the second edition of *Lyrical Ballads* (1800), accompanied by a poem which the recipient described as "the most funny I have ever read; it is quite a caricature of its kind: they ought to have made a parson of him instead of a M.P." The poem may have been that which Lewis afterwards published with the title *The Felon* ("Oh! mark his wan and hollow cheeks, and mark his eye-balls glare!"), since John Wordsworth adds, " 'The Convict' of William's is nothing compared to Lewis's."[64]

Among his distinguished acquaintances Sheridan was the only one whom Lewis hated. At Drury Lane Sheridan gave him rather good grounds for this feeling, but as early as 1793, probably before the two had met, Lewis had suggested to Sheridan in anonymous newspaper verses that he hang himself (see p. 14 above). The verses were ostensibly prompted by a difference in political opinion, but Lewis had even then cause for discomfort at the thought of Sheridan. His own early experiments in social satire, *The Effusions of Sensibility*, *Village Virtues*, and *The East Indian*, must have made him painfully aware of his debt to the elder dramatist's brilliant comedies. His subsequent acquaintance with their author gave him further grounds for dislike. In 1804, when he had come to know the theaters, he described Sheridan to his mother as "the most abandoned Libertine that probably ever existed" (F 55). Lewis, as a Holland House wit, found Sheridan a contemptuous and devastating rival. On at least one occasion as the butt of the latter's ridicule, the "little author became as mute as a fish from the rebuff," in Lady Holland's words.[65] Sheridan's parody is one of the witticisms which circulated to Lewis' discomfiture:

Three Poets in three distant streets dwelt all—
The Strand, New Sloane Street, and famed Leaden Hall—
The first renown'd for Spectres and Bombast,
The next for Plagiary, for both the last.
Exhausted Folly could perform no more,
But made a Lewis from a Cob and Hoare.[66]

Lewis was accustomed to indulgence from society less talented than he or more merciful than Sheridan, but the latter refused to pretend that Lewis' work had any value but a commercial one.

With Tom Sheridan, the dramatist's son, Lewis was on better terms. They were fellow members of the Catamaran Club, together with Theodore Hook, Charles Mathews, the Kembles, Joseph Munden, George Colman the younger, Thomas Morton, and other figures of the theatrical world.[67] But Lewis was quite capable of quarreling with Tom also, as appears from a note by the latter concerning some trifle involving the use of a theater box:

Dear Lewis—

I am conscious of the intense irritability of my Temper when I have drank a certain quantity of wine, for wh: I then deserve to have my head broke and wh: will some time or other be the case I suppose, to this you must attribute my peevishness and ill manners, wh: I acknowledge & regret. Many vexations have latterly crowded upon me & soured my disposition (which you may once remember was cheerful, & wh: still believe me is friendly & sincere tho so much altered for the worse in other respects) and which, while they render me indifferent to the opinion of others, makes me neglect those little courtesies in society wh: are its best ornament.

as to Carpenter you really mistook me, I had no earthly (I could have none) objection to his coming to the Box, but I pride myself upon *speaking out*, and thought it best, at once to say under what understanding the Box was subscribed for (which I consider as belonging *less* to me than any other Person) and what I know wd: be the remark made had *I* began to break thro the Rules agreed upon.—I dare say I did this in an abrupt bad way, but I meant neither more nor less.—I should regret being on bad terms with you, because I think you have many estimable Qualities, you have also many Failings like myself, & we had better take each other as God has made us, than wrangle, at least on my part I wish to remain your Friend

T. Sheridan[68]

Minor literary figures whom Lewis knew included the brilliant and versatile John Leyden, who contributed a ballad to *Tales of Wonder* and who was inspired to write youthful verses by Lewis' sister Sophia. An amusing fragment by Walter Scott, "Criminal

Letters. The King against Sophia Lewis," suggests a lighthearted love affair. In his charge Scott accuses Sophia of assaulting "the person of the deceased John Leyden, late preacher of the gospel" with "divers weapons, called wit, beauty, accomplishments, &c." and announces that "there will be lodged in evidence against you divers poems, in the handwriting of the said John Leyden, all marking the progressive derangement of his understanding."[69] When she was young, the novelist Susan Ferrier often saw Lewis at Inveraray. He wrote several poems for her album and was recommended by her to a friend who needed advice from "some person who is up to the art of bookmaking and bookmending to revise and correct" literary work.[70]

The artist and antiquary Charles Kirkpatrick Sharpe first met Lewis when they supped at the house of Lady Charlotte Bury in Cadogan Place. Lewis "talked so much that I thought he was intolerable," Sharpe recalls. "I afterwards knew better how to value him." He had, Sharpe thought, numberless good qualities of which their hostess could be no judge.[71] Years after Lewis' death, a newspaper announcement of the publication of the *Life and Correspondence* of Lewis filled Sharpe with painful misgivings as, thinking back some quarter of a century, he remembered "much silly poetry" he had included in intimate letters to his former friend. For several days he "ate little and slept less," oppressed by a "fearful apprehension." After reading the new publication and finding that he had been spared, he exclaimed, "I can never be sufficiently thankful to Providence for this escape," and added in criticism of the work, "I detect many lies—but all very innocent ones—all favourable to very unworthy people, the most of whom are dead."[72]

Lewis' name is linked to that of Thomas Campbell by a single anecdote. Once at Kensington among distinguished guests, according to the author Mary Berry, Lewis "gave out a thousand *bêtises* upon the subject of poetry, pretending that he found Homer and Virgil wearisome." During the evening the poet Campbell read a discourse on poetry which "appeared to be made expressly to punish him and to expose the inaptitude of these heterodox opinions. Poor Lewis was in a very bad humour, and did not know where to hide his head during the reading, so he pretended to be sleeping."[73] He was acquainted also with Samuel Rogers, noted, along with more substantial qualities, for his cadaverous appearance. When Lewis visited him one day, Lady Oxford's three- or four-year-old son was present and later reported with the charming hyperbole of infancy that he had been "to see the pretty pretties."[74] Two foreign writers visiting England recorded their impressions of Lewis. Chateaubriand met him twice in London and found him "un jeune membre des Communes fort agréable, et qui avait l'air et les manières d'un Français."[75] Though the American George Ticknor does not mention meeting Lewis, he sat with Byron at Drury Lane in 1815 and saw him in the next box, "a very decent looking man compared with the form my imagination had given to the author of the 'Monk,' and the 'Castle Spectre.' "[76] Incidentally, when Ticknor was sightseeing in Madrid three years later, he was chiefly interested in a few obscure buildings such as the house where Columbus lived, two or three palaces described in *Gil Blas*, and "the convent which Lewis has made the scene of his monk."[77] A tradition, it seems, had been established for visitors to Madrid, where Lewis himself had never been.

During these years, events happy and unhappy were taking place in the Lewis family. In 1799 his sister Maria was married to Henry Lushington, later Sir Henry, eldest son of Sir Stephen Lushington. Sir Henry was appointed consul at Naples and settled his family there. Barrington, Lewis' invalid brother, died in his twenty-second year, soon after Maria's marriage.[78] This loss was a lasting sorrow to Lewis, in whose early letters are several affectionate references to Barrington. According to Medwin, Byron once said, "Lewis had been, or thought he had been, unkind to a brother whom he lost young; and when any thing disagreeable was about to happen to him the vision of his brother appeared: he came as a sort of monitor."[79] In 1804 Sophia Lewis married John Shedden of the Fifteenth Light Dragoons, who later became a colonel.

Meanwhile a quarrel had been brewing between Matthew and his father, having as its storm center the widow of John Poyntz Ricketts, who had been one of Mr. Lewis' friends. It leaves too much unexplained to say merely that the father took a mistress of whom the son disapproved. The account in the biography also needs correction. It is overwhelmingly on Matthew's side and leaves the impression that a despicable person forced her way into the family circle, gained a malign influence over the elder Lewis, and caused him to treat his son with cruel injustice. The impression is strengthened—in fact, largely derived—from Lewis' words: "She has been the cause of almost every quarrel that has happened in our family, ever since I can remember; while they were unmarried, She made the lives of my Sisters miserable; She did all in her power to prevent Maria's marriage; every one of my Relatives except W$^m$ Sewell sees her in the same light that I do" (F 62). But Matthew, as he often insisted, thoroughly despised her and as a principal in the quarrel was naturally led to strong expressions.

References to Ricketts in Mr. Lewis' letters make it clear that the two men had been close friends for many years and that Ricketts and his wife sided with Mr. Lewis in the difficulties leading to the separation of Matthew's parents. In a letter of 1779 relating news of the Jamaica disaster, Mr. Lewis expresses fear to the Secretary at War that the property of Ricketts and his connections has been destroyed.[80] The fear was apparently well founded, since he presently solicits aid for Ricketts, probably a government sinecure. A letter of 1781 breaks through the customary impersonality of the War Office correspondence: "My heart has been too full when I have lately spoken to you, to allow me to give expression to the half of what I feel from your most friendly and affectionate consideration of my family-embarrassments, and your endeavours to make them sit easier upon me. That I do not sink under them I can with sincerity impute to your friendship and that of M$^r$ & M$^{rs}$ Ricketts, and none else."[81] In the spring of 1782 Mr. Lewis writes to the Secretary that had he lost his position as deputy he would have asked no favors for himself but would have gone quietly away to the West Indies: "All I should have said to you then; I will say now; that, as Deputies have usually been considered, after approved Service, I wish my claims to be all transfer'd to my Friend—my very Heart bleeds for Ricketts—Your affecting anything beneficial for Him w$^d$ repay me in the way most pleasing, for every toil that I may have undergone, & for the sacrifice of the Ten best Years of my Life in an occupation not very congenial to my natural turn of mind, & in which I am now rather poorer than when I first was called to it."[82] Whether or not these appeals bore fruit immediately, eleven years later Ricketts was appointed captain-general and governor in chief of the island of Tobago.[83] The next year he was promoted to the same positions in Barbados,[84] where his yearly salary was £3000.[85] In 1796 Mr. Lewis attempted to secure a pension for Mrs. Ricketts,[86] and his will, drawn up a few months after Ricketts' death in 1800, provided for £500 to be paid to his "dear and respected friend" and released the estate of his "late dear friend" from a debt of "22 hundred pounds and upwards and of other considerable sums advanced to the support of his family."[87]

The break between father and son became an open quarrel in 1803, the year Mr. Lewis retired from the War Office.[88] Though Matthew was willing to acknowledge Mrs. Ricketts as an acquaintance, he looked upon her as an enemy, told her so, and refused to call on her as his father requested. Bitter words were spoken. Mr. Lewis declared that Matthew's brutal indifference to the pain such conduct caused him proved he lacked the proper feelings of a son and the generosity of a man. It seems that Matthew was denied the privilege of wine from the cellar at Devonshire Place, and was deeply wounded when, on his twenty-ninth birthday, his father greeted him with a frosty "So; you are there, Sir!" and then dined early and went to a cricket match (F 52). Matthew's allowance was reduced to a thousand pounds a year and then to less (F 57–8). His father "has even refused to keep Saddle-horses for me (though he knows, that riding was the only exercise which I liked, and which had even been prescribed for me as necessary for my health)" (F 59). When told that he was no longer considered part of the domestic establishment, he quit London for a visit to Inveraray Castle with the conviction that he was leaving his father's house forever.

Mrs. Lewis, her brother Robert Sewell, and Mrs. Blake, Mr. Lewis' sister, worked hard to bring about a reconciliation. Matthew was willing to leave a card at Mrs. Ricketts' door, but complained that he was expected to change his sentiments as well as his conduct. "Now a Man's sentiments," he truthfully and wordily declared, "are not in his own power; I cannot think that right, which I know (or at least *think* I know) to be wrong" (F 59). Mrs. Ricketts moreover was reported to have said that Mr. Lewis was only waiting for his wife's death to marry her. "And *ought* a Son to be upon friendly terms with a Person, who He *knows* is waiting with impatience for the death of his Mother . . . ?" (F 59). After two years both sides had made concessions sufficient to end the quarrel formally, though it was never really healed. Matthew says of a

note he received from his father, "He only 'expects kind and respectful attention from me. . . .' Even to my Uncle Robert He
allowed, that He insisted on my changing my sentiments; now, not
a word is said on the subject (F 66–7). This tedious affair at least
illustrates Matthew's stubborn insistence upon principle—he could
never be bullied from what he knew, or thought he knew, was
right, not even at the risk of losing a considerable inheritance.

Lewis enjoyed the luxury of benevolence, a side of his nature
best summed up by Walter Scott: "He did much good by stealth,
and was a most generous creature."[89] One of his regrets when his
allowance was reduced was that it impaired his aid to the Kelly
family. Writers on Lewis have relied upon the biography in their
accounts of Lewis' relations with the Kellys, but it is interesting to
find that a version of the story was published in a now forgotten
book which antedates the biography by thirty years: *London Characters; or, Fashions and Customs of the Present Century. By Sir
Barnaby Sketchwell, Scene and Portrait-Painter to the Argyll-
Rooms, and Other Places of Elegant Resort* (two volumes, London, 1809). This work contains a character sketch of Lewis under
the disguising name "Matthew Monckton, Esq.," which, after a
general comment on his literary work, continues: "His private character is truly amiable; and as free from blame as erring mortality is
capable of being: indeed, instances have occurred, which serve to
shew that his virtue, according to the system of morals adopted in
this age, is as romantic as his ideas, though not so visionary: several
might be adduced; we will beg leave to quote one only, which sufficiently proves the grandeur and disinterestedness of his mind." An
account is then given of the widow of an army colonel who had
written poems and fiction approved by the public. Monckton, who
had never met her, was pleased with her writings and, understanding that she had limited means and a son to support, informed her
through a friend that he would undertake to finance the son's education. When she asked for an interview to express her gratitude
personally, Monckton respectfully declined on the grounds "that
her fine person and his own youth might subject her to the idle
and malevolent slanders of the world."[90]

The widow, unnamed in this account, was a daughter of Captain William Fordyce, carver and cupbearer to George III. She
had married in 1789 Captain Robert Hawke Kelly,[91] whom she

described as "neglected by those on whom he had hereditary claims of protection."[92] There were two sons to support—Fitzroy, born in October 1796, and William, born not more than four years earlier.[93] In 1802 Mrs. Kelly appears to have applied to Lewis, as having influence at the War Office, for help in claiming some accumulated pay which had been due her father. Lewis presented her petition but was obliged to inform her that the money could not be reclaimed. The only authority for the following letter is the *Life*:

August 11, 1802.

Dear Madam,

Your disappointment must have been severe; and I have been turning in my mind how I can possibly serve you. It appears to me that, as you have two young boys, to educate one of them, so as to enable him to become an useful and honourable member of society, will best benefit you; I will therefore do so; and, hereafter, I may have interest enough to place him in the War Office.

I beg you to spare all thanks. When a person of your feelings and character accepts a kindness, you confer, not receive an obligation.

I am, Madam,<br>Your sincere friend,<br>M. G. Lewis.[94]

Lewis afterward recommended her to his own publisher, sent her a plan for a novel and verses for her use, and read some of her work before publication.[95] Her gratitude was rather embarrassing. She wished to dedicate her novel *The Baron's Daughter* (1802) to him, "but *that*," Lewis tells his mother, "I stopped" (F 44); so Mrs. Kelly had to be content to say in her preface that had she not considered the work too insignificant, she would have offered it to "*one* whose genius is only exceeded by his active beneficence."[96] When one of her books was advertised as partly by Lewis, "I immediately wrote to her on the subject," he explained to his mother, "stating that, in consequence, I declined ever reading her future works, previous to their publication."[97] In a letter (F 44) three days later he continues,

It was not merely on account of the advertisement, that I declined seeing any of Mrs Kelly's Manuscripts: But into the bargain She had just published a Novel, in which there was a most flaming eulogium upon the author of the Monk; & the advertisement might have induced people to suppose that I

had written my own praises; Now though I have no objection to other
people's trying to make me appear *wicked or foolish*, I do not chuse to have
it supposed that I have made myself appear *ridiculous*; & therefore I immediately informed Mrs Kelly, that I never could give any public patronage
to a Person who had published an eulogium upon me; & that though I
would continue to take care of her child for another year, I would have
nothing to do with her writings.[98]

The novel with the eulogium is *A Modern Incident in Domestic
Life* (1803), in which two stanzas are quoted which many of
Mrs. Kelly's readers would probably have recognized as extracted
from the "Midnight Hymn" in *The Monk*. They are followed by
this:

> "The lines you have just read are so exquisitely beautiful," said Miss
> Courtney to her young governess, "that I wish you would indulge me, and
> set them to music."
> "Could I give them tones," answered Ellen, "to bear any proportion to
> the beneficence of the spirit that composed them, I might attempt it,—but
> I should only take from their harmony."
> "Indeed! who composed them?"
> "In England he would not need a name, for he lives in the heart of
> *secret sorrow*, and he allows sorrow to repose on his *secret virtues*."
> Miss Mortimer had scarcely concluded the deserved eulogium on one
> whose nature reflects honour on the human kind, before Mrs. Courtney
> entered the gallery.[99]

While this is more cloying than flaming, one can understand
Lewis' feeling that Mrs. Kelly's gratitude was getting out of hand.
The preface to *The Baron's Daughter* states that poetry promised
for that novel will appear in a future work, but Lewis told his
mother concerning this novel, "I gave no poems for it, & mean to
give none for any future work of hers" (F 44).

He suffered considerably more embarrassment through Mrs.
Kelly's son William, who became a lifelong vexation to him.
Sophia Shedden wrote to Scott the year after her brother's death,
"I think that the most prominent of his good qualities was *mercy*.
This was the *Moral* of his *Monk*, and he exemplified it himself in
his conduct to that good-for-nothing young Man Kelly—whose
whole story indee[d] would tend greatly to illustrate my dear
Brother's character."[100] Lewis' continued patronage of this youth
must establish an endurance record for human patience. He paid
for the boy's schooling and got him employment in the War

*Miniature of Matthew G. Lewis by George Lethbridge Sanders.*
*National Portrait Gallery.*

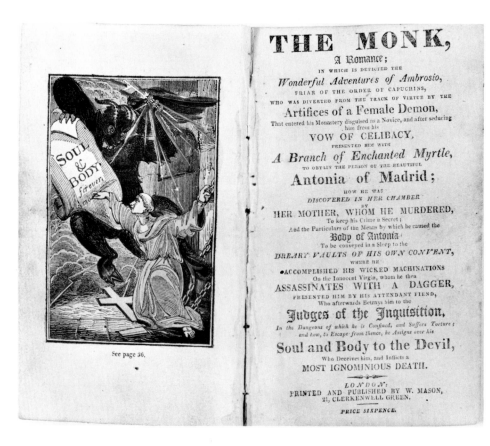

See page 36.

# THE MONK,

### A Romance;

IN WHICH IS DEPICTED THE

### Wonderful Adventures of Ambrosio,

FRIAR OF THE ORDER OF CAPUCHINS,

WHO WAS DIVERTED FROM THE TRACK OF VIRTUE BY THE

### Artifices of a Female Demon,

That entered his Monastery disguised as a Novice, and after seducing
him from his

### VOW OF CELIBACY,

PRESENTED HIM WITH

### A Branch of Enchanted Myrtle,

TO OBTAIN THE PERSON OF THE BEAUTIFUL

### Antonia of Madrid;

HOW HE WAS

DISCOVERED IN HER CHAMBER

BY

### HER MOTHER, WHOM HE MURDERED,

To keep his Crime a Secret;

And the Particulars of the Means by which he caused the

### Body of Antonia

To be conveyed in a Sleep to the

DREARY VAULTS OF HIS OWN CONVENT,

WHERE HE

●ACCOMPLISHED HIS WICKED MACHINATIONS

On the Innocent Virgin, whom he then

### ASSASSINATES WITH A DAGGER,

PRESENTED HIM BY HIS ATTENDANT FIEND,

Who afterwards Betrays him to the

### Judges of the Inquisition,

In the Dungeons of which he is Confined, and Suffers Torture;
and how, to Escape from thence, he Assigns over his

### Soul and Body to the Devil,

Who Deceives him, and Inflicts a

MOST IGNOMINIOUS DEATH.

LONDON:

PRINTED AND PUBLISHED BY W. MASON,
21, CLERKENWELL GREEN.

PRICE SIXPENCE.

*From a pirated abridgment of* The Monk, *watermark 1818.*

Office. After Kelly lost his position, Lewis said, "I could as soon get him into the moon" as re-establish him.[101] Kelly drank, broke promises, and used his patron's name to obtain credit from trades-people. Finally, when after fourteen years of indulgence Lewis had him released once more from jail, he determined that it should be for the last time and informed him that henceforth they must be strangers—unless he would reform. Meanwhile Lewis increased his mother's allowance so that she might aid the young man, an arrangement by which Lewis satisfied both his indignation and his generosity. In a codicil of 1813 to his will he assigned Kelly five £100 shares in Drury Lane Theatre and £1000 to be paid at his maturity, but two years later amended this to a legacy of £104 a year to be paid in weekly installments, since he had "no other means of securing him from starving through his own imprudence & misconduct" (F 120). As late as September 20, 1817, he wrote to his mother from Paris, "My object in the allowance to W. Kelly was to secure him from wanting *bread*, and nothing but bread. . . . I forbade positively his mentioning my name to tradesmen at all. I suppose he will say that he only mentioned yours; but that is the same thing."[102]

Another aspect of the Kelly affair requires mention. In 1938 a biographical account of Lewis declared, in what appears to be the first published statement of the sort, that Lewis was homosexual.[103] The evidence adduced was that Medwin reported Byron to have remarked once, "Lewis was a pleasant companion, and would al-ways have remained a boy in spirits and manners—(unlike me!) He was fond of the society of younger men than himself. . . . I remember Mrs. Hope [Pope] once asking who was Lewis' male-love this season!"[104] The same account of Lewis said that his homosexuality "is quite apparent from his works" because it has been remarked that "the descriptions of female charms in *The Monk*, however voluptuously intended, are in effect cold and merely 'literary,'" and that homosexuality was rife in London society during Lewis' time. Upon these foundations were based the further statements that Lewis visited Mrs. Kelly "and at once fell passionately in love with her eldest son, William, then a lad of about fourteen years old" (actually he was ten or younger) and that "there can be no question that William Martin Kelly was the absorbing passion of his life." Though the *Life,* from which this latter account was derived, furnishes no basis for such an interpretation and sometimes contradicts it, Lewis was nevertheless presented as "the broken-hearted lover" striving to blot the "loved face from memory" and seeking "sorrow's anodyne" in similar intrigues gratuitously furnished on no authority.[105]

So far as it concerns Kelly, the account is fanciful. On the other hand, the statement that Lewis was homosexual, while it would require for confirmation more convincing evidence than has been presented, is impossible to confirm or disprove. Moreover, the term is popularly used to cover such a wide range of phenomena, from the mere enjoyment of the company of one's own sex to the most appalling abnormalities, that a biographer who applies it to his subject would seem to need a careful definition of what he means, to say nothing of strong evidence. To publish the statement with such assurance was rather a pity, because since its appearance it has become fashionable to add piquancy to accounts of Lewis by describing him as sexually abnormal. As for Lewis' descriptions of female charms, whether they are "cold and merely 'literary' " evidently depends on who is reading them. Alexander Dyce noted in one of his copies of *The Monk*, with reference to the scene in which Antonia disrobes to bathe: "Hoppner the painter [John Hoppner, 1758–1810] used to say, that this was the most exciting description he ever read (and *he* was familiar with such descriptions)."[106]

William Kelly drops from sight, but his younger brother, Fitzroy, attended a boarding school and shared a room with the future dramatist, James Robinson Planché. He rose to eminence at the Bar and became Lord Chief Baron of the Exchequer. In 1845 Lady Holland reported the following gossip about him: "It is said he is the son of my poor old friend Monk Lewis. His brother, by the same mother, is acknowledged as such in Lewis's will, who left him a provision."[107] There seems to be no evidence to substantiate this gossip about Fitzroy. Concerning William, Lewis' will contains no such acknowledgment.

Ever since engaging the cottage at Barnes, Lewis had looked for quarters closer to London. In June 1809 he bought for six hundred guineas a suite of rooms at the Albany in Piccadilly, where he could enjoy seclusion in the heart of the city, and retained these quarters until his death.[108] The apartment, subsequently remodeled, probably had four or five rooms and a small reception hall. Though a stairway now leads to the miniature cellar, Lewis was obliged to use a trap door, a detail, in view of some of his dramas, which must have appealed to him. A few years ago there still lingered in the chambers a shadowy and scarcely credible tradition that he concealed in the coal bin the body of a Negro servant he had murdered.[109] Byron once came away from a dinner Lewis gave at the Albany with the determination not to repeat the experience, complaining to James Smith, "I never will dine with a middle-aged man who fills up his table with young ensigns, and has looking-glass panels to his book-cases."[110]

Meanwhile, over two dozen publications and dramatic productions had been keeping Lewis' name before the public in the ten years from 1803 to 1812, to say nothing of printed versions of his dramas and many editions of individual works. *The Harper's Daughter*, a tragedy reworked from *The Minister*, and *The Captive*, an ill-fated monodrama, were performed in 1803. His very popular story, *The Bravo of Venice* (1805), furnished the theme of *Rugantino*, a melodrama performed the same year. *Feudal Tyrants*, a prose translation, *Adelgitha*, a tragedy, and *The Wood Daemon*, a melodrama, belong to 1807; the melodrama *Venoni, or The Novice of St. Mark's*, *Romantic Tales*, and *Twelve Ballads* to 1808. In 1809 the farce *Temper, or The Domestic Tyrant* was acted, and Lewis published a small edition of his *Monody on the Death of Sir John Moore*. Although about the middle of this year he announced that he would probably write no more for the theater, he was persuaded to fashion *Timour the Tartar* for Covent Garden, which with the spectacle of *One O'Clock*, based on *The Wood Daemon*, was produced in 1811, followed in 1812 by *Rich and Poor*, a comic opera taken from *The East Indian*. His last publication, *Poems*, a little collection of verses, appeared in the same year.

# 4

# DRAMAS

During the seventeen years—1796 to 1812—covered by the preceding chapter, eighteen dramatic works by Lewis were published or produced. While this output is not large compared to that of many of his contemporaries, it is certainly varied and in some ways so bold and original that it made him the leading popular dramatist of his day. Although, like the work of all his rivals in this field, Lewis' dramas are forgotten now except by specialists, the chronicle of their successes and failures sheds a good deal of light upon the theater and drama of the time. To group them in one chapter, reserving treatment of his other works until later, will give a clearer picture of his methods and importance as a dramatist than will a discussion of his total writings year by year. Though they do not make stimulating reading, summaries of these brainless stories are dutifully included in this chapter, partly because Lewis' plays are mirrors of the taste of his time and partly in the hope that a brief recounting of the action of each will be useful to students seeking sources or literary influences by indicating what they should read and what they may safely dismiss.

As is well known, these were sad days in the long history of British drama. With the enlarging of Drury Lane and Covent Garden to accommodate greater audiences, intimate and subtle acting gave way to the spectacular. The introduction of gas lighting to the stage and the development of elaborate stage machinery encouraged the emergence of new forms of entertainment, depending for their popularity upon music, pantomime, and gorgeous scenic effects.[1] Authors of the first rank, scornful of the public taste, wrote closet drama or none at all, or at most made only halfhearted attempts to compose for the popular theater. Though Lewis too was perfectly aware of how trivial dramatic entertainment had become, he nevertheless enthusiastically accepted conditions as he found them because they invited experimentation in the very directions in which his talents lay. There is no point in condemning him for abetting the forces working against serious drama. Probably nothing at the time could have restored a high level of dramatic writing to the theater. The contempt so often directed at Lewis the dramatist was really an expression of dissatisfaction with the general state of the popular theater and exasperation over his success.

His earliest dramatic publication made no impression on the world. This was *Village Virtues: A Dramatic Satire*, published in June 1796, a few months after the appearance of *The Monk*.[2] Though he had subscribed his initials to the preface of his romance, *Village Virtues* was completely anonymous. The careful make-up of this little forty-five-page quarto, with its large type and heavy paper, as well as the difficulty of finding copies, suggests a limited edition published at the author's expense.[3] It is a farce, in two parts instead of acts. Lady Mount-Level, a rich widow, disgusted with the city and the vices of society, retires to the country in the expectation of finding virtue and simplicity in rustic life. Her brother Sir David Downright undertakes to disabuse her of this idealization of rural existence, since, as it happens, her retirement would jeopardize the inheritance of his children. He arranges to have her lodge at a farmhouse in Cornwall, where a disagreeable day spent in observing the vulgarity and corruption of Farmer Sturdy's family and of other villagers completely disillusions her. She confesses herself cured, only to find that the events of the day have been preconcerted by her brother's children and friends masquerading as rustics with the purpose of proving to her that humble folk are as full of vice as are members of high society. The satire strikes in various directions—fashionable letter writing, fashionable dress, the increasingly important role of women in public life. Though a few situations are amusing, the illogical conclusion is feeble and the disagreeably class-conscious theme—there had been nothing in Lewis' upbringing to encourage democratic principles—would have had little appeal on the popular stage. He probably composed the farce in Paris in the summer of 1791 at the age of sixteen, the year of *The Effusions of Sensibility* and *The East Indian*, both in the same vein of social satire, and referred to it when he wrote to his mother the next year: "I shall not throw away any more time till I have got one of the things I have already finished upon the Stage" and "I shall also bring two or three other things for you to try your fortune with."[4] It received scant attention from the reviews. "The piece is on the whole very well written" is about as near as it came to evoking enthusiasm.[5] The *Monthly Review* and the *Critical Review* were mildly contemptuous, the latter dismissing it with "Mercy on us! this *thing* is written, 'that every British heart may be firm in supporting our country and our constitution!!' "[6] Thus *Village Virtues* passed from sight. In the notoriety that attended *The Monk*, even its anonymous author may have forgotten it.

In 1793 Lewis had translated Schiller's *Kabale und Liebe* at Bothwell Castle. Subsequently an anonymous English version of the German drama appeared, a clumsy piece of work by a translator who had condensed and rearranged the scenes and repeatedly misunderstood the German text.[7] In April 1797 Lewis published his own version, confidently observing in his advertisement that at least his translation could not possibly be worse than the other.[8] To keep the two distinct, he titled his own *The Minister* and changed the names of all the characters. In every other respect, he said, he tried to keep strictly to the original.

This endeavor is not wholly successful. He makes many small additions to the text and is especially apt to elaborate sentimental passages, most conspicuously in his treatment of the heroine, whom he conceives to be a "lovely unfortunate enthusiast" somewhat akin to his own Crazy Jane. When asked her age, she replies, "On my last birth-day I numbered sixteen years; they have been passed in pleasures, which never must return!"—a rather elaborate translation of "Sechzehn gewesen."[9] More excusable is his habit of adding a few grandiloquent explanatory words at the close of scenes to help the actor off the stage or make clear to the dullest playgoer what is taking place. His omissions, fewer than the additions, are usually unimportant passages he found difficult to translate, such as some of the idiomatic expressions of Miller, the fiery, tenderhearted old musician. When Lewis strays from the sense of the original, his knowledge of German can usually be given the benefit of the doubt, though a few clear cases of mistaken sense occur. The characters under his treatment lose whatever vitality they have in the original. Miller, the only really interesting figure in Schiller's play, Lewis does not try to reproduce; he is content to make him the poor but honest parent and to substitute righteous indignation for full-blooded profanity.

Contemporary reviews of *The Minister* were favorable and, though it did not see stage production, it was published again the following year. The *Critical Review*[10] having pointed out an anachronism in the play—that the Prince of Brunswick, about the year 1580, has been selling troops to serve in America—Lewis inserted in the second edition the footnote: "One of the Reviewers (I believe the *Critical*) very justly censures the glaring anachronism of this passage; but being apt to commit similar faults myself, I can readily forgive Schiller's." With his usual ill fortune at the hands of later critics, Lewis has been accused of originating the mistake and of dishonorably foisting it upon the German author,[11] though his sole fault was in directing attention to the time of the action of Schiller's story by printing the date with the cast of characters.

In an age not lacking in good translations *The Minister* has no value. How much it ever had has sometimes been questioned in view of the freedom Lewis allowed himself in expanding his original. But he took liberties because he knew what was needed for an English performance. *The Minister* has been conceded "the merit of giving the full record, without undue change or omission, of the essential content of Schiller's work."[12]

The first-produced and by far the most popular of Lewis' plays was *The Castle Spectre*, performed at Drury Lane on December 14, 1797. According to his own statement, he composed it not later than 1796. He probably had at least some of its substance in hand as early as 1792, the year in which he wrote to his mother from Weimar that he was struggling to write a romance: "As to my own Nonsense, I write, and write, and yet do not find that I have got a bit further in my original plan than I was when I saw you last. I have got hold of an infernal dying Man who plagues my very heart out; He has talked for half a volume already, seems likely to talk for half a volume more, and I cannot manage to kill him out of the way for the life of me" (F 12). The biography states quite plausibly that this dying man ultimately became Reginald in *The Castle Spectre*.[13] In the prologue to the drama Lewis presents himself as

> A youth, who yet has lived enough to know
> That life has thorns, and taste the cup of woe

and, perhaps building on the Inveraray incident which produced Crazy Jane, explains that while wandering among the ruins of Conway Castle in North Wales he met Romance, a "lovely maniac," who bade him renew the ancient state of the castle. Mindful of the charges of impiety raised by *The Monk*, Lewis submitted the completed play to his sister Maria, who, we are told, "with the delicate tact of a correct judgment, and a pure and pious mind" struck out whatever she thought might get her brother into further trouble.[14]

The Castle Spectre has been recognized as a kind of landmark in Gothic drama, a genre inaugurated by Horace Walpole's *Mysterious Mother*, printed in 1768. In it Lewis "exploited the combined materials of his predecessors and contemporaries, English and German, and out-Gothicized them all."[15] It is a signal example of his ability to seize upon material already at hand and push to the limit its possibilities of public entertainment. The plot is so crowded with minor complications and thrills that a brief summary can give only the main action. Osmond, a gloomy and nightmare-ridden earl, secured his title sixteen years ago by murdering his elder brother Reginald and the latter's wife, Evelina. He now dwells in Conway Castle, which is Gothic to the ramparts, equipped with a ghost and rumors of ghosts, sliding panels, secret passages, mysterious guitar music, and dungeons. In these disturbing surroundings Osmond has confined his ward Angela, in whose arms he hopes to find relief from a guilty conscience. To rescue her, Angela's lover Percy, the young Earl of Northumberland, gains access to the castle. His visit is brief but eventful. He hides in a suit of armor standing in the hall, saves Angela from Osmond's ferocious advances, is held captive by black slaves, and escapes by leaping from a window into a boat on the river.[16] Meanwhile we learn that Angela is the daughter of Reginald, the rightful earl, who, though supposed murdered, in fact recovered and was incarcerated in a secret dungeon of the castle by Kenric, an unwilling partner in Osmond's guilt. Learning this fact, the usurper extorts from Kenric the secret of the hiding place. Since Angela refuses to marry him, Osmond resolves to kill Reginald. Through secret passageways Angela reaches her father; Osmond, arriving a moment later, is deterred from murder by the appearance of Evelina's ghost. Angela mortally stabs him, and Percy, storming the castle with a band of soldiers, arrives in time to hail the rightful earl and offer himself as a son-in-law.

Upon reading *The Castle Spectre* one is hard put to account for its popularity. The language is trite; the characters are well-worn stock figures; the plot is incredibly contrived and crowded with irrelevancies. No one was more aware of its unoriginality than the author, who candidly cited the three works to which the play is particularly indebted—*The Castle of Otranto*, *The Mysteries of Udolpho*, and *Die Räuber*. Of his characters he says in a postscript to the printed play: "To originality of character I make no pretence. Persecuted heroines and conscience-stung villains certainly have made their courtesies and bows to a British audience long before the appearance of '*The Castle Spectre*;' the *Friar* and *Alice* are copies, but very faint ones, from *Juliet's Nurse*, and Sheridan's *Father Paul*, and *Percy* is a mighty pretty-behaved young gentleman with nearly no character at all." He facetiously claims unintentional originality for the Fool, in most plays a sharp and witty knave but in his dull and flat, "as in the course of the performance Mr. Bannister discovered to his very great sorrow."

*The Castle Spectre*, however, is an excellent vehicle for presenting a series of striking scenes of suspense or spectacle—the sudden appearance of the ghost in an atmosphere prepared by forebodings, the ironclad figure in the armory raising its truncheon in threatening gesture and advancing slowly toward the horrified earl, Percy's intricately managed escape beneath the very noses of his guards. Moreover, shortcomings which glare out at the reader were easily remedied in performance. The drama was cut for acting to a little over one half its published length; Kemble and Mrs. Jordan were by all accounts superb in the leading roles; and new costumes, scenery, and decorations were supplied for the opening night.

But the principal reason for its success was the appearance of the ghost in Act IV. Managers, actors, and friends had urged Lewis to forego the apparition, but he had persisted and his judgment did not err. At the end of the act Angela, having successfully repelled Osmond, hears a mysterious voice singing a lullaby to the accompaniment of a guitar. Presently the folding doors of the oratory open and the audience beholds in a blaze of illumination a tall female figure in white flowing garments spotted with blood, gazing and reaching toward Heaven. The specter advances to soft and plaintive music, points at the picture of Reginald, invokes a silent blessing upon Angela, and waves farewell. "Instantly the organ's swell is heard; a full chorus of female voices chant 'Jubilate!' a blaze of light flashes through the Oratory, and the folding doors close with a loud noise." The figure of the Bleeding Nun, popularized in *The Monk*, is here again exploited, this time as a benign instead of an evil apparition. That she accomplishes nothing for the plot, and from that point of view might better be omitted, mattered not a whit to Lewis or the public. Many contemporary accounts testify to the moving power of the scene: the effect was "stronger than any thing of the sort that has been hitherto attempted."[17] Years later James Boaden wrote, "I yet bring before me, with delight, the waving form of Mrs. Powell, advancing from the suddenly illuminated chapel, and bending over Angela (Mrs. Jordan) in maternal benediction; during which slow and solemn action, the band played a few bars" of "unearthly music."[18] The music was the *chaconne* of Jommelli, chosen by Michael Kelly, who records that the scene "rivetted the audience."[19] This scene, presumably, led a newspaper critic of one of the early performances to testify that there was "literally a *magic*" in *The Castle Spectre* which recalled every solemn remembrance of the spectator and appealed directly to the heart.[20]

Reviews gave the play praise mixed with blame, now finding the recital of Osmond's ghastly dream an example of the "sublimely terrific,"[21] now reproving the licenser of plays for not censoring expressions like "Saviour of the world" and "God of Heaven,"[22] and more than one voice was raised to regret Lewis' misdirected talents.[23] The theater was becoming conscious of historical correctness, but *The Castle Spectre* illustrates the rudimentary antiquarianism of the stage managers. The writer of an article who signed himself "An Artist and an Antiquarian" saw a performance in 1799 and, correctly assuming that the time of the story antedates the fifteenth century, amassed a surprisingly long list of anachronisms. The costume of Motley the fool, for instance, included cocked hat, ruffled shirt, short breeches, silk stockings, bells, and long ears. Osmond rushes from his dream of horror in a nightgown. Percy attacked the castle not in armour but dressed as a courtier of Charles I. "It would be more natural," said the writer, "if the castle clock was heard but faintly, and not so dreadfully loud as if the great bell itself was in the chamber."[24] The most notorious incongruity, the introduction of four African Negroes, Lewis justified with such incorrigible indifference to any standard except that of popular applause that it might well have discouraged further censure from serious-minded historians: "I thought it would give a pleasing variety to the characters and dresses, if I made my servants black; and could I have produced the same effect by making my heroine blue, blue I should have made her."[25]

Lewis states that he departed from custom by printing his drama "almost verbatim, as originally written" to disprove assertions that in its early form it was licentious, violently democratic, and crowded with ghosts. Certainly the manuscript copy submitted to the licenser contains nothing to substantiate these charges.[26] The written text is considerably shorter than the one published, because of a reduction of soliloquies, stage directions, and comic dialogue. Three of Hassan's speeches are marked in pencil in the manuscript, possibly because the examiner objected to their anti-slavery sentiments, but these were included in the printed version without important changes.[27] A penciled cross in the margin of the manuscript calls attention to the word "Hallelujah," which is crossed out in ink and appears in the printed play less impiously as "Jubilate."

Comments on *The Castle Spectre* by contemporaries outside the theatrical world are anything but favorable. Lady Holland must have been alone in finding "intellectual interest" in the last two acts.[28] Because of their personal concern with the drama at the time, both Wordsworth and Coleridge gave Lewis' play more attention than they might have otherwise. Whereas Lewis had succeeded brilliantly in capturing public applause, they both had failed in having plays of their own even accepted. Wordsworth, who some six months before had been told by the manager of Covent Garden that *The Borderers* could not possibly succeed if acted,[29] saw a performance of *The Castle Spectre* at Bristol and paid it the ambiguous compliment that "it fitted the taste of the audience like a glove."[30] Later he wrote with a touch of pique, "I am perfectly easy about the theatre, if I had no other method of employing myself Mr. Lewis's success would have thrown me into despair. The Castle Spectre is a Spectre indeed. Clothed with the flesh and blood of £400 received from the treasury of the theatre it may in the eyes of the author and his friend appear very lovely."[31] Coleridge, whose *Osorio* also had been rejected, read *The Castle Spectre* in January 1798 and promptly and acutely analyzed it in a letter to Wordsworth. The style of the serious passages he called "Schiller Lewis-ized—i.e. a flat, flabby, unimaginative Bombast oddly sprinkled with colloquialisms" and could not discover one line that marked even a superficial knowledge of human feelings. "A very fat Friar, renowned for Gluttony & Lubricity, furnishes abundance of jokes (all of them abdominal vel si quid infra)"— jokes "that would have stunk, had they been fresh." On the other hand, he paid tribute to the theatrical merit of the drama, the management of situations for stage effect. "This play," he said, "struck me with utter hopelessness—it would be [easy] to produce these situations, but not in a play for[cibly] as to admit the permanent & closest beauties of style, passion & character. To admit pantomimic tricks the plot itself must be pantomimic."[32]

Before the first three months of its run were over, Lewis' drama was said to have brought eighteen thousand pounds into the Drury Lane treasury.[33] Though the drama was not produced until December 14, the performances to June 18, the end of the season, totaled forty-seven. Playbills are not impartial evidence, but the Drury Lane bills strongly reflect the public's insistent demand by notices like the following: December 18—"The Fatigue attending the representation of some of the Characters renders it impossible to repeat the performance every night in the week"; January 15— "Notwithstanding the great demand for places for the Castle-Spectre; the system of giving as much Novelty as possible at this Theatre necessarily prevents its repetition till Monday next, when it will be performed for the 22nd. time"; March 15—"The Representation of The Castle-Spectre is obliged to be laid aside for some time after this Evening"; March 17—"On account of the very numerous applications for Places, the New Drama of The Castle-Spectre will be repeated for the 32d. time on Monday next, after which it cannot be performed for some time. . ."; March 20—"On

Thursday, (33rd. time) The New Drama of The Castle-Spectre, being positively the last time of its being performed before the Easter Holidays." Evidence that it continued to fill the house at the close of the season is the fact that it was used on four benefit nights in May and June. It was presented over a dozen times during each of the next two seasons and became a reliable stock piece for years. Bell, who brought out the first printed edition in 1798, had published ten more by 1803.[34]

*The Castle Spectre* established Lewis in the realm of the theatre with as much éclat as *The Monk* had put him before the reading public. He was now a dramatist whose work was in demand. Within the following year he published another translation and produced two more plays.

In a letter written toward the end of 1798 he informed Scott of his next dramatic project, a "German work, which is coming out at Drury Lane, and on which a great many cooks are employed; So many that it will be high luck, if the Broth be not spoiled. It is Kozebue's 'Spaniards in Peru'—I am to furnish the *literal* translation, and the Epilogue. Sheridan undertakes the adapting it to the Stage, making a new Catastrophe, and giving a Song or two; the opera house is to supply very splendid dresses; and the present idea is to have the two Heroines played by M$^{rs}$ Siddons and M$^{rs}$ Jordan. Drury Lane needs something as strong as this union, for at present they are playing to Empty Benches."[35] Collaboration with Sheridan proved impossible, however. On January 6 of the next year Lewis wrote to Scott, "I have not quite left off dabbling in Theatricals myself; As to the German Play, Sheridan is so vexatious and uncertain that I want to give up the bargain, and have nothing to do with it."[36] That is what happened. If the initial decision to put on Kotzebue's *Die Spanier in Peru oder Rollas Tod* was Lewis', he showed his usual acumen in recognizing material that would be popular. That it was his choice we may infer from Sheridan's ignorance of German and from Medwin's report of Byron's remark that *Pizarro* was a sore subject with Lewis "and no wonder that he winced at the name. Sheridan, who was not very scrupulous about applying to himself *literary* property at least, manufactured his play without so much as an acknowledgment, pecuniary or otherwise, from Lewis's ideas."[37] Sheridan finally employed a Miss Phillips to supply a translation[38] and from it fashioned *Pizarro*, produced in May 1799, with a success rivaling that of *The Castle Spectre*.

Lewis nevertheless published his own translation in the same year with the title of *Rolla; or, the Peruvian Hero: A Tragedy, in Five Acts*. Since it was not produced it has been given little notice, though as competent translation it deserves at least to be mentioned. It follows Kotzebue's text more faithfully than *The Minister* does Schiller's, partly because *Die Spanier* offers no difficulties of translation comparable to Miller's speeches in *Kabale und Liebe* and partly because *Die Spanier* contains enough bombast and sentimentalism to satisfy Lewis, who was therefore not tempted to make additions. The only significant ommissions are a few references to religion. The diction, as stilted as that in *The Minister*, abounds with inverted word order, lending an unnatural pomp to the most casual remarks; but as a translation it is far superior to that by Anne Plumptre, published the same year, and to Benjamin Thompson's in his *German Theatre* (1800).[39] *Rolla* was favorably reviewed[40] and reached two editions; it might have enjoyed greater popularity had not the success of *Pizarro* at Drury Lane been followed by a number of printings of Sheridan's play.

In the letter to Scott last quoted there occurs the following reference to one of Lewis' dramatic pieces of 1799: ". . . Bannister and I are very busy in cooking up a Farce for his Benefit, which I wrote many years ago, and which He thinks, He can do great things with: However I only mean it at any rate to be played for one night this Season—It is a sort of thing which must either take extremely, or be damned entirely. Bannister is to be on the Stage from beginning to end; He plays *two* characters, one a dissipated drunken Officer, the other a formal sanctified Quaker. The Title is 'The Twins,' and I have trumped up a Prologue for Bannister, which He is delighted with."[41] In the same letter Lewis recommends his friend to Scott: "You will find him one of the most gentlemanlike unassuming Fellows in the world, with more entertainment and sense in his conversation than you find in most people. Let me know whether his acquaintance would be agreable to you; For my own part, I know so much good of the Man, that I have really a regard for him, and shall be thankful for any civility shown him on my account."

Lewis had completed the farce at The Hague, intending it for this actor. Now, five years later, his plan was consummated when *The Twins; or, Is It He or His Brother?* was produced at Drury Lane on April 8 for Bannister's benefit.[42] It was never published but a manuscript copy survives.[43] The twins, Henry and Hezekiah Faulkland, have been separated since infancy. Henry has assumed the name of Melville and leads the life of a military rake. A rich uncle has disinherited him and bequeathed the family fortune to Hezekiah, now a Quaker living in New York. Melville, though he has promised to marry the old maid Tabitha, to whom he is in debt, falls in love with her niece Charlotte, who has been willed a fortune on condition that she marry Hezekiah if he will accept her. With the help of his servant Simon Sly and a Quaker costume, Melville impersonates his brother in order to win Charlotte and save her fortune. Meanwhile, of course, the real Hezekiah arrives from New York and is bewildered by a series of encounters with Charlotte, Tabitha, and others who mistake him for Melville in disguise. Matters are adjusted when Melville reveals himself as Henry Faulkland and a letter from Hezekiah explains that he already has riches and a sweetheart in America and has come to England merely to settle the family estate upon his brother Henry. The aunt resigns her claim, and the lovers are united.

Lewis' biographer correctly states that *The Twins* was taken from the French.[44] Lewis condensed Jean François Régnard's five-act comedy, *Les Ménechmes, ou Les Jumeaux* (1705), to a two-act farce and added a pair of Quakers to the cast.[45] The French play suffers somewhat by the change. The love of Melville and Charlotte, who have met only the day before, and the aunt's sudden renunciation at the end are unconvincing even for farce, and Tabitha's romantic delusions are exaggerated to a tiresome degree. Régnard's hero becomes the typical goodhearted rake; his second twin, a disagreeable country boor, in Lewis' version is a guileless Quaker who wishes to give away his inheritance. Though somewhat sentimentalized, the pompous Hezekiah, whose eccentricities are good-naturedly satirized, is amusing, and Lewis added a further source of fun in a Quaker servant Tobias. As an object of ridicule, the Quaker had appeared in drama years before. Lewis may have had in mind Susanna Centlivre's *A Bold Stroke for a Wife* (1718), in which Obediah Prim, his wife, and Simon Pure speak much in the manner of his Quakers. One may say for *The Twins* that, unlike Lewis' melodramas, it can be read today with pleasure.

The prologue, which delighted Bannister, introduced a medley song beginning with "God Save the King" and including lines from popular ballads of the day. In print it falls very flat, though doubtless it was a pleasing novelty when sung to a mixture of familiar tunes. Contrary to custom, the playbills called attention to the authorship of the farce by advertising it as "written by the author of the Castle Spectre."

The second drama of 1799 was *The East Indian*, the comedy submitted without success to Mrs. Jordan some seven years before. It was now the celebrated actress' turn to solicit the author of *The Monk* and *The Castle Spectre* in a cajoling letter requesting permission to use the play, "as any production of yours would prove of the utmost consequence."[46] Lewis wrote to Scott on March 5: "For my own part I never mean to write another line, as soon as I shall have finished the alteration of a Comedy, which I gave M^rs Jordan several years ago, & which she claims my promise of having acted for her Benefit. The greatest part of it was written at Westminster School, so you will readily beleive, that it can not be a performance to do me any credit; However it will certainly bring her a good House, and I do not intend, even should it escape the damnation which I expect it to meet with, to have it played except for her Benefit."[47] The "greatest part" of the play, then, was written "ere sixteen years had wing'd their wanton flight," as his prologue puts it, but this letter to Scott negates the biography's statement that "he made no further alteration in it" before it was produced.[48]

Prior to the first scene of *The East Indian*, the unhappily married Beaumont, a youth of impeccable sentiments, had left England and traveled to India, where he lived in the home of a nabob whose life he had saved. Here he and Zorayda, the nabob's daughter, fell in love, and in an unguarded moment—though Heaven can witness to his intentions—he seduced her. To escape the father's wrath, the couple fled to England, where we find them at the beginning of the play. Beaumont's wife has conveniently disappeared, and Zorayda lives with his cousin, Lady Clara Modish. Modish and his wife now receive a visit from Rivers, a forgotten relative who has made a fortune in India. To test their charity he pretends to be a pauper and is rudely rejected. When he is warmly received by Modish's poor widowed sister, however, he reveals his true circumstances and shares his wealth with her. Rivers proves to be the nabob, Zorayda's father. A letter announces the timely death of Beauchamp's wife, and father and daughter are reconciled.

Lewis stated in his preface to *The East Indian*, "The Plot of this Comedy, as far as regards Rivers's visits to Modish and Mrs. Ormond, was taken from the Novel of Sidney Biddulph; Mr. Sheridan had already borrowed the same incident from the same source, and employed it (though in a different manner) in the 'School for Scandal.' " Frances Sheridan's *The Memoirs of Miss Sidney Bidulph* (1761) supplied both plot and leading characters. The generous, impulsive Rivers, for instance, easily moved to tears of sensibility, or to anger at an affront which he takes frank delight in revenging, is the exact counterpart of Mrs. Sheridan's Warner; Modish, naturally charitable but subjugated by his shallow, selfish wife, matches Sir George Bidulph. The novel had already been dramatized by Louis Sebastien Mercier as *L'Habitant de la Guada- loupe* (1785), a tedious play which follows its English source in great detail. Lewis owned a copy of *L'Habitant*[49] and in *The East Indian* acknowledges borrowing a witticism from it.[50] A compari- son of his play with Mercier's shows that the latter was open before him when he wrote his own. This might seem to deprive him even of the credit of borrowing from *The Memoirs*, but Mercier's play is so verbose and undiscriminating in its use of Mrs. Sheridan's material that it offers almost as much opportunity for selection and condensation as the novel itself. Lewis at least chose incidents and conversations with good judgment. In pointing out that *The School for Scandal* likewise was indebted to Mrs. Sheridan's novel, he perhaps sought comfort in the midst of heavy indebtedness to Sheridan's play for his pictures of scandalmongering. Though he made no acknowledgment of Sheridan's influence in the first edition of *The East Indian*, in a revision published twelve years later Lewis appended a footnote to one scene: "I am told that there is a speech very like the one above, in 'The School for Scandal," but I do not recollect it myself."[51] One comic incident having no par- ticular connection with the plot was taken with acknowledgment from Molière's *Don Juan*. For a tearful reconciliation between father and daughter, which proved very effective, he seems indebted

to Kotzebue's *Die Corsen*.[52] In the later version of *The East
Indian* he noted that "the Characters of Lord Listless and Miss
Chatterall are evidently copies of Mr. Meadows and Miss Larolles
in the excellent Novel of Cecilia."[53] Fanny Burney's character
Meadows, who never dances when it would be desirable, yawns
incessantly, devotes attention to his teeth in public, and rudely
ignores women in distress, supplied the rules of fashionable conduct
followed by Lord Listless, the most amusing character in *The East
Indian*. Meadows' affected absentmindedness is paralleled by that
of Listless, who in the midst of a sentence forgets what he was going to say.

Thus extracting with the help of Mercier's play a plot from
*The Memoirs of Miss Sidney Bidulph*, stirring in social satire from
Sheridan and Fanny Burney, and adding a pinch of comedy from
Molière and another of pathos from Kotzebue, Lewis produced a
thoroughly unoriginal but reasonably entertaining sentimental
comedy. It was first performed on April 22, 1799, on a benefit night
for Mrs. Jordan at Drury Lane. The author's misgivings concerning
its reception were needless. "This Comedy," said one reviewer,
"will probably appear again with corrections, as it certainly pos-
sesses merit sufficient to ensure it an establishment on the stage."[54]
It was performed once again that season, on Mrs. Powell's benefit
night. Lewis furnished it with an original if inane epilogue. The
ghost of Queen Elizabeth, accompanied by thunder and lightning,
rises through a trapdoor in a flash of fire to explain that Pluto has
permitted her to return to London if the play succeeds; otherwise
she, the poet, and the play must be damned together. When the
comedy was revived the following December, the reviews were not
enthusiastic. The *Monthly Mirror* objected to it on moral grounds:
"*A young lady elopes from her father's house . . . in company with
a married man.* This is the ground-work, and the immorality of it is
unquestionable; for the parties are represented in the most amiable
light in every other respect."[55] It was played four times,[56] but as
Lewis explains in his preface with more good humor than we
might expect: "the succeeding representations did not prove attractive, for which I here make my acknowledgements to Mr. Sheridan,
who blocked up my road, mounted on his great tragic war-horse
Pizarro, and trampled my humble pag-nag of a Comedy under foot
without the least compunction. My Readers must decide, whether

my Play merited so transient an existence; it is unnecessary to say, that I am quite of the contrary opinion."

Busy in 1800 collecting ballads for *Tales of Wonder*, Lewis offered the theater nothing, but in 1801 he published two plays, one of which, *Adelmorn the Outlaw*, was produced the same year. Contrary to the usual assumption, it is probably not his next dramatic composition after *The Castle Spectre*, for he says in his preface that it was written "about six years ago, previous to the performance" of that play. This would place the writing in the first half of 1795, soon after his return from The Hague and before his twentieth birthday.

*Adelmorn* is a "romantic drama" in three acts, songs and choruses comprising about a quarter of the text. Ulric has gained possession of his title and castle by murdering the former count and fixing the guilt upon Adelmorn, the rightful successor. The murder was so managed that even Adelmorn believes himself guilty. Though outlawed, he has returned to Saxony and hides in the forest, where the ruling duke's daughter, escaped from a convent, has joined him. The couple are captured and Adelmorn is condemned to die on the morrow. But that night a well-aimed lightning bolt destroys a dungeon wall in the castle and reveals the long-incarcerated Father Cyprian. This character explains to Lodowick, a servant, that he was Ulric's accomplice in the murder and that Adelmorn is innocent. Lodowick proclaims the news just as Adelmorn is about to be executed. When Ulric denies his guilt, the ghost of the dead man rises from the ground and confronts him with a flaming dagger. With a cry of horror the murderer confesses, and Adelmorn is hailed Count of Bergen.

The similarity of theme to that of *The Castle Spectre* is obvious. *Adelmorn* is as loaded as that drama with Gothic trappings, and a number of the characters in the two plays are similar. Father Cyprian, for instance, as the repentant accomplice corresponds to Kenric and as the victim of incarceration to Reginald; Lodowick is another Motley, the clever servant in *The Castle Spectre*, and in gypsy disguise makes a perilous visit, like that of Percy, to the castle.

*Adelmorn* was in rehearsal by March 4[57] and was presented at Drury Lane on May 4, 1801. The splendid decorations and beautiful scenery were applauded and Kelly's music was encored,[58] yet only strenuous efforts saved the drama from immediate failure. There seems to have been organized opposition ready on the opening night, presumably by playgoers wishing to discourage the further advance of specters on the London stage.[59] But there would have been trouble enough in any case. With Lodowick, Orrila, Herman, and a burlesque musician Hugo, whose humor consists of interpreting everything in musical terms, Lewis found himself with more comic characters than he could use. One execrably tasteless scene, which attempts to mingle comedy and horror, was hissed throughout: Lodowick, eating and drinking with humorous gusto, converses jokingly with the emaciated and dying Cyprian. Another scene which met with misfortune was that of Adelmorn's remarkable vision. The imprisoned hero awaiting execution falls into peaceful sleep and is visited by a dream foreshadowing the triumph of justice. The situation is similar to one in Goethe's *Egmont,* from which Lewis says he took the suggestion. Invisible spirits sing in chorus, the wall opens, and we see Ulric stabbed by an old man representing the murdered count. The latter ascends in a glory and Ulric is carried off by demons.[60] The audience, taught to expect anything, mistook these visionary events for a representation of reality and, having seen Ulric irrevocably disposed of, were totally confused when in the next scene he re-entered as if nothing had happened. This difficulty was not overcome immediately, for an almost plaintive note, possibly inserted by Lewis, appeared in the *Morning Herald* after the third performance: "A very general mistake seems to prevail, with respect to the Dream, in the third act. Many persons suppose that the figures in the vision scene are meant by the Author for so many ghosts; whereas the scene is merely a representation of what is passing in the mind of the *dreaming* outlaw, at the time."[61] In the final scene on the opening night, the ghost with his flaming dagger should have been terrifying, but unluckily he set fire to his drapery and had to return hastily to the tomb slapping himself amid peals of laughter from the audience. After the first night the appearances of the ghost were reduced from three to one.[62]

The play was damned by the reviewers. The *Sun* called it one of the most despicable pieces that ever disgraced a London theater and felt unequal to describing its dullness, folly, and profanation of what ought to be sacred.[63] The *Monthly Mirror* decided that the author had presumed too much upon the favorable reception of *The Castle Spectre*.[64] The *European Magazine* commented, "Without the dialogue, which is wretched, *Adelmorn* would make a tolerable Ballet, or Pantomime; but as a Drama it is far below criticism. . . . When we see such a man at the head of the Concern as Mr. Sheridan, and Mr. Kemble as the Acting Manager, both highly distinguished for classical learning and correct judgment, we cannot but wonder how pieces calculated, like the above, to degrade the English stage, and vitiate the public taste, contrive to gain access."[65]

"In justice to myself," Lewis wrote, "I must say that I never had any sanguine hopes of the success of 'The Outlaw.' "[66] But friends had told him that it was a better work than *The Castle Spectre*, and the Drury Lane management, remembering the latter as their financial salvation, had urged him to supply another of the same sort. With much cutting and revision *Adelmorn* survived nine performances that season. In the following season it was reduced to an afterpiece and performed four times.

Lewis now transferred his allegiance to Covent Garden. His three and a half years with Drury Lane, except for the stunning triumph of *The Castle Spectre*, had not been particularly successful, and some annoyance had attended every play. He had had to defend his *Castle Spectre* ghost from banishment, and when the play had given the company one of its most successful seasons, he had not received his share of the profits. The tradition is strongly established, in fact, that he received none at all. Moreover, he had fallen out with Sheridan over *Rolla*, and *The East Indian* had been crowded from the boards by *Pizarro*. The success of the latter taught Sheridan, who had accepted Lewis' work as a financially necessary evil, that he too could satisfy the public demand for wonders. And finally of course the comparative failure of *Adelmorn* by no means restored Lewis' importance at Drury Lane.

His first offering to Covent Garden was a five-act tragedy in blank verse, *Alfonso, King of Castile*. He wrote to his mother probably late in 1800 or early in 1801, "I have begun a Tragedy in blank verse; But I stick in the third act at a reconciliation between a King & a Princess, the two stupidest people I ever met with" (F 38).[67] By November the tragedy was in rehearsal.[68] Contrary to usual practice, he published it before stage production, because he wanted to forestall willful misrepresentations by reviewers of the first night's performance and because "I have very great doubts, whether even an *excellent* Tragedy, if written in blank verse, would succeed on the Stage at present: of course I do not flatter myself that mine will. . . . I therefore rather wish this production to be considered as a dramatic poem, or (if that be too lofty a character for it) as a short novel in dialogue, divided into acts, instead of chapters."[69]

He chose fourteen-century Burgos for his setting and took a few suggestions from history, but without any attempt to recreate it. The king's general, Caesario, plots the overthrow of the state. Ottilia, a lady of the court whom he once loved, learns of this and uses the information to exact his promise of marriage. He has, however, secretly married Amelrosa, daughter of the king he is about to destroy. Caesario's father Orsino, long ago banished on false charges of treason, inhabits the nearby forest. Though a likely accomplice in his son's conspiracy, Orsino is too noble to take revenge upon his former sovereign and friend. He saves Alfonso's life by divulging the conspiracy a moment before the royal palace is blown up by the conspirators, and when Alfonso's soldiers are defeated, the father kills his son to save his king. There is little mourning for Caesario, for by this time Ottilia and Amelrosa have been murdered also. In the closing scene Orsino, dying of battle wounds, harangues the king's defecting soldiers into obedience, while his words are emphasized by awe-inspiring peals of thunder.

*Alfonso* is a serious attempt at tragedy and the closest Lewis came to writing good drama which can be called his own. "I am working very hard, both in the reading & writing way," he said during the composition, and in his preface: "In writing it, I have spared no pains, I now give it to the public, not as a good Play, but as the best I can produce; Very possibly *nobody* could write a *worse* Tragedy; but it is melancholy truth, that I cannot write a *better.*" Its greatest weakness is the unforgivable one—the characters do not live. The best one can say for Caesario is that he is nefarious without being morbid, a relief after the gloomy Gothic villains Osmund and Ulric. Ottilia, one of Lewis' most unnatural creatures, first pursues Caesario with frantic passion and regards the murder of those who stand in her way as a mere momentary inconvenience. When her love turns to hate she shrieks for his

blood and babbles of racks, whips, and baths of boiling sulphur.
Alfonso is that reliable stock figure, the righteous king, prizing the
love of his subjects above diamonds; both he and his daughter are
sounding boards of sensibility. On the other hand, the play is well
constructed. No useless scenes block the action; everything advances toward a well-marked climax—that the detonation of a
mine marks it only too well let an audience, not a reader, object.
"I am now so thoroughly convinced of my possessing no talents for
humorous writing," Lewis had written with reference to Lodowick
in *Adelmorn*, "that I shall desist from any further endeavours."[70]
This promise he kept in *Alfonso*, to its great advantage. The pentameter lines, metrically flawless, are better able to carry his often
inflated language and the unrelieved intensity of emotion than
the prose of his melodramas. Though it has often been remarked
that *Alfonso* contains passages of worthy poetry, no one has ven-
tured to point one out. The apostrophe by Orsino as he stands before his forest cave shall therefore be offered as a fair example:

> Yes, thou art lovely, World! That blue-robed sky;
> These giant rocks, their forms grotesque and awful
> Reflected on the calm stream's lucid mirror;
> These reverend oaks, through which (their rustling leaves
> Dancing and twinkling in the sun-beams) light
> Now gleams, now disappears, while yon fierce torrent,
> Tumbling from crag to crag with measured dash,
> Makes to the ear strange music: World! oh, World!
> Who sees thee such must needs confess thee fair!
> Who knows thee not must needs suppose thee good![71]

The first performance, expected before Christmas 1801, was
delayed until January 15 of the next year. As usual, alterations and
cuts had to be made, since the drama proved one hour too long in
the acting—some unkind critics said four hours.[72] In the original
version of the catastrophe, Orsino kills his own son; since this was
considered too terrible for representation, Caesario was made to
stab himself in remorse at having fatally wounded his father in
battle.[73] Even though the two meet without recognizing each other,
the fight between father and son caused great offense on the opening night. So many changes were made in the drama that one copy
of the first edition contains the following comment in a contemporary hand: "Since this edition came out, the play has been

altered so much at every representation that a person coming every night would hardly know it. A Gentleman said, it reminded him of a Friend, who having a pair of worsted stockings darned them so often with silk, that they at last become *all silk*."[74]

Reviewers were willing to forgive the author of *Adelmorn*. The *Monthly Mirror* called *Alfonso* "the best tragedy that has been produced in the theatres since Jephson's *Count of Narbonne*."[75] In an amusing article for the *Edinburgh Review* Sidney Smith found passages which even showed the hand of a master, though his praise was mingled with sniping. Why should Caesario, for instance, upon first seeing his father again, begin criticizing the old warrior as a virtuoso would criticize an ancient statue wanting an arm or a leg? ("Now by my life/A noble ruin!") With reference to the explosion, Smith suggested for a future tragedy a waterspout among Lewis' kings and queens or a fall of snow three or four feet deep, the plot gradually unfolding by means of a general thaw. Having read the prefatory note on the morality of the play, "We confess ourselves," he said, "to have been highly delighted with these symptoms of returning, or perhaps nascent purity in the mind of Mr. Lewis."[76] The *Critical Review*, noting that two characters see ghosts and that Lewis apparently violated his inclinations in keeping them off the stage, congratulated him on this victory over his prejudices.[77] Anna Seward, discussing the lack of good tragedies during the past seventy years, found Coleridge, Godwin, and Sotheby disappointing, but had high praise for *Alfonso*. Her criticism is representative. Though surpassed in style by Jephson's dramas and in poetry by Miss Baillie's, *Alfonso* she thought superior in plot to anything these his two rivals had done. It is "busy, animated, and involved, without perplexity," and we "listen with breathless interest to the progress of the scenes, and cannot pretend to guess at the denouement."[78]

The parts were assigned to the best talents in the company and the management bestowed the same lavish attention to properties that Lewis' plays had received at Drury Lane. In his preface to the second edition, while recalling wistfully Mrs. Jordan's Angela in *The Castle Spectre* and Kemble's Rivers in *The East Indian*, Lewis stated that *Alfonso* was the only one of his dramatic attempts the performance of which satisfied him throughout. It had a moderately successful run of ten performances, enough to justify a paragraph by the author in the second edition containing just a trace of malicious triumph, a satisfaction which may be allowed him as part payment for *The Castle Spectre:* "The Tragedy of Alfonso was presented to the Proprietors of Drury Lane, previous to the performance of the Drama of Adelmorn. They rejected the first, and approved of the second. Unluckily for them, the public rejected the second, and approved of the first. Very possibly they were in the right to reject the one, and would have been still more in the right to have rejected both. But, as the case stands, they certainly have been out of luck."[79]

*Alfonso* retained its prestige for years. The languishing state of tragedy in Britain is one of the most frequent themes among the forty-three rejected addresses, published in 1812, which were written to celebrate the opening of the new Drury Lane theater after the old had burned. *Alfonso* alone among contemporary tragedies is named in the *Genuine Rejected Addresses*, where the reference, if not brilliantly poetical, is at least complimentary:

> Too long hath Native Genius been obscur'd,
> French *froth* and German *rant* too long endur'd;
> Too long, a vicious appetite to pamper,
> Britain's Thalia suffer'd Farce to cramp her.
> Divine *Melpomene* a transient ray
> Beam'd—in *Alfonso* beam'd—and past away.
> Then giddy Harlequin and senseless Clown,
> Rush'd forth; and bore all opposition down.[80]

Lewis' letter of January 13, 1803 (F 39, 40), to his mother makes clear the favor he enjoyed with Harris, manager of Covent Garden, and mentions his next two productions:

Alfonso has been played with great applause; so great indeed, that M^r Harris (who was present from the rising of the curtain to its fall) ordered Richard 3^d, which had been announced for the next Tragedy to be postponed, & Alfonso to be repeated instead of it. For what reason I know not, but M^r Harris all of a sudden has taken a fancy for everything that I do. I sent to ask him, whether He would let M^rs Litchfield speak some lines, which I have written, between the Play & Farce—"Anything that you chuse to be brought forward" said He "shall be produced immediately." He has got my after-piece again (but which I like so little myself, that I do not think, that I shall let it appear) and wants it lengthened into a *first* piece, for just now He seems to think He cannot have enough of my writing; Nay, he carried his enthusiasm so far, that when Alfonso was advertised this year, contrary to all custom He put the author's name in the Bills, as if nobody could resist that attraction. How this happens, I am ignorant; but the fact is, that he is as full of civility & compliments, & fine speeches as He can cram—the Lines, which I mentioned to be spoken by M^rs Litchfield, are called "the Captive" & are to be spoken with accompaniments of Music: I believe too, *the Minister* will be played for Johnston's Benefit under the title of "the Harper's Daughter."

In March a Covent Garden playbill announced, "In the Course of the next Week will be produced a *Mono-Drama,* or *Tragic-Scene,* called *the Captive.*" Michael Kelly says of this form of entertainment, known variously as monodrama, monodrame, and monologue, "There was a species of drama at that time [late eighteenth century] much in vogue at Vienna, and indeed all over Germany, called a *Monologue,* and which has since been occasionally introduced upon the English stage. The person who performs, is accompanied between the different speeches by music, made to accord with the different passages of the recitation."[81] Classical themes were often used, but Lewis found other material more to his taste. His scene is a madhouse cell, to which a despairing mother, languishing in chains, has been consigned by her tyrannical husband. She begs the obdurate gaoler for liberty and reflects tenderly upon her loved ones. The stanzas of her monologue end in an incremental refrain through which we observe her progressive madness. When a screaming maniac, escaped from confinement, shakes the bars of her cell and brandishes a blazing firebrand, she collapses shrieking "I'm mad!—I'm mad!" In pantomime her family enter and attempt to woo her back to reason. When she recognizes her little son, "The Father, &c., raise their hands to heaven, in gratitude for the return of her reason, and the curtain falls slowly to solemn music."

*The Captive* was performed on March 22, 1803. A few days before, Lewis had confided to his mother: "The Monodrama comes out on Tuesday; I have not yet been at a single rehearsal. It cannot possibly succeed" (F 43). With the help of Mrs. Litchfield's realistic acting it succeeded rather too well. The biographer describes the effect: it threw part of the audience into hysterics and the whole theater into confusion and horror—"Never did Covent Garden present such a picture of agitation and dismay. Ladies bathed in tears—others fainting—and some shrieking with terror—while such of the audience as were able to avoid demonstrations like these, sat aghast, with pale horror painted on their countenances."[82] This account is amply corroborated. "The *tears* of an audience have generally been accounted the highest species of applause," said one newspaper. "A poet must have an odd taste who would be rewarded with *hysteric fits*."[83] The spectators were thrown into confusion and the only question seems to be how many fits were produced. One account puts the number as high as nine or ten (five or six women, two ladies, and two beaux),[84] though Lewis modestly claimed only two fits during the performance and two more after the curtain dropped (F 41). The piece was announced for another performance, but he withdrew it. In reporting the unlucky affair to his mother next day he observed philosophically that "the only chance was, whether Pity would make the audience weep; but instead of that, Terror threw them into fits; & of course there was an end of my Monodrama" (F 41). It was not separately published, though years later Lewis included it in a small volume of his verses and it enjoyed some popularity as a piece for recitation. Depending so heavily upon acting and stage devices for its effect it may be read, as Leslie Stephen dryly remarked, "with impunity."[85]

On May 4, 1803, *The Harper's Daughter* was successfully produced on a benefit night for Mr. and Mrs. Johnstone. The play as performed at Covent Garden was not published, but the licenser's manuscript survives.[86] It is merely an abridged version of *The Minister*, Lewis' translation of Schiller's *Kabale und Liebe*. Whole scenes are omitted and speeches condensed so that *The Harper's Daughter* is about one third the length of the translation. The prologue, which apparently remained unpublished, has some interest as an early tribute in England to Schiller.[87]

Two years later Lewis scored a striking success at Covent Garden with the two-act melodrama *Rugantino; or, The Bravo of Venice*, presented on October 18, 1805, and performed thirty times. Earlier in the year he had published his translation of Zschokke's prose tale *Abällino der Grosse Bandit* (1794) as *The Bravo of Venice*, a work to be discussed in the following chapter. Recognizing effective stage material in *The Bravo*, Harris asked Lewis to put it into dramatic form. "I shall make no apology," Lewis tells his readers in the published play, "for having employed (or as many may think it, wasted) my time upon a composition of so trifling a nature.—Humble efforts and pursuits are best adapted to moderate abilities."[88] For *Rugantino* he selected the most dramatic scenes from his bravo's career. The hero of the romance keeps up an appearance at court and at the same time, disguised as an outlaw, thwarts a conspiracy to overthrow the state. His dual role is revealed at the end. In the stage version there is further surprise that he is also the Prince of Milan, the destined husband of the Doge's daughter, who already loves him in his character of courtier.[89] The part called for magical transformations which no doubt delighted the audience. On one occasion Rugantino changes in an instant from a bald, white-bearded, and tattered "antient Beggar" to a friar. In the final scene, as the handsome Flodoardo, he turns his back to the audience, "throws off his cloak and helmet, and appears in the habit, and with the countenance, of the Bravo!"—here even the stage directions take fright—then throws off the Bravo's habit and reveals himself as the resplendent Prince of Milan. Lewis added a little, a very little, comedy with two new characters, Memmo, a cowardly conspirator, and an antiquated coquettish duenna, and supplied pathos by a scene between father and daughter which had already proved effective in *Alfonso*.

After attending a performance of *Rugantino*, Lady Harriet Cavendish wrote to a friend, "The Dialogue is flippant and tiresome and one's attention only kept up by claps of thunder and Pistols firing. My head aches so much from this that I can scarcely see to write."[90] Though the dialogue may be dismissed with this, the piece created a great impression as a spectacle. According to a reviewer, the town had "scarcely ever been presented with any thing more costly and splendid. The views of Venice and its environs are exceedingly fine; and the Duke's bed-chamber . . . is executed in a masterly stile. The pomp both of the Catholic and Pagan religions is displayed with the greatest effect."[91] In the middle of Act II a masque was introduced—half of which was later saved for the end of the drama—for which the properties manager and stage machinist deserve praise if they kept pace with Lewis' florid fancy. "The splendour of this part of the entertainment is beyond description," said the writer just quoted. "On the scenery, dresses, &c. immense sums must have been bestowed."[92] We see first a large grotto made of variegated spars and crystals. In the center a porch with richly ornamented folding doors projects far into the scene. Here the Duke sits enthroned, surrounded by lords and ladies, to

observe a masque presented on the random pretext of honoring the
birthday of Thetis. The stage directions in the licenser's manuscript are at this point somewhat more detailed than those published:

A procession Enters—Mars in his Chariot—Warriors—Pan (dancing)
Satyrs and Dryads—Diana (on horseback) with her nymphs—Bacchus,
seated on a Ton: Bacchanals—Mount Parnassus, with the River Helicon,
Apollo at the top Below are the nine muses (represented by Children) playing on various instruments—On one side, Venus, with Cupid, descends in
a rose-colour'd Cloud—and on the other, Minerva in a blue one. They
alight, and while the Clouds re-ascend, the celestial palace comes down
amid thunder and lightning. Jupiter, Juno, Mercury, Iris, Ganymede & Hebe
come out of the Palace, which re-ascends. Memmo, who has advanced into
the middle of the Stage, almost falls thro' a trap-door, which opens suddenly. Pluto and Proserpine rise in a Car, drawn by black horses, breathing
fire—They alight and the Car sinks[93]

Three of the goddesses contend for the golden apple—thrown, incidentally, by Proserpine—and with a burst of marine music the
folding doors open and Neptune and Amphitrite enter, accompanied by Nereids, Tritons, and Sirens.

Last a machine representing a rock of red coral floating on a silver sea, whose
waves are in motion. On the summit of the rock is a brilliant conch-shell,
in which sits *Rosabella*. Artificial *Zephyrs* hang over her, some seeming to
fan her with their wings, others with their breath to impel the rock forwards,
which is drawn by enormous Dolphins, spouting up water, while on the head
of each stands a little *Cupid*, holding golden reins, with which he appears
to guide the animal.[94]

With his next production Lewis returned to Drury Lane. The
year before he had published his tragedy *Adelgitha*, which, had
matters run smoothly at Covent Garden, would probably have been
staged first; but, it seems, when the management suggested the
substitution of Kemble for Johnstone in the leading part, Lewis
peremptorily objected and withdrew the piece.[95] To judge by the
freedom allowed him in staging *The Wood Daemon; or, "The
Clock Has Struck,"* his welcome back to Drury Lane was warm.
This two-act "Grand Romantic Melo Drame" was presented on
April 1, 1807.

Shortly before the opening night the following periodical notice
appeared:

Mr. M. P. [sic] Lewis bas [sic] a romantic melo-drame, called *The Wood Daemon*, forthcoming at Druly-Lane [sic] theatre. According to report, the performers in it may say, with Dryden's Oedipus:

"We play,
For Hell's broke up, and ghosts have holiday."[96]

The quotation would be apt for the title page, for Lewis had racked his brain for wonders and the search had certainly not been in vain. Hardyknute, the usurping Count of Holstein, had made a compact with Sangrida the Wood Daemon, by which he enjoys wealth, power, and invulnerability in exchange for a yearly human sacrifice. He has followed the Gothic formula of murdering the former count, and the young boy Leolyn, the heir, though actually stolen by gypsies, is thought to have been devoured by the Wood Daemon. Leolyn now returns to the castle in disguise as one of a company of entertainers. Hardyknute recognizes him by a birthmark and, since the date is at hand when the count must pay the Wood Daemon her fee or become her victim himself, he confines Leolyn in a "Necromantic Cavern" in the castle and prepares to make the sacrifice. He is delayed during the final moments, however, and Leolyn succeeds in pushing the hand of the clock forward. The fatal hour strikes, Hardyknute is forfeited, and the piece ends with a triumphant all-hail for the rightful heir.

More than any of Lewis' earlier dramas, *The Wood Daemon* depends for success upon stage machinery. It is significant that the opening, originally planned for March 30, had to be postponed because the illness of the mechanic delayed the preparation of scenery, machinery, and decorations.[97] The opening scene calls for a dream more elaborate than that in *Adelmorn*. The stage is filled with brilliant clouds. Auriol, the guardian genius of Holstein, sits among them and explains to the sleeping Una various visions which are disclosed. The cloud beneath him opens and Leolyn is seen in chains, Sangrida with bloody dagger standing near. Leolyn's parents then appear in the clouds on either side. In those above, children in white, crowned with flowers, are revealed, pointing to wounds upon their hearts. Then clouds and visions disperse, and the stage becomes a flower garden with bowers of gilt trellis. "The midsummer-dream, with which the piece opened," the *Monthly Mirror* reported, "was exquisitely beautiful, and the clouds were managed with peculiar ingenuity."[98]

Scene Three presents a magnificent hall, galleries filled with spectators, a large window in the center, two bronze doors with stairs leading to them, Hardyknute and Una on a throne. A pageant of the seasons takes place, each season with appropriate banners, emblems, and attendants. Summer's car is drawn by what the licenser's manuscript calls "Wood Nymps," Autumn's by Reapers, Winter's by White Bears, Spring's by Zephyrs.[99] Presently the guests discover in their midst a female figure thickly veiled in black. Whether this is the Wood Daemon herself or merely her messenger is not clear, but she serves to remind Hardyknute of the date. Horrified he follows her up a staircase and through one of the bronze doors. There is a loud burst of thunder, then total darkness. Next Hardyknute, pale and wild, sword in hand, rushes down. Another thunderclap and the great window bursts open, revealing Sangrida in a car drawn by dragons. She points at Leolyn and ascends in a shower of fire. "Remember!" she cries—indeed, it is hard to see how anyone could forget. "The confusion and apparent horror which ensued after the appearance of the spectre," one reviewer said, "combined to form perhaps the most terrific and sublime scene ever beheld on the stage."[100]

Lewis devised more surprises for the second and final act. The first scene is the State Bedchamber, where Una in the uncertain firelight seeks the way to Leolyn. At the stroke of midnight a blue light illuminates the two portraits of Leolyn's parents. They step forth, kneel before Una, and point to a golden tassel beside the bed. This is the clue she sought. She seizes a firebrand, leaps to the bed, draws the tassel, and cries "Leolyn! I will rescue thee or die! Away!" The bed sinks and the portraits return to their places. The properties of Hardyknute's Necromantic Cavern, where Leolyn is chained to a bronze pillar, include grated doors, a bloody altar around which two enormous snakes curl supporting a golden platter on their heads, and the statue of a giant kneeling upon a pedestal and holding a clock on his shoulder. Above the cave is a gallery along which the audience can see Una guiding herself with her firebrand. During Hardyknute's incantations, blue fire issues from the jaws of the snakes and a gigantic golden head rises from the altar. Candles light themselves. Discordant music sounds. When the clock strikes, Sangrida rushes from behind a rock and stabs Hardyknute, four fiends drag him to the altar, and the snakes twist about him. Altar and figures sink, the whole scene vanishes, and we find ourselves in the great hall of the castle.

*The Wood Daemon* has been recognized as a good example of Lewis' tendency to add to traditional Gothic paraphernalia properties of an alien world—wood spirits, zephyrs, fiends, and the like, had not appeared in earlier Gothic plays. Even details traditionally Gothic are pushed to extremes. The animated portraits, for instance, play a part in the action, and Hardyknute, a Gothic villain in essentials, has acquired magic powers.[101]

The piece received less derision in the public press than might have been expected. It was accepted for what it was—a brilliant exploitation of stage machinery and spectacular effects. "In this melo-drama," reported the *Monthly Mirror*, " 'on horror's head, horrors accumulate.' Every thing is horrible. The machinery is horribly grand and sublime, the plot is horribly interesting, and the dialogue is horribly miserable. Nothing, indeed, can exceed the magnificence and ingenuity displayed by Mr. Johnston, the mechanist, except the contemptibility of the attempts at humour, exhibited by Mr. Lewis, the author."[102] One newspaper records "how impatiently the audience endured the puerile attempts at wit in the first act, which was almost all dialogue, and how gladly they welcomed the second, where scarcely any thing but action was to be found." In the last scene, the account continues, "When the *Count* and the altar sink into the earth, that opens to devour them, there was a general cry of *bravo!* which was redoubled when the piece was announced for a second representation. . . . The intricate machinery did not last night work very well; and in the last scene, particularly, we are fearful that *De Camp* [who played Hardyknute] experienced some hurt in sinking to the lower regions, entwined with serpents; but much allowance must be made for a first exhibition of so complex and elaborate a nature."[103] The comic dialogue in Act I was greatly curtailed for the second performance, and *The Wood Daemon* enjoyed a triumphant run of thirty-four performances, the last of the season being on June 10. "In point of splendour, variety, scenery, machinery, and music, this after-piece," it was said, "may rank with the most admired of its species of entertainment."[104] It was used five times the season following.

At the end of April 1807, *Adelgitha; or, The Fruits of a Single Error* was performed at Drury Lane. This was a drama Lewis had finished and published in 1806. For issuing it, as he had *Alfonso*, previous to stage production, the quite incredible explanation was that the author had sent his manuscript to the printer before rehearsal at Covent Garden because Betty, "the Young Roscius," who was to play Lothair, was able to read print but not writing.[105] As published it had received moderately favorable comment,[106] and a fourth edition had appeared in 1806. Like *Alfonso*, it is a five-act tragedy in blank verse, halfheartedly historical. Anticipating criticism on grounds of historical inaccuracy, he refers his readers to Gibbon, whom he had been reading in 1802,[107] to find out how widely he had departed from history, explaining that first he arranged his plot and characters, then looked for some historical niche in order to give them a local habitation and a name. He says he is perfectly aware that "Githa (who saved her husband's life at the siege of Bari) was a different person from the Princess of Salerno, and that Robert Guiscard is suspected of having made way to the nuptial bed of the second, by poisoning the first." Apparently none of his readers accepted the invitation to consult his source, or it would have been noted that even his summary of Gibbon is altogether confused. It has been suggested by a student of Italian influences in English literature that in choosing an incident from Italian history Lewis "in this as in so many respects, was a true barometer and forecast of the coming poetical weather."[108]

The time of the story is the tenth century. Michael-Ducas, the deposed emperor of Byzantium, has fled to Otranto to enlist the aid of Robert Guiscard in regaining the throne. Despite that hero's efforts in his behalf, the treacherous Michael endeavors to seduce Robert's wife Adelgitha and vainly attempts to bribe the young Lothair, a hero in Robert's army, to murder Robert himself. Adelgitha, a faithful and adoring wife, has kept one guilty secret from her husband: she was betrayed in her innocent youth by false vows of love. Michael, possessing proof of this early misadventure, threatens to expose Adelgitha when she spurns him. She first attempts suicide, then in desperation stabs her tormentor. Lothair is accused of the murder, but, as he is being led to execution, Adelgitha with a dreadful shriek confesses to the murder and reveals that Lothair is her son. Robert forgives her, and to reward his generosity she stabs herself.

The tragedy lacks the uninterrupted and gradually heightening tension of *Alfonso*. Michael-Ducas, the character least void of interest, is a monster of ingratitude and blind rage. Adelgitha is intended "to illustrate a particular fact; viz. 'the difficulty of avoiding the consequences of a first false step,'" or in her own words, "'Tis in man's choice never to sin at all,/ But sinning once, to stop exceeds his power"—a favorite idea with Lewis, as one notes from his imitation of Juvenal's thirteenth satire and from Ambrosio's career. Adelgitha, who slipped once in her youth, is led—though how inevitably seems debatable—to deception, murder, and suicide. The character gave Lewis some difficulty. He liked now and then to permit his heroines to stab villains: Marguerite, a sympathetic character in *The Monk*, plunges a dagger into Baptiste's heart, and Angela stabs Osmund in *The Castle Spectre*. In Gothic drama, however, "good" characters were expected to keep the sixth commandment no matter what the provocation was to break it.[109] Whereas in *The Monk* the incident is brushed aside with the phrase "this horrible but necessary act," in *Adelgitha* Lewis is at great pains to execrate the heroine's murder of the villain, even to the extent of a footnote explaining that she is not to be mistaken for a heroine but is meant to represent merely a woman by nature yet one lacking sufficient firmness of mind to resist the circumstances which lead her gradually from crime to crime until she is overwhelmed.

The verse is as technically competent as that in *Alfonso* and the language as unnatural and inflated, even in casual conversation. When a ship approaches, somebody observes "Swift cuts a bark the billows," and Lothair, remarking that Guiscard will return before noon, puts the information on these stilts: "ere the sun ascends his mid-day chariot,/ The hero's keel will bite Otranto's shore." One concession to popular entertainment not found in Lewis' earlier tragedy is the introduction of songs. In the final act a scene in "a Gothic Hall splendidly illuminated" portrays Guiscard and his knights at a banquet. Here minstrels sing a martial ballad, "Count Hildebrand leapt on his berry-brown steed," at the end of which "The Knights all rise, with their swords drawn in one hand, and their goblets in the other, and repeat the burthen."

The published form of the drama was shortened for the stage by over three hundred lines.[110] With good acting and striking stage sets the play was completely successful. The first performance was a benefit for Mrs. Powell, who had never, it was said, appeared to greater advantage than in the role of Adelgitha. "With all his faults," one newspaper conceded, "Mr. Lewis can interest us: he is too fond of show and situation, but he works up a story with no inconsiderable skill."[111] *Adelgitha* was played nine times that season, three in later years.

On December 1, 1808, Drury Lane produced *Venoni; or, The Novice of St. Mark's, a Drama in Three Acts.* This was Lewis' adaptation of *Les Victimes Cloîtrées,* Monvel's play which Lewis had named sixteen years before as one which would undoubtedly succeed. Monvel's drama may be summarized as follows.

Eugénie loves Dorval, but her mother, disapproving of the match, confines her daughter in a convent. It is soon reported that Eugénie has died. The grief-stricken Dorval, persuaded by the Prior Laurent, enters a monastery adjoining the convent. On the eve of taking his vows he is told by an inmate of the monastery that the Prior intends to kill him for his fortune. He is further informed that Eugénie died for a similar reason after the Prior, in conjunction with the Superior of the convent, had laid unsuccessful siege to her virtue. Confronting the Prior with these charges, Dorval is thrown into a dungeon to die. There he completes the efforts of a former prisoner to break through the wall and finds Eugénie alive in the adjoining dungeon. Meanwhile the scandalous disclosures have been made public, and a rescue party arrives to set the couple free.

Lewis retained the essentials of the French story but combined the first two acts into one. He carefully excised republican sentiments as "by no means adapted to the present times or to the British taste." With no more success than usual he made one of the minor characters a comic figure. He changed the setting from a provincial French town to Messina and made several scenic alterations: the curtain rises not on an interior but on the port of Messina so that we may enjoy a "marine procession," the arrival of a state galley, and a glee by passing fishermen. To Act II is added a procession of monks in a monastery garden equipped with Gothic chapel and rising moon. An entirely irrelevant masquerade introduces the final act.

The early performances were by no means successful. One reviewer, apparently unaware that the work was an importation from France, at least paid the author the compliment of expecting better work: "That a man like Mr. Lewis, who once partly escaped from the delirium of a German brain . . . and wrote one of the most poetical and ingenious tragedies of modern times, should again relapse into its most ridiculous paroxysms, is altogether unaccountable. The mole blundered into a little light, its pureness offended him, and he hurried back to his original gloom. This it is to have the genius of a Poet, unaccompanied by the taste and judgment of a Critic."[112] The dialogue "is without any of his bursts of poetry, or, indeed, any thing above that which is common-place, and unworthy of the author."[113] Reports conflict concerning the acting. The writer just quoted thought Mrs. Siddons' role placed her in a situation in which all her excellence became burlesque, considered Wroughton's acting often ludicrous, and Elliston in the title role anything but impressive: "His appearance . . . excited an universal titter, and some time elapsed before we discovered that this white dress, which clung about his little figure like a wet sheet, was intended for the costume of a *Noviciate of St. Mark's*. . . . He sees Josepha's picture, and much vapouring ensues, which ends in his fainting in Celestino's arms, who with great difficulty drags him off in that laughable situation, for he has all the appearance of a drunken man in his shirt or one caught walking in his sleep."

Contemporary testimony agreed, however, that the third act was a failure. This originally opened with a ballroom scene of music and dancing, followed by another presenting a duet and chorus by gypsies. Neither scene appears in the printed version. The first contained some matter advancing the plot; the second was a mere interlude to allow the stage hands time to arrange the elaborate scene immediately following, as one character candidly states at the end of a song: "I wish they had been encored, for Music fills up the time charmingly and so the Players have found out; for at the Theatre whenever any accident happens, if an Actress an't well, or a Scene wants time for setting, they just whip in a Song, and the audience is generally indulgent enough to accept of the excuse."[114] In this instance the audience was not—the scene was hissed.[115] But the real trouble came with the next scene, which evoked derision. Closely following the French play, it presents the interior of two dungeons separated by a thick wall, in which

Venoni and Josepha, each unaware of the other's proximity, soliloquize alternately until Venoni breaks his way through the intervening masonry. One newspaper reporting the first performance said the "divided cells form a beautiful scene" and objected only that it was painted with a finished front instead of one of broken stone.[116] Another, however, said the scene was ill managed and found the effect "very revolting":

the worst of it is, that these dungeons do not come quite to the front of the stage, and are raised on platforms, so that they look like two dens for wild beasts, an appearance to which certain spikes, placed to prevent their contents from leaping on the stage, very much contribute. When Mr. Elliston and Mrs. H. Siddons appeared in these dens, without seeing each other, and soliloquized alternately, the effect was, in spite of all the horror of the scene, so ludicrous, that we wanted nothing but a showman of the lions in front to tell us which was *Miss Fanny Howe,* and which *Hector:* the scene reminded us of "that useful Toy," a weather-house, in which now the woman pops out, and now the man.[117]

After three performances it was evident, said Lewis, "that unless I could invent an entirely new last act, the piece must be given up altogether—under this persuasion I set my brain to work, and in four-and-twenty hours I composed the last act, as it now stands, both plot and dialogue."[118] Instead of placing his two lovers in their separate dungeons, he introduced a prisoner who had undergone twenty years' incarceration—a resurrection of Reginald in *The Castle Spectre*—and omitted the gypsy scene.[119]

A columnist for the *Morning Chronicle* remarked, "If Mr. Lewis should be successful in the new *third* act of his play, it will only require a better *first* and *second* to make it a tolerable piece."[120] But when it was resumed on December 12 with the new ending it was applauded. The run was cut off at eighteen performances only by the destruction of the theater.

On February 24, 1809, Drury Lane burned to the ground. Friends did what they could for the houseless company. The manager of the Lyceum allowed them to continue their performances at that theater, and Lewis, turning to his portfolio, gave them a farce called *Temper; or, The Domestic Tyrant,* first performed on May 1 at the Lyceum and seven times thereafter. It was never published and, although several contemporary periodicals associate it with Lewis' name, it was not again noticed as his until 1942.[121]

The domestic tyrant is Nicolo Barrasco, an irate doctor, who is determined to marry the daughter of an acquaintance. The friend agrees to this on the condition that Barrasco's daughter Rosella marry Solomon, the friend's stupid son. Both girls objecting to the arrangement, clever servants are enlisted in a plot to thwart it. Mascarillo disguised first as a French dancing master, then as a recruiting sergeant, intimidates Barrasco, who is duped into signing a contract for the marriage of Rosella to a lover of her choice.

A newspaper account of the first perofrmance recognized marks of French origin and called it a translation "said to have been made by Mr. M. G. Lewis; and this report appears the more probable, because a very agreeable song, notoriously written and composed by that Gentleman is introduced in the course of the piece. We must regret that a writer of so vigorous an originality should waste his strength in translating, and particularly in translating such dramas as this."[122] The play from which Temper ultimately comes, Le Grondeur, was written in 1691 by David Augustin Brueys and Jean Palaprat. The French play was no stranger in England. It had been traslated by Sir Charles Sedley as The Grumbler, published in 1702 and produced in altered form at Drury Lane in 1754. An adaption of The Grumbler by Goldsmith had been performed in 1773.[123] Lewis' Temper is a rewriting of Sedley's play, shortened to two acts. Though he rewrote the dialogue entirely, hardly a sentence in Temper is without its counterpart in The Grumbler. The only noteworthy addition might well have been omitted. A recruiting sergeant, describing the doubtful attractions of Madagascar, reads a menu of unpleasant dishes supposed to be typical of that land, at which other characters express appropriate disgust—a puerile effort at gastronomic humor. Lewis also heightened the farce of the closing scene, in which all the characters begin talking at once and form a burlesque group. This rather silly piece may well be one of those he had prepared seventeen years before, when he was seventeen. The Satirist remarked, "Something indeed, called Temper, intended for a farce, and fathered by the town on that father of monsters, Monk Lewis, has been produced at the Lyceum. The public has already passed sentence on it: to enter into its merits here, would be as idle as to try a man for petty larceny already condemned for murder."[124] Of Lewis' gift to Drury Lane, the Monthly Mirror said: "The grati-

tude arising out of this donation, must spring entirely from a re-
fined sense of that hyper-christian maxim, which teaches men to
take the will for the deed;—since we are ready to believe that he
was *willing* to give them a *good farce*. Mr. Lewis is a very clever
poet, but he is without dramatic humour, and poorly endowed
with wit."[125]

About a month after the production of *Temper*, Lewis announced in the preface to *Venoni*, "This will probably be the last
of my dramatic attempts. The act of composing has ceased to
amuse me; I feel, that I am not likely to write better, than I have
done already; and though the Public have received my plays certainly with an indulgence quite equal to their merits, those merits
even to myself appear so trifling that it cannot be worth my while
to make any further efforts at the attainment of dramatic fame—
here then I shall take my leave of the Theatre, probably for ever."
This resolution held firm for over a year, but on December 9, 1810,
he told Lady Charlotte Campbell that he had been "teased into
promising to put together some showy spectacle for Covent Garden."[126] This refers to *Timour the Tartar*, performed about five
months later, which, the preface tells us, was written "to oblige Mr.
Harris, who prest me very earnestly to give him a *Spectacle*, in
which Horses might be introduced." He adds that, having great
doubts of the success of an equestrian performance, he so constructed the piece that it would allow a combat on foot to be substituted for one on horseback.[127] Such misgivings were put to rest
when Harris, in the Covent Garden performance of *Blue Beard* on
February 18, 1811, included a troupe of horses in the cast with
startling success. *Timour* appeared at the same theater on April
29.[128]

This piece has as much narrative as is needed to provide thrills
and spectacles. The settings were said to be more splendid than
anything previously attempted. The scene is Timour's fortress in
Mingrelia. Having captured the kingdom, Timour holds its young
prince, Agib, prisoner and is awaiting the arrival of the Georgian
princess whom for political reasons he intends to marry. The
Mingrelian Zorilda, Agib's mother, impersonates the princess in
order to save her son and to give the signal for a surprise attack
prepared against the conqueror. Timour discovers her identity and
confines her in the fortress. She finds a friend in Oglou, Timour's

father, who brings the young prince to her apartment in the fortress and arranges for their escape at midnight. Timour, however, struck with Zorilda's beauty, has abandoned his former marriage intentions and comes to take her as his bride. When his back is turned, Agib escapes through a window. Georgians now surround the fortress and demand Timour's surrender, but holding Zorilda as hostage he threatens to burn the fortress unless Agib is returned to him. Zorilda plunges into the sea and is rescued by her son. In the ensuing battle the Georgians are victorious and Timour is captured.

Suspense runs high through the piece, particularly in the business of Agib's escape, where stealthy action and spontaneous lies keep one step ahead of Timour's suspicions, until Agib is let down the fortress wall by a curtain cord. At the last moment the cord breaks, but he falls unhurt into friendly arms. The trained horses had a very considerable share in the acting. When Zorilda arrives accompanied by mounted Tartars, the horses pay homage to Timour before retiring. In a lavish tournament scene, when a contestant in a combat on foot loses his sword, his horse leaps the barrier, fends off the antagonist, picks up its master's weapon and returns it to him. When the infuriated rival stabs the beast, it falls and expires. The last scene, replete with towers and hanging terraces, is the fortress by moonlight, surrounded by water. Zorilda throws herself into the sea; Agib leaps his horse over the parapet and disappears. Presently horse and rider rise from the water, bearing the mother to safety. In the ensuing battle, according to a witness of the first performance, a battering ram demolishes a wall of the fortress; some horses leap through the breach; others plunge into the waves and "scud up a cataract with astonishing spirit." "The white horse which carried the heroine (Mrs. H. Johnston) plays admirably. He kneels, leaps, tumbles, dances, fights, dashes into water and up precipices, in a very superior style of acting, and completely astonished the audience."[129] So said the *European Magazine* in a review any horse would be proud to read.

Exhibitions of this sort met with clamorous opposition. One writer sadly remarked, "Amidst the clattering of hoofs, the clangor of swords and spears, and the shouts of an enraptured audience, it is scarcely possible, or perhaps hardly worth while, for criticism to attempt to speak."[130] When *Timour* was first presented a strongly hostile party threw handbills from the upper boxes declaiming against equestrian performances at the regular theater. The bills were loudly hissed and torn to pieces, and when a second performance was announced the horse-hissers were "overwhelmed by most determined and deafening shouts of applause."[131]

A writer in the *Morning Chronicle*, feeling that the degradation of Covent Garden had been consummated in *Timour*, argued that horses on the stage were not justified by the fact that the public wanted them: the public will also flock to an execution, a bruising-match, or a bull-bait. *Bluebeard* had proved attractive without horses, and, in introducing something the public had neither desired nor expected, Harris, the writer maintained, had acted from avarice, not necessity.[132] In the same paper notices occur of a subscription to establish a new theater to be devoted exclusively to the legitimate drama.[133]

Equestrian performances furnished material for a number of burlesque, such as *Quadrupeds; or, The Manager's Last Kick, an Afterpiece* at the Lyceum.[134] This presented a battle scene among journeymen tailors mounted on asses, mules, "foundered horses, &c.," and wielding brooms, shovels, and crutches, the fight concluding with a tremendous discharge of cabbages.[135] Another was *The Quadrupeds of Quedlinburgh; or, The Rovers of Weimar, in Two Acts, a Grand Dressed Rehearsal of Tragico-Comico-Anglo-Germanico-Hippo-Ono-Dramatico-Romance!* played at the Haymarket, an extravaganza attributed to George Colman the younger, which ended with an exhibition of battles, blue lights, and basket-work cavalry burlesquing the final scene in *Timour*.[136] A prelude performed at the Surrey Theatre was entitled "What's a Stage without Horses?"[137] The *Satirist* announced that Lewis was training pigs for a new drama.[138] This never appeared, but by December Covent Garden had brought an elephant upon the stage.[139] Meanwhile *Timour* packed the house and was played forty-four times.

It seems clear that Lewis wrote a romantic drama called *Zoroaster*, since Michael Kelly says he prepared the music for it.[140] Moreover there was gossip in 1812 that "Monk Lewis has composed a new heroic melodrama, in which Kemble is to make his first appearance on horseback, and that he gets up every morning at six o'clock to practice."[141] If the manuscript of this drama is ever found, it may prove to be based on Louis de Cahusac's opera *Zoroastre*, a copy of which Lewis owned.[142]

Though no strictly new drama of Lewis' was produced after *Timour*, there remain to be mentioned two which were revised and offered under new titles. *The Wood Daemon* of 1807 was fitted out with music by Matthew Peter King and Michael Kelly and became "a grand musical romance" in three acts called *One O'Clock! or, The Knight and the Wood Dæmon*. It was produced at the English Opera House, Lyceum, on August 1, 1811. Lewis retained nearly everything in the original *Wood Daemon*, but expanded the dialogue and added minstrels, gypsies, and numerous songs and choruses.[143] It begins with a new scene depicting a cottage in a moonlit forest among mountains. The trees and rocks open, disclosing groups of wood spirits who sing in chorus. Others rise from the ground, the moon turns red, a tempest rises—

> Lo! sanguine clouds the Moon deform!
> Louder and louder grows the Storm!
> Deep Thunders roar! Red Lightnings flash!
> Hark!—'Twas the fall of the Mountain Ash!—

and Sangrida arrives in a black, flaming cloud to announce her bloody mission. At cock crow the spirits vanish and the stage becomes light with day. Another change was further development of the scene in the Gothic hall. The pageant of the seasons becomes a ballet. As the banquet progresses, "by degrees the Music becomes languid, and confused, and at length the Dance ceases abruptly" as the presence of the ominous figure is felt. The end of the scene, when Sangrida makes her terrifying appearance, is cast in operatic form. On the power of this scene one commentator wrote,

there are few scenes in the whole circle of the drama,—scarcely even that appalling one in "Macbeth" after the murder of *Duncan*,—which so inspire an audience with a silent shuddering awe as does that of the Banquet in the second Act: 'tis difficult in fact to imagine that stage-effect can be carried farther, or rendered more grandly impressive. The spectator beholds a magnificent gothic hall, resounding with the "voluptuous swell" of music, crowded with youth and beauty engaged in the lively dance. . . . Gradually, and without any apparent cause, the mirth becomes languid, the music grows discordant and dies away, the dance ceases, a mysterious horror takes possession of the revellers, and a chilling silence prevails. . . . The effect is wrought to a climax by the terrific intrusion of the Wood Daemon, with the subsequent appalling darkness and striking catastrophe.[144]

Overloaded with music, *One O'Clock* extended too far into the night at the first performance and had to be shortened.[145] It was played twenty-five times that season.

At the same theater on July 22 of the following year—1812—the comic opera *Rich and Poor* with music by Charles Edward Horn was presented.[146] Lewis fashioned this piece from *The East Indian,* produced thirteen years before. In revising the comedy he condensed and excised passages to make room for songs. Lady Clara's and Mrs. Osmond's visits to each other are dropped, as is much of Rivers' part, including his plan to humble the rich cousins. *The East Indian* had been branded immoral for the reason that, although she elopes with a married man, the heroine finds happiness, a difficulty Lewis had attempted to remedy by making her deliver a speech of self-recrimination at the close of the play. These lines he now omitted as inappropriate for comic opera. *The East Indian* contains a scene borrowed from Molière's *Don Juan* in which a debtor puts off his creditor by overwhelming him with courtesies. In revising the comedy Lewis was apparently reminded by this situation of another in *The Twins,* in which Melville escapes two importunate creditors by telling each that the other is a lawyer who will discharge the creditor's bill. Lewis now lifted this scene almost without changing a word and incorporated it into *Rich and Poor.* The medley prologue from *The Twins* was also inserted, with a few changes, in his opera, where its jumbled phrases are appropriate in the mouth of a drunken servant. Two other songs are retained from *The East Indian.* As he points out, the words of one song, for which Lewis himself composed the music, consist of two stanzas of Childe Harold's farewell to Spain from the first canto of Byron's poem.[147]

*Rich and Poor* was well received and performed twenty-seven times that season. In contrast to its former jibes, the comment of the *Satirist* was almost mellow: "Mr. Lewis, whose abilities in making the same dish serve twice, with different sauce, has already been demonstrated in the cookery of his Wood Demon, has again been successful in hashing a Comedy . . . into an Opera. . . . There is no writer of the present day so well acquainted with stage effect, and the machinery of the playwright, as Mr. Lewis. The strong interest of this story, however improbable, the rapid succession of incident, the agreeable admixture of grave and gay, and the elegance of the language, must captive [sic] the great majority of an audience."[148] The moral objection, however, was not allowed to die. *The Scourge, or Monthly Expositor*, while avoiding personal abuse, dwelt at length upon the opera as a "sanctioner of female viciousness, which is nightly represented to our wives and daughters."[149] *Rich and Poor* was the last dramatic piece Lewis wrote that was produced or published.

A summary of the works noticed in this chapter is at first glance imposing: a dramatic satire (*Village Virtues*), a monodrama (*The Captive*), two farces (*The Twins, Temper*), one comedy (*The East Indian*), five tragedies (*The Minister, Rolla, Alfonso, The Harper's Daughter, Adelgitha*), six melodramas (*The Castle Spectre, Adelmorn, Rugantino, The Wood Daemon, Venoni, Timour*), a musical romance (*One O'Clock*), and a comic opera (*Rich and Poor*)—eighteen in the space of seventeen years. The total of what by courtesy we may call original works is considerably smaller. *The Minister* and *Rolla* are translations from Schiller and Kotzebue; *Venoni* except for a rewritten third act is a free translation from Monvel; *The Twins* is a reworking of Regnard as *Temper* is of Sedley's translation; *The Harper's Daughter, One O'Clock*, and *Rich and Poor* are adaptations of *The Minister, the Wood Daemon*, and *The East Indian*. Thus the number of original works is reduced to nine, and even this includes *Rugantino*, Lewis' dramatization of his own translation from Zschokke.

A survey of this output shows clearly where Lewis' abilities lay and quite as clearly where they did not lie. For the comic and satiric he had little talent. If we laugh over something in *The East Indian, The Twins*, or *Temper*, we are indebted to an author from whom Lewis borrowed; but when reading the melodramas we do not laugh, at least where we are supposed to, for though in some matters shrewdly understanding of his audience, Lewis could never judge when his comic dialogue would be tiresome. This incapacity is surprising because his prologues and epilogues are sometimes neatly epigrammatic, his letters usually amusing, and his journal filled with unforced humor.

As for serious drama, although the two blank-verse tragedies were well received, only a specialist would read them now. It is, indeed, hard to see how any tragedy successful on the stage of Lewis' day could be memorable in a later age. Dramatic poetry could not compete in the theater with melodrama, and Lewis himself was aware of this as is clear from his preface to *Alfonso* and the presence of spectacle and song in *Adelgitha*. His blank verse, though facile, is bound to the thoroughly stale tradition of imitating Shakespeare, so that the reader is constantly reminded of how unimaginative the language is. Again, tragedy demands insight into human nature and, though often preoccupied with questions of character, Lewis was unable to work them out dramatically and sometimes resorted lamely to editorial explanations of what he had meant to do. Hassan in *The Castle Spectre*, Orsino in *Alfonso*, and Adelgitha are cases in point.[150]

In the Gothic drama, however, it would be hard to challenge his pre-eminence. The history of this native British genre and Lewis' place in that history have been well told elsewhere.[151] Here we may note merely that, inaugurated with Horace Walpole's *Mysterious Mother* in 1768, a special dramatic tradition had been fully developed by the time Lewis began writing for the theater. Its principal elements were the Gothic villain suffering the agonies of a guilty conscience because of some mysterious past event not revealed until late in the story, the persecuted heroine whose function it was to be terrified, the dashing and inept hero, and the conventionalized settings of castle, convent, and cavern. These and other properties Lewis inherited, but he increased their number by additions from regions outside the Gothic world, as in *The Wood Daemon*, and further developed the genre by exploiting the supernatural.[152]

Gothic drama was for him primarily a vehicle for thrills and spectacles; plot, dialogue, character, and history in themselves were of little importance. Such a concept fitted well with conditions in the theater and was indeed largely determined by them. Since lighting and acoustical methods had not kept pace with the accommodation of larger audiences, everything had to be at once simplified and magnified. Lewis' success lay primarily in his ability to arrange arresting effects. A great virtue of his melodramas is their complete lack of subtlety of speech and action and the scope they allow for pantomime. He delighted in conceiving scenes calling for lavish and gaudy costume. As an amateur musician he was well aware of the power of musical accompaniment over the spectators. One wonders whether his fondness for sunrise, sunset, and moonlight scenes and startling contrasts of light and darkness is traceable to an eye condition in Lewis, who was very shortsighted and complained all his life of trouble with his eyes. His knowledge of the theater's new mechanical resources, of what mechanics and carpenters could do if they had to, made him bold in planning spectacles, and managers quickly learned that money was well invested in them.

Amid all this effort to startle the audience with novelty, one finds a great deal of repetition of theatrical devices which had proved effective. In particular, certain scenes with a fundamental sameness of arrangement and emotional appeal repeat themselves in his dramas. This is due partly to the Gothic framework in which he wrote and partly, no doubt, to the expediency of writing pieces that would fit expensive sets in which the theater had already invested. And it certainly illustrates a complacent acceptance, in the interests of popular success, of trite devices. One such scene used three times, a spectacular means of introducing important characters, presents a seaport defined as "the Place of St. Giorgio Maggiore at sunset," "the Port of Otranto, with an extensive view over the Adriatic Gulph," and "the Port of Messina." Presently "a galley passes at a distance," or "the fleet traverses the background," or the approach of ships is announced from a balcony. Twice there are a shouting, celebrating crowd and a chorus or a "marine procession" to greet the prince or viceroy. In four plays Lewis uses a scene of religious pageantry. By moonlight, in the evening, or at sunrise we see a procession of nuns or monks with lighted tapers outside a chapel or illuminated church, and the heroine or the monks themselves receive religious benediction. An interior setting used in four dramas is a room with an alcove and a bed or couch, dimly illuminated by lamps, moonlight, or a flickering fire on the hearth. The alcove, which can be shut off from the room by folding doors or curtains, is usually the lurking place of a ghost or malefactor or a means of secret escape. The bed, located in either the room or the alcove, is no ordinary bed: it conceals a fugitive prince, collapses for comic effect, or is a vehicle to an underground vault. In this scene a sliding panel, portraits, a balcony, and a guitar are optional accessories. Another effective scene fully exploited three times and partially a fourth calls for a brilliantly illuminated banquet in a Gothic hall. There is always a conspicuous entrance such as "folding doors richly ornamented" or "a large painted window" in the backscene, an elevated throne, and a staircase leading to a door above. While the company are enjoying a masque or ballet or the singing of minstrels in an atmosphere of gaiety, a sudden alarm changes the mood to horror and confusion. In *One O'Clock*, as we have seen, the change was accomplished gradually.

The most frequently recurring of these basic scenes is the Gothic dungeon, which Lewis had loaded with excessive horror in *The Monk*. In his dramas it appears five or six times. A composite picture reveals it as dank and cold, with ponderously thick walls. No daylight ever reaches it, but by the dim flame of a small lamp one sees chains, a small jug, a miserable straw pallet, and a grated iron door. The unfortunate captive, usually guiltless, has pined away here from ten to twenty years mourning for his loved ones, without hope of ever again seeing the sun or hearing a human voice. An interesting detail which Lewis used in four of his dungeon scenes and several times elsewhere is an open gallery or passage above the vault and leading to it, along which figures are seen slowly passing, guided by a lamp or torch. In *The Castle Spectre*, while watching Reginald in his dungeon, we also see Angela and Father Philip "through the chasms above, passing along slowly." In *The Captive* "the Gaoler is seen passing through the upper gallery with a lamp," the passage in this instance being visible to the captive. Hardyknute's Necromantic Cavern is equipped with a gallery along which Una lights her way with a firebrand. In the second version of *Venoni*, the gallery again appears, flashing with the light of torches as the hero is conducted to his dungeon.

In addition to these formulated scenes, one could compile a long list of repeated motifs and devices. At least once in nearly every play a bell strikes in token of some fatal hour. A sound equally pleasing to Lewis was that of a bugle or whistle, ranging in significance from a mere summons to dinner to a blast proclaiming a monarch's escape from death. He had constant recourse also to

thunder and lightning, once harnessing the latter so effectively that
it takes an active part in the plot by destroying a dungeon wall.
That his characters divide themselves without demur into several
easily recognized types hardly needs saying. Even their dialogue
could be reduced in some measure to formula. "Guard me, good
Angels!" or "Lead on, I follow!" comes automatically to the lips of
hero or heroine on the brink of perilous adventure, and no villain
could lay hand to sword without exclaiming "This to thy heart!"
Like their fellow characters in other dramas of the time, they are
generous, on little or no provocation, with speeches of trite moralizing, humanitarianism, and, in view of the war with France,
patriotism. In Adelmorn, for instance, the elsewhere unreflective
Herman, aged sixteen, vents the following: "Ah! Maurice, what a
striking proof is he, that riches weigh light in the balance of happiness. If wealth or power could bless, how enviable would be Ulric!
But his frame worn by disease, his mind tortured by anxiety, he
sighs in vain for health of body and repose of mind, those guests
so common in the peasant's cottage!" A moral tag of little or no
relevancy is sewed on to the last scene in three of Lewis' plays to
convince the audience that they have received a wholesome lesson.
One is at a loss to apply the following to anything in Adelmorn:
"When an action seems right, let us consider only the effect, . . .
when an action seems wrong, let us always enquire into the cause,
in hopes of finding there some apology for the error." The French
Revolution will account for the array of kings beloved of their
subjects, among whom even the villainous Hardyknute is momentarily sanctified by the words: "If my people are happy, I am
rewarded amply: Life is only dear to me, while it enables me to
protect you; and when I die, be this my purest praise and proudest
Epitaph, 'Here lies the Sovereign of a happy People!' "

One point, though it applies to much of his other work also,
needs emphasis regarding Lewis' dramas, because it explains their
consistent mediocrity. Except where there is external evidence to
the contrary—for instance, in Alfonso, which does show some
development—it is fairly safe to consider all his published plays to
be products of his teens or twentieth year. When in 1801 he was
smarting under criticism directed at The Monk, The Castle Spectre,
and Adelmorn, he wrote a highly pertinent note which has usually

been overlooked, perhaps because it is buried in a postscript to one of his plays:

Every thing which I have hitherto published, except my Imitation of Juvenal, and the translation of a play of Kotzebue's was written between fourteen and twenty-one; a period which I passed in scribbling Novels and Plays, but which, I am aware, would have been much better employed in reading sense than in writing nonsense. Formerly, indeed, I was of a different opinion; and the consequence is, that I have it still in my power to deluge the town with such an inundation of Ghosts and Magicians, as would satisfy the thirst of the most insatiable swallower of wonders. Whether I shall exercise this power in future, I am not decided.[153]

His subsequent output may be considered a partial fulfillment of this threat to deluge the town. As he gained in experience he must unquestionably have revised and put finishing touches on his early work before stage production or publication, but it is quite erroneous to picture him as an author busily composing one new drama after another. When one was called for, he needed only to thumb through his boyhood manuscripts.

Critics of his day saw in his dramatic work, as they had in *The Monk*, evidence of misdirected talent, but he received more justice at their hands as a dramatist than as the author of the romance. When they condemned his melodramas, they were really decrying the state of popular stage entertainment and could not forgive him his success. They would have concurred with a later critic that "he had the accomplished criminal's faculty of doing his bad things exceedingly well."[154] As for Lewis, he had no illusions about his writing for the stage. The disclaimers of any literary worth or originality with which he studded his plays go beyond the conventional modesty of the ingratiating dramatist. He tried hard in *Alfonso*, perhaps in *Adelgitha*, but so far as the melodramas were concerned, facetious and deprecating comments in the printed editions of his plays make his attitude clear. "I . . . sincerely hope," he says of *Adelmorn*, "that my readers may discover more merit in it than I have hitherto been able to find myself"; of *Rugantino*, "I shall make no apology for having employed (or as many may think it, wasted) my time upon a composition of so trifling a nature"; and *Timour* is a "trifle . . . written to oblige Mr. Harris." He assures his critics: "When they find fault with my Works, I am nine times out of ten of their opinion; but still, until writing ceases to amuse me, I shall not cease to write," and in the preface to *Venoni* he announces that "the act of composing has ceased to amuse me."

Part of this amusement undoubtedly was the satisfaction of being an important figure in the theatrical world. His writing and ideas were in demand. Undoubtedly, too, he appreciated fully the amusement of receiving an income from his efforts. Lewis is conventionally described as rich, and so he became in 1812 when his father died. In the meantime he lived expensively himself and was generous to others, while the estrangement from his father, together with his own pride, limited the elder Lewis as a source of help. It is not entirely a coincidence that he wrote no more for the theater after coming into his inheritance.

# 5

# PROSE AND VERSE

O<small>F</small> Lewis' publications other than dramas, the earliest after *The Monk* was his poem "The Love of Gain." In a letter to Walter Scott of January 24, 1799, Lewis speaks of "having been, and being still, very busy with a sort of Paraphrase of the 13th Satire of Juvenal," of which twenty lines remain to be written.[1] When he asked Lady Holland, she advised him that Mr. Fox would be complimented to have the work dedicated to him.[2] Thus it appeared on February 12 inscribed to the Hon. Charles James Fox "as a trifling Mark of the Veneration in which I hold his Talents and Character, and which his present Retirement from Public Life gives me an Opportunity thus to declare without running the Hazard of subjecting myself to Party Censure."[3] Lady Holland, who found the poem too dull to read to the end, credibly reports that it "was done, as I understand, at the request of his father, who was anxious that he should give a classical turn to his literary reputation, as he laments his ballad and greenroom tastes."[4] Liberal additions make this very free paraphrase over twice the length of the original. Where the Latin poet pictures the conscience-stricken sleep of one guilty of revenge, for instance, Lewis, who had recently cast Ambrosio headlong to a horrible death, finds the opportunity for elaboration too tempting to resist:

> Nocte brevem si forte indulsit cura soporem,
> Et toto versata toro jam membra quiescunt,
> Continuo templum et violati Numinis aras,
> Et (quod praecipuis mentem sudoribus urget)
> Te videt in somnis. Tua sacra et major imago
> Humana turbat pavidum, cogitque fateri.

> Next mark, my friend, his slumbers!—If Repose
> Lists to his suit, and bids his eye-lids close,

Mark what convulsions heave his martyr'd breast
And frequent starts, and heart-drawn sighs attest,
Though Nature grants him sleep, that Guilt denies him rest.
Now groans of tortur'd ghosts his ear affright;
Now ghastly phantoms dance before his sight;
And now he sees (and screams in frantic fear)
To size gigantic swell'd thy angry shade appear!
Swift at thy summons rush with hideous yell
Their prey to seize the Denizens of hell!
Headlong they hurl him on some ice-rock's point,
Mangle each limb, and dislocate each joint;
Or plunge him deep in blue sulphureous lakes;
Or lash his quivering flesh with twisted snakes;
Or in his brain their burning talons dart;
Or from his bosom rend his panting heart
To bathe their fiery lips in guilty gore!—
Then starts he from his couch, while dews of horror pour
Down his dank forehead—wrings his hands, and prays to sleep no more.

The poem received careful attention from some reviewers, but little praise. The *Critical Review* found the verses of Lewis, compared to the strong lines of Juvenal, as he to Hercules: "If Mr. Lewis had published only his Monk, the world would have given him credit for considerable, though misapplied, talents. That work attracted notice by its faults; and the author was abused into popularity. But he is now writing down his reputation."[5]

The most important of Lewis' publications to be noted in this chapter is his next—*Tales of Wonder*, a title which, together with *The Monk* and *The Castle Spectre*, was during his life and still is most frequently associated with his name. Some of the material for this work he probably had in hand as early as 1793, when he wrote to his mother from Weimar of a volume of original and translated poems he hoped soon to publish. At all events he was hunting "marvellous" ballads early in 1798, the year he met in London William Erskine, Walter Scott's literary friend and adviser—a meeting which had important consequences for Scott. Erskine showed Lewis translations by Scott of Bürger's "Lenore" and "Der Wilde Jäger" —exactly the kind of poetry Lewis was seeking. When told that Scott had other ballads, Lewis expressed interest. Scott, then an unknown young barrister four years older than Lewis, was flattered by a request from such a widely recognized literary figure, and, according to Lockhart, placed at his new friend's disposal his translations and imitations of German poems.[6] It is now possible to supplement Lockhart's account with the text of Scott's first letter to Lewis:

Sir

Our freind [sic] Erskine has communicated to me your wish to republish the inclosed Translations in a Collection you are at present forming. I have applied to the publishers for permission which they have granted, and on my own part I certainly feel such an application from the Author of The Monk & Castle Spectre as highly flattering indeed. In the inclosed version of "Lenore" there has been a *petty Larceny* on my part as you will observe from glancing at the preface. May I therefore beg that the acknowledgement and apology of my theft couchd as shortly as you please may accompany the Ballad in a Note or otherways. The Ballads were at first publishd anonymously, I have at present no wish that they should longer remain so. With these little remarks they are very much at your service tho' they can only serve as a foil to your Compositions of many of which I have been long an enthusiastic admirer.

Erskine & Cranstoun, have been teazing me to send you other two translations from the German which have never seen the Light. One is from the "Lied von Treue" of Bürger, the other an imitation of a ghostly Ballad in the "Claudine von Villa Bella of Goethe." I cannot think however of using such a freedom unless the nature of your proposed Collection be more extensive than I at present suppose. I apprehend I shall by means of the Inclosed already occupy too much space.—I would much rather trespass upon your bounds (were your plan to admit it) for the Insertion of a Scots Ballad of great antiquity upon the Recovery of a young Knight who had been carried of [sic] by the Elfin Quene and is redeemd by his Mistress

If the possession of such an ancient Ditty would give you pleasure I shall be happy to communicate that & some others very little known which a long Residence in the wildest part of the South of Scotland enabled me to collect from Tradition. A Farrago of

> Adventures rueful marvellous & deep
> Of fays that nightly dance upon the wold
> And Lovers doomd to wander & to weep
> and Castles high where wicked wizards keep
> Their Captive Thralls.

I have written till I could almost think myself as well acquainted with you as with your Works[.] it is high time I should subscribe myself as the *Spectator* has it

Sir
your sincere admirer
& most obed<sup>t</sup> Servant
Walter Scott
Advocate

Edin. 50 George Street
29 May 1798
M. G. Lewis Esq[7]

The progress of *Tales of Wonder* can be followed through excerpts from a series of eleven letters from Lewis to Scott. The first, in 1798, replies to Scott's letter above and describes the intended volume:

Sir,

    I cannot delay expressing to you, how much I feel obliged to you for your permission to publish the Ballads, which I requested, and for the polite manner in which that permission was granted. The Plan, which I propose to myself, is to collect all the *marvellous* Ballads, that I can lay my hands upon, and publish them under the title of "Tales of Terror." Antient as well as Modern, will be comprised in my design. . . .

He adds that "a Ghost or a Witch is a sine-qua-non ingredient in all the dishes, of which I mean to compose my hobgoblin repast." He has collected thirty or forty ballads so far and asks for more traditional ballads, but not "Tam Lin," a particular favorite of his which he already has. Several people have contributed modern ballads, and he will include thirteen of his own, of which "The Grim White Woman" is "reckoned by those to whom I have shown it, to be much the best of my horrible compositions." The work cannot appear till winter, but he wishes to get it in readiness before leaving for Scotland.[8]

    Three years were to elapse before the hobgoblin repast was served. Lewis reports later in 1798 that he has bargained with Bell, his bookseller, for the publication of Scott's translation of *Goetz von Berlichingen* and grudgingly acknowledges Scott's revision of "Glenfinlas": "I *grumble*, but say no more on *this* subject, though I hope, you will not be so inflexible on that of your other Ballads, for I do not despair of convincing you in time, that a *bad* rhyme is in fact no rhyme at all. You desire me to point out my objections, leaving you at liberty to make use of them, or not, and so have at Frederic & Alice." He then suggests changes in that ballad, "The Chase," and "William and Helen"—other contributions by Scott. Most of his criticism relates to rhyme—Lewis demanded perfect rhymes of himself and expected the same of Scott. He was a little less strict concerning regularity of meter: "Observe, that in the Ballad I do not always object to a variation of metre, but then it ought to increase the melody." He needs a ballad of a "Fire-King" or a "Cloud-King" and wants a contribution from William Erskine (W 23).[9]

On December 15, 1798, we read that Scott's translation is to go to press and Bell is to pay twenty-five guineas, so that *Goetz* "will at least furnish M^rs Scott with the price of a Pad-Nag, and his iron hand many be turned into Horse-shoes." Lewis has promised "(which from my indolent disposition is no small compliment, I can tell you) to overlook the Proofs." Meanwhile the ballad book goes slowly—"Bell talks of publishing them with vignettes, cuts &c, and making one of your *pretty* publications out of them.—I will alter your 'Frederick and Alice' for you with pleasure; But where is my 'Fire-King,' and 'Cloud-King?'—I saw a M.S. Ballad of Southey's the other day, which was *uncommonly* good" (W 15). On January 6, 1799, he praises Scott's ballads "Glenfinlas" and "St. John's Eve." He is awaiting proof sheets of *Goetz* and has begun a poem which later appeared in *Tales of Wonder*: "For my own part I have done nothing in the Ballad way, except that one morning while I was staying at Brocket Hall, every body else being employed in rehearsing a private Play, which they were to perform in the evening, I was left alone, and amused myself in versifying 'The Gay gold Ring' a story, which I beleive, I told you at Edinburgh. However, I have only done a third part of it yet" (W 17).[10] On January 24, he says the first act of *Goetz* is published and that he has given Bell a dressing for not getting on faster (W. 18). A letter of March 5 (W 19) begins,

Dear Scott,
    Do not be impatient for the publication of the Tales of Terror for they are not one jot nearer publication, than they were when I saw you last. There is a sort of Imbroglio about Southey's Ballads, which must be settled, and into the bargain I cannot for the life of me, find a manner of finishing my "Gay gold Ring" sufficiently dramatic. I want too to make William Lamb give me an additional Ballad, which at present He seems inclined to do. Goetz will be published in the course of the next week; It met with an accident while preparing for the Press, for a gust of wind run away with some part of the M.S. & one leaf was lost irrecoverably. However, I managed to provide the German, & translated the passages, which had made their exit by the window.

The *Tales of Terror* mentioned here refers to the work later published with the title *Tales of Wonder*. As for *Goetz*, it is amusing to know that students of Scott have read it unaware that they were also reading—for one page, that is—emergency work by Lewis.[11]

On the last day of 1799 Lewis writes (M 24):

Dear Scott,

I thank you for your Letter, and the trouble which you have taken in stopping the intended publication of Ballads; I have got so far as having sold mine, and consequently they will appear, as soon as the *East Indian* is printed, which is now in the Press, and about which by the bye Sheridan has behaved just as ill, as on former occasions. I have finished the *Gay gold Ring*, & it is much admired; But I am in terrible want of a *Cloud-King*, a *Fire-King* and a good translation of Horace's *Canidia*, to compleat my collection If you will not help me yourself, can you not prevail on some of your acquaintance? In England I have no hopes of finding any help, for Genius seems to have established herself on the other side of the Tweed, and to be as much afraid of crossing the water, as a Cat is of wetting her feet—Could not Mr Tytler be persuaded to do something for me in this way?—Has Mr Campbell no turn for Ghost Ballads? . . . I have desired Bell to advertise the Tales immediately, and to warn all Persons against publishing any Poetry of mine in any shape whatever.

The "stopping of the intended publication of Ballads," especially in conjunction with a later letter from Scott to his friend and future publisher James Ballantyne, makes it clear that Scott, eager to place his work before the public, had arranged to have some of his ballads published by Ballantyne without waiting for the appearance of Lewis' long-delayed book, and that when he told Lewis of his intention the latter succeeded once more in checking his impatience.

But more delays were in store. Lewis was greatly taken with his own scheme of four Elemental Spirits which, however fantastic, had to be worked out logically to the last detail. On February 3, 1800, he writes:

Dear Scott,

I return you many thanks for your Ballad, & the Extract, and I shall be very much obliged to your Friend for the "Cloud-King"—I must however make one criticism upon his Stanzas which you sent me—the Spirit being a wicked one must not have such delicate wings as pale blue ones: It has nothing to do with heaven except to deface it with Storms, & therefore in "The Monk," I have fitted him with a pair of sable pinions, to which I must request your Friend to adapt his Stanza. With the others I am much pleased, as I am with your Fire-King; but every-body makes the same objection to it, & expresses a wish, that you had conformed your Spirit to the description given of him in "The Monk," where his office is to play the Will o' the Wisp, & lead Travellers into bogs &c; It is also objected to, his being removed from his native land to [sic] Denmark to Palestine, and that the office assigned to him in your Ballad has nothing peculiar to the "Fire-King," but would have suited Arimazes, Beelzebub, or any other evil Spirit as well.

However, the Ballad itself I think very pretty[.] I suppose, you have heard from Bell respecting the copies of the Ballads, I was too much distrest at the time to write myself—I hope, you will dispense with the proofs of your Ballads being sent to Scotland as it would delay the publication very much —I shall have the work put in the press, as soon as I receive your Friend's Ballad—I have almost finished a new one myself, in which all the four elementary Spirits are to appear, and Count Albert's brand is to make a conspicuous figure—

He then gives sample stanzas which he thinks particularly happy (W 26). The friend who supplied "The Cloud-King" was John Leyden. The distress Lewis refers to sprang from his brother Barrington's death on January 13, 1800.

The next letter is of February 20. John Leyden's "Cloud-King" has arrived. Lewis is pleased but objects that

the Cloud-King cannot possibly have *blue* wings, blue being the very reverse of Clouds; besides in the Monk, He is described with *black* wings, for which in my *own* Ballad of the Cloud-King, I have given a reason.

"My eyes furnish lightnings; My wings *cloud* the air,"

which you will allow blue wings cannot possibly do—Now in my opinion the whole scenery, story, & Personae Dramatis of this Ballad (as well as the phraseology are much more applicable to Scotland than to any other Country, and therefore if He has no objection, I wish the Ballad to be published under the title of "the Elfin-King," with whose Scotch character the seven-years wandering, the *greensward ring*, & many other circumstances suit; the elfin, or elf-king, will do equally well for the metre, & the Spirit may then have wings as blue as he pleases.

The long-delayed collection he intends to send to the press immediately, and Scott shall receive the proofs he apparently requested (W 27). On April 22 Scott wrote to James Ballantyne: "I have your favour, since the receipt of which some things have occurred which induce me to postpone my intention of publishing my ballads, particularly a letter from a friend, assuring me that 'The Tales of Wonder' are actually in the printer's hand. In this situation I endeavour to strengthen my small stock of patience, which has been nearly exhausted by the delay of this work, to which (though for that reason alone) I almost regret having promised assistance. I am still resolved to have recourse to your press for the Ballads of the Border, which are in some forwardness."[12] On May 29 Lewis was obliged to inform Scott that *Tales of Wonder* could not appear before the following season, only seventeen of the sixty ballads being yet printed (W 30). One more reference to their collaboration occurs in Lewis' letter apparently written soon after the appearance of *Tales of Wonder* in 1801 (W 31):

Dear Scott,
    I send you Sir Agilthorn, for doing which you ought to think yourself much more obliged to me, than if I had sent you something worth having. As this Ballad has no merit, my suffering its publication is a much stronger proof of my anxiety to comply with your requests, than if I had given you a composition, which flattered my own vanity. However, the Ballad will serve to augment the bulk of your volume & the list of your Contributors; To do this, & to show my gratitude for your kindness respecting my late publication are the only purposes it can answer. I hope, you got your copies —Remember me to Professor Stewart, & wish Erskine joy from me.
Yours truly
M. G. Lewis[13]

"Sir Agilthorn" duly appeared in the third volume of Scott's *Minstrelsy of the Scottish Border* (1802–03). The words "my late publication" and "your copies" refer to *Tales of Wonder*, the work projected to Scott in 1797 or 1798 and at last published in 1801. Scott's patience had not been entirely equal to the delay. To help his friend James Ballantyne, who wanted material for a small book which would exhibit his skill at a printer, Scott had given Ballantyne nine ballads which were privately printed at Kelso in 1799 as *An Apology for Tales of Terror*, a title suggesting Scott's impatience over the delay of Lewis' book. Three of the ballads were by Scott, three by Lewis, two by Southey, and one by John Aikin. Of these nine, three of Lewis', one of Scott's, and one of Southey's were later included in *Tales of Wonder*. It may seem unsporting of Scott to have released for publication material intended for Lewis' book; however, only twelve copies of the *Apology* were run off, and these were not for sale but were intended merely as specimens of printing.[14]

    Lewis is usually granted the distinction of having influenced Scott's early poetry. Scott himself readily testifies to this, though one must keep in mind Lockhart's warning that Scott was rather disposed to hold popular favor as the surest test of literary merit and continued throughout life to overestimate all talents except his own.[15] Scott said his youthful interest in ballad poetry was re-

awakened by poems in *The Monk:* "finding Lewis in possession of
so much reputation, and conceiving that if I fell behind him in
poetical powers I considerably exceeded him in general information, I suddenly took it into my head to attempt the style of poetry
by which he had raised himself to fame."[16] He never lost this regard
for Lewis' ability. In 1797 he had sent his own version of Goethe's
*Der Erlkönig* to a friend with the remark, "I assure you, there is no
small impudence in attempting a version of that ballad, as it has
been translated by *Lewis*,"[17] and over thirty years later he recalled
that Lewis, although a martinet in the accuracy of rhymes and
numbers, "had a right to be so, for few persons have exhibited more
mastery of rhyme, or greater command over the melody of verse.
He was, therefore, rigid in exacting similar accuracy from others,
and as I was quite unaccustomed to the mechanical part of poetry,
and used rhymes which were merely permissible, as readily as those
which were legitimate, contests often arose amongst us, which were
exasperated by the pertinacity of my Mentor, who, as all who knew
him can testify, was no granter of propositions."[18] Scott told Archibald Constable that he had received much instruction from Lewis,
though he added that "it related almost entirely to the rhymes, in
which he was greatly superior, and to the structure and versification,
for which the poor monk had a most excellent ear."[19] He wrote on
the margin of Byron's diary that Lewis "had the finest ear for the
rhythm of verse I ever heard—finer than Byron's."[20]

Literary influence is difficult to measure, but a kind of evidence
is provided by the extent to which Scott accepted Lewis' editorial
suggestions for improving six ballads, five of which were published
in *Tales of Wonder.* As we have seen, Scott made alterations in
"Glenfinlas" but the editor grumbled at the revision. In "Frederic
and Alice" Lewis pointed out fifteen flaws, eleven of which were
removed from the *Tales of Wonder* version. Of this ballad Scott
wrote years later, "It owes any little merit it may possess to my
friend Mr. Lewis, to whom it was sent in an extremely rude state."[21]
To "The Wild Huntsman" Lewis made seven objections, all of
which Scott satisfied. Lewis made some thirty-four suggestions for
improving "William and Helen," but Scott adopted none, a fact
which probably accounts for the absence of the ballad from Lewis'
book. It cannot be shown that Scott changed "Glenfinlas," though
Lewis reported two suggestions made by friends to whom he had

read it. Of the five faults Lewis found in "The Eve of St. John," Scott attended to only one.[22] The evidence from these six poems is enough to suggest that Scott quickly made himself independent of his friend's judgment, wisely no doubt. Though individually justifiable, Lewis' suggestions when followed in quantity could change a border ballad or an imitation of one into something exceedingly artificial. But Lewis' discipline, though "severe enough, perhaps," as Scott later said, was something "for which I was much indebted to him, as forcing upon the notice of a young and careless author hints which the said author's vanity made him unwilling to attend to, but which were absolutely necessary to any hope of his ultimate success."[23] Lewis' lectures "did not at the time produce any effect upon my inflexibility, though I did not forget them at a future period."[24]

When *Tales of Wonder* finally appeared late in 1800 or early the following year, the public was disappointed.[25] Scott gives as reasons for this the false hopes raised by the delay, the fact that the popularity of ballads and ballad-mongers was already waning, Lewis' misguided sense of humor, and that, by the inclusion of many well-known poems, the work was expanded to two substantial and expensive volumes.[26] The first edition was in royal octavo, on heavy paper, in large uncrowded type with generous margins, and sold for a guinea. Of the sixty pieces in the collection, about two thirds had been published before, many in generally accessible eighteenth-century works like Percy's *Reliques*, David Herd's *Ancient and Modern Scottish Songs*, James Johnson's *Scots Musical Museum*, Thomas Evans' *Old Ballads*, and in editions of well-known poets like Dryden, Parnell, Gray, and Burns. Of the published sources for *Tales of Wonder*, Percy's *Reliques* was the most useful—in fact more useful than Lewis felt obliged to indicate. For "The Marriage of Sir Gawaine," "King Arthur's Death," "Fair Margaret and Sweet William," and "The Boy and the Mantle," he cites the *Reliques* as his source; "The Witches' Song" from Ben Jonson's *Masque of Queens*, "Admiral Hosier's Ghost," and "The Witch of Wokey" he attributed merely to Jonson, Mallet, and Glover, but the presence of Percy's notes betrays the source of all three. Moreover, Percy's collection presumably supplied "Margaret's Ghost" and "Sweet William's Ghost," since both are to be found in the *Reliques* respectively assigned, as in *Tales of Wonder*, to Mallet and to Ramsay's *Tea-Table Miscellany*. Lewis' book was soon known as *Tales of Plunder*, many people feeling, as Anna Seward did, that the editor had dishonestly imposed on the public, a charge against which Scott later emphatically defended Lewis.[27] The Irish poet Thomas Dermody published, under the name of Mauritius Moonshine, *More Wonders! An Heroic Epistle, Addressed to M. G. Lewis, Esq.* (London, 1801) with the happily chosen motto "The time has been/ That when the brains were out the man would die." The free use Lewis had made of the work of others inspired in Dermody the following dream:

> When ev'ry sense by pow'rful Sleep was seal'd,
> And o'er the brain his poppy-dews prevail'd
> In my lone Study, lo! methought, I sat,
> Grave as an Owl, and pensive as a Cat;
> Before my sight, in pompous garment gay,
> Fresh from the Press, thy "*Tales of Wonder*" lay,
> And much I gloated, with lascivious eyes,
> On its white form, gilt edge, and comely size:
> When, sudden, from the lab'ring shelves around,
> I heard, at first, a small, still, solemn sound,
> That louder wax'd anon:—and, now, I view'd
> Descending from their cells, the motley brood,
> An animated host of various hue;
> Pale yellow, chestnut brown, caerulean blue,
> And glowing red, as if inflam'd by rage;
> All cover'd with the rev'rend dust of age!
> Fierce they approach'd, and (oh! extremest grief,)
> Each from the stranger-volume tore a leaf,
> Indignant tore; and while my anxious mind
> Quick doubts involv'd, scarce "left a wreck behind;"
> Then, to their sev'ral seats, alertly fled,
> Mutt'ring low curses on thy fated head.
> Curious to know, what lucubration rare
> These vellum-vested knaves would deign to spare
> Thy Tome, all tatter'd as it was, I took:
> Good Heav'n! how much unlike the former book!
> For they had pick'd the meat, but spurn'd the bone,
> And, only left thee, S[outhe]y's, and—Thy Own.[28]

History seems to have decided it enough to remember of *Tales of Wonder* that it contains early poems by Scott. Nevertheless, let us glance at Lewis' original poems, his translations, his adaptations, and one or two editorial points.

Of his nine original poems, "Alonzo the Brave and Fair Imogine" is not completely forgotten, nor does it deserve to be. This
macabre ballad of a warrior so brave and a virgin so bright had
been reprinted in periodicals after its first appearance in *The Monk*.
The subject matter has not the merit of much originality, the old
theme of the broken pledge and appearance of the dead lover's
ghost having already been popularized anew by Bürger's "Lenore";
and Lewis could have found in "Des Pfarrers Tochter von Tauben-
heim" by the same poet meter and rhyme scheme quite similar to
those of "Alonzo." For all that, this little ballad is in its way
perfect—prosodically flawless, it is a ghost story told with economy,
proportion, and a unity of tone which Lewis seldom achieved. One
does not begrudge it its place in *The Oxford Book of Eighteenth
Century Verse*. It is pre-eminent among the "Gothic ballads" of the
time, a genre of which a critical study is still wanting. After the
appearance of "Alonzo," anonymous Gothic ballads began to sprin-
kle the pages of contemporary periodicals. Several writers tried the
form, Southey perhaps most successfully. He was early in the field
with a number of short metrical tales of terror contributed to the
*Morning Post* in the years 1796–1798, though none of them appeared before "Alonzo." Of his "Mary, the Maid of the Inn" he
noted that he had "adopted the meter of Mr. Lewis' Alonzo and
Imogine—a poem deservedly popular"; and later, "The metre is
Mr. Lewis' invention; and metre is one of the few things concerning which popularity may be admitted as a proof of merit."[29]

Whether or not he agrees with Southey, the reader of *Tales of
Wonder* is impressed by the variety of metrical feet, stanzaic forms,
and rhyme schemes displayed in Lewis' poems. Usually preserving
strict regularity in all these throughout a single composition, he allowed himself freedom in "The Gay Gold Ring." It seems affected
by the magic of "Christabel," which was then in the air, although
Coleridge's poem was not published until 1816:

> In silence the maid
> The knight obey'd;
> Low on his pillow her head she laid:
> But soon as by hers *his* hand was press'd
> Changed to ice was the heart in his breast;
> And his limbs were fetter'd in frozen chains,
> And turn'd to snow was the blood in his veins.[30]

In subject matter these nine poems are highly miscellaneous, ranging from the moral peudo-oriental tale of "The Princess and the Slave" to "Giles Jollup the Grave," Lewis' own reworking of a newspaper parody of *Alonzo*. The inclusion of "Giles Jollup," the anonymous "Cinder King," and George Colman the younger's "Maid of the Moor," all written in ridicule of Gothic verse, must have been a stroke of that misguided humor to which Scott alludes. Of the *bona fide* ballads in *Tales of Wonder*, some represent the Gothic manner at its most violent. One is the grotesque and repulsive story of Bothwell's Bonny Jane, an innocent maiden assaulted and drowned by a villainous abbot who might be Ambrosio's brother and who in turn falls into the clutches of a gigantic and unconvincing fiend. "Osric the Lion" presents a riot of physical horrors when a murderous uncle is seized by a whole company of devils. In "The Grim White Woman," an ingenious tale of sorcery, the horror is again overwrought and the effect of the poem is marred by moralizing. This propensity for pointing a moral no matter what the artistic cost Lewis could seldom resist.

Eight ballads are translations by Lewis from German, for five of which he turned to Herder's *Volkslieder*. Though he has been blamed for not citing his source, he acknowledged in two conspicuous notes his use of the German poet's collection for four of the ballads, probably overlooking the fifth. Some of these five do him credit, though not usually as translations. Since his purpose clearly was to produce a neat, polished, metrically perfect little poem, he never hesitated to depart entirely from his original in stanzaic form and rhyme scheme and to repair a fragment or complete a stanza by adding new matter. The result is a handful of Gothic ballads which, if faulty as translations, are decidedly more pleasing than those in which he enjoyed unrestricted choice of content. His greatest offenses as translator are inappropriate elegance of diction, sentimentality, and a fastidious counting of syllables, refinements which obliterate whatever folklore tone survives in Herder. Take the opening stanza of "Elver's Hoh":

> The knight laid his head upon Elver's Hoh,
> Soft slumbers his senses beguiling;
> Fatigue press'd its seal on his eyelids, when lo!
> Two maidens drew near to him, smiling;

> The one she kiss'd softly Sir Algamore's eyes;
> The other she whisper'd him sweetly,
> "Arise! thou gallant young warrior, arise,
> "For the dance it goes gaily and featly!"

Except that the third person instead of the first is used, the translation is reasonably faithful, but "Fatigue press'd its seal on his eyelids" is rather elaborate for "Mein Augen begannen zu sinken," as is "Arise! thou gallant young warrior, arise" for "Steh' auf! Du muntrer Jüngling, auf!" Also, the perfection of meter turns the poem into a carefully machined product. "The Sword of Angantyr," only roughly metrical in the German, brings out his skill in meter and rime, although, as he confessed, the translation is very free and the conclusion his own addition. Warned that to touch the magic sword will mean her death, Hervor nevertheless compels Angantyr's shade to surrender it. Here the original breaks off with just a suggestion of the catastrophe, but Lewis could not resist adding eight stanzas in which Hervor bursts into flame and dies shrieking.[31]

His best translation from Herder is "King Hacho's Death Song." In this he faithfully presents the content of his unmetrical and rhymeless original in well-packed iambic couplets free of pretentious diction, and he preserves the restraint of the conclusion:

> Since to the gods the king hath fled,
> Heroes and valiant hosts have bled:
> The bones of friends have strow'd the sand;
> Usurping tyrants sway the land;
> And many a tear for Hacho brave
> Still falls upon his honour'd grave.

That his choice of meter and stanza was not always wise is painfully emphasized by the next two ballads from the *Volkslieder*. Anapaests are not the foot for "The Erl-King's Daughter," of which the opening line, "Herr Oluf reitet spät und weit" becomes "O'er mountains, through vallies, Sir Oluf he wends," suggesting a galloping camel. Herder's blunt and effective ending becomes flabby as Lewis fills out his own stanza:

> Die Braut hob auf den Scharlach rot,
> Da lag Herr Oluf, und er war todt.

Sore trembled the lady, so fair and so gay;
She eyed the red curtain; she drew it away;
But soon from her bosom for ever life fled,
For there lay Sir Oluf, cold, breathless, and dead.

In reworking "Der Wassermann" as "The Water-King" he committed himself to a stanza requiring four lines for every two of German and was forced into ludicrous repetition intended to do duty for the incremental repetition of folk balladry:

Oh! mother! mother! now advise,
How I may yonder maid surprise:
Oh! mother! mother! now explain,
How I may yonder maid obtain. . . .

He bound his courser to the door,
And paced the churchyard three times four.
His courser to the door bound he,
And paced the churchyard four times three.

Two translations are from Goethe. Lewis' version of *Erlkönig* is creditable, though he introduces inappropriate patches of bright color: "Manch bunte Blumen" becomes "Fine flowers . . . white, scarlet, and blue" and the Erl-King's daughter is dressed in "purple and gold." Again he sentimentalizes an effective final line: "In seinen Armen das Kind war tot" is exchanged for "Life throbbed in the sweet baby's bosom no more." On the other hand, "Der Fischer" has probably never received a better English translation than Lewis gave it.

*Tales of Wonder* contains four English or Scottish folk ballads, "Clerk Colvin," "Willy's Lady," "King Henry," and "Tam Lin." The first three he took from the so-called Brown MS, a collection of ballads belonging to Walter Scott's friend Alexander Fraser Tytler. Lewis' version of "Clerk Colvin" seems indebted also to that published in David Herd's *Ancient and Modern Scottish Songs* (1769, 1776). Of "King Henry," which first appeared in print in *Tales of Wonder* with the title "Courteous King Jamie," Lewis notes, "I have altered and added so much to this ballad, that I might almost claim it for my own."[32] "Tam Lin" he found in James Johnson's *Scots Musical Museum* (1787–1803). One scarcely expects his treatment of ballad texts to show—and it certainly does not show— the antiquarian's veneration for what is genuine or the scholar's for what is accurate, virtues to which Lewis as a ballad editor did not pretend. As in the translations, he adapts and polishes, counts syllables, contrives rhymes at the price of unnatural word order, and, rather than leave anything to the reader's imagination, fills gaps which are often highly effective in the original narrative. Such changes, made when textual tampering was no sin, may be condoned, as may occasional slips in the glossing of words at a time when Scottish-English dictionaries were less accessible than now.[33] But the incongruous mixture of diction and of idiom, Scottish and English, old and new, would be an artistic offense in any age.

We need not evaluate here the nineteen pieces by Lewis' contemporaries, but the presence of Southey's eight ballads raises an editorial question. Scott's account of the contributors to *Tales of Wonder* is as follows: "I readily agreed to contribute the ballads of *Glenfinlas* and of *The Eve of St. John*, with one or two others of less merit, and my friend Dr Leyden became also a contributor. Mr Southey, a tower of strength, added *The Old Woman of Berkeley*, *Lord William*, and several other interesting ballads of the same class, to the proposed collection."[34] Southey's collaboration was less enthusiastic than this implies. Lewis in his letter of December 15, 1798, already quoted, mentioned having recently seen an "*uncommonly good*" ballad by Southey. Probably some time later he sought permission to publish this and others by the same author, for on March 5, 1799, in a letter also quoted, he spoke of "a sort of Imbroglio about Southey's Ballads, which must be settled." On May 30, 1799, Southey told William Taylor, "Lewis, the Monk-man, is about to publish a compilation of ballads, a superb quarto, I understand, with prints. He has applied to me for some of mine."[35] In the same month he wrote to his friend C. W. Williams Wynn, who acted as intermediary, "I should not wish Lewis to print either 'Lord William' or 'Jasper,' because they have not appeared with my name; and this previous publication would perhaps lessen the sale of the volume, in which I should hereafter print them. If you think this an insufficient reason, act as though it were so, and let him have them. At any rate, he may have 'Rudiger' and 'Donica,' if he likes them; but alter a word he must not."[36] Presumably Wynn considered Southey's reason for withholding "Lord William" insufficient, for, with "Donica" and "Rudiger," it was included in *Tales of Wonder*, though "Jasper" was not. Lewis also printed five other ballads by Southey, "The Old Woman of Berkeley," "Bishop Bruno," "The Painter of Florence," "Cornelius Agrippa's Bloody Book," and "St. Patrick's Purgatory." These had already been published in the *Morning Post*, and all, save the last, with Southey's name, so that Lewis hardly needed permission to use them. He attributed each to Southey except "St. Patrick's Purgatory," the authorship of which he did not know.[37] Nevertheless, Alexander Dyce recorded in his copy of Lewis' book, "Wordsworth (whom I have heard quoting & laughing at Lewis' *Alonzo the brave*) told me, that, when this book first came out, it used to be called *Tales of Plunder*, because there was so little new in it; and that Southey felt rather indignant at Lewis for having reprinted *his* ballads in it without permission."[38] One notes in this connection that, whereas the ballads by Lewis' other contemporaries in the first edition of *Tales of Wonder* were retained in the second, all eight by Southey were omitted. But if unfriendly feeling arose between the two men, it was, as we have seen, gone by 1805 when Southey contemplated writing for Covent Garden.

Though Lewis aimed at popular appeal in *Tales of Wonder* and did not pretend to the antiquarianism of Percy, Ritson, or Scott, his meddling with the folk ballads seems pretentious. A modest collection of contemporary Gothic verse, however disturbing to susceptible readers, at least would have produced an unequivocal book; but the editor pillaged past and present without remorse. The real trouble lies in his ill-advised choice of a unifying principle —the long train of ghosts and goblins. No reader can shudder throughout two volumes. Although one reviewer's exclamation ("all is hideous—all is disgusting"[39]) is unfair, it does express the total effect of *Tales of Wonder*.

Lewis' collection was criticized and parodied unmercifully— Mauritius Moonshine was not alone. It was pilloried in *English Bards and Scotch Reviewers*, but that, after all, put it in very good company. A less scornful and therefore more telling satire than Byron's well-known passage was circulated in manuscript and later published anonymously as *The Old Hag in a Red Cloak. A Romance. Inscribed to the Author of the Grim White Woman*. It is attributed to George Watson Taylor.[40]

> Matthaeus was little, Matthaeus was young,
> Of wonders he chanted, and quaintly he sung.

Matthaeus, in the act of pursuing a phantom in Parliament Street, meets a beggar woman, but

> "I'll give thee no sixpence to buy thee thy bread,"
> To the Hag in a Red Cloak Mat cruelly said;
> Then down to the House in a huff strutted he,
> (Sure all the world knows little Mat's an M. P.)

In the dead of night the hag appears before him and reveals herself as Mother Goose and his own mother by a German romancer. When she angrily threatens him for encroaching upon her domain of nonsense, Little Mat, terrified, renounces his claim to the field, pleading only for certain concessions—

> Mother Goose thus confirm'd in the rights of her throne,
> Kindly spared to her son what was justly his own,
> And left him in future to trifle his time,
> In Epilogues, Sonnets, and Lady-like rhime.

"The Wonder-King: A Tale of Wonder," a parody of fifty-five lines, apparently unpublished and attributed to either Scott or Southey, describes the parentage and birth of Prince Lewis, the Wonder-King's son, ending with these stanzas:

> Sweet Child! twixt a Fish & a Beast & a Chick,
> It could lap, it could suck, it could peck, it could pick
>     With an odd sort of Mouth, made for either:
> It could bark, it could mew, could whistle, could howl,
> Could roar like a Lion, or hoot like an Owl;
>     Or could make all these Noises together.

> So to fit the young Prince to rule over the Nation,
> The Wonder-King gave him a right Education,
>     And worthy the Wonder-King's Heir:
> He taught him these Howlings & Hoots to write down,
> And the Book it is publish'd in wise London Town,
> And sold for a Guinea, tho' not worth a Crown—
>     The Delight of the Gay & the Fair.[41]

Still another parody, *Tales of Terror; with an Introductory Dialogue* (1801), seems destined for immortality, not as literature but as a bibliographical hazard. Four separate works have at various times been confounded—Scott's *An Apology for Tales of Terror* (1799), Lewis' *Tales of Wonder* (1801), the anonymous *Tales of*

*Terror; with an Introductory Dialogue* (1801), and Henry Morley's
*Tales of Terror and Wonder Collected by Matthew Gregory Lewis;*
when the tangle was unraveled in 1894,[42] the error of attributing
*Tales of Terror* to Lewis had already found its way into standard
bibliographies and literary histories and persists today. *An Apology
for Tales of Terror*, as already explained, was printed in 1799 by
Ballantyne at Scott's suggestion; the title alludes to Lewis' long-
delayed collection first intended to be called *Tales of Terror* but
published as *Tales of Wonder*. The latter was shortly followed by
the anonymous *Tales of Terror; with an Introductory Dialogue*
(1801), a deliberate parody of *Tales of Wonder*. Although this parody was sold by Lewis' publisher Bell who, moreover, issued it and
the second edition of *Tales of Wonder* in uniform size and advertised the two works as good companion volumes, *Tales of Wonder*
and *Tale of Terror* seem not to have been confused in Lewis' day.
By 1839, however, his biographer attributed *Tales of Terror* to
Lewis, without giving an account of the book, and in a "List of
works published by M. G. Lewis" included "Tales of Terror; 2 vols.
1807," an interesting description in that, despite its brevity, it
contains three errors—the attribution of the work to Lewis, the
number of volumes, and the date.[43] Then in 1887 there was included in "Morley's Universal Library," with the generous latitude
suggested by the title of the series, a new work entitled *Tales of
Terror and Wonder Collected by Matthew Gregory Lewis*, a volume made up from a defective copy of *Tales of Terror* and a second
edition of *Tales of Wonder*. A descendant of this book created by
Morley is *Tales in Verse of Terror and Wonder* (1925) in the Haldeman-Julius Little Blue Book series.

    *Tales of Wonder* was followed by a second London edition in
1801; derived from this was a Dublin edition in the same year.
Another in Dublin appeared in 1805, but apparently no more in
London until 1817, the year before Lewis' death. The contents of
the work show a tendency to dwindle through the years. The second London edition reduced the number of ballads from sixty to
thirty-two; an edition of 1836 contains twenty-three; and the 1925
catchpenny only eight of the original sixty.[44]

    During the four years following the publication of *Tales of
Wonder*, Lewis bestowed his attention principally upon plays, as
already noted. By the end of October 1804, however, he had also

translated Heinrich Zschokke's youthful prose tale, *Aböllino der Grosse Bandit* (1794). This is the story of the exiled Neapolitan Count of Obizzio, who, disguising himself and assuming the name Abaellino, joins a band of bravos in Venice, betrays them, and becomes the only professional assassin in the city. He terrorizes the populace and is employed by conspirators plotting to overthrow the government. Meanwhile the doge promises the hand of his daughter Rosamunda to a young Florentine noble named Flodoardo, lately arrived at court, if the latter succeeds in capturing the bandit. Flodoardo and Abaellino prove to be the same person, who now exposes the conspirators, produces the friends of the doge whom the bandit was employed to murder, and as savior of Venice wins the hand of Rosamunda.[45] Lewis published his translation of this story in 1805 as *The Bravo of Venice. A Romance: Translated from the German.*[46] Among the liberties he confessed taking with his original is the addition of a final chapter, in which he sketches the hero's earlier history and hints that he may later offer the public a book on that subject. This he never did, despite the success of *The Bravo*, one of his most frequently reprinted works.

The following year another translation appeared, *Feudal Tyrants; or, The Counts of Carlsheim and Sargans,* a four-volume romance of feudal times "taken from the German"—more specifically, from *Elisabeth, Erbin von Toggenburg, oder Geschichte der Frauen in der Schweiz* (1789) by the once-popular German writer, Christiane Benedicte Eugenie Naubert (1756–1819).[47] *Elisabeth* blends medieval historical traditions of Switzerland with a series of adventures in castles, cloisters, and catacombs told by several narrators in the form of letters and memoirs, the stories being woven into a complex plot not easy to keep in mind. Over a hundred characters are named. Most of the narrators are women, as obviously the readers were meant to be. Tyrannical lords and scheming churchmen persecute innocent ladies until their one desire is to escape the world forever in the sad peace of the convent. One senses something disingenuous in the author's opposition of feminine saintliness to fascinating masculine cruelty; the modesty and indignation of these ladies banish what they sue for. Of his treatment of the German Lewis says only, "The real name is *Toggenburg;* but as this would have sounded harsh in English ears, I have taken the liberty of softening it a little; and in several parts of this work I have changed the names of places and personages entirely."[48] Though he neither introduces nor omits important characters or incidents, he treats the text freely, adding, deleting, occasionally transposing phrases and short passages, and, rightly judging the narrative too complex, supplies retrospective transitions. The portion of the German represented by his fourth volume shows the most rearrangement and condensation. Throughout the work he carefully omitted passages disparaging religion.[49] It seems likely that his translation was part of the literary toil which preceded the publication of *The Monk* and that it was laid aside for years and then published on the strength of his reputation.

The critics found *Feudal Tyrants* dull. Never, said the *Monthly Review*, "was heard any thing so dismal as the direful croaking of this German raven!"[50] A writer for the *Critical Review*, noting that the title page omitted mention of *The Monk* among Lewis' works, wondered whether the author hoped to be forgotten or was certain of being remembered for a work which the reviewer considered in some respects Lewis' best, having "more merit and less morality than any of his other productions." *Feudal Tyrants* is held up to ridicule in an amusing four-page summary.[51] Despite these unfavorable opinions, a fourth edition had appeared by 1807.[52]

The next two publications to be mentioned serve to introduce Lewis as a writer and composer of popular songs. Numerous songs, glees, and choruses from his dramas and several independent ballads saw separate publication with musical accompaniments. The *Life* states that he supplied many ballads also for the use of other dramatists.[53] Analyzing *The Castle Spectre* for Wordsworth, Coleridge said, apparently with reference to the verses "How slow the lingering moments wear": "There is a pretty little Ballad-song introduced —and Lewis, I think, has great & peculiar excellence in these compostions. The simplicity & naturalness is his own, & not imitated; for it is made to subsist in congruity with a language perfectly modern—the language of his own times, in the same way that the language of the writer of 'Sir Cauline' was the language of *his* times. This, I think, a rare merit: at least, I find, I cannot attain this innocent nakedness, except by *assumption*.[54] An editor of *One O'Clock* remarked that Lewis' songs always rise far beyond the level of those generally found in operatic dramas.[55]

A number of his songs written for dramatic works, and some of his ballads, sold well in the music shops and were sung by street singers so constantly that people grew tired of hearing them, surely a criterion of success in this province of music. "The Banks of Allan Water," arranged by Charles Edward Horn, was sung in Lewis' comic opera *Rich and Poor* (1812) and was remembered for years. "The Wife's Farewell, or Oh No My Love No!" immediately became a favorite when introduced in Thomas John Dibdin's *Of Age Tomorrow* (1800).[56] Michael Kelly, who composed the music, called it the most popular song of the day, found upon every pianoforte and, as a great favorite with the ballad singers, heard in every street.[57] Another for which Kelly composed the music, "What though Fate forbids me offer," was always encored in Thomas Holcroft's *Deaf and Dumb* (1801).[58] When requested to compose an English ballad expressly for the Regent, Kelly applied to Lewis for verses and the latter wrote "Tomorrow; or, The Mars, Captain Connor," another favorite. Harriet Abrams composed music for "The Felon," a ballad on social injustice, "The Soldier's Grave," "The Orphan's Prayer, a Pathetic Ballad," and "Crazy Jane." The last two proved exceedingly popular and are the only titles now associated with her name in music encyclopedias. Two other ballads separately published were Lewis' "Original Cossack Air," introduced at Drury Lane in 1813,[59] and "He loves and he rides away." The latter, supposedly composed for his sister Sophia,[60] was popular enough to be pirated. He consequently published it with the title *He Loves and He Rides Away, a Favourite Ballad, the Words and Music by M. G. Lewis, Esq., with an Accompaniment for the Harp or Piano Forte. . .* [61] and the following illuminating prefatory note:

This Ballad was composed above six Years ago, and it was my intention to delay its publication till its appearance with eleven others now Engraving—It will still form a part of this larger work; but I find myself compelled to give a separate edition, in consequence of its having been published by Messrs Goulding & Co without my *consent or knowledge,* The sale of this imperfect Edition has since been discontinued: but although the general Idea and many of the most marking passages were retained in the Music, as such material alterations were made in parts of it as almost to constitute a new Air, I thought it necessary to publish a correct copy of the original Music without delay. In consequence of various Frauds & impositions I am obliged to caution all Persons from employing my Verses either in Musical or other publications without my express permission, as they will subject themselves to prosecution; and I hereby warn all Music Dealers &c. against purchasing such verses, no Person being authorized to make any such sale. May 22ᵈ 1808                                        M. G. Lewis.

The larger work appeared a few weeks later as *Twelve Ballads, the Words and Music by M. G. Lewis.*[62] These twelve are predominantly pathetic, humorous, mournful, or patriotic. Some, of knights and fair ladies, are in their artificial chivalry musical cousins of *Alonzo the Brave,* but none are macabre. "The Fisherman" is Lewis' excellent translation from Goethe; it had been first sung at Drury Lane in 1800 by Mrs. Bland, who also introduced "Evelina's Lullaby," another of the *Twelve Ballads,* in 1802 at the same theater.[63] "Sir Agilthorn and Lady Eva" is taken from the ballad Lewis contributed to Scott's *Minstrelsy.*

In 1808 *Romantic Tales* appeared, a four-volume miscellany of seven ballads, one long poem, and five prose stories, largely translated and adapted from foreign literature. "I find it difficult," said Lewis in his preface, "to point out exactly, what portion of the following work is my individual property. Even in those Tales, which are least my own, I have made so many and such important alterations, omissions, and interpolations, that it would have been less trouble to write an entire new work.[64]

Among the ballads are two translations from Spanish—"The Admiral Guarino" and "King Rodrigo's Fall," in connection with which are to be noted four similar ballads, "Durandarte and Belerma" in *The Monk* and three published in the biography— "Alatar," "The Loss of Alhama," and "Zayde and Zayda." The likelihood is that he made all six translations at about the same time, inserted one in *The Monk,* two more in *Romantic Tales* twelve years later, and one in his journal in 1816. The two not used were published by his biographer in the *Life,* together with "Zayde and Zayda," which had already appeared in the *Journal.* Lewis' advertisement in *The Monk* states that "Durandarte and Belerma" is "translated from some stanzas to be found in a collection of old Spanish poetry, which contains also the popular song of *Gayferos and Melesindra,* mentioned in Don Quixote." The editorial flavor of this statement suggests that Lewis, as was his wont, copied the information. In the *Journal* he gives his source for "Zayde and Zayda" as *Las Guerras Civiles de Granada.* But wherever he found his originals, these six translations testify to his ability to preserve in competent English verse the tone of a poem in another tongue.[65] They are far from being word-for-word translations but retain all important details of the Spanish narratives without the addition of embellishments. The alternating eight- and seven-syllable lines are skillfully economical; making his task harder but the result more pleasing to English ears, he replaced the original *asonante* with alternate rhymes.

The ballads from German fare less happily. "Bertrand and Mary-Belle" and "The Lord of Falkenstein" are, Lewis explained, "in a great measure taken from some fragments of old German Ballads." By this he means "Ulrich und Aennchen" and "Das Lied vom Herrn von Falkenstein" among the *Deutsche Lieder* in Herder's collection.[66] In reworking the first he doubled its length. Aennchen's statement, for instance, "Da droben auf jener Tannen/ Elf Jungfrau'n sah ich hangen" becomes an elaborate vision:

> Methought all in the dead of night,
>     E'en in this very vale,
> I saw nine maids in garments white,
>     Their faces wan and pale.
>
> With solemn steps advanc'd the band
>     And on her breast each maid,
> Imprinted by some cruel hand,
>     A ghastly wound display'd.
>
> I heard their hollow voices swell,
>     And this was still their song;
> "Thy hour is near! come, Mary-Belle,
>     And join our mournful throng."

Lewis lengthens and sentimentalizes the Falkenstein ballad, freely changing it to achieve a unified effect; but his phrase "in a large measure taken," if it implies some originality in essentials, is hardly justified. He acknowledged Herder as his source for the Lithuanian ballad of "The Dying Bride," to which he added seven stanzas to give the knight and bride ample space for a pathetic death scene.

For the three remaining poems in *Romantic Tales* Lewis was less indebted to others. "Sir Guy the Seeker," he tells us, is "founded upon a tradition current in Northumberland" and was written during a visit in the neighborhood of Dunstanburgh Castle.

The story is of a knight who, seeking shelter at the castle during a storm, is invited by a wizard to enter and attempt to rescue a lady imprisoned in a crystal tomb. He is offered the choice of a sword or of Merlin's horn, with one of which he can effect the rescue. Making the wrong choice, he finds himself outside again and thereafter until death seeks in vain the lady and the irrevocable opportunity. There is a clutter of wondrous and incongruous details—the wizard with his crown of flames, wand of burning iron, and red-hot chain for a girdle, the candelabra fashioned of severed arms, the giant skeletons—but the story and setting are well handled, particularly the description of Dunstanburgh Castle, and the subject had enough antiquarian interest to prompt a separate publication of the ballad in 1844.[67] "Bill Jones, a Tale of Wonder" is Lewis' grisly ballad of a sailor who, killed by his brutal captain, continues his seaman's duties as a ghost and drives the captain to suicide. Lewis had heard the story from Scott and includes in his preface Scott's note concerning it. The ballad was once recited at the Lyceum Theatre.[68]

The remaining poem in *Romantic Tales* is "Oberon's Henchman; or, the Legend of the Three Sisters," a narrative of some eight or nine hundred lines in iambic pentameter couplets which Scott thought beautiful.[69] He himself had tried and abandoned the same subject in his "Bothwell's Sisters Three: A Fragment." In prefatory verses Lady Douglas requests Lewis to explain three rocks at Bothwell Castle known as the "Three Sisters." Lewis obligingly supplies a fanciful tradition in the form of a fairy story suggested by a theme in *A Midsummer Night's Dream.* Oberon's Indian boy Zelim, who loves Lillia, one of the three daughters of the Earl of Bothwell, has by Oberon's jealous contrivance killed the Earl during a hunt. One midnight the three daughters visit a witch who can make their wishes come true. One sister asks for the heart of a disdainful youth whom she adores; the second for vengeance upon her father's unknown slayer; the third, Lillia, that Zelim may never prove faithless to her. A fay summoned by the witch instructs them to kill a spaniel to be found on the banks of the Clyde. When they do so they behold the spaniel's form change to that of Zelim and recognize with consternation the fulfillment of their wishes. The fay then explains—as need not be done here—the circumstances which have led to Zelim's fate. Finally Oberon, incensed over the death of his henchman, condemns the fay to live as a spaniel for six hundred years—the very spaniel now owned by Lewis' hostess Lady Douglas—and changes the sisters into the three rocks. The poem is filled with fancy and successfully combines Shakespearian fairy lore with the witchcraft Lewis delighted in. A notable description is that of the witch and her noisome cottage where eft and viper have been

> Compelled by charms in slime and deadly gall
> To smear Hell's secrets on the wizard wall

and from which the sisters emerge to feel the fresh air of dawn on their cheeks and to see the morning star shining and dew on the grass.

The five prose pieces in *Romantic Tales* are as miscellaneous as the verse. Four of them, Lewis tells us, are "of German origin." Of the first and longest, "Mistrust; or, Blanche and Osbright," he adds: "In particular, the idea of 'Mistrust' was suggested by a Tragedy, from which I have borrowed a great part of the plot, and one of the most striking scenes: I have also occasionally inserted in my Narrative such speeches as pleased me."[70] His source was Heinrich von Kleist's five-act tragedy *Die Familie Schroffenstein*, published anonymously in Bern, 1803, having for its subject a disastrous feud, kept alive by jealousy and false suspicions, between two noble houses. When Lewis admits borrowing one of the most striking scenes, the reader can only wonder which, of a generous number of possibilities, he had in mind. The first seven chapters of "Mistrust" reproduce rather closely the story in Acts I through III of the drama, with the usual addition, omission, and rearrangement of details. From Act IV he took only Kleist's cottage scene, in which Ottokar (Lewis' Osbright) meets the country girl chanting spells and stirring the witch broth. To this scene he devoted Chapter VIII, omitting, surprisingly enough, the pointless but melodramatic episode of the hero's imprisonment and escape. Act V of the tragedy contains but one scene, the cave in which, through mistaken identity, Ottokar is killed by his father and Agnes, Ottokar's beloved, by hers. This act, frequently objected to by critics of Kleist, Lewis rejected entirely. Perhaps he considered it too abrupt an ending, for he concludes "Mistrust" with a crescendo of thrills sustained through four chapters. At one point it becomes difficult to follow what is happening; at another, the story seems to veer dangerously toward an incongruously happy ending. A timely assassination and a suicide prevent this, however, and the leading characters are variously consigned to convent, pilgrimage, and grave.

Lewis changed the names of Kleist's characters and for the most part exaggerated their leading traits. He took advantage of the greater freedom allowed by the narrative form to explain the stormy emotions of two of them, Rupert of Schroffenstein (Lewis' Rudiger) and his natural son Johann (Eugene). As presented by Kleist, the former is driven to commit murder by an inordinate passion for vengeance, yet suffers bewilderment and horror when the deed is done. Following this path, Lewis devotes several pages to analyzing Rudiger's motives. When this character takes an active part in Lewis' narrative, however, he loses all semblance of humanity and leaps up before us like a ludicrous nightmare. Kleist's Rupert, solemnly swearing vengeance in the presence of his supposedly murdered child, is tame compared with Lewis' Rudiger, who in a paroxysm of grief and rage plunges into the open grave, rips open the coffin, and holds the dead child aloft. His appearance, exhibiting the peculiar vividness and distortion which Lewis could achieve, is no less startling than his actions:

With involuntary horror the friars started back, and then as if changed to stone by a Gorgon's head, they remained gazing upon the dreadful countenance, which presented itself before them. Count Rudiger's stature was colossal; the grave in which he stood, scarcely rose above his knees. His eyes blazed; his mouth foamed; his coal-black hair stood erect, in which he twisted his hands, and tearing out whole handfulls by the roots, he strewed them on the coffin, which stood beside his feet.[71]

Kleist's Johann, frustrated in love, loses his mind with unconvincing suddenness. Lewis leads up to Eugene's insanity by supplying a life history. Eugene's mother, he tells us, broke conventual vows to elope with the already married Rudiger, but, overcome by remorse, disappeared after the birth of the child. Ten years later the boy, already strange and melancholy, was shocked by the return of his unknown mother, who at the point of death told him the secret of his parentage. This episode and the death of his younger half-brother prepare his way to madness.[72]

"The Anaconda, an East Indian Tale" is a short story skillfully set in a frame. Young Everard Brooke, returning from Ceylon with a mysteriously acquired fortune, is on the point of losing his friends and the girl he loves because, through a misunderstanding of his Ceylonese servant's broken English, gossip has spread the delicious rumor that Everard has become rich by killing one Ann O'Connor —the servant's pronunciation of "anaconda" was no closer than that. Everard clears his name and wins his bride by relating what really happened. His employer in Ceylon, it seems, was one day besieged in his pavilion by an enormous anaconda. This vigilant and determined creature thwarted every attempt to rescue the master until, having gorged an animal driven into its path, the serpent was dispatched as it lay helpless. Rescue came too late, however, for the very breath of the anaconda had so poisoned the air in the neighborhood of the pavilion that the master soon died, leaving Everard a fortune. A devoted wife who defies danger and swoons in turn and a courageous native servant contribute more sentimentality than present taste enjoys. All the characters, in fact, are bores except the anaconda; but the anaconda invites even further attention.

The story depends for effectiveness upon the reader's ignorance and credulity respecting these creatures. Lewis' serpent is endowed with personality, deeply malevolent yet with a touch of skittishness. She gambols and sports among the palm branches at a speed the eye cannot follow and with high-arching neck describes "a large or small circle, as her capricious pleasure" prompts; now and then she becomes motionless and in a listening attitude looks behind her—one almost expects to be told, over her shoulder. Besides the pestilential vapors which issue from her jaws and lethally infect the neighborhood, Lewis equips her with a tongue capable of separating flesh from bone and eyes "blazing with their own vindictive fires," which shoot "lightnings through the gloom of night" and from the reflection of which in the window glass of the pavilion the serpent herself recoils as if affrighted.

It has not been noticed that a principal source of Lewis' story is an article published in *The Scots Magazine* for 1768, signed "R. Edwin" and headed "Description of the Anaconda, a monstrous species of serpent. In a letter from an English gentleman, many years resident in the island of Ceylon, in the East Indies."[73] *The*

*Scots Magazine* gives as its source a London paper for the same year; the letter was reprinted in *The Lady's Monthly Museum* forty years later.[74] Although it professes to be an eyewitness account of how an anaconda killed and gorged a tiger and was in turn dispatched by Ceylonese natives, several details are impossible, as for instance the anaconda's "monstrously large eyes," its use of the jaws to tear and grind the prey during constriction, and its ability to swallow a tiger "of a monstrous size, not lower than a common heifer"; nevertheless, the account is realistic in intent and some details are still matters of herpetological disagreement.

Lewis' story makes use of everything in this account. A notable description of the gorgeous and intricate marking of the serpent brings Keats's Lamia to mind, though the details are not similar. One would like to credit the passage to Lewis as a striking product of his fondness for riotous colors, but the description comes almost verbatim from the published account. In one instance he reduced in length the material he borrowed: the writer of the letter lingers painfully over the death agonies of the tiger, which endure for hours, whereas Lewis' anaconda kills her victim (a bull, a noble beast which puts up a spirited fight) in fifteen minutes. More often, mere suggestions in the letter are elaborated in Lewis' story, as when "a small animal of the fox kind" devoured by the original anaconda becomes "the little Psyche, a beautiful Italian greyhound," by which the isolated employer vainly hopes to send a message from the pavilion. Many outright additions, which make the story eight times longer than the letter, include an abortive attempt to frighten away the serpent by fire, Everard's use of a sounding-board to communicate at a distance with his employer, and a servant's attempt to pass safely within range of the anaconda, in the manner employed by elephant hunters, by slowly advancing beneath a disguise of shrubbery.

In the preface to *Romantic Tales* Lewis names "The Anaconda" as one of the stories "of German origin." Some German writer may have used the account of the anaconda as the basis of a story which Lewis then translated; yet the similarity of Lewis' description of the serpent's coloring with that by "R. Edwin" seems too close to be the product of translation. Possibly he combined materials from a German story with the letter which he found either in *The Scots Magazine* or in *The Lady's Monthly Museum*.

"My Uncle's Garret Window," a pantomimic tale, is the third story "of German origin." If it comes from foreign literature, Lewis has adapted it to English readers by a reference to Drury Lane; but his source is still to be discovered. It is a cheerful narrative of a family next door, told in the form of a series of observations made through a pocket telescope. From the silent evidence of gesture and action the narrator with apparent ingenuity conjectures the conversations and emotions of his neighbors and shows us the development and happy outcome of a domestic quarrel. Iffland's drama *Frauenstand*, performed three times during Lewis' stay at Weimar, has been suggested as the major source for the motifs and the rough outline of the action.[75]

For the fourth story Lewis turned to Klinger's *Der Faust der Morgenländer*, first published in 1797.[76] Klinger's work is in the form of a dialogue between the warm-hearted and impulsive Caliph of Bagdad, his cynical Vizir, and Ben Hafi, an unknown wanderer whose conversation excites the admiration of the Caliph and the contempt of the Vizir. For twelve nights Ben Hafi relates the story of Abdallah, a Sultan's vizir of high ideals, who in order to administer justice more efficiently and further his philanthropic plans allies himself through magic with a supernatural spirit. The spirit is a personification of calculating prudence which coldly reveals to him every human motive and demonstrates the futility of generosity and good works. The result of this blighting knowledge is a series of disasters which drive Abdallah to ruin and attempted suicide, until, free of the spirit at last, he again finds contentment. Ben Hafi introduces himself into his narration as a son of Abdallah, banished under false charges by an elder brother. In similar circumstances the Caliph, influenced by corrupt councillors, had himself banished a beloved brother. Ben Hafi, of course, throws off his disguise and to the Caliph's amazement, but to nobody else's, reveals himself as that brother. The two embrace, the wicked Vizir is banished, and the feeling heart wins complete victory over mere prudence—or, to put it cynically, sentimentality drowns common sense.

Klinger was more interested in the ethical questions raised by the story than in the story itself, which his Caliph and Vizir frequently interrupt with pages of moralizing. Lewis balanced more evenly the philosophical and narrative elements by dropping most of these passages, together with many excerpts from the Koran with which Klinger's Caliph embellishes his remarks; he also omitted minor incidents and condensed pages of action into a single paragraph. By these means he reduced Klinger's leisurely story to about half its length. He added nothing important but made several changes: his Ben Hafi appears as a Hebrew; the form of the spirit, in the German work a beautiful youth, is in Lewis' story a woman; and as usual most of the characters are renamed.

"The Four Facardins, an Arabian tale," the remaining prose piece in *Romantic Tales*, is Lewis' translation of Count Anthony Hamilton's *Les Quatre Facardins*, a fairy story written in parody of Oriental tales. Lewis had made the translation years before and had originally intended it for publication by Bell.[77] It follows the French quite faithfully and preserves the sparkle of Hamilton's wit.[78] Since the original was left incomplete, Lewis supplied a conclusion of his own. His comment on this addition is modest, not to say abject: "the brilliance of colouring, the playfulness of imagination, those easy graces and that felicity of expression, which give such a charm to the French tale, I well knew to be quite beyond my reach, and I have not even attempted to imitate them. My utmost aim has been to finish those adventures by some means or other, which Count Hamilton had left imperfect; and conscious that to rival the First Part in wit would for me be a hopeless attempt, I have only endeavoured to make the Second surpass it in extravagance." Though successful, the endeavor was hardly worth while. The extravagance becomes tiresome; and, although Lewis' conclusion displays ingenuity in untangling and neatly braiding the threads of Hamilton's complicated beginning, the labor is supererogatory, for the absence of logic and resolution is part of the humor of *Les Quatre Facardins*—as Lewis himself noted, Hamilton probably never intended to finish the tale. The fairies, elves, dwarfs, jeweled chariots, conches, birds of paradise, and other exotic properties with which Lewis loads his continuation suggest the influence of Wieland.[79]

*Romantic Tales* at least has the virtue of variety, and the aftereffects are pleasanter than those brought on by *Tales of Wonder*. Better no principle of selection than a bad one. The book received favorable comment in the reviews but less attention than Lewis' ballad collection. The *Gentleman's Magazine* believed that no other living author was "capable of producing pictures equally awful, new, and sublime."[80] Despite this opinion a second edition seems not to have been published during Lewis' lifetime.[81]

Of the two remaining publications to be noticed, the first is Lewis' monody on Sir John Moore. In January 1809 Lieutenant-General Moore lost his life in the unsuccessful peninsular war. The failure of the expedition roused criticism, and there was sentiment in favor of a parliamentary inquiry into the conduct of the campaign. But to the public Moore was a hero, and on February 14 the monody in praise of him was recited at Drury Lane by Mrs. Powell habited like the mourning Muse.[82] It was said to have been hastily written for the occasion,[83] and Lewis probably had no intention of printing it. The performance was applauded and repeated but on the third night inexplicably prohibited by the Lord Chamberlain. Political reasons arising from the Spanish campaign may have been the cause or, as the *Monthly Review* suggested, a disinclination of Sir John's relatives to have his fame puffed by theatrical recitation.[84] Official objection could hardly have been directed at anything in the monody, which consists of some forty heroic couplets of utterly conventional praise. The incident seemed closed, when nearly three months later George Tierney, addressing the House on May 9, censured a disposition among the ministers to conceal the merits of Sir John Moore and mentioned the suppression of the monody as an illustration of this injustice. Lewis perhaps winced for his reputation when the monody was prohibited; when the incident was mentioned in Parliament, he quickly decided to print the work, "lest," as his preface explains, "the Public should suppose that it contained something objectionable either in a moral, religious, or political view."[85] Thus the *Monody on the Death of Sir John Moore*, with a preface dated May 13, 1809, and a dedication to the Princess of Wales, appeared and disappeared and was forgotten. But any indignation felt by the shade of Sir John Moore was appeased a few years later by enduring lines from the pen of Charles Wolfe.

The last book of which Lewis supervised the publication was his little volume called *Poems*, published in May 1812, for which, his advertisement explains, he "selected from a great mass of Verses such as appeared to myself and my Friends to be the least discreditable to their Author; I have endeavoured to remove such faults as were pointed out to me; and indeed have bestowed more time on their improvement, than such trifles can possibly be worth." This modest collection is quite different from his other books, the majority of the poems being graceful neoclassical odes and lyrics. The metrical variety is remarkable: the twenty-seven poems exhibit over a dozen stanza patterns, all prosodically flawless and with scarcely a forced line. Beneath the eighteenth-century frigidity of conventionalized diction and personification, one detects currents of personal feeling. There is pathos, for instance, in the ode "To Vanity." He included a handful of popular pieces like "Crazy Jane," "The Orphan's Prayer," and "The Captive." "Homer in a nutshell" was C. K. Sharpe's phrase.[86] He wrote to Scott, "Lewis lately sent me a little book of his poems printed last May, in which there are some pretty things. There's always a violet among his weeds."[87]

# 6 ⚖

## JAMAICA

Matthew had not resumed very friendly relations with his
father after their superficial reconciliation in 1805, since it was
impossible for the son to approve of Mrs. Ricketts. While this was
the real difficulty, the elder Lewis had other reasons for being disappointed in Matthew. He had been sent to The Hague to learn
diplomacy and had written *The Monk*. He had obtained a seat in
Parliament and had produced *The Castle Spectre*. Moreover, the
father disapproved of the son's indulgences toward Mrs. Lewis.
Thus matters rested until November 1811, when Mr. Lewis became seriously ill and continued so for several months. Matthew
was deeply concerned for both his father's health and his father's
feelings toward him. "Maria told him," Lewis wrote to his mother
at the end of March 1812, "that his illness had affected me extremely; on which He said (with kindness and interest)—'Ah! He's
a foolish Boy.' From all this, I have some little hope, that his illness must have softened him a little towards me."[1] The habits of
his life, he reflects with melancholy, will not be affected by the
loss of his father: he will have few remembrances of his affection,
will not miss his presence at the table, the morning welcome, the
affectionate goodnight.

Often and often in my early days, when I quite doated upon him, I have
thought, that my heart would break, if I were ever obliged to attend him
on a death-bed. Nine years of constant harshness or indifference on his
part have now made us Strangers to each other; But still I dread so much
the thoughts of witnessing his sufferings, that I scarsely know, whether for
my *own* happiness I ought to wish for a reconciliation *now*. . . . In a mercenary view a reconciliation may be desireable for me; but in what other?
Good God! To have his affection restored to me, merely that I may instantly
lose it again for ever, it seems shocking to me. . . . (F 96–97).

That is his only mention of the possible loss of the inheritance. He returned briefly to Devonshire Place, and about ten days before the end received his father's blessing. For this final benediction he felt indebted to the Reverend Cyril Jackson, who had interceded in his behalf. Mr. Lewis died on May 17.

Any fears Matthew may have felt regarding the family fortune were unfounded, for with the exception of small bequests to servants, £100 to each of three executors, and £500 to Mrs. Ricketts, the father had left everything to his "beloved Son," and Matthew, at the age of thirty-seven, found himself a rich man. That the will had been drawn up in 1800 and never changed as it affected the principal bequest is evidence, if any is needed, that Mr. Lewis had at no time during their quarrel seriously considered disinheriting his son.[2] Upon receiving a copy of the will, Matthew immediately wrote to his mother, expressing more satisfaction over the affectionate reference to him than over the legacy, and requesting her to relieve the anxiety of a relative unmentioned in the will whom Mr. Lewis had been in the habit of helping financially.

"Matt Lewis, is now a Man of business," his aunt Mrs. Blake observed, "having a vast sight of *family* Matters on his hands. I trust, & hope, he will have no time to *write another Timour* God forbid!"[3] Her hope was fulfilled. *Poems*, appearing in the month his father died, was Lewis' last publication. Now he himself drew up a will, in which he bequeathed £1000 a year to his mother during her life, to be paid before all other considerations.[4] The Reverend Cyril Jackson and his uncles William Luther Sewell and Robert Sewell were named executors to manage his plantations and to pay one half of the profits to his sister Maria or her children and half to Sophia and hers. In a codicil dated January 16, 1812, he directed that the Jamaica property should be divided not equally between the sisters, but in proportion to the number of their children at the time of his death.[5] Still later he again changed the bequest, leaving the estate of Cornwall to Maria and that of Hordley to Sophia, to prevent dispute.[6]

After three months he found time to write a letter to Charles Kirkpatrick Sharpe. He was beginning to take breath after attending to "law business, Jamaica agents, letters to relations, and, above all, a cursed mortgage of £24,000 on my estates to be provided for."[7] He now probably gave his mother an allowance of £1000 a year, since he had so provided for her in his will, and she established herself near Leatherhead, Surrey, in a cottage which received a long, fatuous description in the *Life* and was later more briefly and quite adequately characterized as "truly dinky."[8] Lewis himself continued to live alternately at Barnes and at the Albany. Records of his social life become less numerous than formerly; he and the fashionable world were growing tired of each other. His aunt Anna Blake wrote in 1815 to their mutual friend, James St. Aubyn:

So, *Mother Goos'es Son* has become scarce! Every body makes the same complaint even to his own Brother in Law. He is only *at home*, when he *professes* to be at home. This is vast nonsense, and very like some of his former Tales. I wrote to him the other day, & I therein mentioned the universal complaint that reached my ears, of the *scarcity* of his appearance, and yet strange as it may be, we have very fine weather altho' this said most enlightened body, has *not appeared*. Well my dear St Aubyn, one of these days (if he has not already) he will *feel* the whole of his happiness to be *but* ideal. He pos[sess]es Money it is true, but I am pretty certain, it does not, make him a *happy* Man. I thought once that if ever Matt Lewis was a *rich Man, I* should be better off than I was. I do not think so *now.* . . . He has a *new* friend for every Month in the year. How fond he was of you when he was last down here! pressing me to *insist* on your coming or to pretent I shou'd be affronted & now he has forgot you![9]

His friend Lord Holland wrote of Lewis in after years: "As he advanced in life he grew exceedingly tedious, especially upon all that related to himself; so that contrary to the usual course of things, the peculiarities and egotism which had been in some degree pardoned to his genius and youth, *when poor* became intolerable, and were, in fact, not tolerated in society when he succeeded to a large property in Jamaica."[10] This growing coldness of his acquaintances will partly explain why he spent so little of his three remaining years of life in England and chose rather the self-exile of a Continental tour. Moreover, his new responsibilities in Jamaica left little time for dining out. His slaves became his chief occupation.

Opposition to the slave trade had begun in England before Lewis was born, and during his life public sentiment against it had steadily increased. Thomas Clarkson's essay had appeared in 1786, a committee against slave trade had been organized the following year, and Denmark had abolished the trade in 1792. Whether

England should do likewise was a question repeatedly debated in Parliament during Lewis' membership, though no bill proposing abolition of the trade succeeded in passing both houses until 1807. Meanwhile there had begun a new movement, of which Wilberforce was the great champion, for the emancipation of the thenexisting slaves, an object not attained until 1833. Lewis' West India experiences, then, give a glimpse of the situation between these two reforms, eight years after abolition of the trade, when people were wondering whether and how emancipation ought to be accomplished. It is pleasant to record that Lewis played a small but honorable part in the great slavery question.

Of his opinion of the trade there is not much doubt. The humanitarianism displayed in *The Castle Spectre* by Hassan, the anachronistic African, may be discounted as dramatic convention. And it is true that Byron, who delighted in setting Lewis and Madame de Staël to quarreling, is reported by Medwin as having said that she and Lewis "used to have violent arguments about the Slave Trade,—which he advocated strongly, for most of his property was in negroes and plantations."[11] Byron was a cynic and Medwin often an unreliable reporter, but if these arguments did occur, one need not take Lewis' stand very seriously. He loved a perverse position in dispute, and Madame de Staël was one to put him on his mettle. His Holland House associations identify him with the group hostile to the slave trade. The elegiac lines of 1806 laud Fox for his efforts to abolish the trade, and Lewis later added the note: "Great fears were entertained, that Mr. Fox's death would occasion the continuance of the Slave-Trade; but these apprehensions fortunately proved unfounded."[12] His *Journal* of 1816 speaks in retrospect of "the execrable slave-trade."[13]

Concerning emancipation he had probably reached no conviction before visiting Jamaica, though his feelings in 1803 are expressed in a letter to Moore: "among other things I have read a book . . . on the subject of Colonial Policy, which really made my blood run cold while I perused it, for it stated very clearly that the inevitable consequences of the independence of St. Domingo would be the ruin of the other West Indian colonies, and of Jamaica in the first place; in which case, *Morbleu!* I should be in a pretty pickle."[14] Like most Jamaica property owners of the time, his father opposed emancipation. In 1788 he sent to the Secretary at

War an extract from a letter speaking in strong terms against the growing movement for freeing the slaves "by one of the most respectable and most opulent Gentlemen of Jamaica: He is both a Planter & Merchant, and Attorney to several considerable Estates."[15]

Lewis' Jamaica property consisted of two estates, one on the western and one on the eastern extremity of the island. The first, in the parish of Westmoreland, was about four miles from the port of Savannah la Mar. The two plantations of Cornwall and Black Morass of which it had originally consisted had been united to form a single plantation of 1607 acres and 250 slaves known as the Cornwall estate.[16] Of the second, Hordley, in the parish of St. Thomas in the East, Lewis was a part owner with a Mr. Scott. Before his death Lewis bought out the latter's share, making his holdings at Hordley some 1670 acres. Before this purchase he seems to have owned about 140 Negroes at Hordley; at his death they numbered 278.[17]

It was customary for nonresident landowners in Jamaica to leave their estates in the management of an attorney or agent, usually a merchant or an experienced planter, who was paid for his service either by a six per cent commission on all sales or purchases or by a fixed salary. On each estate an overseer subordinate to the agent was responsible for planting the crops and managing the Negroes. Under the overseer were "bookkeepers" who superintended the Negro labor more directly and served apprenticeships of five or seven years to the overseer. Since an agent was sometimes responsible for as many as ten or fifteen estates, the system was open to abuse and mismanagement.[18] Lewis, who expressed very little interest in his profits, nevertheless was deeply concerned with the safety and comfort of the slaves and therefore determined to investigate his Jamaican affairs at first hand. It was not entirely "to suck his sugar canes," in Byron's phrase,[19] but to face his responsibility for some four hundred human lives that he set out for Jamaica late in 1815.

He sailed from Gravesend November 10 on the *Sir Godfrey Webster*, a vessel of six hundred tons, He left without taking leave of his mother, explaining that the scene "would have been so very painful to myself, and probably to you, that I thought it infinitely better to spare each other the unnecessary agony."[20] The voyage lasted nearly two months but was reasonably tranquil. After four days of sickness and headache Lewis read, wrote, and drew as comfortably as if he had been on shore.[21] On the fifth day out, he managed to walk into an open hatchway, narrowly escaping a deep fall to the bottom of the ship. Thereafter, occasional foul weather and a very real danger of pirates were the principal sources of excitement.

The ship reached Jamaica on New Year's day, and Lewis arrived at his Cornwall estate on January 2. The works were instantly abandoned, he reports in the journal he kept, and everything that had life, including hogs, dogs, geese, fowls, and turkeys, flocked to the house from all quarters: "Whether the pleasure of the negroes was sincere may be doubted; but certainly it was the loudest that I ever witnessed: they all talked together, sang, danced, shouted, and, in the violence of their gesticulations, tumbled over each other, and rolled about upon the ground" (J 60–1).

In the first weeks of his visit he went the rounds of the plantation, observing the process of sugar making, inspecting the hospital and the Negro dwellings. After a month at Cornwall, he made a ten-day trip through other parts of the island, visiting Spanish Town and Kingston, and returned to Cornwall on February 11, 1815, by way of the north shore after "an excursion the most amusing and agreeable that I ever made in my life" (J 173). He mixed as much as possible with the Negroes, distributing silver dollars and many indulgences to win their confidence and satisfy his own craving for kindnesses given and received. A revealing comment occurs in his description of the Negroes' gratitude:

All this may be palaver; but certainly they at least play their parts with such an air of truth, and warmth, and enthusiasm, that, after the cold hearts and repulsive manners of England, the contrast is infinitely agreeable. . . .

I find it quite impossible to resist the fascination of the conscious pleasure of pleasing; and my own heart, which I have so long been obliged to keep closed, seems to expand itself again in the sunshine of the kind looks and words which meet me at every turn, and seem to wait for mine as anxiously as if they were so many diamonds (J 90).

The immediate results of all this indulgence were not uniformly gratifying. Upon his arrival he granted the Negroes a holiday to celebrate the event: "The singing began about six o'clock, and lasted without a moment's pause till two in the morning; and such a noise never did I hear till then. . . . At twelve, my agent wanted to dismiss them; but I would not suffer them to be interrupted on the first holiday that I had given them; so they continued to dance and shout till two; when human nature could bear no more, and they left me to my bed, and a violent headache" (J 80–1). When several runaway Negroes, some of whom had been absent from the estate for months, returned to the fields during his visit, he would not allow them to be questioned (J 109). Another deserter, who returned only to profit by a distribution of beef, rum, and jackets, improved the occasion by stealing a sheep and a turkey. He was sent to Lewis for discipline, "But, as this was the first offender who had been brought before me," Lewis writes, "I took that for a pretext to absolve him: so I lectured him for half an hour with great severity" (J 132–3). The Negroes were quick to appreciate the relaxation in discipline: the hospital began filling upon Lewis' arrival, and in three weeks contained thirty invalids, "of whom only four were cases at all serious; the rest had 'a lilly pain here, Massa,' or 'a bad pain me know nowhere, Massa,' and evidently only came to the hospital in order to sit idle, and chat away the time with their friends" (J 122). He cured them by announcing a distribution of presents at his house that evening. Before he had been in Jamaica a month, his agent declared that the Negroes had "never conducted themselves so ill before; that they worked cheerfully and properly till my arrival; but now they think that I shall protect them against all punishment, and have made regularly ten hogsheads of sugar a week less than they did before my coming upon the estate" (J 140–1).

In treating the slaves with kindness Lewis was carrying on a family tradition. "My father was one of the most humane and generous persons that ever existed," he wrote; "there was no indulgence which he ever denied his negroes, and his letters were filled with the most absolute injunctions for their good treatment" (J 116). Lewis found no evidence that the Negroes on the Cornwall estate had been abused. Though they overwhelmed him with requests for favors, none complained of ill treatment, hunger, or overwork (J 111). Their quarters were comfortable and well equipped; he was assured that many were rich. The presence of very old slaves on the estate and the fact that several manumitted

Negroes were in the habit of returning to visit Cornwall he considered strong evidence of past good treatment (J 108–9). During
his first stay in Jamaica he found no opportunity to inspect Hordley, his estate in the east, but at least was informed by the agent
that for a long time the cartwhip had been used there not more
than twice a year, and then only lightly.

Lewis' incidental favors to the Negroes were of no importance,
but the reforms he established were. Among these, the abolition
of the lash is probably the one most agreeable to modern minds,
though it seemed madness to many of his contemporaries: "I am
indeed assured by every one about me, that to manage a West-
Indian estate without the occasional use of the cart-whip, however
rarely, is impossible; and they insist upon it, that it is absurd in me
to call my slaves ill-treated, because, when they act grossly wrong,
they are treated like English soldiers and sailors. All this may be
very true; but there is something to me so shocking in the idea of
this execrable cart-whip, that I have positively forbidden the use
of it on Cornwall" (J 119). The agent silently shook his head, but
Lewis preferred to have the estate go to rack and ruin than to
leave the cheerful creatures with whom he had lived subject to
lashing—"besides," he added, "they are excellent cajolers, and lay it
on with a trowel" (J 119–20).

He discharged three bookkeepers for maltreating the slaves,
though the charges were not serious against them. Upon hearing of
the first dismissal, the Negroes "one and all, sprawled upon the
ground in such a rapture of joy and gratitude, that now I may
safely say with Sir Andrew Aguecheek, 'I was adored once!' " (J
155). In judging another bookkeeper, he admitted the testimony
of five slaves against the white man's word, a radical departure in
the methods of Jamaican justice (J 196–7).

The slaves, by law, were free from work on Sundays and alternate Saturdays, and had three days at Christmas for themselves.
Lewis increased the allowance to include every Saturday, as an aid
in cultivating the provision grounds, and three extra play days each
year, on Good Friday and the second Fridays in July and October.
The first was to be in honor of the Duchess of York, Lewis instruct-
ing that the slaves on this occasion were to drink a health to Her
Royal Highness and give her three cheers. The July play day com-
memorated his own birthday. Since the abolition of slave trading

had made the Negro birth rate important to planters, the third holiday was dedicated to the mothers in an attempt to dignify their state. Lewis hit upon the scheme of giving each mother a scarlet girdle with a silver medal for every child born, to be worn on feast days, when it would entitle the wearer to respect among the Negroes and to certain privileges from the overseer.

As an antidote to Lewis' early reputation for impiety, his biographer quoted an excerpt from the *Journal* in which he instructs a disconsolate Negro in the ways of God.[22] As a matter of fact, although he christened their children and for a time conducted Sunday services for as many as cared to come, he saw clearly that Christianity to the Negroes was merely a magic superior to Obeah. He looked upon their promiscuity and crude conceptions of marriage with undisturbed good humor, and declined to subscribe to a plan of religious instruction drawn up by the ecclesiastical commissaries at Kingston because it proposed compulsory church attendance: "Sunday is now the absolute property of the negroes for their relaxation, as Saturday is for the cultivation of their grounds; and I will not suffer a single hour of it to be taken from them for any purpose whatever. If my slaves choose to go to church on Sundays, so much the better" (J 141).

Lewis' first visit to Jamaica lasted three months, at the end of which period the Cornwall Negroes declared themselves perfectly happy and well treated. On the other hand, Lewis frankly confessed that before his arrival they had produced thirty-three hogsheads of sugar a week, that within a fortnight the weekly total dwindled to twenty-three, and during his last week to thirteen. For this problem he offered no solution, but was content to draw up a code of laws to control and protect the Negroes during his absence. A new lying-in hospital was to be built, and patients in the old building were to be segregated to discourage pretended illness. A record of all punishments inflicted was to be kept, with the names and offenses of the culprits, and a note of each entry was to be given to the Negro to enable him to seek redress from the attorney or proprietor if he thought himself unjustly punished. No Negro was to be struck or punished in any way except by the express order of the trustee, nor in any case was punishment to be inflicted until twenty-four hours after the offense had been committed. A white person proved guilty of impropriety with the wife of a slave was to be dismissed.

Lewis later told William Wilberforce that he had come by chance upon an anonymous pamphlet on the management of slaves and being greatly struck with it had carried it to Jamaica and left it with his attorney as a guide.[23] He does not, then, claim originality for his reforms. But inventing them was not important; putting them into practice was.

It was Lewis' destiny to stimulate hostile criticism in whatever sphere he entered. His fellow proprietors were quick to denounce his methods. And at the opening of the assize court in Cornwall county two months after Lewis' arrival, the presiding judge remarked to the jury that many people out of Jamaica, and some in it, had thought proper to interfere with established systems and by insidious practices and dangerous doctrines to endanger the peace of the island (J 220–1). This subsequently proved to be directed principally at missionaries who were disturbing the Negroes, but Lewis had heard from a number of quarters that the reference was to him. He was told, but did not believe, that a song declaring his intention of setting all the slaves free was circulating among the Negroes of neighboring estates. "However, my agent here says, that he has reason to believe that my negroes really have spread the report that I intend to set *them* free in a few years; and this merely out of vanity, in order to give themselves and their master the greater credit upon other estates. As to the truth of an assertion, that is a point which never enters into negro consideration" (J 226). Somebody "positively assured" him that an attempt had been made to persuade the grand jury at Montego Bay to present him for overindulgence to his Negroes. "It is a great pity," he remarks, "that so reasonable an attempt should not have succeeded" (J 236).

Though we now side with Lewis' humanitarian cause, this widespread disapproval was not altogether unjustified. Stories of Lewis' indulgences were doubtless exaggerated as they spread over the island. Several runaway slaves from other plantations petitioned him personally to intercede for them with their masters, and Lewis was consequently looked upon as a protector of disobedience. His own slaves, childishly proud of their good fortune, undoubtedly spread a feeling of discontent in neighboring estates. The whites in Jamaica at the time, outnumbered almost ten to one, lived in continual fear of an insurrection, which might have annihilated the entire white population; like other proprietors, Lewis himself felt that total emancipation would end in a general massacre of whites (J 173–4). During his second visit he expressed himself on this question with finality: "Every man of humanity must wish that slavery, even in its best and most mitigated form, had never found a legal sanction, and must regret that its system is now so incorporated with the welfare of Great Britain as well as of Jamaica, as to make its extirpation an absolute impossibility, without the certainty of producing worse mischiefs than the one which we annihilate" (J 402).

He left Jamaica on April 1, 1816, to the very evident sorrow of his Negroes, and arrived at Gravesend on June 5. He continued his journal during the voyage, composed several poems, one of eight or nine hundred lines, and wrote down some Annancy stories he had heard on the island.[24]

Lewis had found Wilberforce's policies a common topic of conversation in Jamaica and mentions the philanthropist several times in his journal, never very cordially. But unwilling to overlook any source of enlightenment in the management of his slaves, he now wrote to Wilberforce and talked with him, a conference briefly noted in the latter's diary, dated only 1816 in its published form: "Monk Lewis dined with me, to talk over Jamaica. I went again to town to see him; he is I hope in earnest in writing to me to secure the happiness of his slaves after his death; I am quite anxious to try to do some good through this channel."[25]

Lewis remained in England only a few weeks. His aunt Mrs. Blake, ever critical of her nephew, wrote to a friend, "He returned from the West Indies & I am sorry to say, so much *dis*improved (a word of my own) that I think I may say, with perfect justice & truth, that, his friends in general wish He were among his Black Slaves again as being the only Creatures fit to bear with his Nonsense and Vanity. He returned, the most altered Man I ever knew and so very disagreeable that there was no bearing with him."[26] Just before leaving for the West Indies he had expressed to his mother an intention of visiting Italy,[27] and he now took the opportunity afforded by his new resources of making a Continental tour that was to last a year and a half. Unfortunately the journal he kept on this trip has disappeared, but his itinerary can be partially reconstructed.[28]

He visited Byron at the Maison Diodati in Geneva during August.[29] Here he met, probably for the first time, Shelley, Mary Shelley, Claire Clairmont, and John Polidori. Hobhouse, who joined the party later, had been introduced to Lewis in 1811;[30] to his host, of course, Lewis was well known. The weather had been bad at Geneva that season, and the company had often been confined to the house, where they amused themselves with ghost stories.[31] It is well known that Byron, the Shelleys, and Polidori agreed each to write a tale of the supernatural, a project resulting in Polidori's fragmentary Vampyre and Mary Shelley's Frankenstein. Polidori notes in his diary that by June 17 all the stories were begun with the exception of his own.[32] Lewis could not possibly have been at Geneva so early and therefore, contrary to what is often thought, had no hand in the origin of the plan, though his presence may well have served to keep it alive. Lewis enjoyed a considerable reputation as a storyteller, and some of the supernatural tales he told were taken down by contemporaries.[33] At Diodati he found a receptive audience. The twenty-four-year-old Shelley was particularly impressed and recorded five of Lewis' stories in his Geneva journal, which begins with the paragraph: "See Apollo's Sexton, who tells us many mysteries of his trade. We talk of Ghosts. Neither Lord Byron nor M.G.L. seem to believe in them; and they both agree, in the very face of reason, that none could believe in ghosts without believing in God. I do not think that all the persons who profess to discredit these visitations, really discredit them; or, if they do in the daylight, are not admonished, by the approach of loneliness and midnight, to think more respectfully of the world of shadows."[34]

Byron wrote to Samuel Rogers the following year, "I forgot to tell you that, last autumn, I furnished Lewis with 'bread and salt' for some days at Diodati, in reward for which (besides his conversation) he translated Goethe's Faust to me by word of mouth."[35] The incident has often been mentioned, involving as it does the question of the indebtedness of Manfred to Faust. It has been felt that the impression on Byron of Lewis' readings was deep and lasting and that no other work of foreign literature ever left so strong an impression upon him as *Faust*.[36] Reviewers of *Manfred* made much of Byron's debt to Goethe, and the latter took it for granted that Byron had seen his poem. On the other hand, Byron told his publisher, "*Faust* I never read, for I don't know German; but Matthew Monk Lewis, in 1816, at Coligny, translated most of it to me *vivâ voce*, and I was naturally much struck with it."[37]

During his stay at Geneva, Lewis made frequent trips to Coppet, sometimes with Byron who "set him by the ears with Madame de Stael about the slave-trade."[38] Ever since his visit to Jamaica he had been troubled by the question of protecting his Negroes from abuse after his death. He now wrote a codicil to his will, ordering that the future owner of each estate, or a son, brother, or husband of the owner, pass three months on it every third year on pain of forfeiture to the next heir, except in circumstances amounting to a legal impossibility, such as dangerous illness or rebellion in Jamaica. According to this document, the owner is empowered to make regulations likely to ameliorate the situation of the Negroes, but anyone who dares to diminish the comforts and indulgences they already enjoy shall lose his share in the estate. The sale of any Negroes is forbidden, and a solemn curse is put upon anyone who transgresses these injunctions. "I trust that I have expressed myself so clearly," Lewis writes, "that there can be no doubt as to my *meaning*; and I also trust that the law will not suffer that meaning to be defeated through any quirk or quibble, or trifling informality."[39] The codicil was dated August 20, 1816, and signed by Byron, Shelley, and Polidori as witnesses.

Before leaving Geneva Lewis caught a bank agent red-handed attempting to overcharge him for a bill of exchange and came away with the opinion that in that city "the people are all rogues from the first to the last, and nothing can equal their rascality except their impenetrable stupidity."[40]

Lewis must have left Diodati soon after the codicil was signed, for on September 1 he wrote to Byron from Como.[41] There perhaps he paid his respects to the Princess of Wales, who was living at the Villa d'Este in Como that month. In northern Italy he visited other towns—Milan, Pavia, Genoa, and Parma; at Parma he was presented to Maria Louisa, daughter of Francis I of Austria and Napoleon's second wife. On October 1 he informed his mother that Upper Lombardy was, next to Holland, the ugliest country he had

*Matthew G. Lewis, drawn by George Henry Harlow,
engraved by J. Hollis.*

CASTLE SPECTRE.

*Earl Percy escaping from the Castle.*

Published by J.Bailey, Chancery Lane, London. *vide page* 11 &12.

*Frontispiece of* The Castle Spectre: An Ancient Baronial Romance
*by Sarah Wilkinson, founded on Lewis' drama, circa 1820.*
*British Museum.*

ever seen, "and the Singers at the Opera bawl in a manner, that
would get them hissed off the Stage in England. I am, therefore,
not only glad to have seen all that I have seen, but delighted to
think, that there never can be occasion for my seeing it again. But
the Pictures and Statues exceed all praise!" (F 102). This letter
is dated from Florence, where he again met Madame de Staël, as
is clear from Byron's note to Moore written a few years later: "Our
dear defunct friend, Monk Lewis, who was too great a bore ever to
lie, assured me upon his tiresome word of honour, that at Florence,
the said Madame de S was open-*mouthed* against me."[42] Lewis
was still there on October 11, but by December 16 seems to have
been in Rome for some time, according to the Duchess of Devonshire: "M. Lewis till last night has never appeared. Here, as at
Florence, he shuts himself up to hold converse only with the departed."[43] Whether or not he visited Venice and Dalmatia at
that time, he was in Rome at the beginning of 1817: "I am still
greatly amused with Italy, and wonderfully so with Rome. But the
People are insupportable, and I shun them like wildfire," he wrote
to his mother. Since his last letter, he says, he has "Kissed the Pope's
hand (not his Toe) and now have nothing more to do at Rome.
I shall probably go to Naples soon, but my stay is very uncertain"
(F 103).

He set out for Naples a few days later, to visit his sister Maria
Lady Lushington.[44] Some twelve years previously, when the
estrangement between Lewis and his father was widest, Maria's
husband Sir Henry Lushington had been an intermediary and had
conveyed the father's orders to the son in a manner which the
latter found extremely irritating and which, since Lushington's
sympathies were entirely with Mrs. Ricketts, perhaps contained a
trace of malicious satisfaction.[45] Because of this old quarrel with
his brother-in-law, visiting the Lushingtons entailed some embarrassment for Lewis, but, according to Charles Greville, his ingenuity was equal to the problem: "Melbourne told me the other day a
queer trait of Lewis. He had a long-standing quarrel with Lushington. Having occasion to go to Naples, he wrote beforehand to him,
to say that their quarrel had better be *suspended,* and he went and
lived with him and his sister (Lady L.) in perfect cordiality during
his stay. When he departed he wrote to Lushington to say that
now they would resume their quarrel, and put matters in the 'statu

quo ante pacem,' and accordingly he did resume it, with rather more acharnement than before."[46] His prejudice against Lushington was not very deep, or at least he had confidence in his judgment, for in a codicil to his will written four years previously he had left all his "Letters, journals and *written papers* and books of all descriptions to S^r Heny Lushington requesting him to burn all such as he may judge improper to be seen. If there are any which he wishes to keep for himself or for my sister he is at liberty to do so."[47]

Lewis stayed at his sister's home about nine weeks. "I . . . never thought it possible," he told his mother in a letter of March 13, 1817, "for me to be so much delighted with any place out of England. The climate is delicious, and the beauty of the Scenery beggars all description. . . . I am determined, that if Jamaica should fail, or anything happen to make England odious to me, I shall ship myself off for Naples, and fix myself there immoveably. Rome did not agree with me; and in particular my eyes troubled me a good deal: But at Naples I have been (for me) singularly well, and I shall quit the place with the greatest regret" (F 105–6). He speaks of Naples as the extreme point of his travels and intends to be homeward bound in two days, though he does not expect to reach Paris for several months (F 106). He remained at least another week, however, and gave a ball at which Stendhal, then visiting Naples, was a guest. "Que je suis fâché," the latter wrote in his *Rome, Naples, et Florence*, "de ne pas pouvoir parler du bal charmant donné par M. Lewis, l' auteur du *Moine*, chez madame Lusington [*sic*], sa soeur! Au milieu des moeurs grossières des Napolitains, cette pureté anglaise rafraîchit le sang."[48]

Lewis may next have visited Greece, but his travels fade from view until July 1, when Byron wrote to Murray, "Mr. Lewis is at Venice, and I am going up to stay a week with him there—as it is one of his enthusiasms also to like the city."[49] Lewis lived on the Grand Canal,[50] and visited Byron at the Villa La Mira. He had arrived by July 10, and Hobhouse found the two together at the end of the month.[51] From La Mira, Byron and his guest used to ride out along the Brenta, Byron going before to guide his shortsighted companion through the twilight. Once he absent-mindedly passed over a ditch without giving warning, and Lewis went into it. "Thrice did I lose him in the gray of the Gloaming," Byron wrote, "and was obliged to bring to to his distant signals of distance and distress. All the time he went on talking without intermission, for he was a man of many words."[52] Lewis continued his storytelling at La Mira,[53] and give at least one piece of literary advice which Byron followed and acknowledged. The latter had been planning *Marino Faliero* ever since February, and now asked Lewis' opinion of jealousy as a motive for Faliero. "If you make him jealous," Lewis said, "recollect that you have to contend with established writers, to say nothing of Shakespeare, and an exhausted subject:— stick to the old fiery Doge's natural character, which will bear you out, if properly drawn; and make your plot as regular as you can."[54] Byron was composing *Childe Harold* also and gave Lewis the fourth canto to read.[55]

In August Byron wrote his "La Mira Separation Document," intended to show that, far from wishing to suppress Lady Byron's charges against him, he had encouraged a statement of them, especially since they were unknown to him. This he entrusted to Lewis, to be circulated among friends in England, though Hobhouse disapproved of the step.[56] According to a report based upon letters by Lady Byron and Augusta Leigh, the paper was written at Lewis' instigation. Mrs. Leigh wrote that Hobhouse found Byron and Lewis together and the paper just written and sealed, and that Hobhouse "had tried *Heaven & Earth*" to persuade Byron "not to give it to Monk Lewis (whom he abused) *in vain—* & that only the hour after it was *gone*, Byron expressed regret he had given and written it!"[57] The document was found among Lewis' papers after his death and first published in 1869.[58] It is supposed that he suppressed it. Quite possibly his remaining time in England was too short and too occupied with legal matters and preparations for his second journey to Jamaica to permit him to circulate it.

It may have been at Venice that Lewis engaged Giovanni Battista Falcieri, known as Tita, the servant who accompanied him on his subsequent visit to Jamaica and was with him when he died.[59] Tita afterwards served Byron. He was described by Shelley as "a fine fellow, with a prodigious black beard, who has stabbed two or three people, and is the most good-natured looking fellow I ever saw."[60] Lewis had great respect for him and relieved some of the boredom of his second voyage to Jamaica by relating to the passengers a romantic adventure of how he and Tita first met. Tita, it seems, aided Lewis' escape from Italian banditti.[61]

Lewis left Venice in the second week in August. Though he afterwards wrote to Byron, the two never met again. "Lewis was a good man, a clever man, but a bore, a damned bore, one may say," was Byron's verdict. "But I liked Lewis: he was a Jewel of a Man had he been better set. I don't mean *personally*, but less *tiresome*; for he was tedious, as well as contradictory, to every thing and every body."[62] In accounts of Byron, Lewis usually appears as a little comet that swam for a moment in the poet's orbit, an amusing eccentric who served as a target in *English Bards* and told ghost stories at Diodati. But he was more than that to Byron, behind whose habitual joking lies respect for the elder man's talents and judgment.

From Venice Lewis made his way, probably through the Tyrol and Switzerland,[63] to Paris, where on September 20 he wrote to his mother, "I shall probably be in London before the end of next month, but say so to *Nobody*."[64]

He was in London on October 16, composing a long letter to Wilberforce about his slaves. A year earlier, Lewis had written from Florence to his agent in London concerning a new Jamaica purchase and his dissatisfaction over his joint ownership with Mr. Scott of the Hordley estate. Half of the Negroes at Hordley were Lewis' property:

It is my *duty* to make them as happy as it is in my power; and they have a right to enjoy, as many advantages from me, as are enjoyed by my negroes upon Cornwall. Upon Mr. Scott's refusal to sell his share, I offered to go on jointly, provided I might have the power of increasing the various indulgencies of the negroes, as I had increased them at Cornwall and introducing such laws respecting them as I chose to do, and that without controul; As to the cultivation of the soil, etc., *that* He might order, as he pleased. He refused this proposal, and was pleased to deprecate my coming upon the Estate with such intentions, as utter ruin, etc., etc. With ideas so different, we never can go on together.[65]

From the same letter we learn that Lewis had proposed to buy Scott's share, that their joint agent had made an evaluation, and that Scott had refused to sell, except at a figure which Lewis found too high. The only course left open was to divide the estate, an expensive procedure for both, since they would be obliged to build a new set of works—"However, there is no remedy," Lewis writes, "for I *must* have my own negroes under my own controul." In the event of such a division, he insists that the slaves be shared evenly: "I do not wish to have a single Negro more than belongs to my own half; but I will not give up a finger, no, not so much as an hair of any one, who ought to belong to me, I also wish the business to be arranged by the end of next year; and I am determined to visit Hordley early in February 1818 [?] for the purpose of assimilating the management of my own share of it with that already established at Cornwall." He expresses some faint hope that Mr. Scott will change his mind before October 1817. The division of Hordley did not take place; either Scott lowered his price or Lewis met it, for articles of agreement by which Lewis contracted to buy the rest of Hordley were executed on or about October 31, 1817.[66]

He refers to this transaction in the letter of October 16 to Wilberforce when he writes that he has "just been worried into making a fresh large Jamaica purchase."[67] He regrets the philanthropist's absence from town and asks for suggestions for the future protection of his slaves. With the Geneva codicil he is not satisfied—an attorney had asked him how he could be certain that the proprietor would not be their greatest tyrant, and he could give no answer. As to freeing the slaves at his death, he thinks the step would be ill advised; he is unwilling to change their state at present because they are contented—they have even sent him a message to that effect. An eyewitness has told him that since his visit to Cornwall the Negroes have behaved so well that his agent is reconciled to Lewis' methods of inducing them to work through good will instead of terror. The red sashes are having their expected effect upon the birth rate, only two children have died, and the crops have increased withal.

After a brief stop in England, his last, Lewis sailed again for Jamaica, on November 5, on the same ship and under the same captain as before. Again he avoided taking leave of his mother, writing to her instead: "If you have any thing pleasant ever to tell me, send it to the Albany, when an opportunity occurs, I shall order letters to be sent to me. But tell me nothing that can *possibly* agitate me, or you will be the death or the blindness of me,"[68] and to another correspondent, "I leave my Mother in such good health, that I have little apprehension that this note should be of use.—Still I may as well say that *should* any thing happen to her, I request you on no account to inform me of it.—It would affect me too heavily and might Kill me in such a Climate."[69] The ship met particularly stormy weather, and it was reported that of other vessels starting at the same time sixteen were lost. The voyage was a month longer than the first. However, Lewis had provided himself against boredom by bringing aboard an old-fashioned piano and a collection of modern books, including novels by Scott.[70]

Arriving on January 24, Lewis found the Cornwall estate running smoothly, though his account is less enthusiastic than the one he had given Wilberforce upon hearsay. An unhealthful season had killed a number of his Negroes, though other estates in the parish had suffered more heavily. But after three weeks, during which he made inquiries and invited the slaves to voice their complaints, he could not find one with even an imaginary grievance. All assured him that his code had been followed implicitly, except that, to punish actual crimes, in a few instances the lash had been used.

After six weeks at Cornwall, Lewis traveled the length of the island to pay a first visit to his Hordley estate. The journey, hazardous under the best conditions, was accompanied by inconveniences of every sort and took five days. Stopping off at Kingston one night he attended the theater, "and I may reckon it among my other misfortunes on this ill-starred expedition, that it was my destiny to sit out the tragedy of 'Adelgitha,' whom the author meant only to be killed in the last act, but whom the actors murdered in all five" (J 363-4).

Instead of the perfect paradise he had expected, he found Hordley "a perfect hell," full of tyranny, discontent, and general ill will (J 365).[71] Not anticipating such conditions, he had allotted only a week to attend to the estate. He dismissed a bookkeeper, another fled, the black governor was demoted, and a humane proprietor of a neighboring estate was appointed as the Negroes' protector to whom they might appeal in cases of injustice. Then the Cornwall code was read to the slaves and became their law; two dances and a distribution of money were granted; and Lewis set off hurriedly for Cornwall. The return proved more perilous than the journey out. He sums up the two trips in what was probably his last letter to his mother (F 107-8):

... I begin to beleive (like Macbeth) that so long as I stay in Jamaica, "*I bear a charmed life.*" I have been climbing over Mountains with knocked up Horses; fording Rivers which an Irishman would call "impassable"; been benighted without Moon or Stars on a road bordered by precipices & Swamps; crossing Bridges, whose supporters had rotted & tumbled into the Ravine beneath; Sitting at Midnight in violent perspiration for an hour at a Gate with Dew falling and Wind blowing on me (which is your only true receipt for getting a Jamaica fever) carried away Horses Carriage and all by a Mountain Torrent; Driving along the Sea, whose roaring frightened my young Horses, one of whom tumbled into the Waves, while the off-wheel flew up into the air; & thus the Chaise balanced backwards & forwards till luckily the Postillion pulled up the Horse again, or we should all have gone over into the Sea and been drowned to a certainty. . . .

The hospital Lewis had ordered built at Cornwall was now complete, and, thanks to his regulations, it was said by the physician to give less trouble than any other in the parish. Expecting many years to elapse before his next visit, "if indeed I should ever return at all," Lewis left with his attorney a code regulating punishments of the most common misdemeanors of the slaves, to prevent disproportionate and arbitrary punishments by the overseer. "I have at least exerted myself while here," his last entry in the *Journal* reads, "to do everything which appeared likely to contribute to their welfare and security during my absence" (J 403).

He was entitled to this satisfaction. The part he played in Jamaica brings out the best in his character—his humanity, common sense, and courage. By putting his reforms into effect he anticipated general practice in Jamaica by nearly eighteen years.

His system justified itself from a practical standpoint as well. In a letter of 1834, Richard R. Madden, appointed by the Crown as magistrate to supervise abolition in Jamaica, described the Lewis estates as valuable properties, whereas many others had by that time gone to ruin.[72] Both of them, he reported, "are now in the hands of his heirs, and not under the superintendence of the Court of Chancery. One of the proprietors, the son of Sir Henry Lushington, is now on the island, following the example of Lewis; seeing with his own eyes how the management of his properties is going on."[73] After summarizing Lewis' reforms, Madden adds: "Such were the means Lewis took to *improve* his plantations: he looked beyond the crops of this year or the next, and he accordingly improved the conditions of his negroes, well assured that in so doing he was serving his own interests better than by making it his only study to exact the utmost labour, and to obtain present advantages at any sacrifice of future interests."[74] The writer is presenting an argument that will convince his correspondent: in crediting Lewis with a vision of future crops, he is probably wrong. Lewis seems to have given scarcely a thought to the profits from his estates either for himself or for his heirs. That his kindhearted efforts bore tangible fruit in a later day is merely poetic justice.

In a letter of March 1815 from Cornwall during his first visit, he mentions "a sort of journal I have *in petto*, and which, indeed, I have already begun; meaning it for publication on my return to England."[75] He brought it to a close at the end of his first trip and just before starting on his second offered it to the publisher Murray at the rather startling price of £2000. Though Murray thought highly of it, Lewis received no reply.[76] Meanwhile he wrote the second part. In the year following his death his sister Sophia told Scott of a manuscript of her brother's worthy of publication and asked, "Is there not a method of bargaining with a Bookseller, to sell the Copyright for only a term of years? the family keeping possession of the original MS?"[77] Nothing was done with the journal at the time, but fifteen years later, on June 26, 1833, Charles Greville noted in his diary that he had got from Sir Henry Lushington "Monk Lewis' journals of his two voyages to the W(est) Indies (one of which I read at Naples), with liberty to publish them, which I mean to do if I can get money enough for him. He says Murray offered him £500 for the manuscripts some years ago. I doubt getting so much now, but they are uncommonly amusing, and it is the right moment for publishing them now that people are full of interest about the W(est) India question."[78] By July 12 Greville had concluded a bargain with Murray and sold the journal for four hundred guineas, the manuscript to be returned to Lushington with fifteen copies for the latter and five for Greville. Murray promised publication within a fortnight.[79] It appeared in 1834, with the title *Journal of a West India Proprietor, Kept During a Residence in the Island of Jamaica. By the Late Matthew Gregory Lewis, Esq. M.P.*

Coleridge found it delightful: "it is almost the only unaffected book of travels or touring I have read of late years. You have the man himself, and not an inconsiderable man,—certainly a much finer mind than I supposed before from the perusal of his romances, &c. It is by far his best work, and will live and be popular."[80] Coleridge was right. In the same year of its London publication it appeared, with a few squeamish deletions (mostly relating to childbirth among the slaves), in the American Select Circulating Library; and in 1845, somewhat abbreviated, as the *Journal of a Residence among the Negroes in the West Indies* in Murray's Home and Colonial Library, a text reissued in 1861.[81] The original text appeared in America in 1929 with a good biographical introduction.[82]

Unlike other works by Lewis, the *Journal* presents reality and gives free play to his talent for clear and lively description of everything he observed, whether it was a distant mountain range or two halves of a centipede running away from each other. The book is rich in literary allusions but never strains for effect. Verbal echoes in the letters to his mother show that he recorded events as they occurred. He reflects upon the unpredictable and preposterous behavior of the slaves with kindliness and humor. Though he sometimes expresses shrewd opinions concerning Jamaican life or British colonial policy, he does not attempt to speak with authority on matters beyond the limits of his two estates. To historians of the West Indies, nevertheless, the *Journal* has been a valuable source of information. In the words of a recent writer on Jamaica, "No fairer picture of tropical slavery was ever done by a man whose personal interests were involved."[83] After noting the insignificance of Lewis' earlier literary achievements, the *Edinburgh Review* observed that the *Journal* "seems to afford evidence which is difficult to resist, that the writer was not only a pleasant companion, but a sensible and practical man—keen-sighted without bitterness—a good-natured noter of passing absurdities, without any cynical disposition to censure—seeing things through no discoloured medium of sentimentality or romance, but taking a plain, correct, man-of-the-world's view of all that passed around him."[84]

Some dozen short poems occur in the *Journal,* one of which, "Zayde and Zayda," from *Las Guerras Civiles de Granada,* was probably composed years before. Others were inspired by the day's occurrences and served to while away the weeks on shipboard. The "Song of the Tempest-Fiend" is an effective blood-and-thunder ballad in the "Alonzo" meter, having a shipwreck as the source of horror. "When summer smiled on Goa's bowers" is one of Lewis' most graceful and delicate songs. The poem entitled "Landings," which he might have polished had he been granted more time, has personal interest. After his first arrival in Jamaica, following two months on a ship peopled only by men, he was moved to write the verses upon hearing once again the sound of a woman's voice. It was a Negro's and "each phrase the tortured language broke," but that did not matter. It led him to put on record his final peace with womankind:

> Once raven locks my temples wore;
> Time has pluck'd many, sorrow more:
> Through forty springs (thank God they're run!)
> These weary eyes have seen the sun;
> And in that space full room is found
> For flowers to fade, and thorns to wound.
> But now, (all fancy's freaks supprest,
> Each thread-bare sneer and wanton jest,)
> With hand on heart in serious tone,
> With thanks, with truth, I needs must own,
> Wide as I've roam'd the world around,
> Roam where I would, I ever found,
> The worst of Women still possess
> More virtues than of Men the best.     (J 72–3)

For some days on the first outward voyage he was exceedingly seasick and between eight on a Monday morning and twelve the following Thursday brought up, as he puts it, nearly one thousand lines with rhymes at the end of them. This production, in heroic couplets, is *The Isle of Devils: A Metrical Tale*. He had the story from "an old Italian book, called 'Il Palagio degli Incanti.'" It is a grotesque and ugly narrative of a maiden who on a voyage to Lisbon is shipwrecked upon an enchanted island inhabited by monsters and devils. Carried off by a loathsome giant, she is forced to live with him and bears him two children, one a monster. When at last she escapes from the island, the giant, who has done his best to win her affection, dashes himself from a cliff in despair. Coleridge called it "a fever dream—horrible, without point or terror."[85] It was published separately in Kingston, Jamaica, in 1827, before the publication of the *Journal*, and in London in 1912.[86]

Lewis gave his Cornwall Negroes a farewell party on May 2 and closed his *Journal* with the words ". . . I am certain that there cannot be more tractable or better disposed persons (take them for all in all) than my negroes of Cornwall. I only wish, that in my future dealings with white persons, whether *in* Jamaica or out of it, I could but meet with half so much gratitude, affection, and good-will" (J 408). He was on his ship by May 4, where he wrote his last letter:

> Monday. 10 o'clock [May 4, 1818]
> On board
>
> My dear Hill,
>
> I knew, there was something which I particularly wished to say to you, and coud not recollect what it was. I am [writing] about a young Book-keeper on Cornwall, named Blackeston; he was obliged to leave Malta on account of insanity. He has been on Cornwall more than two years: about a Month ago He had a return of his complaint, is wasting away hourly, and must die, unless He leaves The Island. I advised his doing so, but did not like to speak *too strongly*, because (being Proprietor) I was fearful of hurting his feelings, and making him think that I wanted to get rid of him. Now I should be greatly obliged to you, if *you* would see this youth, and tell him, that I have spoken to you respecting his bad health (*not hinting at his insanity*, observe) generally; and that you (as well as myself) are convinced, that He never will recover in Jamaica, and by speaking to him in a kind and friendly manner convince him of the [necessity] of his return-ing to England *as soon as possible*. Probably, such an attention from a Gentleman would please his feelings and soften the advice, at the same time that from you (who are not burthened with him) He could not mis-interpret the advice, as He might when coming from me who am his Employer. Excuse my giving you this additional trouble, and accept my thanks for all the other kindnesses which you have done me—We are now getting under weigh, & my Boat is in sight; But we have just had a Mutiny among the Sailors, who declare, that so many Sailors have been lost one way or another, that they have not hands enough to work the Ship! There is no end of our disagreeables! and I broke a wine-glass last night, which *every body knows* to be a very bad omen!—Remember me kindly to your Wife
>
> > Ever yours most truly
> > M G Lewis

I told Cubina to desire Plummer to order that Catalina (the Madwoman) should be maintained by the Estate, and that her Husband should have nothing to do with her; and also Cubina is to repay Sully a Dollar, which I borrowed of him—will you be kind enough to remind Cubina of the one, and tell Plummer of the other, if the Negro should have forgotten his in-structions?

Pray, remind Plummer "not to forget to put up the paradosical piece of Deal Board in the Mill, which is to cost nothing, and prevent the Feeders

from falling forwad,—This is serious, observe, *and really so.* I want the
Board put up, and the sooner the better.[87]

After the hardships Lewis had undergone on the return from
Hordley he suffered a slight attack of yellow fever, then prevalent
in Jamaica. When the wine glass broke it was a portent that the
protecting charm he had enjoyed on the island would no longer
be in force. He died thirteen days later.

A fellow passenger, "Miss F.," supplied Lewis' biographer with
a description of his last hours and death. Another passenger, who
was "a mere child, almost an infant" at the time, published in *The
Court Magazine* sixteen years later her impressions, colored by a
good deal of adult moralizing. Both accounts are to be found in
the *Life*,[88] but from the second the biographer omitted one passage
which, since *The Court Magazine* is not readily available, may be
reproduced here:

[Lewis] also possessed an old-fashioned piano, bound with brass bands for
travelling; and often did he while away the dreary hours ever attendant on
a long sea-voyage, by his exquisite touch on that instrument.

When we were passing the islands of the Cayman, some of the natives
came alongside of our vessel in their boats, with parrots, shells, and live
turtles, for sale—he purchased several of the latter, intending to present one
to the Prince of Wales, and another to the Duchess of York.

Though his general manner was serious, yet he would sometimes relax;
and become animated even to gaiety,—on one occasion when sitting down
to dinner, he observed (probably owing to some mistake of the steward) that
there were four dishes of kid on the table, all, however, dressed differently,
—"What!" exclaimed he, without moving a muscle of his face, and drawling his words out in a most ludicrous tone—"Is this all that we're to have?
kid at the top, kid at the bottom, kid at the side, and kid in the middle!
Why, it's kid all over!" This caused a great deal of laughter, particularly as
they were almost the first words some of the persons present had heard him
utter; and there was such a comic surprise expressed in his manner of
delivering them. During Mr. Lewis's stay in Jamaica he had been made the
subject of many a strange anecdote; among others it had been reported that
he was in the habit of giving dinner parties to his own black slaves, presiding in person at the head of the table, and conversing with them in the
most familiar manner (always remembering to place his driver at his right-
hand side); besides which condescension, it was said that he constantly
shook hands with the negroes, when visiting them at work in the fields.
This may be true, or it may be only a fable; but if true, how far he was
right or wrong in so doing, it will be difficult for anyone to pronounce; and,

besides, is not to be gravely considered, since who can account for the freaks of genius?[89]

The narratives by the two passengers concerning Lewis' end agree in essentials. The *Sir Godfrey Webster* had several cases of yellow fever aboard; Lewis was already ill when the ship sailed on May 4. He became obstinate and irritable, refused to remain in his berth, and paced the deck for hours, spouting Italian and German poetry with violent gestures. On May 10 he insisted, against advice, upon taking an emetic. This further weakened his condition, and he died, apparently after great suffering, on the sixteenth. His aunt Mrs. Blake wrote: "He died of an Inflamation of the Stomach and of perseverence in doctoring himself in his own fashion. He was reading but the instant before he breathed his last."[90] Hobhouse noted in his diary, "His servant told my servant that just before he died he wrote his will on his servant's hat."[91]

Two years before, having contemplated the elaborate marble and ebony mausoleum of his forebears in Jamaica, Lewis had written, "It is a matter of perfect indifference to me what becomes of this little ugly husk of mine" (J 102), and Fate took him at his word. For the protection of the other passengers Captain Boyes ordered a sea burial. The body was placed in an improvised coffin, which was wrapped in a sheet with some weights and dropped into the ocean to visit the bottom of the monstrous world. But Lewis' aptitude for astonishing effects did not desert him even then. After the first plunge the weights slipped out and the coffin reappeared, to float spectrally upon the surface, and the loosened sheet, acting as a sail in the wind, guided it slowly off toward Jamaica until it was lost to sight.

The news of his death, reaching London in June, caused no stir.[92] It was remarked that no one so well known in the circles of literature and fashion ever created so little sensation by his death. Michael Kelly attributed this to Lewis' absence from society during his last years.[93] Sir William Gell's comment to Lady Charlotte Bury may stand for the attitude of the fashionable world: "To think of the poor dear Monk's being thrown overboard and eaten by the fish! Truly it vexes me, and I am sure so it will you. To whom did he leave all his worldly goods?"[94] The cause of his death was variously reported. It was widely rumored that he had been poisoned by his own slaves because he had promised them freedom at his death, an explanation which, satisfactory in its logic and irony, developed picturesque details: he was poisoned on ship-board by his three favorite slaves whom he was bringing to England to make them free British subjects.[95] The newspapers, sometimes spelling his name wrong, noted that he had been called to Jamaica solely to ascertain the happiness of his slaves, "by whom, as well as by every friend of humanity, he will be sincerely lamented."[96] The *Gentleman's Magazine* ran a decent obituary.[97]

One parting shot of defamation was fired by the press. An anonymous writer for the London *Courier*, journalistically sensing a good story, seized the opportunity of resuscitating the almost forgotten scandal of *The Monk* and its author's old reputation for satanism. The account, published on October 31, 1818, as a "just estimate of this writer's character," is astonishing in that, after a quite plausible opening, the writer, in pursuit of a moral lesson, presents an irresponsible and totally false picture of Lewis as an evil man struggling for publicity and acclaim and being chastised by Sisyphean frustration:

> Lewis came into life with unusual advantages, a competence, a sufficient rank in society, an understanding cultivated by education and travel. If his talent was not of the first order, he had great dexterity in its application. If his taste was inferior to his talent, it was equal to the requisitions of his time. It was his fortune to come forward when all rivalry was past or unborn; the powerful splendours which have since lightened over the whole region of poetry were then below the horizon; and his feeble and wandering fire was brilliancy in the dimness of that misty solitude. England had then no poet, no dramatist, no novelist of distinction; like our ancestors, in the day of our distress, we were forced to invoke the aid of the barbarians, and our literature was at once inundated with the ferocious fantasies of Germany. Lewis was a leader in this northern invasion, and he triumphed in the common degradation of the English genius. But he had native claims; his occasional tales had a vigour and a pathos new to our degenerate poetry. His first drama of *The Castle Spectre* was unequalled for dramatic artifice, and his firs[t] novel of *The Monk* was the model of high-wrought language and seductive story to its tribe. But his first celebrity was his last. His setting was as rapid as his rise. He had devoted the first fruits of his mind to the propagation of evil, and the whole long harvest was burnt up. As if a retributive judgment pressed upon him, he struggled continually down-wards; his efforts were perpetual, his failures were unvaried; he rolled that eternal stone upwards, and it was his punishment to be at once urged to that cheerless labour, and broken by seeing it all to be begun again; still he

went down, till at last he had perished into total obscurity. There is a moral in the life of this man, and it may be well for his successors in popularity and vice, if they read it before it comes to be inscribed on their own early graves. He was a reckless defiler of the public mind; a profligate, he cared not how many were to be undone when he drew back the curtain of his profligacy; he had infected his reason with the insolent belief that the power to corrupt made the right, and that conscience might be laughed, so long as he could evade law. *The Monk* was an eloquent evil; but the man who compounded it knew in his soul that he was compounding poison for the multitude, and in that knowledge he sent it into the world, priding himself in the subtlety of the venom whose diffusion was to be his boast, fame, and fortune. Than this there can be no deeper crime, if the depth of crime is to be measured by its effects. The homicide is grasped by the law, and there his mischief ends. The author of a licentious book propagates evil as far in the present as vice can attract, as far in the future as man exists; his ability shoots out the death but with the greater force, he enlists our natural admiration of genius against our purity; the brilliant and seductive writer bewilders us by the natural means of illumination; in our passage across the "sea of troubles" that make life, we are led astray by the stars; the natural refreshment of the human spirit is turned into mortality; in our travel across the Great Desert the wells are poisoned. If Lewis's literary oblivion is looked on as a trivial punishment, let it be remembered that authorship was his ambition, that it was the labour of his life, and that his daily labour issued in his daily discomfiture. The man knows little of human morbidness, who will not believe that the deadliest blow might be given on this naked and diseased sensibility. He has now passed away, and it must be his happiest fate to be forgotten.[98]

Lewis had never expressed, as Southey did of himself, the conviction that his memory would smell sweet; but he could have hoped for a memory less noisome than this. The account was copied by the *Weekly Dispatch* and Galignani's Paris *Messenger*. Sir Henry Lushington was shocked and exasperated when he came upon it in the latter periodical. Sophia Shedden sent Walter Scott a copy of the article together with a reply which had been published and urged him to defend her brother's reputation: "It will be a great pleasure to all the family, if you will kindly fulfill your original intention, of inserting some little memorial of my dear Brother in the Quarterly [R]eview. Any thing from your pen, will indeed my dear Sir, be highly valued by us all; but more especially by myself!"[99] It appears that Scott intended to say something of Lewis in an article on *Tales of the Dead,* but the review being assigned to another, his friendly intention was not fulfilled.[100] Sophia's letter continues, "I am indeed hurt at any *injustice* done to my Brother's memory! I was his favourite Sister [;] he *owned* it; not as he said 'that you are more amiable, or more sensible, or that you love me any *better* than Maria does, for you are *not* so.—But I do love you the best, because you love me more as *I like to be loved*. Your Sister loves me with reason & good sense. *You* love me with devotedness, & docility, which never waits for reason & good sense."

On July 17, 1818, Lewis' aunt Mrs. Blake answered the query of a friend:

It is indeed our poor friend Matt Lewis whose death you read of and of whom you have been kind enough to make your inquiries. . . . He has left many to regret his oddities among which I am sure I ever shall remain altho' during the last Twelvemonth we were not the best friends but I know full well how to attribute all his faults. Peace be to his ashes!—

Matthew has died very rich. He has provided very liberally for his beloved Mother who mourns his loss beyond the expression of words. She really does suffer as one wou'd imagin, she who loved a Son as Mother never loved more fondly, wou'd do.—To his two Sisters he leaves his Estates & personal Property.[101]

Perhaps no final estimate is needed, but years after his friend's death Lord Holland supplied one which few of Lewis' acquaintances would have disputed:

He had a clear and even a strong understanding, imagination amounting almost to genius, and indefatigable industry. As a poet he was endowed with an excellent ear and a command of elegant language. But his mind was vitiated with a mystical, though irreligious, philosophy; his taste in reading, writing, and thinking, corrupted by paradox; and his conversation disfigured by captious perverseness in controversy or sickly affectation in sentiment. His efforts at pleasantry, which were continual, were very unsuccessful. He had no talent for humour. He was sincere, affectionate, and generous; but his vanity was inordinate and more troublesome than diverting.[102]

To these qualities let us add integrity and courage. Hobhouse, who found him more fond of contradiction than any man he ever knew and called him the "completest egotist in the world," nevertheless recognized him as a man of principle and attached to truth.[103] When he stubbornly insisted upon a ghost for *The Castle Spectre* (and was right), there was not much at stake. When he repudiated his father's domestic arrangements, he lost what was left of his home and could have lost his inheritance. In Jamaica, against the advice of experienced agents, the hostility of neighboring proprietors, and the temporary discouragement of diminished crops, he persisted in humanitarian policies which were approved by a later generation. Moreover, it has not been sufficiently understood that much of what seems in him pure affectation sprang from an extremely sensitive temperament housed in a body never robust and often troublesome. "I am so constituted," he once wrote, "that I beleive, I never felt a painful sensation, which I could afterwards efface from my memory, however strongly I may have wished to do so" (F 62), and again, "In my opinion, the acuteness of pleasure in this world bears no proportion to the acuteness of pain" (F 42).

If today there is anything to be forgiven him, it is that, with very considerable natural gifts, he devoted so much of a short life to producing ephemerae. That he had such gifts can be seen in the fantastic world of *The Monk*, in the real world of the *Journal*, and in a handful of verses. His importance as an influence in the literature of his time is increasingly recognized, but one could wish that he had left us more works than he did which can be read for their own worth. Critics have been puzzled that, aside from the *Journal*, nothing else he wrote was as good as *The Monk*, completed when he was only nineteen; it almost seems that he exhausted his talent on his first attempt or somehow enjoyed beginner's luck. His unfulfilled promise as a writer becomes understandable if we suppose that his precocious and intense passion for authorship, in the period before he entered the world of society and became a public figure, was followed, after the publication of *The Monk*, by a compensating disinclination to take literary accomplishment seriously. Having achieved his boyhood objective, he lost his incentive— such enthusiasm simply could not be maintained. He continued to write, but without direction, without a goal, amusing himself in various genres, and, by happy accident, finding one at the last in which he could show himself at his best.

There is an appropriate tone of finality in the sentiments of his aunt Anna Blake, who shall have the last word:

Thus, then, closes the short career of one with whom we were ever pleased to pass an idle hour, but who for ever more is lost to us!—'Tis sad, my dear St. Aubyn, to reflect that such things are, and still more so, that it may be our own fate any one moment that ensues. God bless us all, & send that die when we may, we may die in Charity with the whole World!"[104]

# Selected Letters

# SELECTED LETTERS

Of THE following letters, the texts of those from Lewis to his mother are taken directly from the originals in the Forster Collection at the Victoria and Albert Museum and later studied in photostat. The letters appeared wholly or in part in the *Life*, but with so many alterations that a more reliable text seems desirable. For about one fourth of Lewis' letters published in the *Life*, however, that work must still be consulted.

Lewis' unpublished letter to John Plummer and the letter from Sophia Shedden, Lewis' younger sister, to Walter Scott, formerly published in part, are from photostats of the originals at the Institute of Jamaica and the National Library of Scotland respectively. The late Frank Cundall, secretary at the Institute of Jamaica, kindly brought the Plummer letter to my attention. From manuscripts in my possession I have added ten unpublished letters from Lewis to James St. Aubyn, one presumably to Sir Thomas Durrant, second Baronet, and selections from letters by Lewis' mother and by his aunt Anna Blake.

I have tried to reproduce the texts exactly, preserving the writers' misspellings and inadvertencies (unaccompanied by *sics*), but the following editorial points may be noted. Cancellations are not recorded unless they are of at least slight interest. When the writer's intention concerning capital or lower-case initials seems impossible to determine, I have followed conventional usage. Portions of text missing because of mutilation, mounting, or inking out by a later hand are supplied within square brackets. Many of these conjectural readings have the support of visible portions of the script, and all take spacing into account. Square brackets in the headings of letters, however, indicate editorial expansions of dates and addresses. Lines under superior letters and figures have been removed, and the position of date lines and signatures has been standardized. Postscripts, wherever they appear in the manuscripts, are placed after signatures. The full line ellipses in nine letters by Anna Blake and in one by Lewis' mother indicate omission of matter entirely unrelated to Lewis.

Other letters or parts of letters by Lewis, aside from the text of the present work, will be found in the following:

Robert Isaac Wilberforce and Samuel Wilberforce, eds., *The Correspondence of William Wilberforce*, ed. by his sons (London, 1840).

Lord John Russell, ed., *Memoirs, Journal and Correspondence of Thomas Moore* (London and Boston, 1853).

Alexander Allardyce, ed., *Letters from and to Charles Kirkpatrick Sharpe* (Edinburgh and London, 1888).

John Gibson Lockhart, *Memoirs of the Life of Sir Walter Scott* (Boston and New York, 1902).

A. Francis Steuart, ed., *The Diary of a Lady-in-Waiting by Lady Charlotte Bury: Being the Diary Illustrative of the Times of George the Fourth* (London and New York, 1908).

Mabell, Countess of Airlie, ed., *In Whig Society, 1775–1818* (London, 1921).

D. F. S. Scott, *Some English Correspondents of Goethe* (London, 1949).

Karl S. Guthke, "C. M. Wieland and M. G. Lewis," *Neophilologus*, XL (July 1956), 231–233; "Die Erste Nachwirkung von Herders Volksliedern in England," *Archiv für das Studium der Neueren Sprachen*, CXCIII (Apr. 1957), 273–284; "Some Unpublished Letters of M. G. Lewis," *Notes and Queries*, N.S. IV (May 1957), 217–219. With respect to the last, see also "M. G. Lewis," by "A Friend of Accuracy," *Notes and Queries*, N.S. IV (Sept. 1957), 389.

Friday April 1st 1791.

My dear Mother,

You might be certain that if I had received your letter I should have written to you before, since I knew that when you was ill, the assurance of affection would be doubly acceptable, but the stupid rascals at the Post-Office mislaid your letter, and it was some time before they could find it; however the moment I had read it, I sat down to assure you that nothing but ignorance should have prevented my writing to you; but now I have sat down, I have resolved to write you a very short letter, for I have at present so much to do (as this is the time when we are examined) that I have not a moment unemployed; I say I have *resolved* to write you a very short letter; but whether my regard for you will not oblige me to break my resolution, [I] will not answer.

You gave me pain by saying that every body had forgot you. I thought my constant attention would have exempted me at least from the accusation, and my poor Barrington has but too good a reason for not writing to you. His illness I am sorry to say continues to grow upon him, and the least exertion does him harm. This is what I am informed, for as he is not able to come to Town, and I do not find it possible to go to Chatham, it is long very long since I saw him last: indeed I am so selfish as now hardly to wish it, and for his own sake as much as my own; since to see him in pain would distress me, and my melancholy would only contribute to make him uneasy. however I write to him very frequently, though he is not permitted to answer me. I need not tell you (and yet it will give you pleasure to have it told you) that he is gratified in every wish; your letter must have given him a great deal of pleasure, for the highest satisfaction he now has is to receive letters, and I am sure therefore you will write to him again immediately.

I need not tell you how much how very much concerned I am for your illness, and it affords me a fresh obligation to my Father. I shudder to think at what would have been your situation had he refused my request. Without money, without friends, sick, in a foreign country. Oh my Mother! The remembrance of your being in pain and sorrow often clouds the pleasures I enjoy, and I hardly conceive myself justified in partaking amusements, when you perhaps may be in want of common comforts. God bless you, my dear Mother, and may you soon return to this Country, where whatever happens, you may at least have those you love, and who love you near to assist you.

Yet unless you return very soon I fear it will not be in my power to see you for some time. I shall go to Town on April the 15th, and return on the 4th; and then shall not be in London untill Christmas, as I intend passing the intermediate vacation on the continent. but however wherever I am, it will make me easier to think that you are among your Country men, and where are some who will ever be willing to assist you as much as is in their power.

I sent a letter-case to York House, Dover, as you desired me. I must be very poor indeed if I could not afford to present you with such a trifle, and beleive me I find myself and ever shall in having it in my power to show you my readiness to oblige you.

The direction to my Father's is No 9 Devonshire Place, Upper Wimpole St. I do not know whether I told you that it was a very good house, and fitted up very elegantly; the preparations for war paid entirely for the expence of it, and [as] a war[1] with Russia is expected, I hope he will make a tolerable year of it. I am sure no one deserves success more than he does.

My Sisters are perfectly well. Sophy is wonderfully pretty, but very little. She is so childish, so heedless, so inattentive, that she provokes every body; and when any body talks to her, she will cry vehemently and play with the Cat's tail all the while. She dances very prettily, has a very good ear for musick, and a charming voice. in short She may do very well if She will. Maria improves every day; She is a charming and interesting Girl. She plays really finely, and her understanding is infinitely superior to Girls of her age. She is very tall, and has a very fine figure. She has quite outgrown me, I promise to be a remarkably little personage. here have I run on to you, whilst I ought to have been crossing the Hellespont with Xerxes, or attending to the pleadings of Cicero; but when I once I begin to write to you, I never know when to stop. I will now then only assure you of the tender love and affection of

M. G. Lewis.

[1] "A war" seems a correction of "the war."

Paris, September 7th [1791]

My dear Mother,

I have this moment received your letter, about which I began to be uneasy, fearing my parcel had miscarried. I am very happy to find that the Farce[1] may perhaps be of some service to you, and I wish sincerely it was in my power to be of more. As yet however I can be of very little use to you; but be assured that whenever it is in my power, you shall be convinced that my wish has ever been to manifest to you, how great a regard and affection I entertain for you. You say "you wish you had it more in your power to shew yours for me". Ah my dear Mother, you have it in your power; you shew it every moment. Nothing can give me so much pleasure as the offering me an opportunity in which I can fulfill the first and dearest duty of humanity, and enabling me to shew how great a regard I feel for the name of Mother. Love your Son therefore, as tenderly as He loves you, and every trouble it is possible for me to take will be paid with excess. "You may perhaps serve me in the course of your life." Is it not then a service to assist me with your counsels, to help me to correct my faults, and to procure me the most sensible of pleasures in making me conscious that my existence is not entirely unprofitable to my Parent? Believe that my heart is conscious in cherishing you, that I fulfill a duty, that I procure myself a pleasure, and that I can never equal my obligations to you. As to the Farce it was at your option to cut it as you pleased. The Explication I am conscious was rather long, but I endeavoured rather to put it into three or four short speeches, than into one long one. I wished to make the character of Caroline as entertaining as I could, from the idea that if it was accepted at Drury Lane M^rs Jordan might think it worth accepting: All the story therefore about the Governess was purposely introduced to enliven the character of Caroline, though the story was not necessary. However I read it over but once, and I dare say you have altered it for the better. I trust as soon as you have offered it, you will not delay letting me know what success you have had. As to the Novel[2] I have nearly written the 2 first volumes; for the 1^st I managed cleverly about, and lost: I was consequently obliged to write it over again. I shall take care to finish it before I leave France, but if you choose to begin it immediately, I will send you the first Volume by the next post. I think the Faulcon in itself very interesting, and its simplicity is the greatest beauty. It is easy to keep the canvass and plan of the scenes, and write the dialogue over again, only preserving the points already written of which there are several worth keeping. In the style in which it is written, it will not do for more than one act. the simplicity will not have any charms after that period, and if you mean to extend it, you must write it in a new style, and make it broad Farce; which in my opinion will destroy the beauty and simplicity of the subject. If however you persist in your first idea of lengthening it, I have found a play which may assist you. It is called "Le Faucon, et les Oyes de Boccace." You may perhaps know the Story of Father Philip's Geese. I will however just give you an idea of the play I speak of. Frederic despairing to make Clêtie love him, leaves the capital, and assumes the habit of an Hermit whose cave he takes possession of, together with the Servant who has been brought up by the Hermit without ever having heard the name of Woman. In this situation [, Clêtie's carriage breaks down][3] in the wood[.] She is searching for Frederic to demand the Faulcon which He has carried off with him, but his retreat being unknown to everybody, She is returning home without the Bird. Guillaume who sees the Women arrive, enquires of his Master who they are. He tells him that they are Geese, but the most savage creatures that can be imagined: notwithstanding which Guillaume has a great desire to catch one of these Geese, and tame it. He meets a young Shepherdess who undeceives him, and there are some of their situations which are amusing enough. Clitie in the mean while hears talk of a Woman-Hater, and discovers him to be her Lover, by the Cottager who has received her, vaunting the agility of the Faulcon. The rest of the plan is the same, and Guillaume is united to Sylvia. I prefer the plan of the one I sent to you, but if you think it necessary to make it broader farce, the plan of Guillaume (Harlequin in the other play) & Sylvia will afford you an opportunity of introducing it. This however there is no need to be in an hurry about, & when I return I can shew you the other play if you are resolved against the first. I will at any rate enclose the songs which I have written for it, but luckily they are so very commodiously written that (like Bayes's verses which served for prologue or Epilogue, Tragedy or Comedy, with equal merit) my songs will do for either one play, or the other. If you adopt the other plan [,] It is necessary to write more songs since you had better make it a Comic Opera in 2 Acts; but I think the first plan will not only give you less trouble, but is much the prettiest. Let me hear from you very soon, to say whether you wish me to send you the beginning of the Novel, & what you think of the verses. Observe that I have not written them with regard to the poetry, but merely to give an opportunity to the Musician to write pretty Music upon them. My Sisters are well; My Father writes me word that Barrington fancies himself better from his journey to Margate, but that *He* perceives no amendment. You speak of *rings*; I am so afraid that Barry's desire to have something to hang to his watch should have escaped your sight, that I repeat it. Tell me seriously did the Farce make you laugh, did it interest you the first time you read it? I need not repeat to you my entreaties never to let the least hint drop to any body (particularly to any of my Uncles) that I had the least idea of writing any thing belonging to the Theatre.

Beleive me, my dear Mother,
Your most affectionate Son,
M G Lewis

I shall endeavour to send this by the Courier, as I did the last, by which means I suppose you got it free; at any rate I have written with a crow quill that it might take up the less room. Write to me by the next post I entreat you. Adieu, my dear Mother.

1 Probably *The Epistolary Intrigue.*

2 Probably *The Effusions of Sensibility.*

3 A line of the MS is covered by mounting. The reading in brackets is from the *Life* (I, 55).

Oxford. Thursday the 8th. [March 8, 1792][1]
I should have written to you before my dear Mother but I have been very unwell for this last fortnight and still am obliged to take medicines three times a day However I am considerably better and doubt not but in a little time I shall be perfectly well. As my head-ache however is still painful to me you will excuse my writing you a very concise letter though indeed I generally begin with that resolution and find myself at the end of my paper before I am aware to what a length I am arrived. It is very provoking that the Farce should be returned and I do not understand Lewis's reason.[2] However He only said it could not be brought out this season Why not ask whether he will accept it for the next unless indeed you chuse to try Colman's. I shall be in Town I beleive about the 25th or 26th but in-

tend going to Chatham in Passion Week I shall then return and stay a fortnight and if (as you intended) you take a lodging shall be with you as much as I possibly can but as I am ordered for my health to ride every day that will necessarily take up some part of my mornings every moment however that I can command I shall be happy to pass with you. I am finishing Felix as you desired and will bring it and the Music to Town with me I read over what I had translated and I began to fancy it not uninteresting You will judge of it however whether it will do when I see you in Town but I must beg you to transcribe it for that I find the most troublesome part of the business and besides I write an hand which is not legible to vulgar comprehension. I shall also bring two or three other things for you to try your fortune with and if they do not produce money I am sure they will find amusement for *you* who will be partial to every thing I either write or do. I will not specify what are the contents of my budget till I see you when I hope to read them to you myself, which I suppose will give you double satisfaction. Sophia has got the hooping cough and Maria is consequently expected to catch it. Barrington is tolerably.

Beleive me my dear Mother
your most affectionate Son
M G. Lewis

I forgot to say that concerning the Story you told me I do not see well how a dead body can be brought upon the Stage besides which it does not merely consist in writing an Opera which will succeed when acted but the difficulty lies in getting it acted I know at least twenty French Operas which if translated would undoubtedly succeed but after Kemble's refusing Blue Beard the most interesting production of that kind I quite despair. There is an Opera called Le Souterrein where a Woman is hid in a cavern in her jealous Husband's house and afterwards by accident her Child is shut up there also without food and are not released till they are perishing with hunger. the situations of the characters the Tragic of the Principal Characters the Gaiety of the under pa[rts,] and romantic turn of the Story make it one of the prettiest and most affecting things I ever saw but I shall not throw away any more time till I have got one of the things I have already finished upon the Stage. Les Victimes Cloitrees of which I spoke to you is another which would undoubtedly succeed. As I have written so much after my signature you may perhaps have forgotten that this comes from

Your affectionate,
M [. G. Lewis]

1 Between October 1791 and March 1792, Thursday fell on the 8th only in December 1791 and March 1792. The reference to Passion Week (March 25–31 in 1792) indicates March.

2 The farce is probably *The Epistolary Intrigue*. The actor William Thomas Lewis (1748?–1811) was deputy-manager of Covent Garden Theatre.

Ch: Ch: Sunday 25th [Oxford, March 25, 1792]

My dear Mother,

I have the pleasure of informing you that on my arrival in Town my Father has promised to give me the twenty pounds which you desired for as He gives me no settled allowance I am obliged to apply to him for any thing extraordinary[,] not receiving above a few guineas from my Tutor at a time which would be inadequate to furnishing you with any sum which you might want. The little presents I have occasionally made you have been merely what I have either spared from my pocket money or by fortunate success at play (which however I use but seldom) and have been enabled to dispose of in the manner which was most agreable to me. None can be more agreable than that of giving you satisfaction and supplying you with conveniences which you may happen to want but had I a fixed income I should be happy to be considered merely as your Banker and would sacrifice to you not only what might be wanted for pleasure but what would be absolutely necessary but I own being obliged to apply so frequently to my Father is very painful to me It is always a disagreable and humiliating task to ask for money but it is much more so when one is conscious of the Person to whom we apply having been most liberal and generous. That my Father has always been so I have ever heard you acknowledge and if you accuse me of being more partial [to] my Father than to you beleive me one of his first qualities in my eyes is the readiness with which He grants my requests and [b]y that means puts it in my power to show my affec- tion towards you. This was the case with regard to my present demand but [I] was so sensible of my encroaching upon his bounty and that [p]erhaps it might be necessary for me to do so again shortly that I entreated him to let me have a fixed allowance and that then I should be enabled to assist you without applying to him [a]nd if I was too extravagant my own necessity would give me the punishment I deserved by depriving me of luxuries and obliging me to purchase the pleasure I experienced in releiving your wants by sacrificing gratifications which might be dispensed with. He refused my request and I inclose you his [a]nswer that you may see at the same time his readiness to [ob]lige me and kindness towards me in every thing and at the [s]ame time how decidedly every body is of the same opinion [u]pon a point which I will not mention for to that it is [I] am clear that He alludes. So much for this subject with [w]hich I shall have done when I have told you how much pleasure I promise myself in seeing you My intention is to come to Town on Tuesday go to Chatham on Sunday [a]nd return that day week when I shall remain a fort-night in Town. As to the Farce do as you think best about it but I shall bring Felix to Town with me and perhaps it might be as well (if you approve [of it) when] you send it to Lewis to mention a word about it in the sam[e] note. I am more anxious than ever to get something upon the Stage for you since I shall receive a double satisfaction in thinking your satisfaction and ease was the effect of my industry for in a Translation I cannot call it abilities. Suppose you were to ask Lewis what line of dramatic writing would be most acceptable. At any rate however I have begun something which I hope and am inde[ed] certain will here-after produce you a little money though it will be some time before it is compleated from the length of it and the frequent interruption and necessity of concealment I am obliged to use in writing it. It is a Roma[nce] in the style of the Castle of Otranto but though I have been ever since my return from Paris (when I first thought I might be of service to you by writing) employed about it from the above-mentioned causes I have not yet quite finished the first volume. I hope however to get it done time enough to read it to you during my stay in Town[.] I have just read the Excursion[1] and could not help fancying it was just the kind of Book you would have writte[n,] the style was so like your common language. I like it much in some parts but one struck me particularly a[s] a most excellent stroke of Nature It is the sanguin[e] account which Maria writes to her Sister of her havi[ng] past an Evening in the very *best* company with the most amiable and worthy people &c. It is so na[tu]ral for a young ardent mind just entering the world to paint every thing in the most vivid and brilliant colours. I liked the Book as to the rest of it merely I beleive from those few sentences. I have had no return of my headaches & thank you for your kind solicitude about them. Perhaps though you do not take a lodging you will be able to see me before my going to Chatham Why not at the place where Miss Poulter is when She is in Town I should think she might find out some place among her acquaintance. This however you will settle and as I beleive you are as anxious to see me as I am to see you I am sure you will take the earliest opportunity of doing so.

Bele[i]ve me my dear Mother
Your most affectionate Son
M. G. Lewis

[1] A novel by Mrs. Frances (Moore) Brooke (1724–1789), published 1777.

London. Wednesday 28th [March 28, 1792]

The date of this letter my dear Mother will inform you that I am safely lodged in Town for which peice of news you may perhaps have been a little anxious. On my arrival I found a blank sheet of paper from my Father enclosing the twenty pounds I had requested of him and I wish to know whether I shall send to you by the same means that you receive this or what other you prefer. When I had written my last to you I recollected that I had burnt the letter from my Father which I wished you to see but I remember the particular expressions which struck me were these. The question is not whether you shall deny yourself pleasures to give satisfaction to others but whether you shall continue to supply wants which perhaps are not necessary to a person to whom I have already been very liberal. If you continue to be found an easy exchequer there will be no income I can allow you will be sufficient to satisfy their avidity who are imposing upon your Mother. As to what you say about my calling myself your Nephew do about it as you think proper. I remember once you desired me when in company to speak of my Father as my Uncle and you may wish me to call myself your Nephew for the same reason at present but for my own part it is immaterial to me. When I do not say that I have a Mother living I do it to give the shortest answer and save myself from an explanation which must be very unpleasant to me. You will therefore do in this case just as is most agreable to yourself. I am not likely to get you lodgings as the parts of the Town where I go are not those in which it is probable for me to find that kind of thing but if accident should bring it in my way I'll let you know. I am in a great hurry as you will perhaps perceive by the rambling Stile I have used. Adieu my dear Mother I am very anxious to see you and till then remain

your most affectionate Son
M. G. Lewis.

Weimar. 30th July. [1792]

As I know my dear Mother, you must be anxious to hear that I have escaped all sorts of perils and dangers, both by land and by water, women labouring with Child, all sick Persons, and young Children, I take the very earliest opportunity of letting you be ascertained that I arrived safe at Weimar three days ago.[1] I should have written to you on the moment that I arrived, had it not then been too late for the Post, as I know your affection for me must have made you anxious to receive the assurance of my being safe. I had a very disagreable journey, being very sea-sick in crossing from Harwich to Helvoet; and the Roads were so bad, the Postillions so stupid, and the time I was obliged to wait at the Post for Horses so long, that at last I began to be quite out of patience, and to despair of ever arriving at the place of my destination. I am now knocking my brains against German as hard as ever I can: I take a lesson every morning; and as I apply very seriously, am flattered with the promises that I shall soon speak very fluently in my throat, and that I already distort my mouth with extremely tolerable facility. The place is at present rather dull, most of the people who compose the society being gone to different places, some to their Country Houses, and others being with the Duke and his army at Coblentz. However [I] am not sorry for this; since as the common conversation of the Town is German, I wish before I enter the routine, to know a little what people say when they speak to me; which you will acknowledge to be a very reasonable desire. The few people who are still here are however extremely polite, and I doubt not when I know a little of the language, I shall find the place extremely agreable. Among other people to whom I have been introduced, are the Sister[2] of Schroeter, the Composer, and Mr de Goethe, the celebrated author of Werter: so that you must not be [s]urprized if I should shoot myself one of these fine Mornings. As to my own Nonsense, I write, and write, and yet do not find I have got a bit further in my original plan than I was when I saw you last. I have got hold of an infernal dying Man who plagues my very heart out; He has talked for half a volume already, seems likely to talk for half a volume more, and I cannot manage to kill him out of the way for the life of me.—I have had no news of Maria since I left England, but She was infinitely better when I left her. (perhaps that might have done her good.)—I may safely beg you to "honour me by laying your commands on me"; since I do not conceive it possible for you to have any to lay; and indeed I should as soon expect you to lay eggs: But you will beleive me when I tell you, could I find any opportunity to do anything which would give you satisfaction, I would offer my services as readily as I do, when I can find none. Let me hear from you soon, and tell me what you have done about the Farce, the Comedy,[3] &c.

> Beleive me, my dear Mother,
> your most affectionate Son,
> M. G. Lewis.

Not being certain of the number of your Lodging I am obliged to put the Mistress's name upon it to avoid mistakes but I shall be obliged to you to mention what it is in your answer

[1] The *Life* (I, 70) tones down this frivolous application of the Litany by omitting "women . . . Children."

[2] Corona Elizabeth Wilhelmina Schröter (1751–1802).

[3] Probably *The Epistolary Intrigue* and *The East Indian*.

Sept$^r$ 17$^{th}$ [Weimar, 1792]

I began to be extremely uneasy about my not hearing from you, my dear Mother, and was upon the point of writing again, when I received your letter. I suppose you waited for M$^{rs}$ Jordan's answer; but I was anxious to know that you had received my letter, and that you was still in good health. I am glad to be assured of this, and I hope you will in future write to me more frequently. You see I answer your letters the moment I receive them; and beleive me nothing can give me more sincere pleasure than to know you are happy and comfortable, and have met with some fresh satisfaction. I felt this pleasure from your last, which informed me of your reconciliation with your Brother Robert; upon which I congratulate you, and hope it will be productive of many good consequences; it cannot be of more, than I desire.—M$^{rs}$ Jordan's letter gives me great satisfaction, but how, my good Lady, did you manage to read it? for the seal was unbroken. Perhaps you have a secret for lifting wax, have learnt to play with the cups and balls, and have made no inconsiderable proficiency in the intricacies of Legerdemain.—I expect no small pleasure on my return to England, from the exhibition of all your tricks and contrivances. As to the Music for the Play, I have managed most awkwardly about it. I intended to have got it, whilst in London; but poor Maria was so ill, that I forgot every thing. The consequence is, I am now obliged to send to her for the two airs with some others, as if for a Lady in Germany; they must first come to Weimar, and then return to You; So that it will be at least a month before Mrs Jordan will receive them. I have, therefore, written to her to excuse this delay, and I inclose you the letter unsealed, that you may read it.—I think you had better send it to her by the Penny Post, as you now know how to direct to her; and it will be as well to send now and then [to] Ibbotson's Hotel, to know if any letter has been left there [b]y her.—Did you observe her letter was sealed (and probably [d]irected) by the Prince? It is the most cruel, unjust, barbarous, [s]avage, and inhuman proceeding, I ever was a witness to, the telling me you have "done something" with the Farce, and not [e]xplaining what; I can conceive "doing something" with it, to be [n]othing but putting it into the Fire; but as you have "done [s]omething" likewise with your own work, that cannot be the case. I hope you will in future condescend to be more intelligible. [I] know it is extremely vulgar, but yet, I must say, I think it more agreable—I receive nothing but the most delightful accounts about my brother; Maria is quite recovered, and Sophia (as I am told) a very little tiny bit mended. I will try to "boil yo[u]r egg for you;" but I will not take "my bible oath upon Messalina's poems," (as Congreve makes the Chamber-maid say) that it will be in my power to execute your commission First, because the Music which I hear (nowhere except at Court) is almost entirely instrumental of Haydn & Pleyel, which can be got better in England than here;—Secondly, because the little vocal Music I hear, is entirely from the Italian operas. However the Comedie will begin in October, and then perhaps I shall have an opportunity of hearing some German Airs. I have endeavoured to execute the same commission for Maria, but have not as yet procured a single [s]ong. I suspect the air you mean, to be one by Pleyel, sold in London under the Title "Of Lady Isabell's Lamentation;" [a]nd begins, "Sleep, poor Babe, ill-fated Boy." It is the sweetest [a]ir at present existing in the "varsal world!"—Les Sages entendent a demi-mot, mais il faut des mots entieres pour [le] demi-Sage. Write to me soon[,] I beg you. I am in a great hurry, But still I must tell you that my situation is very pleasant here. Nothing can be more polite than the people belonging to the Court; the two Duchesses are extremely affable, and condescending; and we have nothing but Balls, Suppers[,] and Concerts. Thank God! I weary myself to death; but it is always some comfort to think, I am wearied with the best Company; and I really beleive the fault is in myself, and not in other people.—I have nearly finished my second volu[me] and have written over half the first; But I found such faults upon faults, that I have actually almost made it all ov[er again] but I find the [st]yle grows better as I get farther on[.] I wis[h] much to know what you have done with your Book. Have yo[u] printed it at your own expence? or what?

> Beleive me ever,
> your most affectionate Son,
> M. G. Lewis

*Matthew G. Lewis by Henry William Pickersgill.*
*National Portrait Gallery.*

The Albany. April 22.
1815

Dear S.ʳ Aubyn,

My Sister tells me, that the other night you made great complaints of me: I have been, and am likely to be, so rarely in Town, except for a single night that I have never been lucky enough to be at home when you called; but I beg you to observe, that I have been _twice_ this year to Lincoln's, but to look for you; once indeed I had no card; but the second time I left one, though I suppose, that by some accident you did not see it — I hope, this will exculpate me fully from the charge of intentional neglect, which I assure you, I do not deserve.

Yours truly

M G Lewis

Do you usually write your letters without mentioning time, place, or even putting a signature? It is the fashion, I suppose.

Dec$^r$ 24$^{th}$ Weimar. 1792.

My dear Mother,

You may possibly be aware, that there are certain means of arranging certain words in a certain way, so as to leave the Reader perfectly uncertain as to the sense intended to be conveyed by them; and in one of the phrases of your last Letter you have succeeded most happily in the clairobscur style of writing. You tell me you "are surprized at not having received the Songs in all this Time"; by which I am left perfectly at a loss to discover whether you have, or have not received my letter (inclosing one for M$^{rs}$ J.) giving an account of the causes, which made it probable that you would not receive them for a considerable period. You may possibly, however, mean by "all this time," the time which has elapsed since your receiving the letter, which I have just mentioned; But I beg you to write to me immediately upon the receipt of this, and let me know whether you are now actually in possession of the Songs, which have now been full a month upon the road to you. It is very possible, that you are not; for as I have a knack at *losing* things as well as other people (N:B:) a slight hint to a certain Person, who shall be nameless) I entirely lost all recollection of the number belonging to your Lodging in Shepherd St. I therefore was obliged to direct it at a venture to No 14, nearly opposite Bond St, and I put upon the cover in case the Person should not be found, that the Letter must be sent back to me. It is therefore possible, that it has not reached you; I hope however, that it has, and at all events, I beg you to send to the foreign Post Office immediately upon the receipt of this, and enquire whether such a letter has not been left there for you. I hope you will let me hear from you in answer to this with all possible expedition, as till then I shall be not a little uneasy. I am very happy to find, that your situation is comfortable, and likely to be more so: But I cannot however say that I am very happy to hear, that your good spirits have altered your looks: for in that case perhaps when we meet again, your features may be quite unknown to me, and we may stare at one another, like the Old Woman in the print, who cries out "Oh? Gemini! is this my Daughter Anne?" I trust however that your countenance will not be so very much altered, as to make you quite irrecognisible; and that I shall find you on my return to England, at least with the same heart, and the same affection for me. I beleive in all probability I shall not return to England till March or April: But my Father saying He did not wish me to hurry home in case of a War breaking out, I have written to him, to beg that in such a case He would permit me to return to England immediately. In fact though I am at present perfectly well satisfied with my situation, I should not like to be shut up in Germany, the Lord above only knows how long; and more especially should I be uneasy, in the present disposition of the English Populace, at being at so great a distance from my Family. I trust there is nothing to apprehend; but still when one is so far off, every trifling accident becomes a serious and alarming affair. I continue to be well enough contented with this Town. There are some things to be sure which are not quite so elegant and well ordered as in England; for instance the Knives and Forks are never changed, even at the Duke's table, and the Ladies hawk and spit about the rooms, in a manner the most disgusting: but as the Duchesses are very affable, and everybody is extremely obliging, I put up with every thing else, and upon the whole amuse myself tolerably well. I have also made a little excursion, since I wrote to you last, to Berlin. I staid there but a very few days, and as I arrived there without having any acquaintances, at first I found the societies into which I entered extremely wearisome and insipid: I beleive however had I staid a little longer I should have been well enough satisfied with my stay there, for I began to know the greatest part of the Persons I met, and nothing could be more polite and attentive than our Envoy there, Sir Morton Eden, was to me. Though a great part of the Court was in the country, and though the King, the Princes his Sons, and many others were at the army, I was perfectly astonished at the crouds of Princes, and Princesses, Dukes, and Duchesses, which were poured upon me from every quarter. It put me in mind of Foote's observation upon France, that "every mangey Dog He met, was either Duke, or Marquis." I was at some[1] Court or other to Supper every night, that I passed in Berlin; and I verily beleive it would be possible to stay a year in that Town, and sup with a new Highness at least six days out of every seven. Then there are crouds of Excellences; for observe, that not only all Ambassadors, Generals, &c bear that title, but also the Wives, Daughters, Aunts, and Grandmothers of such Generals, and Ambassadors: so that I reckon upon the whole, there is to be found more *soi-disa[nt]* excellence in Berlin, than any other Town upon the face of the [earth. I] have moved heaven and earth in order to make a little collection of Songs for you, and I have already near a dozen, and have hopes of more. It is possible however that you may not like them; but you will at least like my readiness to obey your wishes. I have translated the German words into English, so that may possibly appear in your eyes as a recommendation; and there is at least a very beautiful Overture from an Opera of Mozar[t's,] which I think cannot fail to please you. I heard from my Father this morning, and He informed me, both my Sisters and Barry are in perfect good health. Adieu; Write to me as soon as it is possible, and beleive me, my dear Mother,

Your most affectionate Son,

M. G. Lewis.

[1] "Some" may be "one," as in the *Life* (I, 81).

Weimar. Feb^y 8^th 1793

My dear Mother,

I have this moment received yours of the 17^th of Jan^y and hasten to reply to it but I must first observe that it was highly necessary to mention how I should direct to you in Berkeley Square as you had not given me the slightest informa[tion] in your former Letters. I consequently directed my last to No[.] 11 Shepherd St. where you will most probably find it by sending thither in case you should not already have receive[d] it. As to the profits of the Play[1] I confess I never entertained so high an idea of them as you appear to expect them to tur[n] out and consequently never thought about the matter. The idea never entered into my head that M^rs Jordan instead o[f] giving it for her Benefit would offer it to the Manager[s] and have it acted upon her own account. In the first case[,] I supposed that when She had made use of it She would return the Copy to me and then the Managers would either app[ly] for it to me or would not apply as they thought the play promised to turn out. In that case the Profits evidently belonged to myself. As however She has not thought proper to adopt this plan She has the Game in her own hands an[d] it is not possible for me to take any active part in the matter. The best way for us is to wait patiently and se[e] how it will all turn out. There are a number of chances in our favour. It is possible, that She has only taken the compliment to herself without any idea of appropriating the profits. That She is pleased with the *air* of *patronizing*, and having brought it upon the stage as the character was written expressly in reference to her talents will give up every thing else to the Author. She brought out a farce last year, but it was for her benefit and it was never acted afterwards. Should on the contrary my Play be brought out as a simple Comedy and not as a piece merely composed to serve for a Benefit Night, it seems to me to be of good augury as to the Managers opinion of it. At the worst Should She take it entirely to herself I should think the right of printing would undoubtedly belong to me. By right, I mean not the positive right of the law of England, but what the law of politeness and open-disinterestedness dictates and which is the only one to be followed here. It is possible also that She may insist upon sharing the emoluments and though I should of course at first reject such an offer by a good deal of pressing I *might* be *prevailed* upon to accept it. Setting money out of the case It certainly will give the play a much better prospect of success if it is represented as other new plays instead of a Benefit for People are rather prepossessed against Benefit-Plays. Another reason is that many Actresses would then play in it who from pique against M^rs Jordan.[2] Besides it's being the first appearance of this favourite Actress will give the play a good deal of éclat and not a little prepossess the audience in favour of it. This therefore is my decided opinion. As M^rs Jordan is reported to be not without generosity to let her act just as She pleases and gaurd a profound silence on the matter and even should She think herself entitled to take no notice of any claim of the Author's upon the profits, I shall willingly abandon to her my first play as a reward for the trouble She has taken in bringing it out and I shall gain the great point of insuring the performance of a second play. You did not deceive yourself my dear Mother when you supposed I intended the profits of the Play (if any profits there should be) to be applied to your use. I trust however that your "hopes will not be baulked" should I not obtain a farthing from the "East Indian." I trust I have a much surer prospect of making you a little present than depends upon the humour of a Gallery. The Volu[me] of Poems of which I spoke to you in my last lett[er is almost]³ compleated and by July I tru[st I shall have it written] out fair and in a fit manner to [publish. I have no] doubt of selling it for Walter at Charing [Cross (even though] We have little prospect of the Book's success) [has promised to] give me a good price for it out of gratitude to [my Father, to] whom He is indebted for the liberty of printing . . . a liberty which you know without doubt is extremely [valuable.] I shall have no scruple of putting my name in the Title Page[,] for my Father insists upon my reciting verses of my own composition at the Oxford encenia and I may as well print th[em] as speak them. This Volume will consist partly of originals p[ar]tly of Translations most of which are admired Poems in German and my translations of them have been applauded by the Authors themselves. which is no slight proof of their being tolerable. Whatever this work produces you may reckon upon every farthing of it as your own. If the "East Indian" succeeds I shall set out arranging "Adelaide" for rep[resen]tat[ion.] The opera of "Felix" would easily be brought out upon the score of my first Play In short I have a number of Irons in the fire and I think some of them must answer my purpose. I should not be averse myself to getting a little money which I might throw away according to my own will and pleasure. Among other things I have a great wish to have Maria's picture well-drawn and also to give [her] my own. There are several other things which would please me and [whic]h my conscience will not permit to employ my Father's money in obtaining. But whatever happens I am resolved to consider the first of my productions which succeeds as *your* property and you may rest assured my dear Mother I shall always remember that you have a right to be served before myself. Be careful I beg that nobody finds out I am the Author of this Comedy. I would not have it known at present for any thing upon earth

Beleive me your<br>Most affectionate Son<br>M. G. Lewis.

¹ *The East Indian.*

² For "who from pique against Mrs. Jordan would otherwise not do so."

³ Ten lines are mutilated in the MS. The conjectural readings at least indicate the approximate space the missing words occupied. The lost portion between "printing" and "a liberty" could have held some fifteen letters.

Ch: Ch: Monday [May] 20th 1793.[1]

My dear Mother,

I now send you the verses which I mentioned to you in a former letter, and which I wish you could get put into the papers. I should n[ot] even scruple paying a guinea and an half but not more if the Editor will not put them in for nothing. I should prefer "the True Briton" and if you succeed in getting them inserted Do not fail to let me know in what days paper as all the papers I read in ordinary are "the Morning Herald" The St[ar] and the Sun none of which (as I before mentioned to you) would answer my purpose. It is not decided whether I shall go abroad this summer or not[.] Much will depend upon who is to fill the Embassy which Lord Auckland ha[s] quitted or is on the point of quitting at the Hague. I once thought of Brussells but Lord Elgin is by all accounts a cold unpleasant Man and by no means likely to make the place agreable to me. Upon the whole I am rather incli[ned] to believe that I shall pass my three months vacation in England. My Father talks of taking a Hunting Box at Barnet or Hogsden or Ne[w]ington Butts or some such place where He can place my Sisters during their vacation and whip down to see them on Saturday and Sunday but this plan is much too quiet and dull for me and I rather think I sha[ll] beg leave to cut it come what come may. Have you seen this new Com[edy] of "How to grow rich?" It has a mighty pretty title at least. I should lik[e] to know what Mrs J. means to do about the East Indian. You shou[ld] positively go to see the new Comic Opera of "I Zingari in Fiera". The Music (which I heard in Germany) is most beautiful and Storace has a Character which must suit her to a T. You should really indulge yourself in this amusement for it is well worth your money and I should think after your illness hearing such a quantity of delightful Music would go a great way to your recovery.

My Father has just sent me[2] two letters of Maria's written in Italian and very prettily I assure you[.] I think after all it will be very hard if She does not turn out very accomplished. Adieu my dear Mother You write to me always very concisely and never half frequently enough. However all I can do is to tell you what satisfaction I receive from your letters when they do arrive and that to get them oftener would give great pleas[ure] to your affectionate Son

M. G. Lewis

[T]he Verses are on the other si[de]


To C. J. F—Esqr
on the mention made of the Empress of Russia in the House of Commons
by Mr Sheridan on Thursday April the 25th


Well may the angry Edmund roar
"The age of Chivalry's no more,"
Since Sheridan's detected
In railing at that royal Dame,

Of warlike and of amorous fame,
Till late by Whigs respected.

Would none defend the Spoiler's cause,
And give her lawless deeds applause?
Didst thou, too, F— abuse her?
Could not thy artful brain produce,
To serve thy Friend, some lame excuse
And baffle her Accuser?

How when this news of strange import
Shall reach thy once-loved Russian Court,
Will anger shake the Palace?
Inflamed with rage, imperial Kate
Shall doom thy bust to high estate,
And fix it on a gallows.

Oh! were it not thy head of stone,
But that black mass of flesh and bone,
Which grows between thy shoulders,
That perched on Temple Bar, might fright,
And yet the gazing Mob delight,
What joy for the Beholders!

I know you long have strove to gain
A Patriot's name, but strove in vain;
From me then take a favour:
To gain that name I'll teach you how,
For hang yourself, and we'll allow
A Patriot's, your behaviour.

By throttling show your public zeal;
Your death shall prove your country's weal,
And end all strife and wrangling;
Parties shall join the deed to praise,
And national subscriptions raise
A gibbet for thy dangling.

Then Englishmen shall say, who view
Your patriot legs in air, to you
Their gratitude expressing;
"Though various crimes his annalls blot,
"Now be those various crimes forgot,
"His death's so great a blessing."

Thus shall They say; Then haste to swing
To praise upon the hempen string;
And famed in British Story,
England shall long retain your name,
Your faults and life esteemed its shame,
Your parts and death its glory.


But to compleat Britannia's feast,
Your Gibbet must (a patriot Beast)
Consent to carry double,
That you before, and Dick behind,
At once the road to Hell my find,
And save Jack Ketch the trouble.

The Ghost of Col: Titus.

1 Postmarked May 22.

2 "My . . . me," inked out by a later hand, is legible, though "Father" is not
certain. The *Life* (I, 96) reads "I have received two letters of Maria's. . . ."


Bothwell Castle. Sunday 12th [December? 1793]1

My dear Mother,

I shall just write a few lines to you to thank you for your letter, and
inform you of my future motions. I leave this place on Friday next, shall
sleep that night at Dalkeith a seat of the Duke of Buccleugh's, and then
proceed to London as soon as possible. I do not however expect to reach
*the Village* till the evening of the sixth day from my quitting Bothwell;
as a little Boy of Lord Douglas's is to make a third in the Chaise with
Charles and myself, and consequently, the fear of making him ill, will
necessitate us to make our day's journey conclude at a much earlier hour,
than would be the case, were we left to our own guidance. I shall probably
pass a few days in Town, and a few days more with my Aunts Brownrigg and
Whitelocke. What then becomes of me is not certain; Lord Valentia has
sent me an invitation to join his Christmass party at Arley; But I do not
think my Father wishes me to accept it. His Lordship is mad, that there
is very little [d]ou[bt] of, but I think him rather the more entertaining for
that circumstance. I must not omit telling you of a curious blunder, which
I made in reading his letter. Being fully persuaded of his delirium, and
finding that He wrote a very bad hand, I gravely read instead of "will
you join my Christmas party at Arley," "will you join my Curst mad party
at Arley." Nothing is as yet settled [a]bout my going abroad, and that event
will certainly not take place till after Easter. I have been passing my time
very agreably in Scotland; I like every individual of the family in which I
am living. Lady Douglas in particular is the most sensible and entertaining
Woman, that I almost ever met with. I have been no where else, except

for one week to Wood-Hall; during which time the Duke of Argyle's family arrived there on the way to Town, and passed a couple of days, which of course enlivened the society not a little. However, in spite [o]f all this amusement, I have not been totally idle. I have translated part of the German Tragedy, which you have heard me extoll so highly, and have already made some progress in the fourth Act.[2] So that I have some hopes of being able to finish it. I am sure you will like it, for both the Characters, incidents, and style of the whole play seems exactly adapted to your Taste. Barri[ngton I a]m informed is gone to M[r. Bucknell']s: I shall inclose this letter to him for two reasons. First, because I have burnt your letter, and forgot the name of the particular Street in which Miss Ingall lives; and secondly, because by that means you will have only to pay for the postage from Oxfordshire instead of that from Scotland, which becomes somewhat heavy. As you have taken up an oeconomical plan, I must not be the first to make your exertions fruitless.—Your next letter will probably find me in London. Let me know whether you are likely to be there; I dare not flatter myself with the hopes of finding that you make it your abode at present. My Father in his last tells me, that "He has som[e] idea of *ruining* me by giving me an annual allowance. I confess, this step will be by no means disagreable to me, though I should then not be able to spend half the money, that I do at present. However, I should at least know m[y] own expences, and for your sake I wish very much that my Father may execute his threat. I should have an opportunity of assisting you in any little exigency; and I hope you would make no scruple of applying to me, as our interests should ever be considered, like the French Republ[ic,] to be one and indivisible. I might then too take some cred[it] to myself, if by any self-denial I enabled myself to procure you any trifling convenience or pleasure. At present, I get money so easily and in such plenty, that I can derive no merit from assisting you[,] since I must be conscious, that I do it with my Father's money, not my own. Write to me soon, and believe me your most affectionate Son,

M. G. Lewis.

[1] The year can be only 1793; the reference to a Christmas party suggests December. Lewis' date must be in error, for in 1793 Sunday fell on the twelfth only in May.

[2] Schiller's *Kabale und Liebe*, which Lewis translated as *The Minister*.

Oxford, Wednesday [late 1793?]

My dear Mother

I have the pleasure of acquainting you that my Father has granted your request[.] As it shews how unjustly you have accused him of having altered his opinion with regard to you I shall transcribe that part of his letter which relates to you. "What you desire in your last is reasonable and proper for you to ask. The mode of changing the payments is the only

difficulty I wish your Uncle William would undertake it I would regularly
pay the money in advance or otherwise into his Banker's hand. The only
other Person who occurs to me is M^r Trotter but any explanation from me
to him would be unpleasant In short I am ready to do it in any proper
mode but desirous of having that mode settled without my personal interference M^r Bishopp I understand is in a very dangerous state of health
but illness is not an excuse for incivility. I suppose He wishes to be rid of a
thankless office attended with trouble. I must observe that whatever agreement
was made about applying certain sums to be retained in Bishopp's hands for
that purpose to repay some money advanced I know not what must be transferred to the Person who shall pay the allowance in his stead. Let me
observe that I am *not* r[ic]h enough as M^r B: was pleased to say to add
to your Mother's allowance I am not yet out of debt and when I shall be so
there is much to be done in order to make an adequate provision for your
Sisters (poor Barry I must think out of the question) who would not be left
in a very desireable situation were any accident to happen to me Not that I
have any fears of your kindness to them but independence is the best security
for affection in Families and I should wish to leave them a sufficiency without the necessity of your sharing with them what will come to you as a
matter of right Whenever I find I can with propriety spare a further sum
for your Mother it shall be *your* gift to her." I hope my dear Mother the
kindness with which this letter speaks of you will give you satisfaction
that your suspicio[ns of] my Father's behaviour being chang[ed toward]
you are unjust. I hoped to hav[e heard] from you whether you got th[e] . . .[1]
or not as I am afraid it [may have] missed you and you may h[ave been]
distressed but I trust y[ou will write] immediately upon the rece[ipt of
this.]

Believe me my [dear Mother,]<br>
Your most affecti[onate Son]<br>
M G Lewis

[1] A portion of MS large enough for ten letters is lost.


[late 1793]

My dear Mother,
    I was not conscious of shewing any coolness or reserve when I saw you;
Believe that my affection is still as warm for you as ever, but since you
desire me to tell you my thoughts, I will openly confess to you that I feel
many very different sensations upon your subject. I feel for you the greatest
regard, the most eager desire to do any thing that can give you even the
most trifling satisfaction; but at the same time I cannot help recollecting the
pain and anxiety you have occasioned to my dear my worthy Father, and
that it is owing to your conduct that my Sisters are deprived of maternal care
and attention, and, of receiving the benefit of those little instructions and ob-

servations, so necessary to make young Women accomplished, and which are in the power of a Mother alone to point out to them with success. You ask me how much I know of your difference with my Father, and whether I could publickly make allowances for you; you suppose my Father has been giving me instructions. you accuse him unjustly; He has never said a syllable to me with regard to you, and my behaviour is entirely such as is dictated by my own heart. If that is good, as yourself has often told me, my conduct must be the same; if my conduct is wrong, my heart is the same, and it will be worth no one's while to seek to have a share of it. No; I will own to you openly I could not declare in public that I can make allowances for you: In my heart I can excuse you, and believe that your own innocence and the deceit of others may have been the occasion of your errors; but these are arguments never received by the world, which is always eager to believe the worst side of every thing. But, saying I have arguments to bring [a]gainst your adversaries, though I swear to you on my soul I know of no adversaries that you have, I never could bear to talk coolly upon the subject; but let me put a case to you, and make you remember a circumstance which must speak to your own feelings. My Sisters are now in the age when their minds are most capable of receiving lasting impressions; they have been taught to regard me almost as attentively as their Father, and from my being more with them, and entering into their amusements with more vivacity than people who [a]re not so near their own age can do they readily adopt any sentiments they hear me declare. Can you openly confess that you wish your conduct to be followed by your Daughters? I will not [s]ay your conduct is to be condemn'd, but I cannot call it [c]ommendable, when I know the anxiety it has occasioned and still occasions to my Father, and which at your separation [w]as perfect phrenzy. As to the two lights which you say I *may* regard you in, the light in which I do regard you is [c]omposed of both; I feel the love and respect for you which [y]ou state is the first; I conceive your heart to be so good, your mind so enlightened that I am astonished that you could be led into those errors, when the strength of your understanding must have shown to you the calamities you were bringing upon yourself, and the excellence of your heart have made you feel for those your errors must bring upon the people whom you declare were then, and still are the nearest to your heart. You tell me that I ought to hear your arguments as well as those on the other side. I have heard neither on one side or the other; and you ought to consider it as a mark of generosity, that [whilst it was in my father's power to have][1] made my [mind re]ceive any impressions he chose to give it, he did not take the opportunity, but left me to draw my own sentiments from what I might afterwards hear and feel myself; for in these circumstances the heart must be the best and most impartial judge. You have put me into the most distressing and embarrassing situation in the world; you have made me almost an umpire between my Parents; I know not how to extricate myself from the difficulty; I can only believe neither of you to be in the wrong, but *I* am not to determine which is in the right. only believe that my affection for you is as great as ever, and that there is nothing which I can do to oblige you which shall not be done with the greatest readiness. When I am obliged not to see you I deny myself a pleasure and be convinced that I should not do it without good reaso[ns.] There are many which make Oxford an improper abode fo[r] you. it is an uncommon thing to see a Lady arrive there by Herself and as there are People who have a right to enqui[re] into my actions I should be subject to many unpleasant questions and what answer would you have me give them. You wish to spend the Ten Pounds I offer you at Oxford and you tell me your difficulties are over but t[hey] may recur and I imagine you would not wish positively to throw away Ten Pounds. I must now beg you to have done with this subject never let me again be obliged to write such a letter so embarassing so distressing I really think it unkind to accuse with[2] a coolness a[nd] reserve of conduct which I have not merited, and I am not conscious of having failed to you in any on[e] point of affection; The rage[3] also and manner in wh[ich] you put it was not a fai[r] on[e.] You [must] h[ave] been conscious that I could not decide in your favour and to decide against you would give me infinite pain But I have now done with this painful subject. I must beg you to pursue the line of conduct with regard to Barrington which I mentioned to you, to write to him often and feed him with distant hopes of meeting, not to make the excuse of his health preventing you for it would make him fret and his spirits will not bear it I have just heard from M^rs Brownrigg who says that his not having received a toothpick case which I was to get for him has made him fret a great deal this little circumstance will convince you that He cannot bear the emotion of seeing you the more I think of this the more I am convinced that the flurrying his Spirits so much would be absolute madness. I have the pleasure to inform you that my my Uncle William is in Town he will remain a Month but He says he is very busy at his office. He asked if you was coming over soon I told him I believed so I did not tell him you were arrived because I did not know where you would chuse to have him directed to. He asked if you had received his letter and was surprized you had not answered it. If you send a letter for him Tomorrow morning to Devonshire Place He will receive it at dinner as He dines here. The Servant will give it to him as I dine out.

Believe me your most affectionate<br>Son M G Lewis.

[1] A line is covered by mounting, but the reading, taken from the *Life* (I, 106–7), appears to be correct.

[2] For "me with."

[3] "Rage" is uncertain. The word is clearly not "way" as in the *Life* (I, 108).

December 25th [1793]

Your letter, my dear Mother, has given me very serious uneasiness because I am not conscious that *my* Letter contained any expressions which deserved to be treated with so much anger; nor do I think you judge fairly when you put my pride in opposition to my affection for you, and say that the former over-balances the latter. Change pride for *reason* and your proposition will stand right; and that it ought to be put in that way, yourself acknowledges since you say my arguments were both right and natural. If I was conversing, I should then perhaps through warmth and thoughlessness shew that inconsiderate affection (without any regard to reason) which you think so proper, and wish so much to see; but when I take up my pen upon reflection, and can have an opportunity of looking calmly upon what I have said, and if wrong correcting it, I must then give the preference to reason, which stares me so broadly in the face. You cannot suppose that *I* should think your conduct blameless, when you yourself do not think it so. I can make every allowance for your intentions and your heart, but that does not prevent my seeing that you [h]ave erred in practice, however right you theory may be. As to what you say about my shewing a want of affection in the letters I formerly wrote to you, you ought not to *wish* me to be so much blinded by affection as to overlook Common sense, propriety, and every other consideration. In those letters in answer to the many arguments which occurred to me in my own vindication [(a]nd which you could not confute) I do not remember one that [y]ou [u]sed to me which could exculpate yourself. The contents were [co]nstantly the same; you owned that you had done wrong, but [s]aid that I ought not to think so; you declared my head [w]as better than my heart, and that I ought to follow [b]lind affection instead of common-sense; you wished me to [c]onsider your provocations (which must be *obscure* to every [b]ody but yourself) as glaring, and your errors (which are *clear* [to] every body) as trifling; and in short you concluded by saying [t]hat if I did not beleive your conduct to be perfectly blameless [y]ou would throw away all affection for me, and never care [a]ny farther about me. These were not arguments, and I remained consequently unconvinced; but in whatever means [I] could shew my affection for you in making you more easy [o]r comfortable, I was ever happy and ready to take the opportunity. If I were to declare your conduct blameless and justifiable, I should think the punishment deserved, if my [o]wn Wife and Sisters fell into the same errors. You must [h]ave been very angry when you wrote your last letter, [f]or your arguments are easy to be confuted, and you seem wilfully to have mistaken several parts of my Letter. You say that you ["]never thought otherwise than that such a [conne]xion was ineligible". that is extraordinary, since you though[t] "their arguments were reasonable, and you merely came to England to see your friends before you took the Step". This is a contradiction. "My Pride is stronger than my affection." My affection for you is very strong, but I never said it was stro[n]ger than my love for my Sisters, whom I still think would be hurt by your living again with my Father. You said once that "you could give me many reasons why it would be advantage[ous] to them". I will give you mine, why it would not be. Your re-un[ion] with my Father would certainly introduce you again into Society. but still many Women would be shy of coming to your house. this would be a disadvantage; but the great one is that it would be a material obstacle to their establishment. I must give you an example of this in a conversation which I once was present at, and which cut my pride (if you will have it so) and my feelings for my Sisters most severely. Lady Jersey has had many slurs thrown upon her character, but She has never been separated from her husband, nor made so very public a subject of discourse. She was then the topic in a large assembly, when somebody said, "It is very fortunate for her to have married her Daughters so advantageously." Yes, answered another, and very extraordinary too; for there should not be another Girl in the world, before I'd marry the Daughter of a Woman who has been talked of so freely". This was in a large assembly, and I fear the opinion of three[1] parts of the world is the same. This then is a reason why I should feel more hurt than pleased at your reconciliation with my Father; add to which I was certain it would be impossible to take place, and tho' I wish most earnestly to preserve your regard, I am still anxious not to lose my Father's. Instead of thinking Miss Knowles's conduct amiable, I think it weak and selfish; since for her own gratification She compelled two people to enter into an engagement which could produce nothing but unhappiness to them: Such a reunion must constantly be embittered by reflections upon the past, and the Husband and Wife like two Dogs tied together must be continually pulling different ways. Besides this my *fretting* would be to very little purpose, for my Father's heart is not so easily shaken to what his reason does not approve. I would do any thing in the world to make you both happy in your separate situations, but I see so many obstacles, and even impossibilities to a reunion taking place, that it is idle to think of it. You tell me that I have two faults which you can discover; I have two thousand which any body may perceive at the first glance (I do not reckon my obedience to the dictates of reason as one of them) but when you tell me that I restrain them, that circumstance I confess piques my curiosity, makes me own you have made a discovery, and beg you to tell me which of my many faults I have got so well under command; since the first step gained, I may perhaps succeed in totally subduing them. I suppose you mean Pride and Conceit; I know that I have a great deal of the first and I am not ashamed of it, when it has the sanction of Common Sense; and it should only be despised when exercised in a bad cause, and proceeding from a bad principle. As for Conceit I know that I have more than other people with less reason for it, and I have not a word to say in my vindication of it. You wish my letter had been a pathetic address; you might as well have desired it to have been a sentimental one; either would shine in a Novel, but would be perfectly ridiculous and out of its place when writing seriously and upon actual circumstances. Besides which it is not the nature of a Man to write Pathetics, but to express his sentiments as strongly and forcibly as possible. I did not sit down to think what I should write, but to write what I thought; and since you acknowledge what I have said to be right and natural, I do not think it would have been much more to the purpose, if my letter had been stuffed with Ohs and Ahs from the beginning to the end. If you will not beleive that I have a great affection for you, nothing that I can say will be able to persuade you of it. I can only repeat my assurances that while you retain your regard for [me, mine wi]ll never decrease, and tha[t] I shall always be de[lighted] to have it in my power to give you proofs of the interest I take in your welfare and happiness. You mistook what I said in my last about threa[tening, and] if you read it again you will find it conveys a very different [sen]se from that in which you now con[strue] it. I thought it n[ecess]ary to specify that threats [were very far fro]m my intention, l[est] you should construe it that way, [as you have appare]ntly from what you now design, since I had hear[d you declare] rather a singular maxim; "that if any thing was mentioned [to you w]ith threats, you would reject a proposal however [libera]l and proper, and prefer any other however disad[vanta]geous. It was on this account that I was obliged to warn [you not] to consider what I said as a threat. I have written you a very long letter, and I hope it will convince you that [it was] very far from my intention to use any manner that might be unpleasant to you; and if after having read this you still [per]sist in your opinion, I can do nothing else than assure you I am very sorry for having displeased you, and very sincerely beg your pardon. Maria has got a sore throat which has confined her to her bed since Sunday, and She is not yet permitted to see any body, lest it should be infectious. All parties to the Play therefore are deferred for some time at least. On Wednesday I will be at M^rs Lonsdale's by twelve o'clock unless I hear anything from you to the contrary.

Beleive me yours most affectionately,<br>M. G. Lewis.

1 Or "those."

[postmarked Oxford, March 15, 1794]

My dear Mother, I will not delay a day in sending you the following letter from M^rs Blake, as I am sure the contents & sentiments conveyed in it will give you pleasure, & convince you that there are some people in the world, who entertain the opinion of you, which every body ought to do. I shall write (Turn to the last page) [a rep]ly immediately, to say how much her letter gratifie[d me, and tha]t I shall ever esteem those to be my best Friends w[ho consider] my Mother in a favourable point of view, & that I shall endeavour to make up to *her* Children the kindness which She is inclined to shew to *my* Parent.—I must observe to you, that since her kindness to you, I have taken much notice of her Son, & never seen him without giving him a Guinea. I have done the Same thing by Br^1

Sewell, as I thought you might possibly (though not probably) reap some benefit from it. I shall say something to M^rs B. about giving Robert Sewell a favourable idea of you, making him write to you &c. I do not mean in money matters, but in fraternal regard; for in the first, whenever I have any fortune of my own, I shall be too proud to let you be indebted to anybody but myself for assistance. I believe that in 2 weeks I am going abroad; If so, I hope that you will pass in town the few days during which I shall be there. I will let you know as soon as my plans are settled, that you may make your arrangements accordingly.—I hope, you got my letter, inclosing the paper for the "True Briton", but was rather surprized, at not hearing from you to-day, to say that you had received it. However by tomorrow's post, I expect without fail to hear from you. God bless you, and make you feel happy & contented.

> Believe me ever, ever,
> Your truly affectionate Son,
> M. G. Lewis.

[The preceding letter is written on the margins of the following from Mrs. Blake.]

> Jamaica, 20^th: January 1794.

I consider myself as guilty of an extreme degree of neglect in not having sooner acknowledged your kind letter, but do me the justice to believe my dear Matt, that in no shape whatsoever did it arise from an indifference either to your correspondence, or good opinion. I rejoice, that the gratification of my own feelings, shou'd have been deserving of any acknowledgements from you. I wish to God! I cou'd have seen you on the subject previous to my departure from England Many circumstances, that passed, I cou'd have wished to have communicated to you, particularly a conversation between your Father & myself on the subject. I do interest myself in the cause of your Mother I must confess with no small degree of earnestness. I cou'd think and talk on the subject untill I became perfectly melancholy, because I think she has merits, that are not fully understood and I think also, she has Relations that are not as serviceable to her as they might be. Good God! when I think of this World or rather the *ways* of it, I almost wish myself out of it—I have been & still am very ill with a complaint that wou'd very easily have rid me of all my uneasiness about this world but I fancy like the old Man in the Fable that call'd out for death to relieve him of his pains, I shou'd find out that I only wanted him to help me up with my bundle of Sticks. Seriously tho', I have been very ill, and am still so unwell as to be very weak and my Spirits too low to bear any exertion therefore, I shall not fatigue you with any length of Letter. Whenever my dear Matt, you can spare time to scribble me a few lines, the attention will be soothing, and I shall be very thankfull.

I beg you to accept my best acknowledgements for the Ear-rings you were good enough to send me. They are infinitely admired & to me are more valuable from the idea of their being tokens of your remembrance & satisfaction of a triffling act on my part, but which notice in you, proves the goodness & tenderness of your Heart to a very great degree, the impression of which, I shall always think of with pleasure. If you are now in England remember me kindly to your Sisters, & assure them, of my earnest wishes for their Happiness.

Believe me My dear Matthew
Your truly affectionate Aunt
& faithfull Friend
A Blake.

¹ "Br" is not certain.

$\frac{11}{D}$ The Hague, Sunday May the 18th [1794]

My dear Mother,

As you must undoubtedly be anxious to know that I have crossed the water in safety, I sit down to give you early intelligence of my being arrived at the Hague. I had a remarkably good passage of four and twenty hours; The weather was uncommonly fine, and the Sea so calm, that the movement of the Vessel was scarce perceptible. I was not in the least sick, which I am in general to such an excess, that I never enter the Packet but with fear and trembling; though my apprehensions are not for my life, but for my stomach. I am at present inhabiting an Inn, but in the middle of next week I shall remove to very tolerable Lodgings, which I have procured near the Ambassador's Hotel. I arrived at the Hague on Thursday night; and have already dined twice with Lord St Helens, who was excessively polite. I have not as yet been presented at court, but shall be on Monday; After which as I understand, I am to send about my cards to all the principal People in the place, and I shall have immediately as much, (if not more), society as I can wish for. At present, as I know nobody here, I cannot therefore supply you with much information respecting the Hague, or much anecdote respecting its Inhabitants. I must not however omit to inform you, that you may have some notion of the poetical ideas, and tender nature of the Dutch, that my Landlord, though He is nothing more than a Grocer, displays a sign, representing an altar on which repose two Hearts pierced through by a flaming arrow! Show me an English Grocer, whose shop can boast so allegorical an ornament! There are very few English here at present, but the few who are, seem to be remarkably pleasant. I hope that you got a letter, which I wrote to you from Harwich [r]especting the Habit-Maker; but as I left it to the care of an Inn-Keeper, it may not have reached you: I, therefore, mention the circumstance, lest you should accuse me of inattention. I have again taken up my Romance, and perhaps by this time Ten years I may make shift to finish it fit for throwing into the fire. I was induced to go on with it by reading "the Mysteries of Udolpho, which is in my opinion one of the most interesting Books that ever have been published.¹ I would advise you to read it by all means, but I must warn you, that it is not very entertaining till S^t Aubert's Death. His travels to my mind are uncommonly dull, and I wish heartily that They had been left out, and something substituted in their room. I am sure, you will be particularly interested by the part when Emily returns home after her Father's death; and when you read it, tell me whether you think there is any resemblance between the character given of Montoni in the seventeenth chapter of the second volume, and my own. I confess, that it struck me, and as He is the Villain of the Tale, I did not feel much flattered by the likeness.[2] I hope that you will write to me soon, for I am impatient to hear, whether you have done anything with the Poem, or got any answer from those two tiresome Devils, Colman and Kemble. I favou[ra]ble one I do not expect, but I confess, I should like to have one of some kind or other. I left poor Maria in great distress at my going, and I could not help being Fool enough to shed some tears upon quitting her. However I have just written to her a long letter to comfort her. Of course, you will send your letters to my Father, and I beg, that They may be long ones.

Believe me, my dear Mother,
you most affectionate Son,
M. G. Lewis.

[1] For "ever have" the *Life* (I, 123) reads "has ever," a well-intentioned but misguided attempt to improve Lewis' grammar; and a particularly unfortunate one, since the sentence, having importance for the history of Gothic literature, has often been quoted from the *Life*.

[2] "Montoni had been otherwise engaged; his soul was little susceptible of light pleasures. He delighted in the energies of the passions; the difficulties and tempests of life, which wreck the happiness of others, roused and strengthened all the powers of his mind, and afforded him the highest enjoyments, of which his nature was capable. Without some object of strong interest, life was to him little more than a sleep; and, when pursuits of real interest failed, he substituted artificial ones, till habit changed their nature, and they ceased to be unreal. Of this kind was the habit of gaming, which he had adopted, first, for the purpose of relieving him from the languor of inaction, but had since pursued with the ardour of passion. In this occupation he had passed the night with Cavigni and a party of young men, who had more money than rank, and more vice than either. Montoni despised the greater part of these for the inferiority of their talents, rather than for their vicious inclinations, and associated with them only to make them the instruments of his purposes. Among these, however, were some of superior abilities, and a few whom Montoni admitted to his intimacy, but even towards these he still preserved a decisive and haughty air, which, while it imposed submission on weak and timid minds, roused the fierce hatred of strong ones. He had, of course, many and bitter enemies; but the rancour of their hatred proved the degree of his power; and, as power was his chief aim, he gloried more in such hatred, than it was possible he could in being esteemed. A feeling so tempered as that of esteem, he despised, and would have despised himself also had he thought himself capable of being flattered by it." *The Mysteries of Udolpho* (London, 1794), II, 52–54. The passage occurs in Vol. II, ch. III, which in the first edition is misnumbered XVII—hence Lewis' reference.

Hague. Tuesday. July 22d 1794.

My dear Mother,

Before I tell you any thing about myself and my present proceedings, I shall mention that the way in which Robinson proposes to publish the Poem, by bits and fits[1] in Magazines, is by no means to my liking; and if He has accepted it for that purpose, I beg you to break off the bargain at any rate. This is the sure way of not having it taken notice of, and it would steal out of the world in as shabby a manner as it stole in. I should sacrifice a few Guineas to the publishing it at my own expense, were I not deterred by the idea, that the Booksellers discourage such conduct and do all in their power to prevent the sale of a Book which has not past through their hands. However at all events I wish you would find out what the expense of printing, Advertising, &c would come to altogether. If it were not a great deal I feel very much tempted to risque the money though at present I am obliged to oeconomize very much. The Hague is the most expensive place possible; My Father allows me £400 a year, and out of this I am actually obliged to Keep House; I stare sometimes to see in the Bills what an immense sum is run up every week for trifles, such as Oil, vinegar &c, and find it very difficult to live within my income. It is true, that my Father says, if I want money He will give me as much more as I chuse; But this liberality makes me anxious if possible to do with the sum already allotted to me. I am not, therefore, very desirous of throwing away my money; but if the expense should not be very exorbitant, and if I thought the poem likely to be *read* (for that is at present my only aim) I should be tempted to try my fortune. Whether the verses were liked or not, the consequence would be beneficial. If they were praised, it would please my vanity; If abused, I should be convinced that I had no talents for Authorship. Should I adopt this plan, I think, I should let Walter of Charing Cross into the secret, let him publish it, and I think, He would from his obligations to my Father, do all in his power to promote the sale. Much of this plan depends upon your answer repecting the price. I did not send my German translation[2] to any body—I did it in Scotland, and brought it to you the moment that I arrived in London. The Author of the Robbers has written several other Plays. Why did you send the Epistolary Intrigue to Harris, which He had already refused?—I have written a little Farce,[3] which I wish to offer to young Bannister for his benefit, and mean to send it you for that purpose by the first opportunity. It would be too expensive to send such a parcel by the Post. It is calculated solely for his acting, and is on the subject of two Twin Brothers, one a Rake and the other a Quaker who are constantly mistaken for each other; and I have so arranged the scenes, that as the Brothers are never both on the Stage at the same time, they may be played by the same Person, who of course must be Bannister. So much for Authorship; You see I am horribly bit by the rage of writing—you will be sorry to find, that I am not more pleased with my situation, than when I wrote to you last; I have nothing in the world to do, and I am certain that the Devil Ennui has made the Hague his favourite abode. I have not as yet found a single soul whom I ever wish to see again. There is hardly any society of any sort or kind, and I cannot express to you with what impatience I wait for a recall to England. Of this, however, I am afraid that there is at present no hope; I am tyed down here, and I assure you, I have need of all my patience and fortitude to keep myself from falling into low spirits, which when I have them, with me become a serious malady. I have been very unwell for this last week; But this probably is occasioned by the extreme heat of the weather, which is said to be unequalled, and is the more unfortunate since the dryness of the season prevents an inundation from taking place. You doubtless know, that the security of Holland depends in a great measure upon the Canals, which resource at this moment it is impossible to make use of. You may perhaps be a little alarmed for me, when you hear of the progress of the French; I shall assure you therefore that at the Hague there is no possible danger of our being visited by the Carmagnols. Every body here is in perfect security upon their own accounts; But of course their faces are very gloomy from the bad success of the combined Armies. I hope, you recieved a letter from me some time ago, inclosing some verses which I wished you to get inserted into the Times. As I am dying for want of amusement, in spite of the little which this letter must afford you, I hope you will not neglect to answer it with all possible diligence, and not to send me a less quantity of writing than was contained in your last. My Sisters are well, & gone on a visit to M^rs Gen: Cuyler at Portsmouth. Farewell, my dear Mother, write to me soon, and believe me your most affectionate Son,

M. G. Lewis.

1 "Bits and bits," as in the *Life* (I, 126), may be correct. Lewis obviously speaks of a single poem, evidently one of some length—possibly the lost translation of *Oberon*. The *Life* (I, 126) changes "verses" to "poems," presumably to support the error (*Life* I, 129) that Lewis refers to the collection of poems he made at Weimar.

2 *The Minister.*

3 *The Twins.*

Hague. Sept^r 23^d 1794.

My dear Mother,

You lament in your last that it is always your lot to send me disagreable intelligence; It is true, that you sent me a whole budget of disappointments: and nothing would console me under them, but the idea that it is sometimes in my power to send you letters calculated to produce an effect exactly contrary. This I imagine will be the consequence of your reading the letter from M^rs Blake which I inclose. It will prove to you, that every body is not unjust in their way of thinking upon your subject; and more particularly will it give you pleasure to know, that my Father is not one of the number who censure you harshly, that He wishes you well, and will be happy to know that you are comfortable and easy. I intend to write to her, and beg her to tell me what past between her and my Father; as also to enquire, whether He named *what* might be done to better your situation, and whether I can be of any use in it. There was another sheet to her letter, but it contained nothing that would be interesting to you. I have not therefore sent it. I must now thank you for your very long consequent[l]y very acceptable letter. I can only do, as a Child fed with sweetmeats, cry "More[!] More!".[1] I am happy to find that you have been passing your time so pleasantly since I left England. As for me, the Hague and the Dutch are as insufferable as ever; But of late I have cut the society of the place, and got into a very agreable Coterie, which assembles every other night at the House of one of the cleverest Women I ever met with, a Madame de Matignon. She is the Daughter of the celebrated Baron de Breteuil, who lives with her; We have also the Marquise de Bebrance, the Princesse de Leon, the Princesse de Montmorenci, the Vicomte de Bouillé, the Duc de Polignac, the *beau* Dillon (of whom you must certainly have heard) and in short the very best society of Paris. This you must suppose is pleasant. Every body is at their ease. Some play at Tric-trac; others work; others "font la belle conversation", and so well, with such wit and novelty of thought, that I am much entertained by it. You will easily conceive, that after such a society the Dutch Assemblies must be dreadful; I therefore seldom go near them, and indeed a late proof of their stupidity would have terrified a Man possessed of more courage than myself. An unfortunate Irishman known by the name of Lord Kerry, being the other night at one of the Dutch Assemblies, and quite overcome with its stupidity, yawned so terribly that He fairly dislocated his jaw: It was immediately set again; But He has suffered much from the accident, and is still confined by it to his bed. He is a Man upwards of fifty, and consequently must have been frequently ennuied before; But such peculiar Ennui was more than He had bargained for, or had power to resist. You may think this a made Anecdote; but I assure you that I have told you the plain matter of fact. There is a Duchesse de la Force here, a sort of Ideot, whom I wish you could see; She would entertain you much. Her conversation is composed of the same set of phrases, which She vents upon all occasions. One of them is, "Et les détails?"—She said the other day, without minding her question or his reply—"Eh bien! M\r Dillon, y a-t-il quelque nouvelle?" —"Il n'y en a pas, Madame".—Vraiment; Et les détails?"—When they told her that the Queen of France was dead, She asked for the "détails"—She would make an excellent character in a comedy. Talking of that, I see that M\rs Jordan is engaged at Drury Lane. Perhaps She will bring out the *Play which She accepted*; I now rather wish that She would not; I was reading it the other day, and it seemed so bad that it cannot miss being damned. However, it is most probable that She has forgotten the Comedy and every thing about it. I long to hear your opinion of the Farce, which I sent you lately.[2] I know that you will like it because written by me; but I want to know which parts pleased you most. They say, that practice makes perfect; If so, I shall one day be a perfect Author, for I practise most furiously. What do you think of my having written in the space of ten weeks, a Romance of between three and four hundred Pages Octavo? I have even written out half of it fair. It is called "The Monk", and I am myself so much pleased with it, that if the Booksellers will not buy it, I shall publish it myself. Since I wrote to you, I have payed the Army a visit, and passed a week at Oosterhout with great pleasure. I was presented to the Duke of York, and dined with him one day; He was very civil, and seems uncommonly good-humoured: But I should have liked him better, had He not been so very like Lord Stopford, who in my opinion is one of the most disagreable Men in the world. I was also presented to Prince Adolphus. This little expedition made me only feel the Hague more stupid and insupportable than ever. As you are a novel Reader, you ought to read "Caleb Williams"; It is in a new style, and well written: Unluckily the Author is half a Democrate.—I shall inclose this to Miss Ingall, and send it to Devonshire Place. As to my Bills, I must let them go on as they can, for I know not what are the points with which I *ought* to find fault; and if I pitch upon the wrong, it gives the Servant a disagreable advantage over me. I long to know, what it is that you are writing, or perhaps I should say, *were* writing, for as you are something inconstant in your paroxysms of Authorship, you may possibly have laid it aside by this time. Part of the character of your Maitresse d'Hotel I have observed sometimes in myself, though not taken up with the idea of deceiving. You say, that She remarks what is said, and the next day produces your sentiment as her own. Now I have often after disputing on the Sunday upon a subject, taken the contrary side on the Monday, and used the arguments which were used against me: However, I never found this succeed very well, for as I seldom knew more upon that side of the question than what I picked up from others, it was no difficult matter to put my reasoning in disorder. You need not be under any alarm about me at the Hague, with respect to the visits of the Carmagnols: You may dep[en]d up[on] it, that I shall not wait for their arrival, and to avoid a disagreabl[e] visi[t] in a way somewhat unusual, I shall take care to be at home not to [r]eceiv[e] them. I allow your receipt against ennui to be a very good one; But you mistake in supposing me to have anything to do with him. With my pen, my pencil, my Book, my fire, and above all my Dog who is beautiful, I am never weary of solitude: It is only when I go into Dutch company that I am bored. However, with this French coterie I am never in want of society. You may judge what Animals the Dutch must be when I tell you, that They brick up their Chimneys during the summer; and that till the month of November no power on earth would prevail on them to light a fire. For my own part I have never been for a week without one, and now write to you by a very comfortable blaze. Let it console you, and put you into conceit with your Spinnet, to know that Queen Elizabeth played upon no better an instrument. Mrs Cuyler is the Wife of the General, which is all that I know of her. My

Sisters are now at Broad-stairs with Mrs Brownrigg. I hear that Barrington is in wonderful health. Certainly you may direct your letters to my Father. Write to me soon and beleive me

you most affectionate Son,
M. G. Lewis.

1 Cf. "diejenigen . . . die gleich den Kindern . . . mit grossem Respekt um die Schublade umherschleichen, wo Mama das Zuckerbrot hineingeschlossen hat, und, wenn si das gewünschte endlich erhaschen, es mit vollen Backen verzehren und rufen: Mehr!" *Die Leiden des Jungen Werthers*, Am 22. Mai.

2 *The Twins*.

Stoke Farm. August 29th [1797][1]

My dear Mother,

I was unexpectedly summoned to Oatlands on Saturday last; where I remained till the end of this week, and during my absence my letters were all kept for me at Stoke Farm. Consequently I could not obey your wishes of writing to you by [r]eturn of Post, and not being in Town I could not discharge Bernard's bill, which otherwise I would have done most readily. I am very glad to be releived from my fright respecting the things in Gerrard St; I assure you, I gave them up for gone.—It certainly was *not* very *easy* for you to tell me what you did not know yourself; and therefore you are most satisfactorily exculpated from the charge of having unnecessarily kept me in hot water. However, on any future occasion, pray remember (when other circumstances do not make an immediate comnunication necessary) [tha]t I prefer knowing the whole, or nothing; for I have an admirable talent at tormenting myself, and the truth can never be worse, that what I imagine when left to myself. the party at Oatlands was very large, and very gay; we had excellent Music every night, and the Egham Races every morning; But unluckily, I was so extremely ill during the whole time with head-achs and a vile stomach complaint, that I could enjoy nothing—the Duke of Clarence (to whom I had never been presented, nor had even dined in his company in my life) came up to me on the Racecourse, called me "Lewis" *tout court*, talked to me as familiarly as if He had known me all his life, and before we parted, He told me "that He meant to ask the Spanish Deputies to dinner, and that as I was a Man of Romance and Sentiment, He should invite Me to meet them at Bushy Park." I dare say though, that He will forget the invitation; He dined, however, at Oatlands the next day, and was extremely civil to me. Dinner is on table; So I must go and dress.

Your affecte Son,
M. G. Lewis

1 1797 is probable, since the following letter, written three days later, seems to anticipate the first performance of *The Castle Spectre*, which occurred on Dec. 14, 1797.

Stoke Farm. Sept<sup>r</sup> 1<sup>st</sup> [1797]

My dear Mother,

I wrote to you lately, but cannot recollect the particular day. My letter mentioned my having been at Oatlands; If it has not reached you, pray, take measures for getting it from the Post Office, Lewes, to which place it was directed, as I have a great dislike to having my correspondence read by the Clerks of the Post Office. As to Miss L—'s[1] situation, every thing has its good and its bad side; and having now gone so far, that it would be difficult to retire, it would surely be most prudent to look only upon the first: you know, I never advised her going upon the Stage, nor indeed had much hopes of her success. But *now* what can be done? It seems by your account, that in the Country She has been very successful; and supposing that She were to give up this profession, and anything were to happen to you, what would She have to depend upon?—as to a School, do you think such an employment would have suited her, and that She would have been contented in it?— As it is, the profession, in which She is engaged, has many drawbacks; but it certainly has two advantages, which are the most essential to *Her*, and which surely must be the most consolatory to You; It makes her happy and satisfied at the present, and ensures her a livelihood for the future—and I cannot but think in this point of view, that She is better situated, than if She were engaged in an employment uncongenial to her wishes and disposition, and in which She would consequently have been discontented. By a *temporary separation*, certainly I did not mean "giving her up entirely"; You may remember, when we found it so difficult to procure her an engagement, and when you said, "that it weighed upon her spirits to think, that your Friends must consider her as a dead weight upon you," that I answered, "She ought to be assured, that your Friends were quite ready to allow, that her attention to you, and the pleasure which you derived from her society, were a sufficient compensation for any expense which She might be to you, and that as far as regarded *their* feelings, they would rather wish her not to go upon the Stage, because it would in some measure deprive you of that pleasure." But *your* interest and Miss L's are on this occasion a little at variance, and in consideration of her future subsistence, I think, that you ought *occasionally* to submit to sacrificing the pleasure of her society. this would only be for the summer months; while She is at Drury Lane, and living in your House, there is nothing to be objected to; and the separation in question is in fact nothing more, that is required from *every* person, who is not fortunately situated enough to be able to do without a profession. —We cannot have things exactly, as we would wish them; we can only make the best of what we have. Of course, you will understand that in saying all this I am only pointing out what appears to me to be the *reason* of the thing; as to what you or Miss L *do*, of that you must be yourself the only proper persons to decide. My Servant is out, and I cannot ask him, how much He gave Bernard, or indeed be *quite* certain, that He *did* give it: But I have every reason to beleive, that I saw a Guinea charged to her in his

Books. I think too, that She came to me and thanked me for it; but of this I am also not *certain*. I know, I told him to give her that sum.—I am still at Lady Charlotte Campbell's; and shall remain here for some days longer. I was unjust to my *new Friend*, when I suspected him of forgetting his promise to invite me to meet the Spanish Deputies; for yesterday morning I received a command from the Duke of Clarence to dine with him at Bushy on Sunday next. Twelve miles to go and twelve miles to return is rather a heavy penalty to pay for a dinner; Luckily, it is a penalty, which is not exacted often, and the *honour* of the thing must console me for the trouble; I am sure, the *pleasure* will not—the rest of my motions are so very uncertain, and depend so much upon those of other people, that I cannot at present give you any account of them. However, I am glad, that you are removing into the neighbourhood of London, as it is probable, that I may shortly come there for a day or two. I have not yet been to my Uncle Robert's: William wrote to me again the other day, and in *all* his letters He desires to be remembered to you with affection. Tom Sheridan was at Oatlands, and assured me *positively*, that my Piece should come out before Christmas.[2]

your affec<sup>te</sup> Son.<br>M G. L.

It *was* either a pound, or a Guinea, that was given to Bernard.

[1] Throughout this letter the initial L (for Lacey) is inked out by a later hand.
[2] Probably *The Castle Spectre.*

[To Sir Thomas Durrant, second Baronet (1775–1829)?]
My dear Sir,

I thank you very kindly for your obliging offer, & would gladly avail myself of it, if, having been at Yarmouth all day yesterday, I was not otherwise engaged. Perhaps, I may look-in upon you this or Tomorrow evening (but not till *after* Dinner), & we may then be able to arrange some other day, mutually convenient, for our Drive; as, I dare say, notwithstanding a very warm & pressing invitation from my friend Mr. Turner, I shall not quit Lowestoft for his abode till the end of this or the beginning of the ensuing week.—Allow me to repeat my Thanks to both Lady Durrant & yourself for your hospitable & friendly attention, & beleive me always

My dear Sir<br>Very truly your's<br>M. G. Lewis[1]

Wednesday Morng

[1] If "Lady Durrant" refers to Sir Thomas' wife, the date of his marriage—Sept. 28, 1799—gives a *terminus a quo* for dating the letter.

Barnes. [early 1801][1]

My dear Mother,

I return a letter. I am contented with Barnes, till I can get a place to purchase, and therefore make your Leatherhead arrangements, as suits you best. Before you leave it, I mean to pass a day there with you, but had rather come nearer the time of your departure than just at present, as I am working very hard, both in the reading & writing way. Have you read Cowper's "*Task*"? It is a long Poem, making part of one of the volumes of his Poems: If not, read it; It will suit *your* taste exactly; It is not *quite* to mine (though I like it much) as you will find, when you read it. I must apprize you though (lest you should triumph too much) that I understand, the author died stark staring mad, and rather *too* mad to have it mistaken for inspiration.[2] Godwin's Enquirer, & Behmen's prophecies will make a charming Salmagundi of your ideas. I forget, whether I have heard from M^rs Riddock lately. I am truly sorry to hear of your late illness, but as you do not mention your arm, trust, it is got quite well. If not, pray have some advice, and from having that advice, I earnestly request, that you will not let *money* be any consideration; nothing would give me greater pain, than to suppose any pecuniary idea made you treat your health slightly, while I possest a single guinea.

your affec^te Son,
M. G. Lewis

I have begun a Tragedy[3] in blank verse; But I stick in the third act at a reconciliation between a King & a Princess, the two stupidest people I ever met with.

[1] The reference to the composition of *Alfonso* indicates early 1801, since the tragedy was submitted to the proprietors of Drury Lane before the production of *Adelmorn* on May 4, 1801 (see *Alfonso*, 2nd ed., London, 1802, p. xii).

[2] Cowper died Apr. 25, 1800.

[3] *Alfonso*.


Sunday[1]

My dear Mother,

I send a letter from M^rs Blake to me, being certain that the kindness of what She says, will make you take it in good part; and I shall only say *for myself*, that I agree with her *entirely*. I *depended* on a line from you this morning (written yesterday) to say, that you had seen D^r Baillie a second time, and I was quite disappointed at your silence. Pray, do not omit a *single* day the letting me have a *single* line at least. I shall not be in Town till Thursday.

Your affec^te Son,
M. G. L.

[1] This letter is written on the margin of the following one from Mrs. Blake. It seems impossible to date and is placed here on the very poor chance that it refers to the same illness mentioned in the preceding letter.

[To Lewis from Anna Blake]

Saturday

My dear Matthew

As the *pretty* Novel writers say, "impute my silence to any thing but neglect."—I am much obliged to you for your letter. I did not care much, about the orders and as you will soon have an opportunity of obliging me in this respect I dont mind it *at all*.—Caroline, as you imagin, is *delighted*, and declares, in *good* time, "that she *cant bear* going to *Covent Garden*" I went to the Castle-Spectre, because both your Uncle and I, had nearly forgotten it, & we wished Caroline to see it. We were very much pleased with it, and very glad that we went. I am much grieved to find your Mother has had a relapse. She has seen Dr Baillie at which I rejoice but I regrett to find that on Baillie's calling again she *declined* seeing him. I know Baillies time to be so very much engaged that He is obliged to decline seeing many *new* patients, when he will call on those whom he has once seen, and he wou'd not have called on your Mother had he not thought it Necessary to make some further alteration or observation necessary for her *certain* recovery He *told* her, "her recovery wou'd *not be speedy*." Yet, because she felt *relieved* in the course of *Two* Days, wou'd imagin, that she cou'd do without seeing him *any more*. Had he done her *no* good, I cou'd have reconciled it but, I am, as it is, quite concerned at her standing so in the way of her own good. I have known Dr Baillie many years and had a great deal to do with him and I do declare, I know not a more *dis*interested Man any where, or one more, humane & considerate in not putting himself *in the way* of taking *one* Guinea unnecessary to the *patient*. Your Uncle has seen her, & says, He does not like, her appearance, & thinks there is cause to be alarmed at the stile of her Cough, if it is not soon cured. [I] paid the Twenty Pounds y[ou] desired me to give her.—

Believe me am most affec[tionate aunt]

A B

Pray tell me the first words of the Glee you desired Caroline to learn.


Barnes. Jany. 13. 1803.

My dear Mother,

I return you Mrs Sewell's letters & verses. I had a letter from her myself yesterday, stating that She meant to publish her Poems by *Subscription*: I wish, you would put down my name, & when the book appears, I will trouble you (if you will let me know of its publication) to transmit £5 to her, either for my copy, or for as many copies as will amount to that sum, whichever, you think, will appear the most civil to her; but I particularly wish my name *not* to be put down for *more* than *one* copy. I have had so much flattery & censure for the last eight years, that I am quite indifferent about both, & therefore cannot say with truth, that I am very grateful; However, if you chuse to take the *sin* of the falshood upon your own shoulders, you are welcome to say, that I am highly flattered by the verses &c. As to the verses, they are neither good, nor very bad. I hope, She does not mean to publish them: But if She does, you should apprize her, that She has got the *names* wrong; Angelina should be Angela, & Oswald should be Orsino. If She does not correct this fault, People will suppose that She never read the plays in question, but was determined to praise me *á tort et á travers*— "the beauteous form" clearly belongs to the Muse, not to me; but you are quite right that the title of her poem should be "To the Muse, on reading the Tragedy of Alfonso by M. G. Lewis". When I read the lines, *I* too thought that She imagined the Play to have failed; but in her letter She asks, whether I "wondered at its having succeeded": I now beleive that *It* relates to *the Tower*; but this is so obscure, that every body would suppose, that the Play had been damned, which is the only possible supposition which I am anxious to avoid. In fact the two lines had better be left out, for the second is an errant plagiarism, it having been already been said of old Oaks or old Statues, (I forget which) that they were

Graced by defect—& worshipped in decay," which is nearly the same idea & words.—But I hope, these lines will not be printed; the more praise, the more envy; and the first in my opinion does not balance the second in *value*, & certainly does not in *activity*.[1] Alfonso has been played with great applause; so great indeed, that M<sup>r</sup> Harris (who was present from the rising of the curtain to its fall) ordered Richard 3<sup>d</sup>, which had been announced for the next Tragedy to be postponed, & Alfonso to be repeated instead of it. For what reason I know not, but M<sup>r</sup> Harris all of a sudden has taken a fancy for everything that I do. I sent to ask him, whether He would let M<sup>rs</sup> Litchfield speak some lines, which I have written, between the Play & Farce—"Anything that you chuse to be brought forward" said He "shall be produced immediately". He has got my after-piece again (but which I like so little myself, that I do not think, that I shall let it appear) and wants it lengthened into a *first* piece, for just now He seems to think He cannot have enough of my writing; Nay, He carried his enthusiasm so far, that when Alfonso was advertised this year, contrary to all custom He put the author's name in the Bills, as if nobody could resist that attraction. How this happens, I am ignorant; but the fact is, that He is as full of civility & compliments, & fine speeches as He can cram. The Lines, which I mentioned to be spoken by M<sup>rs</sup> Litchfield, are called "The Captive" & are to be spoken with accompaniments of Music: I believe too, *The Minister* will be played for Johnston's Benefit under the title of "the Harper's Daughter". But do not mention *either* of the above circumstances to any body for particular reasons. I do not know anything about W. Sewell, not having been in Town for some time: You quite mistook me about him; I alluded to his general behaviour, not to any particular circumstance which had occurred lately. Maria is quite well; I dine with her tomorrow being my Father's birth-day, for which I shall go to London.—If I can give Miss Parsons orders for Alfonso, I will; but as I have no *right* to give them this season, & only am upon *sufferance* in that respect, I am obliged to restrict myself to a certain number. Sophia is just returned to Town, in good health & spirits, but rather in the dumps at her Sister's not having yet succeeded in getting an Opera-Box.

your affec[te] Son

M G Lewis

Pray, let M[rs] Sewell know that I answered her letter directing simply to Chertesy, for I burnt her letter before I examined the particular address.

[1] Lewis' hope was not fulfilled. In the same year there appeared *Poems*, by Mrs. G. Sewell, relict of the late Rev. Geo. Sewell, rector of Byfleet, Surrey, 1803, containing a thirty-four line effusion (pp. 261–263), in which, except for the title, Mrs. Sewell observed Lewis' corrections. The verses begin:

To M.G.Lewis, Esq.

on reading his tragedy of Alfonso.

1803.

*Sweet* Muse! and hast thou found the honour'd way,
Where holy Truth bestows her golden ray?
Tho' clouds appear, and Terror's dreadful storm
Rends the fair drap'ry from thy beauteous form. . . .

Friday—18th March 1803[1]

My dear Mother,

I will not lose a moment in expressing to you my sorrow at your late illness, and in thanking you for your compliance with my request. Our opinions certainly on the subject of my last letter seem to be very different; for I hold, that a Woman has no business to be a public character, and that in the proportion that She acquires notoriety, She loses delicacy: I always consider a female Author as a sort of half-Man; But as this is a subject on which it is not likely we should coincide, and as your ready acquiescence with my request makes it unnecessary to discuss it, I shall say no more on that head. I return you many thanks for your kind intentions in writing the letter to the Morning Herald, but am full as well pleased with its not having been inserted; I had *rather* not be mentioned at all without necessity; but otherwise the Newspapers may insert what paragraphs they please, & I had just as soon be called M[r] *Monk Lewis* as anything else: this is a subject of all others on which I profess the most total indifference. It was not merely on account of the advertisement, that I declined seeing any of M[rs] Kelly's Manuscripts: But into the bargain She had just published a Novel, in which there was a most flaming eulogium upon the author of the Monk; & the advertisement might have induced people to suppose that I had written my own praises; Now though I have no objection to other people's trying to make me appear *wicked or foolish*, I do not chuse to have it supposed that I have made myself appear *ridiculous*; & therefore I immediately informed M[rs] Kelly, that I never could give any public patronage to a Person who had published an eulogium upon me; & that though I would continue to take care of her child for another year,

I would have nothing to do with her writings. She wanted too to dedicate to me, but *that* I stopped, as I should have done her eulogium had I been aware of it.—I gave M^rs Kelly the plan of a Novel, but She did not adopt it in the Baron's Daughter: at least I beleive not, for I only read the 2 first Vol^s. I gave no poems for it, & mean to give none for any future work of hers. The paragraphs only appeared within these two Months, & the Baron's Daughter was published last May (I beleive). The paragraphs therefore could not apply to that work; Her last was called "The Modern Incident;" the one She is now about (of which I have not seen a line) is "The Secret;" & the title of the supposed Novel is "The Father & Mother." —I never before heard of your being *accused* of having written *The Monk:* this goes nearer to put me out of humour with the book, than all the fury of The Pursuits of Literature &c. What the world knows I care not, provided *I* do not know it; But I cannot remain ignorant, if I find the Morning Post, or Morning Herald filled with offensive Paragraphs which I have read, & see lying upon every breakfast table. Lady Buckinghamshire's expression was "that She was related to the *Sewell* family": but this subject is equally painful and unnecessary to discuss; Let me hope, that it will drop here, & not be resumed. I am quite of your opinion when you say "that it would be better for you as a Woman to write a dull sermon, than the *Monk;*" & that not merely on the score of delicacy, but because a dull work will prevent its Author's being much talked of, a point (in my opinion) of all others the most desireable for a Woman to attain; but surely it is not worth while to take the trouble of composing a Work, when *"to avoid the dangers of authorship your only safety perhaps would be in the want of Genius in its composition."* You will equally avoid those dangers by *not* publishing your work, & at the same time have the advantage of keeping your want of Genius a secret. *Au reste*, I should much doubt there being at present a single soul existing, who thinks the Monk was written by any body but myself; & as I said before, till now I never heard of such a suspicion. Again I thank you for your acquiescence, & rejoice in your finding such good effects from the air of Tunbridge. The Monodrama comes out on Tuesday; I have not yet been at a single rehearsal. It cannot possibly succeed.

your affec^te Son,
M. G. Lewis

[1] The *Life* (I, 278) gives 1804 and omits Lewis' reference to the monodrama (I, 281), which would have betrayed the change.

Wednesday. [March 23, 1803][1]

My dear Mother,

The Papers will have already informed you, that the Monodrama has failed: It proved much too terrible for representation, and two people went into hysterics during the performance, & two more after the curtain dropped. It was given out again with a mixture of applause and disap-probat[i]on; but I immediately withdrew the peice. In fact the subject (which was merely a picture of Madness) was so uniformly distressing to the feelings, that at last I felt my own a little painful; & as to M$^{rs}$ Litchfield, She almost fainted away. I did not expect that it would succeed, and of course am not disappointed at its failure; the only chance was, whether Pity would make the audience weep; but instead of that, Terror threw them into fits; & of course there was an end of my Monodrama. I thought, you might like to hear this account from myself, & therefore write these few lines. I hope, Tunbridge continues to agree with you. Read *"Rosella"* if you have not done so already; I am delighted with it.

> your affec$^{te}$ Son
> M G Lewis

I have just received your letter, & open mine to say a few words in answer; but I am in haste, & shall be as brief as possible.[2] You did *not* "give me the least pain by what you said about the Monk;" I meant the word *accusation* to be understood in its literal sense, & on this point perfectly agree with you, that it would not do credit to a *female* pen. So different however are our opinions & ways of seeing the same thing, that I confess, they meet upon no other point of your whole letter. In my opinion, the acuteness of *pleasure* in this world bears no proportion to the acuteness of *pain:* I requested you to sacrifice the *chance* of receiving *pleasureable* sensations from your work being well received by the public to the considera-tion, that your publishing at all would *certainly* give me very *painful* ones, whether your work succeeded or failed—though *you* may think it [un]neces-sary to consider the feelings of a person, who (you say) [ha]s stabbed you to the heart, you will allow that *I* ought to consider them, and be doubly anxious that they should not be wounded by *you*, more than by any other person. I did not expect you to consider the feelings of the Lushington family, but Maria's interest; which certainly is that She should be loved and respected by her Husband's Relations; & from what I know of them, I am persuaded, She would not be thought the better of by them for having an Authoress for her Mother. Observe at the same time, that Lady Lushington was consulted before Maria visited you, & not only approved of it, but (I beleive) offered, if there was any occasion for it, to accompany Maria herself, an offer which Lushington thought it unnecessary to accept. Observe, I am not positive about this last circumstance. Of course, It is not that Lady L— thinks unworthily of you in your present character; but if you dashed forward as an authoress, from her ideas I am sure that She would be displeased, & being a Woman of strong passions, Maria most probably would feel the effects of her displeasure. I have *not* met with any paragraphs concerning you; I wrote, from the fear that I might hereafter; from the pain which I felt even at the *idea*, judge what I should feel at [the] *reality*. The very paragraph which you have copied out, would [have] been enough to make me miserable for a week: But I observe in it, that the compliment of "a rational & inoffense life" is annexed to a "life of retirement" & a "Tragedy *not* intended for publication". I doubt not, you will always be loved & respected by those who live with you, and are sufficiently intimate to know the good qualities of your heart; but Those who alone know you by report, can only know that you formerly took a step in defiance of the declared principles of society (in taking which step, the more genius that you prove yourself to possess, the less excuseable will they think you) and that now you take another very bold step for *any* person but especially for a Woman, in declaring yours[elf] a candidate for public applause.—The reason why I should have employed Maria to speak to you on the subject of writing was because I thought you would take it more gently from [*her*], than from *me*: You say, that I am too haughty in my manner, & I hoped, you would find Maria's more delicate. As it is, I fear, from the style of your Letter that mine offended you: I can only solemnly assure you, that it never was, & never will be my design to give the least pain to your feelings, when I can avoid it. Again I thank you for your acquiescence, & trust, that you will not withdraw it.

Your affec<sup>te</sup> Son<br>M G Lewis

You will observe that the Morning Herald continues to call me *Monk-Lewis*, & to abuse me as much as formerly.

¹ The monodrama *The Captive* was performed on Tuesday, March 22, 1803.

² This addition after the signature is printed in the *Life* (I, 282–285) as a separate letter.

Wednesday [late 1803]¹

My dear Mother,

I will not let a day pass with[out] releiving you from any anxiety which you may be under respecting the loan, which you wish to make. £65 shall be ready for you as soo[n] *after* January as you please, but as I *give* no interest for the money, of course I can *take* none. Having said this, suffer me to remin[d] you of my peculiar situation, which will not *always* admit of my lending large sums wit[h] as much facility, as I can grant your presen[t] request. I have no fixed allowance; my money is not paid into my own hands, but is paid upon drafts upon my Father, which drafts are open to his inspection, and liable to his enquiry as to the occasion which I had for particular sums[.] If in addition to the sums which I draw for my own use there should be a large sum lent to another person, it might naturally lead him to ask to what use I had applied it, and on hearing the answer He might *as* naturally enquir[e], what right I had to lend *his* money without previously asking whether He *chose* to lend it: I cannot therefore but own, that it would not merely be *inconvenient* to me to lend large sums out of *his* money, but in my opinion absolutely *wrong*. Whatever is my *own* I shall be always happy to accomodate you with; but I have no right to make the same use of what is my Father's. The little sums, which I have been able to assist you with from time to time, have been my own property;

either taken from the produce of my writings, or what I thought I had a right (from having been moderate in my expenditure for a month or two) to bestow on my own pleasure, than which I could have none greater than contributing to yours: It is from the former of these sources, that I am now able to promise you the loan which you request; Bell the Bookseller owes me about £200, part of which I shall receive by the end of January, and with the use of part of which I shall readily accomodate you, and you may replace it at your own convenience during any period of the ensuing year: But if I had not luckily had this fund to resort to, I own, I should have felt considerable inconvenience in managing the business; since I must either have done what I have absolutely no right to do (viz: lent you my Father's money unknown to him) or else have asked of Him the loan of it for you as a favour, which would have been [ex]tremely distressing to me, as at present it would give me great pain to be obliged to ask a favour of him. However, as it is, I can accomodate you without either of the above inconveniencies, and whenever you let me know *after* January that you want the money, I will send it to you. I intended to have gone to Lord R$^t$ Spencer's, but various things have detained me in London, or rather at Barnes, for I stay in London as little as possible; I did not, however, think it necessary to answer your last letter on that point, as you desired me not, "unless I should be free from engagements"; instead of which my time is so wholly occupied by different things but part[icularly] by my being obliged to run the gaunt[let] of invit[ations thro]ugh the whole of Capt: Sheddon's . . .[2] family, that [I have had hardly] a day to myself. [However,] I hope now to make my escape ti[ll the] marriage draws near, as M$^{rs}$ Whitelocke presses me very much to come down to Portsmouth, and perhaps my coming as soon as the marriage is over, (which will be some time in January,) I shall probably join L$^d$ H. Petty at Bath, and remain there till the end of the Month. Sophia on her marriage goes to Twyford Lodge; & I beleive, it is her intention to request you to pay her a visit there, in which case I shall if possible meet you—an additional reason for my being unwilling to make more use of my Father's money, than I can avoid, is that He really has not ready money himself; a proof of which is, that He only pays Sophia the *interest* of her fortune, and She is not to receive the *capital* till his death; though on Maria's marriage He paid the whole of *her* fortune down. Maria is quite well; I have no opera coming out, nor anything but Alfonso.

your affec$^{te}$ Son M. G. Lewis

[1] Sophia Lewis' marriage (Jan. 18, 1804) is in prospect.
[2] "Large"? Space for five letters is torn away.

Tuesday. [late July or early August 1804]

My dear Mother,

Surely I wrote you a few lines acknowledging the receipt of the £5; at least I persuaded myself, that I had done so. You will be sorry to hear, that all the disputes are beginning again, or rather are *ending*. Some time ago, my Father through Lushington enquired, whether *"not out of duty*, but out of affection to him I would be on the same terms with M^rs Ricketts as with any other acquaintance," previous to which He had also sent me word, "that though He was satisfied with my behaviour towards himself, He should never restore his affection to me, till I had been to visit M^rs Ricketts." —My answer to this question was "that I had never declined acknowledging her as an acquaintance, when I met her; that whenever She came to his House, it was my duty to receive her, if He chose to order me to do so, and also to take care to do nothing which could make his house disagreable to her while She was in it; But that I could not be on the same terms with *her*, as with any other acquaintance, Because I had no other acquaintance, towards whom I had the same feelings, and of whom I entertained the same opinion: I therefore declined being on any other terms than the above-mentioned, and concluded by expressing everything the most kind and affectionate towards himself personally." Since this He has treated me in the coldest manner possible; He wrote to Sophia, that He should endeavour to become totally indifferent to me (which I firmly beleive, was a work that could cost him little trouble) and when He went to Portsmouth He did not inform me that He was going out of Town, and made Frederick Ricketts his *compagnon de voyage*, though I should have been very glad to have accompanied him, and probably my aunt Whitelocke would have been more pleased to see *me*, that the Boy.[1] Yesterday however I received a note from him, telling me that "He had ceased to consider me as part of his domestic establishment; that after what has passed, it was disagreable to him, that I should remain an inmate of his house, and desiring me to [move out][2] before his return from his T[rip to Portsmouth].[3] I cannot omit mentioning (though it is [a trifle], that] where-as hitherto I had been supplied with [wine from his] cellars, He tells me, I shall have this little [privilege no] longer; I suppose, the quantity altogether [amounted to] four dozen in the course of the year!—[He said when I] requested to know my fault, for which [I am to suffer] this banishment; You shall know the [reason later.] you see, how little good has arisen fr[om your] humbling yourself to soliceit M^rs Ricket[t's] interference. Maria has inoculated her C[hild, who] is doing well, & She is going into the country . . . ay[4] much recovered; Sophia is in Town for a few day[s], the Reg^t being on the march to Winchester; She expects to be confined in December. Shedden has forbidden her visiting M^rs Ricketts, & She resides at her Brother-in-Law's, purposely to avoid the necessity of being much with that Lady, which would result from her inhabiting Devonshire Place. My Uncle William is in Town, and says, He wishes to see you; He dined here yesterday.

Your affec^te Son,<br>M. G. Lewis

[1] For "than the Boy."

[2] A corner torn away affects thirteen lines.

[3] The "T" is doubtful.

[4] There is space for about seven letters.

Tuesday [early August 1804]

My dear Mother,

M^r Martin's Cottage will not do on account of the £300 required for the Lease, and which it would cost me near £900 to raise: otherwise it would do very well. The Cottage in Middlesex must be too large a concern for me; there are *seven* bed-rooms. I should like to know the rent of that at Hanwell as soon as you get an answer, pray send it to me; Perhaps it might do for a year, though the "very small portion of garden-ground" sounds as if it were not very retired. I begin quite to despair of success; I shall go to Scotland next week, and what is to become of me when I return, I know not; However, I [ca]n remain at Barnes till the end of the year. —During my absence perhaps you or M^rs Ingall may hear of something such as I wish; and I have no fear of your *neglecting* or *forgetting* my commissions. Continue to send your letters to Devonshire Place. Nothing that you can write to M^rs R— at present could be of any service; nor untill My Father has *actually* withdrawn his protection from me, would I participate in anything, that could possibly offend him. If you think, you can do any good, you are the best Judge, nor can I prevent your doing it; But for my own part I am persuaded of the contrary.—Nothing but absolute submission to M^rs R— would be of the least use towards making my Father *endure* me. She wants to separate him from me, and will succeed by hook or by crook. I came up to-day to dine with M^rs Whitelocke in D— Place; and I found an order from my Father "that as M^rs R— was to dine there, I must not offend *him* by my appearance either at dinner or in the Evening."—In haste—I do not wish you to write what I mentioned to you, till I have *actually* left my Father's House for ever.

Your affec^te Son
M G Lewis.

Inveraray Castle. August 18^th[1804]

My dear Mother,

When-ever I mean not to be annoyed for any time, I always order my letters to be detained: the consequence of which is, that through this fear of getting disagreable news, yours of the 13^th and 22^d did not reach me till this day, when on my arrival at Inveraray a large packet was put into my hands of which your epistles formed a constituent part, and they are the first which I sit down to answer. The House at Hanwell (it is clear) is *not* the Rectory, and *does* stand in a row; It cannot therefore be so very eligible, as to induce me to take it six months before I should want to inhabit it. I think, I shall certainly not return to England before December, and I have taken my rooms at Barnes on till the end of January; So that I shall have those two Months to look about me. In the mean while you will oblige me by keeping your eye upon the look-out; I should like (if possible) to find something on the plan of your Cottage at Leatherhead, for which I recollect you paid so much a year for so many years, with a liberty of giving it up at stated periods, but not paying any money down for the Lease. If I could meet with such a thing as this, I would take it immediately; otherwise, if I can only take the House by the *year*, it would be silly to take it before Christmas. Should any accident lead you or M^r Ingall into the neighbourhood of Hanwell, perhaps you might as well just look at M^r Glasse's; But it would not be worth while to go on purpose. the date of this Letter is an answer to the part of your letter respecting M^r Auker;[1] you must say to M^rs Parsons from me, that had I been in London I should have been very happy to have made his acquaintance, and that I feel extremely indebted to her and to Miss Parsons for their civilities; I trust, that I shall never again quit Great Britain; but if anything should ever take me to Demmark, I shall not fail to make use of Miss Parson's permission to pay her my compliments. With regard to my Father and M^rs Ricketts, things are worse than ever; I will not repeat to you the various modes in which He showed his resentment, and, I must say, his hatred of me; for that He does *hate* me now, I am quite convinced. I will only mention, that the ninth of July being my Birth-day, He met me on the Stairs, said—"So; you are there, Sir!" and past on: Nor did I see him any more, though I dined at home with nobody but M^rs Whitelocke; But though it was my Birth-day, He preferred taking an earlier dinner by himself, and then going. . . . to a cricket-match![2] If you wish to know the *kind* manner, in which He expresses himself about me, you will see it in the following extract from one of his Letters to Maria—"Your Brother is still in my House, pursuing the same *steady* conduct as before; His indifference as to the pain He has occasioned me, and continues to give, is brutal; and must operate to convince me, that He wants not only the proper feelings of a Son, but the generosity of a Man."—Would not any body think, that I had committed some great crime? Or at least, that I had disobeyed some command of his? On the contrary, I have never disobeyed him; I am ready to do anything, but *lye*; the whole extent of my offense[3] is, that I think ill of a Woman, to whom He is attached, with whom I *ought* to have nothing to do, and whom I look upon as my most bitter Enemy.—As to what you say, "about leaving my card," with all my heart; I am not only ready to do this, but anything which can be included in the proposal which I have already made to him, and which follows.—"I am ready to do anything that my Father chuses, provided it can be done consistent *with Truth*."—I think, *you* will not wish me to make a more ample declaration; I have made it to him through my Aunt Whitelocke; I have desired Maria to make it again, accompanied by a *denial* of my *indifference* as to his renunciation of me, and an assurance of my having felt equal *pain* with himself; I now offer you, for your own satisfaction to cause the same proposal to be made to my Father through your Brother William, find out through *him* to what extent of *friendship* towards M^rs Ricketts my Father wishes my conduct to be carried, then ask yourself (but remember you are upon *honour* with me, and that you must not make an *heroic sacrifice* of truth to your wish to bring about a reconciliation) how much of what is required you can in conscience ask your Son to submit to, and what you say shall have *much* weight with Me. One thing you must bear in mind; From my own knowledge of it, and from positive facts, I never can entertain any other real sentiments of M^rs R's character, than the most profound contempt and aversion;[4] I therefore am content to *endure* her, but I never can with *sincerity* be *cordial* with a person, of whom think so ill.[5] I can *forgive* injuries so far as never to *revenge* But I cannot, however I may *wish* it, *forget facts*. Now weigh all this well; then apply to your Brother William, and say to him what you may think fitting. A thought has just suggested itself to me, which if you think any good can arise from, you are at liberty to adopt. Let her be informed by my Uncle William (who is her Friend, and therefore from whom it will come most palatable) of the true state of things; She hates me, that is certain; I despise her, that is equally sure; My Father wishes us to be reconciled, and that is in *fact* quite impossible. But if She is once positively informed, that I never *willingly* will be on other terms with her than those which exist at present, and if She has really that regard for my Father's tranquillity to wish to make him easy on the Subject, the business may be easy to manage. I shall have no objection to call on her, provided She will have the goodness to order, that I shall never be let in; whenever She dines in D— Place, She can easily let me know secretly, and I will always dine somewhere else; But She must upon no account expect me to *behave cordially* to her, because with the opinion which I entertain of her, and after the pain which She has been the means of causing me, it is *impossible* that I should ever feel the least *cordiality* towards her. If any compact of this nature could contribute to my Father's happiness I am ready to enter into it; I can reserve my sentiments to myself, but I cannot feign those which I do not feel: Do *you* wish, that I should? Talk over this business with W^m Sewell, and let me know the result.—I rejoice to hear, that my Uncle Robert is attentive to you.—I have been very unwell of late, my headachs being returned with increased violence, and almost without intermission. Direct to me *under cover* to Lord J. Campbell, M.P. Inveraray Castle, Argyllshire, N.B.

Your affec^te Son,<br>M. G. Lewis

1 Or "Anker."
2 The dots are Lewis'.
3 Or "offence."
4 Lewis canceled "abhorrence" and substituted "aversion."
5 For "I think so ill."

Inveraray. Sept^r 28 1804.

My dear Mother,

I wrote a few lines to you the other day, being afraid from your silence that my first letter had not reached you, and I was unwilling to have it fall into the hands of a Stranger. Your answer reached me this morning, and I lose no time in apprizing you of a mistake which you seem to me to have made, probably from having mislaid my letter. The first step in my opinion should have been to ascertain what my Father wished to be done, not what Mrs Ricketts would consent to do. If what would content him proved to be no more than leaving a card at her door or some such trifles, then it would be worth while to enter into a negotiation with her, in order that my obliging him might not be misinterpreted, and that we might satisfy him without being obliged ourselves to submit to society which we hate (for I am certain, She hates me as heartily as I do her, and indeed when I have told my Father so, He has never contradicted it only assured me, that She was willing to be reconciled) But if on the other hand He will not be satisfied without my being on *friendly* and *intimate* terms with her, having a formal *reconciliation* and giving her my hand with a promise of future *amity*, you must be sensible that it it impossible for to submit[1] to lye so grossly, for such conduct must be a lye as long as I entertain my present opinion of Her, and of her conduct: It would therefore in this case be superfluous to make any application to Mrs Ricketts; and therefore I could wish you (before you have any sort of intercourse with her either through William Sewell or anybody else) to ascertain the utmost extent of my Father's demands, and to do this, there cannot be a more proper person than Wm Sewell. You need not tell him *what I am determined not to* do, but desire him to ascertain with how much compliance my Father would be satisfied, "in order that *you* may persuade me (if it appears to you possible) to consent to my Father's demands." I must, however, acknowledge to you, that I wish to ascertain this point from other reasons, than from the hope of bringing about a reconciliation; for since I wrote to you, I have made again an offer through Maria "of doing anything He chuses which is not inconsistent with truth." His answer was "that I had lost the moment for regaining his affection, and that now no compliance of any kind would be of any use."—He has said nearly the same thing to Sophia, and therefore I have finally given up all hopes of a reconciliation. But still you will *oblige me much* by finding out through Wm Sewell, exactly what it is that my Father requires of me. I do not beleive my Uncle Robert knows her; I know, that She does not visit Mrs Blake; You may as well look for a white Crow, as for an Individual of our Family who does not view Mrs Ricketts in the most contemptible light, or who would accept of "her partiality," Wm Sewell excepted; theref[ore] I still t[hin]k, that if anything were to be done, it mu[st] be through *Him*, but my Father's speech to Maria [seems] to me to put an end to the business. Pray, ascertain my Father's demands, as soon as you can, and let me know them without delay. Lady Bath's House at Twickenham costs her £5000 a year. Mr Glasse (I take it) lives *himself* at the *Rectory*, and the House which He has to let in Hanwell is a different one from that in which He resides. He wrote word to you, "that He did not answer your letter, because you had positively objected to an House in a row;" His not answering you therefore proved, that his *was* in a row, and therefore would not suit you. Lushington *is* very inconsistent frequently, and I told him so, respecting his Wife's receiving M^rs Sewell, and not M^rs Blake. My illness has only been continual headachs, which I am tormented with more than ever. You do not mention your own health; I hope, it is good.

Your affec^te Son
M. G. L.

Who is the Drury Lane Opera said to be written by?—A Madman called "Corri,"[2] brought me just such a plan once with the same title.

[1] For "impossible for me to submit."
[2] Domenico Corri (1746–1825).

Inveraray [postmarked October 22, 1804]

My dear Mother,

I thought, I had mentioned in a former letter, that as I had engaged my rooms at Barnes for three months longer, till the end of January I did not want to take anything at present unless it was such, as I should be likely to continue in; you say yourself, (and the account of the place confirms what you say) that the Twickenham Common House would only do for something temporary; and as the rooms are so small, there would not be space enough to put away my Books, which is my chief object in quitting Barnes. Trees too are indispensible. I wish you to enquire about different places while I am absent, and then I can look at them when I return; But I do not wish a House to be taken for me, unless I hear of one *quite* what I am in search of. Being near London (if possible not more than four Miles) would be a great recommendation to me; Twickenham Common is too far off, unless I could find something very eligible indeed.—I keep the addresses of all Houses, which I see advertised, and mean to enquire about them when I return to London.

It is about a year and an half ago, that Corri called on me, and wanted me to write the Dialogue of the Opera in question; I thought him mad from his manner and conversation, and also from the extreme absurdity of the plan which He described to me: It appeared quite impractable, but That was only one of the objections to it. The first Act (according to his account of it to *me*) was to be in Holland, not China. I should doubt much, Cherry's having promised to write the Dialogu, at least upon Corri's plan; and if He *has*, the merits of "The Soldier's Daughter," do not induce me to expect very good Dialogue; nor does such of Corri's Music as I have heard (with the exception of Storace's Song in The Cabinet) lead me to expect any very good Music. It seems to me very unlikely, that the Proprietors should have accepted an Opera, before it is written; for as to their accepting it on account of the merits of the *Music*, I doubt much there being any among them very capable of judging of Music in Score.— Another reason I had for thinking Corri mad was having heard a good many anecdotes of him from the Buccleuch Family who patronized him in Edinburgh, and were highly amused with his oddities. I rather beleive, He taught some of the Ladies Montagu; when I go to Bothwell, I will try to find out, what sort of a Teacher He is, for I can say nothing as to that. Miss Mortimer of Covent Garden was his Pupil, and I have heard, that She complains of him; but I am not certain of this, and rather beleive that her complaint regards money, not skill.

I must give you a caution about Miss L[ace]y[1] She will find the Theatre a very dangerous place for a young Person; Many of the Women with whom She must associate are of the worst principles and conduct; and many of the Men are insolent and depraved to an excess. You ought also to be made aware, that not only Sheridan is the most abandoned Libertine that probably ever existed, But that Graham (though a very good-natured worthy Man in other respects, as far as I know) passes for having very few scruples when Women are in the case.—If therefore She is to have anything to do with the Theatre, you ought to take care of providing some elderly *and* discreet Woman to accompany her there and protect her; otherwise however good may be her own principles and regular her conduct, She will be continually exposed to a thousand insults.—A Theatre is in fact a place, in which no woman of delicacy ought to set her foot (behind the scenes, I mean) unless protected by the presence of an Husband. I hope, you will find this kind of life answer for Miss Lassy,[2] but I fear the contrary much; For a Man the case is very different.

your affec<sup>te</sup> Son

M. G. Lewis.

I am very curious to know, both what William Sewell [will] answer you, a[n]d what He has already answered. When [you] direct to me under cover to Lord J. Campbell, do not om[it] the *cross* under the outer seal. Whereabouts is your Lodgi[ng] in Town, and what does it cost you?

[1] Canceled by a later hand.
[2] For "Lacey."

Barnes. Wednesda [1805][1]

My dear Mother,

All that *you* require me to do, I have done already; But you are not aware, what *is* required of me. It is not merely to alter my *conduct* towards M<sup>rs</sup> R—, But my *sentiments* respecting her and her proceedings, on which that conduct was grounded: Now a Man's sentiments are not in his own power; I cannot think that right, which I know (or at least *think* I know) to be wrong; and if I were to say that my sentiments are altered, when in fact they remain the same, I should tell a lye. It is also expected of me, that I should say, (observe this, and frame the answer.) the whole of my conduct has been *wrong* in this business; as I shall answer it before God, I declare that I beleive that the whole of my conduct in this business has been perfectly right; Can I then make the acknowledgement expected of me? Would it not be telling a most absolute and wilful falshood? Can you really ask me to become a *Lyar*, for that would be my proper appellation?—Now hear what I *have* done, and you will allow, that it is not an *apology* to my Father that is expected from me, nor is it *pride* that prevents me from effecting a reconciliation. I have given up every point regarding *conduct*; I have promised to sacrifice my own feelings so far, as to consent to meet this odious Person at my Father's House, and have engaged to meet her with a fixed determination not to say or do anything, that can possibly offend her. I have made a declaration to my Father, that "I am ready to obey him in every thing in which I can and ought to obey him."—I was told that some passages in my letters had offended him; I made the humblest apology, assured him over & over again that they were not *meant* to offend him, that since they had had that effect I wished they had not been written, and I begged his pardon. I have also told him (with regard to his insisting on my "owning the *whole* of my conduct to have been *insulting to him* and *improper*") that I was ready to acknowledge, that if I had either said or done anything which appeared to him insulting or which gave him the least pain, when I could *possibly* avoid it, in so far my conduct had been extremely improper, and that I was extremely sorry for it, assuring him at the same time that nothing which I had said or done was intended to produce that effect. Could I say more? Would you really wish me to say—"I declare, that I have been entirely wrong;" when in truth I feel, that I have been entirely right?—Yet even this I have profest myself ready to do; I have told him, that it is not in my power to think myself wrong; But that if He chuses to degrade me so far as to insist on my telling a falshood, and *saying* that I think what I do *not* think, I will do so, if it can contribute to his satisfaction. Now have the goodness to let me know, what more you would wish me in conscience to do. The business about Mrs W— is quite given up; She acquiesces in the propriety of the observation of my Sisters, that it would be best to be introduced to them only as *acquaintance*. With regard to *myself* I assure you, I am quite easy on the Subject; all that I wish is to spare my Father the unpleasant sensations, which He may hereafter feel, should He sacrifice me to the wish of gratifying Mrs R—. I have long perceived that He loved me no longer; Sophia too has just sent me a letter of his, in which He says plainly that He has no longer any affection for me, and does not think (even should He be reconciled to me) that He shall ever feel any again.—I cannot therefore expect much *pleasure* from his society even when I can have it without Mrs R's, and I suppose *you* will not *expect* me to feel *very* happy in *her* society, when I know (and my Father has justified the speech to Sophia) that She has said—"My Father was only waiting for my Mother's death to give her the greatest proof of his regard." and after this, considering the light in which She is at present looked upon, can anyone doubt that the news of your death is expected by her with impatience and will be received by her with delight? And *ought* a Son to be upon friendly terms with a Person, who He *knows* is waiting with impatience for the death of his Mother, and who has had the imprudence to avow, that She is doing so?—If I ever *am* obliged to submit to her society, certainly I shall be miserable while I am in it; My Father's society will not be at all a consolation, since I know that He has no affection for me, and firmly beleive that He had rather my throat should be cut, than that Frederick Ricketts should lose a joint of his little finger; on the terms on which we shall be together, I can never ask any of my own Friends to his table; In his resentment He has assigned me an income less than my expenditure has been for several years, and of course I shall not ask him to increase it; He has even refused to keep Saddle-horses for me (though He knows, that riding was the only exercise which I liked, and which had even been prescribed for me as necessary for my health) and turned away the Groom, telling me that if I chose to have them now, I must pay for them myself; What then am I to gain by a reconciliation? Nothing for myself, but I would willingly spare *Him* the painful reflections which may hereafter come across him, should He now throw me off so totally without cause. Pray, answer this soon, and tell me, what *more* you think I can do, than what I have done. Was not your letter (go to the first page[2] written in consequence of one from Maria? I *suspect* it. Observe, that no apology to Mrs R— has been ever asked of me. I have never said or done anything to insult her; I am only charged with having treated her with *coldness* and *distance*, and I am required to receive her with *warmth* and *pleasure*: Is that possible?—"*Manner*" is the chief thing complained of.—You did not date your letter.

your affecte Son
M G L.

[1] This letter and the five which follow it, all dealing with the quarrel between Lewis and his father, appear to belong together in the order here adopted. None is dated by year and only one by month. One is watermarked 1805, and another, dated Sunday, Feb. 24, indicates that year, since between 1804 and 1808 Feb. 24 fell on a Sunday only in 1805.

[2] All that follows "page" is written over the date line.

[1805]
[M]y dear Mother,

On reading your letter again I find one expression, which requires an observation—that Mrs R— is my "*Foe*" and hates me is true enough; But I deny that *I* am *her* Foe, or any body's Foe. I think it wrong to *hate* any one; but I heartily despise Mrs R, and would not do her any service; But on the other hand I would not do her any injury. This is the expression which I have used to my Father;—"As Mrs R— is your Friend I will not be her Enemy; But as She wishes for the death of my Mother, I will not be her Friend." Surely that is moderate—after reading "what is required of me by my Father," I wish you to frame [suc]h an apology as can be at all *consistent with truth*; and if it is *possible*[,] I will transcribe it, and send it to him. Can you ask more?

M G L.

Friday. Barnes. [1805]

My dear Mother,

I must *in justice* lose no time in setting you right in *one* particular; M^rs R— did not say bluntly, that She *wished* you dead; but She said (what in my opinion is equivalent) "that my Father was only waiting for your death to give her the strongest proof of his regard"—and after this, considering her situation, and the light in which She is looked upon, can there be a doubt, that your death would be the most welcome news that She could possibly receive? And knowing this, ought I to seem happy to see a Person, whose bosom is filled with such wishes, and to be gay and pleased in her society? In fact, this is the whole point, for I have offered to come into her society, if my Father insists upon it, But what He wishes is, that I should come into it voluntarily, and as if it was of my own seeking. However, you will be pleased to hear, that my last letter has had some effect, and that I have had a tolerably kind answer from my Father, in which He luckily mentioned a circumstance, which had displeased him, and which it was in my power to make an apology for. He expresses an inclination to forgive what is past, but waits for my next letter; I have written one as humble and conciliatory as I could, allowing his right to ask whom He pleased to the House, and that when I met them there, I ought to do nothing that could possibly offend his guests, allowing also his right to make *me* receive them, if He thought proper. Observe, that all along I have said, that if He chose to *command* me to stay in M^rs R's society, I should obey him; as to M^rs R, (by name) and her speech, I past them over in silence, as well as my sentiments of her: He must know them, and I think *She* cannot mistake them, and therefore there was no use in repeating them.—As soon as I hear from him again, I will inform you. If Maria did not tell you anything of this business, surely my Uncle William did; what I told you, was not sufficient to inform you of all that you knew, when you wrote to Me. I cannot "set out anew" with M^rs R— I know too much of her ever to be at my ease in her society; She has been the cause of almost every quarrel that has happened in our family, ever since I can remember; while they were unmarried, She made the lives of my Sisters miserable; She did all in her power to prevent Maria's marriage; every one of my Relations except W^m Sewell sees her in the same light that I do; Many years ago my Sisters refused to go into Public with her, and in consequence the Opera-Box (which before they had jointly) was divided into alternate weeks; as to myself, She has profest the most decided hatred against myself frequently, and how then can I "set out anew with her?"—all this I can *forgive* so far as not to wish her any injury; but I cannot *forget* it, and thus by putting myself in her power, give her an opportunity of injuring *me*. What you have sent me to transcribe is an hundred times *weaker*, than many things which I have said; If I were to send it, instead of being pleased, my Father would call it an *insult*; Indeed, He wrote me word, that "*any* compromise was an insult."—Do not think me *vindictive*, when I say, I cannot forget injuries; To *forgive* them is in one's power; But we can no more *forget* them at pleasure, than one can cease to love at pleasure. Memory is not quite so obedient, as to retain all the pleasant things, because we wish to retain them, and wipe out all the disagreable ones, the moment that we wish to lose them: as for myself, I am so constituted, that I beleive, I never felt a painful sensation, which I could afterwards efface from my memory, however strongly I may have wished to do so. To *forgive* injuries means a resolution not to retaliate on the person who injured us; that is in a Man's power; But to *forget* them is in no Man's choice, and if it ever happens, it must be entirely the work of Time. You know, Macduff in Shakespeare says—(speaking of the murder of his Wife & Children)

"I *cannot* but remember, such things were,
and were most dear to me!"—

—I *have* tried "not to associate at all with M^rs R"—but that is not now to be permitted; I told my Father, "that if I had wished to insult her, I should have sought her society, instead of shunning it; but that while I kept out of her way, it was *impossible* for me to offend her." However, this had no effect.—How can I "bury *everything* in oblivion respecting M^rs R—" when I entertain such an opinion of her character in general? If She does at all wish for my society, I am sure, it can only be for the purpose of tormenting and mortifying me, conscious that in my Father's presence my hands must be bound. I wish her no ill; But I heartily wish, I may never see her again.

Beleive me, my dear Mother,
your affec^te Son, M G L.

You will be gratified to know, that in consequence of his attention to you, I have endeavoured to show as much as I can to your Brother Robert. When I went to Portsmouth, I sent for one of the Boys from the academy, made him dine at Gen: Whitelocke's, & gave him some money. I believe, They were pleased[.]

Tuesday. [1805]

My dear Mother,

I shall just write a few lines to thank you for your *very* kind letter; but my spirits are too much sunk with disappointment, and my thoughts too much occupied with disagreable subjects, to permit my writing more than a few lines, at present. I meant to have communicated to you this fresh instance of my Father's *paternal affection* for me, when I came to Town; for I thought, there was no need to be in a hurry to write what was so disagreable; and I knew well, that you would feel no less mortification than myself. When I left his House, He wrote to me in the most positive terms—"your income from this moment is £1,000 a year." Could any engagement be more express? Yet He breaks it without thinking it necessary to use on word of regret for being obliged to inflict on me so severe and so unexpected a mortification! Nay more; I have since written to him a most humble letter, acquiescing without a murmur in his arrangements, thanking him for a hope held out of restoring my income at some future period, assuring him that I would chearfully submit to every privation rather than exceed the sum, which He said it was convenient for him to allow me, and professing for him undiminished affection! Of this letter has He not deigned to take the slightest notice!—I have been obliged to tell poor Mrs Kelly, that after this year I cannot pay for her little Boy's schooling: She has written me a very kind answer (rather too enthusiastic, indeed) but the step has given me very great pain. With regard to yourself, my dear Mother many thanks for your kind schemes[,] but be assured, I am only anxious, that you should be able to make your income serve for your own expenses, as (I fear) from the narrowness of my present prospects It will not be in my power to afford you assistance. I had flattered myself with the contrary persuasion, and this is one of my airy Castles, the destruction of which gives me the most pain and disappointment. I assure you, it is a great source of satisfaction to me to think, that at least you have a comfortable House, where you are secure from vulgar intrusion, and vulgar occurrences; and I cannot but think it cheaper for you to have taken your House, than to be eternally changing your Lodgings, and be exposed to the impositions and various vices of ill-bred Landladies &c. For my own part, I must say, that I had rather dine with you upon bread water[1] in Gerard St, than upon the best possible dinner in a Lodging. I know, it will also give you satisfaction in your House to be told, that it is really a great comfort to me to be *certain* of a place, where I can find a kind reception and sympathy for my vexations, whenever compleat solitude becomes insupportable to me. In which case, I can always come up to Town, and take my dinner with you in Gerrard[2] St which I shall do very often; *provided*, that you give me *absolutely* the same dinner that was provided for yourself, though it should consist of bread and cheese. For my other Friends, I am frequently too melancholy, or too ill-tempered to have recourse; but I am sure with *you*, that I shall be welcome with all my sorrows and all my faults. Pray, let me know, when you hear, that my Uncle Robert is going out of Town.

yours affecte Son,

M. G. L.

[1] For "and water."
[2] Or "Gerard."

Sunday. Feb^y 24^th [1805]

My dear Mother,

As to there ever being *real* harmony between my Father and myself, you know, I look upon that as being out of the question because I am convinced, that He has not the least affection for me. As He is conscious (He told M^rs Blake so) that this dissension is of detriment to M^rs Ricketts, perhaps for *her* sake He may chuse to be on *apparently* good terms with me; but He will not for *mine*, be assured. I premise this, in order that you may understand that my proceedings are not founded on the vain hope of recovering his affection. In the first place I must say, that I agree *perfectly* with you in every word of your last letter, respecting my Father's note, and shall act accordingly to it, if He will permit me; but I shall not be surprized, if He *first* obtains as much for M^rs Ricketts from me as He can; endeavours to make it *appear* as if I was reconciled to her, in order that She may be no longer accused of being the cause of his anger; and *then* by demanding that I should confess my *principles* to have been wrong (which thinking them right, I cannot do without telling a lye) to make *that* refusal the pretence of his continued displeasure, and thus have an excuse for saying that M^rs R. has nothing to do with the quarrel. Pray, keep this letter, in order that if this scheme should be put into action, I may prove, that I previously protested against it. Only observe, whether I do not receive a declaration from my Father "that whenever I am come to such a proper sense of the respect that is due to him as to allow myself to have been wrong, and to repent of the conduct which has displeased him, as well as to assure him that it shall never be repeated, He will then *forgive* me and receive me as his Son; *but not till then*". This I shall not be able to do, and then M^rs Ricketts will swear, that *She* is not the cause of quarrel, for that I have called upon her, and everything is made up between us. Now you are to know, that upon receiving my Father's note, I was in doubt whether I *should* call in Baker S^t or not; However, M^rs Blake prest me so anxiously that I went and left my card last Sunday. I then wrote to my Father that I had called; I assured him of my undiminished affection and respect, I told him, I was very sorry, if I had caused him any affliction, not only during the last twelvemonth, but the whole course of my life, but that I denied having ever been the *voluntary* cause of affliction to him even for a moment. I finished by saying, that if there was anything else I could do to gratify him, I should consider his telling me what I was to do as laying an obligation on myself. To this He has not condescended to answer a line himself; but instead of doing that, or sending me word through M^rs Blake (as I think, He *ought* to have done) yesterday came a letter from Lushington saying "He was authorized to tell me, it was my Father's *wish* that I should call on M^rs Ricketts, ask for her, and see her, if She was at home: and that no explanation would be expected." In answer to this, I have sent my Father word, "that a *wish so exprest* was the same as a *command*, and I should *obey*."—You know, to call upon her *by my Father's desire* without any wish exprest of my own, or any apology for

having cut her for three long years, is no breach of sincerity, and I have
said for the last eight months "that I was ready to do anything that was not
inconsistent with sincerity." Besides this, you must know (but do not
mention this to *any human being*) to put the thing past doubt, before I
even left my card, I wrote to her, and told her in respectful but *positive*
terms "that I should call on her *merely* because my Father wished it"—"that
when I last met her in D— Place, I did not mean to be *rude* to her, but
I certainly *did* mean to be *cold* and distant"—"that I knew She hated
me, and that She had told my Sister so"—"that the speech (which She
owned having made) *comprized* in it a wish for my Mother's death, and that
her making it had placed a barrier between her and the Son of that Mother."
—"that *She* was the *only* cause of the existing dissension"—"that I was not
her *Enemy*, but neither was I her *Friend*"—and that "as She had sent me
word by W. Sewell that She was ready to do anything I would point out,
I begged her to try to persuade my Father, that it would be better for her
and me never to meet again." All this was said in the most *civil* manner
possible, but the deuce is in it if it was not plain speaking; and after reading it, I wonder, how She can *submit* to receive me; But that is her affair
and my Father's; I shall call upon her the first time I go to Town. Lushington's letter (whether intentionally, or not) was exactly calculated to make
me *refuse* to do what was desired of me; He talked of my having "gained a
great victory over myself." "That I had only to make more struggles"—
"that I ought not to mind humiliating myself before Mrs R— (if it was an
humiliation)"—"that it was a sacrifice of feeling, not of principle" &c &c
—I have requested my Father in future not to convey his orders through
Mr Lushington. I send you a letter from Mrs G Sewell, as it contains many
civil things about you.

your affecte Son
M. G. Lewis

Barnes. Wednesday [1805]

My dear Mother,

    This inclosed is a copy of a letter from my Father to me, written upon
my informing him, that Lushington had declared himself "authorized to
say that my Father *wished* me to call on Mrs Ricketts, and see her, if She
were at home." Upon receiving this answer, I considered things to be
worse than ever, and quite gave up the point in despair; But in order that
my Father should no longer have it in his power to assert, "that I had
insulted a Woman in his house", I determined to address to *her* what
I had already said to *him* repeatedly; viz "that I had not intended to treat
her with *rudeness* in D— Place; and that if my treatment had worn that
appearance I was very sorry for it": I added "that if we should ever be placed
*in a similar situation,* I would studiously endeavour to convince her, that
it had not been my intention to insult her"—you are to observe, that I had

already written her word, "that I had not meant my manner to be *rude*, though I *did* mean it to be *cold* and *distant*"—This letter I submitted to my Uncle Robert's opinion, and He very kindly consented to show it to my Father, and ask him, whether He thought such an apology sufficient for *that particular* occasion. He acknowledged it to be so; but asked, what security M^rs Ricketts would have for my not behaving rudely to her in a third place? To this my Uncle answered, "that it was not my intention to treat her with *incivility* meet her where I would;" But He gave him not the slightest reason to suppose, that I would show her the *least civility* or *attention*; on the contrary, He said that it was *not* my intention to visit her. This interview finished by my Father's saying "that He should not *forbid* my writings to him." Accordingly after sending this letter to M^rs Ricketts (every syllable of which by the bye She had already read in my letter to her, though perhaps My Father did not know it, as He did not desire her to show him my letter) I wrote to him as kindly as I could, saying "that my Uncle assured me, that the letter which had been communicated to him had given him some degree of pleasure, and that I hoped to obtain similar assurances on future occasions; that nothing had prevented my seeking his society since my return from Scotland, except thinking that my presence would be disagreable to him, and that the slightest intimation that my visits would no longer produce such an effect would make me renew them." M^rs Ricketts was not mentioned, nor a syllable relating to these disputes. Half an hour ago I received a very gracious letter from him, in which He says, that "He is satisfied with what I have said and with my manner of saying it; that He *relinquishes* all displeasure at the past," (*not* "*forgives* it" observe) in hopes that in future He shall not experience similar displeasure." He even apologizes for not offering me to live in his house again, hoping "that I will not consider it as unkind, but that He acts from motives *totally unconnected* with the subject of our disagreement." He does not mention one word about "change of principles"—"change of sentiments"— nor of "the claims which persons dear to *him* have upon *my* friendship" —on the contrary He says, that He only "expects kind and respectful attention from me, and that He as little wishes for servility on my part, as systematic opposition". There's a contrast for you with the note, which I inclose! I can scarcely recover from my surprize! Even to my Uncle Robert He allowed, that He insisted on my changing my sentiments; now, not a word is said on the subject. He finishes by telling me "that I shall be welcome, if I will meet Sophia in D— Place on Friday," and of course I mean to go. Unfortunately, I am persuaded that this reconciliation is only apparent, and that every spark of real affection for me is extinguished in his bosom. However, I shall endeavour to make the best of it. As I knew the pleasure which this news would give you, I lose no time in conveying it to you. M^r Lushington is now M^rs R's professed Supporter. Not contented with asking her to his own house, He came to Shedden the other day to persuade him to suffer Sophia to meet M^rs R— at dinner in Bedford Square, where He had kindly assembled a *family* party to meet her.—In short, He has been currying favour with my Father as much as possible, and trying to make his treatment of M^rs R— a glaring contrast to mine and Shedden's, who will not suffer Sophia to accept M^rs R's invitations

your affec^te Son<br>M G Lewis

Pray, return the inclosed note. Nothing can be kinder than M^rs Blake and my Uncle Robert have been on this occasion, and it is entirely owing to them, that matters are adjusted.

Barnes. Wednesday 7^th [1805][1]

My dear Mother,

I return many thanks to you for the trouble, which you are taking about my never-to-be-found Cottage; But that which you describe in your last will be of no use, as it has no advantage whatever over the one, which I inhabit at present. You make a mistake in saying, that it has one room more than *my* present residence; I *have* five rooms; what I want is a sixth. I collect too from what you say, that the Owners inhabit some rooms in it, and also reserve the garden (or at least part of it) for themselves; these are the only inconveniencies, which I have to complain of at Barnes. It will therefore be quite unnecessary, that I should go to look at this Cottage; But you will oblige me by thanking M^r Ingall for his offer to walk to it with me—the House, which I should have liked so much near Acton, belongs to one Salmon a Butcher, the corner of Bond S^t He said, that He should have been very glad to have had me for a Tenant, had He had not let it only a month before to a M^rs Howard for three years, & that it had been frequently advertised in the Herald, & Morning Post. Is it not strange, that we should neither of us have observed it? after all, perhaps the price might be too high for me, for I do not know what rent He asks. He said that I should have the refusal of it, in case of M^rs Howard's giving it up, and that at the end of the three years He *thought* of selling it. Now could not M^r Ingall call upon him, (but *not* as coming from *Me*) and try to find out, whether his price is likely to come within my compass; whether it is freehold, leasehold, or what; and whether He would sell it to me *now*, so that I might be *sure* of having it at the expiration of the three years? In which case, I would find something that would do for those three, & comfort myself for being inconveniencied at present with the thoughts of being comfortable at a *certain* period. M^r I— will greatly oblige me, if He could make any progress in this business; of course, it does not signify, if it were not done for a month.—I am very glad to find, that you are more comfortably situated than you were, and that your mind is relieved from former anxieties; It will always give me the greatest pleasure to find, that any endeavours of mine to produce that releif, have in some degree been attended with success. I thank you for the offer of your apartments; but you forget, that I am in possession of my Uncle Robert's House during his absence. When you write to him, ask after William Robertson; the poor Boy cut his hand dreadfully at Eaton with a penknife, & it was feared, He would be obliged to lose his finger; But He came to London to have it looked at, got nearly well, & is gone down to Felpham.[2]—As to my Melo-drama,[3] it is no *particular* secret; But still it is better not to talk more about it, than can be helped. Harris is highly pleased with it, & means to bring it out, the first piece in the Season; probably in the middle of October: the Scenes and dresses are already preparing, & it is to be brought out with great splendour. I have also given him the Spectacle,[4] which Sheridan stopped at Drury Lane for Ali Baba, and which I then took away: Harris has accepted it with great joy, & praises it extremely. But I rather wish its appearance to be deferred till another Season.

Your affecte Son,<br>M. G. Lewis

[1] Apparently about the middle of 1805, because of the probable reference to *Rugantino*.

[2] In Sussex. But the word may be "Feltham" (Middlesex, Somerset) or "Felsham" (Suffolk).

[3] Probably *Rugantino*, first produced at Covent Garden, Oct. 18, 1805.

[4] Probably *The Wood Daemon*, first produced at Drury Lane, Apr. 1, 1807.

Inveraray Castle. August 14th [postmarked 1807]

My dear Mother,

As I know, that your affection will make you anxious to hear, that I am once more in harbour, I lose no time in announcing to you, that I arrived here this evening without having met with any accident, or indeed any inconvenience; bating one of my old Companions the Head-ach, who paid me a visit two days ago, and has but just quitted me. Nothing could succeed better than the journey. We travelled in the Duke of Argyle's Landau, which formed a very pleasant open Carriage, when it was fair, and Shut up very close, when it rained; not to mention the advantage of being able to stand up, whenever we pleased, with as much ease and security, as if we had been walking (which could not be done in a Phaeton) and thus we were never subjected to the irksomeness of remaining in the same posture. I never travelled in a Landau before, and was quite delighted with it.—We coasted the Lakes of Cumberland and Westmoreland, which (though I had seen them twice before) are so beautiful, that I always see them with fresh pleasure; then we took the opportunity of a very fine day to visit the Falls of the River Clyde near Lanark, and on Tuesday reached Ardincapel, an estate belonging to Lord John Campbell. We past a night at Glasgow, where the Duke went to hear Mrs Mountain and Mr Bellamy in "Love in a Village"; but we had travelled all the preceding night, and I was too sleepy to accompany Him. I found afterwards, that He had himself occasionally fallen asleep during the performance, and (as He says) should have taken a very sound nap, had it not been for the construction of the Theatre; for all the audience-part of it is described as being built with coved backs and ceilings, the consequence of which is, that the slightest whisper runs audibly round the whole House, the letting down a seat sounds like thunder, and if a person calls the Box-keeper to open the door—"Box-keeper!—Box-keeper—Box-keeper" —is reverberated from every part of the theatre for the space of several minutes. In short, they say, that nothing except the Mansion of the Winds was ever known to be so noisy as this Temple of the dramatic Muse, where everything can be heard distinctly; *except* the Performers. From ardincapel, we crossed the Clyde to Roseneath, a seat of the Duke of Argyll's, where He is building a most magnificent Mansion, which (without the furniture) will not cost him less than £60,000. and here we heard a little anecdote so pretty, and so much in *your* taste, that I would not upon any account omit relating it to you. About ten days ago one of the Farm-keeper's Wives was going homewards through the Wood, when She saw a Roebuck running towards her with great speed. Thinking, that it was going to attack her with its horns, She was considerably alarmed; but at the distance of a few paces the animal stopped, and disappeared among the bushes. The Woman recovered herself, and was proceeding on her way, when the Roebuck appeared again, ran towards her as before, and again retreated without doing her any harm. On this being done a third time, the Woman was induced to follow it; till it led her to the side of a deep ditch, in which She discovered a young Roebuck unable to extricate itself, and on the point of being smothered in the Water. The Woman immediately endeavoured to rescue it, during which the other Roebuck stood by quietly; and as soon as her exertions were successful, the two animals galloped away together. Now this is really a matter of fact; and if all matters of fact were as pretty, I should think it quite superfluous to read Romances and much more to write them. at [Ard]incapel we found Tom Sheridan and General Bligh, whom the Duke had engaged to accompany him to the Western (Well, upon my honour, that is the very best ale that I ever tasted, for you are to know, that all this while I am at supper) the Western Islands on a fishing and shooting expedition; but as I neither fish nor shoot, and am always sea-sick, previous to my leaving London I stipulated with the Duke, that when He went to the Islands, I should take possession of Inveraray Castle, where accordingly I arrived this Evening, and would not suffer a single Post to pass, without giving you some news of me, and requesting to hear some of you in return; but I desire, that that news may be *good*.— During my journey I abstained from reading so compleatly, that during the whole seven days that it lasted, about ten Stanzas of Ariosto formed the utmost extent of my reading; and in consequence I fancy, that my eyes are already greatly benefited. I mean therefore to read as little as possible; but as I am now the sole Inhabitant of the Castle, I cannot avoid readin[g a good] deal just at present. However, when [the] Duke [returns and] the expected party gssembles[1] (which [will] consist o[f some th]ree dozen of people) I shall be able to exchange my books for their society; though between ourselves, I am persuaded, that in point of *amusement* I shall lose by the exchange: and yet all the persons, of whose coming I am as yet aware, are people whom I am much disposed to like. I inclose a letter from M^rs B[lake],[2] which has been a great Traveller; for it has come five hundred miles to reach *me*, and will go back five hundred more to reach *you*; independent of which, it not only travelled from Felpham to London, but General Brownrigg's head being full of the expeditions, He made a little mistake, and forwarded it to Me *at the Baltic*, from whence it is but just returned, (I hope) much improved by its travels. Pray, let me hear from you soon. My comp^ts to M^r Ingall and. . . .[3] You know, as soon as they can eat (not M^r I— or . . .) the puppies are to be sent, one to Lady C. Lamb at Melbourne House, & the other to George S^t for M^rs B[lake].

your affec^te

M. G. L.

[1] For "assembles"—with "gathers" in mind?
[2] Canceled by a later hand, and so in the final sentence.
[3] Canceled by a later hand, and so in the next sentence. "Miss Lacey"?

Inveraray Castle. Sept^r 22. [1807]

My dear Mother,

If you should find this letter full of blunders, inconsistencies, and con-tradictions, you are not to be alarmed at any supposed derangement of my intellects, but ascribe it to the confusion and noise, with which I am at present surrounded. This is the Duke's birth-day, and all the blackgaurd children of the Town are hallooing round the Castle, firing squibs and crackers, and making such a diabolical noise, that we cannot hear each other speak. when the Duke came into the breakfast room just now, in-stead of wishing him "many happy returns of this day," I could not help telling him, that I wished to the Lord, that He had never been born at all." I can not give you a very favourable account of my health in any respect; and indeed the irregular life, which I am at present leading, is by no means calculated to make any improvement in my constitution; for we remain so long at table, that unavoidably I eat and drink too much, and dining at eight, supping at two, and going to bed at four in the morning, cannot possibly tend to strengthen my nerves, my eyes, or my stomach; all of which are undoubtedly worse at present, than they were in England. and yet you are to understand, that I am very regular in my mode of life, compared to most of the other Inhabitants of the Castle; for many of them seldom go to bed till between six and seven, and between four and five in the morning is the time generally selected, as being most convenient for playing billiards. The other morning I happened to wake about six o'clock, and hearing the billiard balls in motion, I put on my bed-gown, and went

into the Gallery; from whence looking down into the great Hall I descried
Tom Sheridan and M<sup>r</sup> Chester (who had not been in bed all night) playing with great eagerness. Fortunately, Tom was in the very act of making a
stroke, on which the fate of the whole Game depended, when I shouted to
him over the ballustrade—"Shame! Shame! a married Man!"—On which
He started back in a fright, missed his stroke, and lost the game. M<sup>rs</sup> T.
Sheridan is also here at present, very pretty, very sensible, amiable, and
gentle. Indeed, *so* gentle, that Tom insists upon it, that her extreme quiet-
ness and tranquillity is a defect in her character; above all He accuses her
of such an extreme apprehension of giving trouble, that (He says) it
amounts to absolute affectation. He affirms, that when the cook has forgotten her duty, and no dinner is prepared, M<sup>rs</sup> Sheridan says—"Oh!
pray, do'nt get dinner on purpose for me; I'll take a dish of tea instead!"—
and He declares himself certain, that if She were to set her cloaths on fire,
She would step to the bell very quietly, and say to the Servant with great
gentleness and composure—"Pray, William, is there any water in the
House?"—"No, Madam; but I can soon get some." "Oh! dear, no! It
doesn't signify! I dare say, the fire will go out of itself."—Many thanks
to you for your care about my Dog; I have heard of the safe arrival of the
Puppies at their respective destinations, and am assured, that *both* are
reckoned beautiful. Jessy begs to be remembered to Fatty, and says, "that
She would write, only She hurt her right paw the other day in running
after a Roebuck—and besides, truly, what with one thing or another, She
has so much to do!"—Edward Bligh, whom I mentioned to you, is a
Brother of L<sup>d</sup> Darnley's; He is gone away, and I make no doubt, is totally
ignorant, whether He ever had a great Grandmother or not. I like him very
much, but He is not an intimate Friend of mine: However, his Sister is
married to Charles Stewart, one of my greatest Friends, and when I return
to London, I shall certainly endeavour to establish a relationship with Her,
through the medium of your genealogy. Since the Duke's return from the
Hebrides (which took place about a month ago) every nook of the
Castle has been occupied by Visitors of all ranks, colours, and descriptions. Among the most distinguished have been Lord and Lady Holland,
the Marquisses of Ely and Downshire, and the Duke and Duchess of
Bedford. With the two latter I am perfectly charmed. The Duke was
always a favourite of mine; He is remarkably good-humoured and well-bred[,]
with the pleasantest smile possible; and when He get[s] a[t] his ease (for
He is uncommonly shy) his conversation [is] enlivened by a number of
well-selected anecdotes, which He tells with peculiar point and neatness[.]
The Duchess is very pretty, lively, good-humoured, and obliging; but
when She went away, She did something by me so *very* good-tempered,
that it quite won my heart. She had brought with her a Novel called
"Corinne,"[1] of which She had read only the two first volumes. [As] I
wished to read it[,] She left me these first volumes; but when the Duke of
Argyll's Horses returned from conveying her the first Stage, She sent
me by the Groom the *third* volume, though She had not read it herself,

for the leaves were still uncut. M^rs Sheridan says,—that "this was a piece of good-nature, which She could not have prevailed on herself to show to the person She loves best in the world." Send me some theatrical news. Has Miss [Lace]y[2] been acting during the Summer? Is She likely to get any business at Drury Lane? Is there any talk of doing either Adelgitha, or the Wood-Daemon? Are any new pieces in rehearsal?—How is your health?

—Your affec^te Son,

M. G. L.

I am told, that my Father has *not* been at Worthing.

[1] Presumably Mme. de Staël's novel, published 1807.

[2] Title and name canceled by a later hand.

[postmarked Aug. 6, 1808][1]

your own judgement coincides with, or differs from it. I past four days at the Duke of Bedford's very pleasantly, and was much prest to stay longer; which I like on *first* visits, as it at least proves that I am not thought to have stayed too long already. The House, grounds, and mode of living are all in a style of magnificence truly princely: We had Turtle, venison, burgundy and Champagne in profusion every day; and as an instance of the ordinary splendour I shall tell you as peculiar to Wooburn,[2] that at breakfast every person had a silver tea-pot appropriated to his own use. The party in the House was very large, and most of them, not merely people whom I like, but whom I am very intimate with; among others, Lord & Lady Holland, and the Duke of Argyll. On Sunday last I came to Lady Charlotte Campbell's in Buckinghamshire; This is a Villa in a different style from Wooburn Abbey, but nothing can be more beautiful in its kind. It is a long low white House, all over Virandas, and rustic colonnades and creepers, with fruit and flowers in profusion. For myself, I inhabit a small Cottage about a Stone's throw from the House, consisting of only three rooms, opening into a flower garden, and so quiet and pleasant that one would think, that it had been built with a view to my living in it. I have heard twice from young William Sewell, who is coming home, and in both his letters He begged to be remembered to you. I have ordered my Music to be left for you in Gerrard S^t

your affec^te Son

M. G. L.

[1] The last page of a letter.

[2] For "Woburn."

April 24^th[1] [1809]

My dear Mother,

*Probably*, I shall be in Gerrard S^t myself on the 1^st of May; and certainly either Betty or Cartier will be here, and I shall give directions about receiving the money, and paying the note.—As to letters, it really does very often happen, that they are several days without reaching me: not a month ago M^rs Blake sent me one requesting me to forward it *instantly*; It was a fortnight at least in reaching its destination; and I wished to gaurd you against any such accident. I sometimes go into the Country for a day, order no letters to be sent to me, and then stay on from day to day for a month—and also when I am going to any very pleasant place, I order my letters to be kept till my return, in order that I may not receive such as would put me out of humour. Once I returned from Scotland, and by this means found at once the letters of ten weeks. I mention all this merely to show you, that this is no new whim of mine, but a system; I receive so many more unpleasant letters, than pleasant ones, that sometimes I like to put my contentment out of the power of the Post. What I said, about Cartier's carrying your letters, had *no reference whatever* to your last letter to [Miss Lacey.][2] But I wished you to know, that I would not answer for his being able to leave them. I have so much for him to do, which will not admit of delay, that I cannot find time to send him out of his beat; If your commissions are in his way, He shall do them readily; or if by accident He should be unemployed; But there is scarcely a day that He has not to go as far as Paddington, besides other messages.— Betty's name is *Spiller*.—The Bricklayers are gone; the wall between the two Houses nearly tumbled down; It has been done up again new.—I am sorry for Lady S—'s[3] ill-humour; but I cannot beleive it to proceed from any of the reasons you give: unless perhaps, being ill, She might rather wish to be quite alone. As it is, it is a pity, that your visit was not made earlier; but you could not foresee her caprice. If I were you, I should tell W^m S. that I wanted a fire in another room, and offer to pay for it. I send the Bill for the taxes. Betty knows nothing of a Man with a demand for £2-11. 0.—I continue to lead the same life, and really begin to long to be a little by myself again: I have only dined at home once since you went, and am engaged till Sunday next; and I never get to bed till three or four. Hitherto, I have had very good health, but I begin to feel bilious. Here has another great Lady taken it into her head to shower down her civilities upon me. On Friday the Princess of Wales (who *sans rime ou raison* has not spoken to me for these five years) chose to send for me into her Box at the Argyle Rooms made me sup with her, asked me to dinner yesterday and kept me till three o'clock in the morning, and was extremely good-humoured and attentive. To-day I dine at York House, and then sup with the Princess of Wales at the Admiralty: So that for these two days I shall have had a dose of royalty. Pray, write to M^rs Mitz; Tell her, that in consequence of her long friendship for you, I *immediately* on receipt of her letter wrote to L^d J. Campbell; but the agency was already given to M^rs Donaldson

your affec^te Son[4]

---

| | |
|---|---|
| [1] Or "26th." | [2] Canceled by a later hand. |
| [3] The initial is not certain. | [4] Unsigned. |

Wednesday [May ? 1809]¹

My dear Mother,

I have not given any orders, nor did I think it right in the present state of the Performers, that I *should* give any. Into the bargain, the Benefits have commenced, and the Farce is played no longer. Otherwise I would have given M[iss Lacey]² some orders with pleasure. I am told, that the Theatre closes on the 10th of June. When there are *two* constructions to be put on my conduct, I confess, I am surprized, that you prefer putting the most unfavourable one; especially as in the present instance, you put the wrong one. It was not out of *hauteur* that I did not write to Mrs Mitz myself; but in the first place, because as I only asked the favour for her out of consideration of her being *your* Friend, I was willing, that *you* should have the merit with her of my having asked it; for as to her being "the Daughter of my old School-master," whom I did not care for, and scarcely remember, it would not weigh a straw with me; and "long acquaintance" without the least intimacy being produced by it, would weigh with me just as little: In the second place if I had written to her myself, I must have exprest a great deal of "pleasure if I had succeeded" and "sorrow at having failed", of neither of which I felt a grain, and this I wished to avoid: and into the bargain, I hate writing, and *you* are fond of it. But as to your charge of "thinking it beneath me to answer her," you could not well have hit upon one more totally unfounded. I dined with both my Sisters yesterday, who are quite well; and Maria dines with me tomorrow at Barnes, to meet W. Scott the Poet. Cartier is a little better, and flatters himself, that He shall be able to keep his place; I fear not, but shall go on with him, as long as I possibly can.—The Newspapers *come* very irregularly, but I have spoken about their being sent as well as they can be: I kept back one from a particular motive for a day, but *only* one. The Examiner has not been sent for the two last Sundays, and Cartier's dropsy prevent his going about to enquire the reason at the Publisher's. I beleive, the Queen took away the Poem more from curiosity to see what was said about the Duchess &c than for the purpose of admiring the penmanship: So that I fear, Mr Ingall must not look for preferment from Windsor in consequence. Tierney abused Minister³ in the House of Commons, about my Monody (I think, I told you this before) So I am printing it, and will send you a copy soon: It is dedicated to the Princess of Wales, who accepted it very graciously. With *real pain* I inform you, that the bugs and Fleas are in compleat possession of your whole House, not excepting the Drawing-room; they have kept me awake for the two last nights; I have sent for the Bug-wash, but I fear, the attempt to get rid of them is a desperate one. My best compts to your associates.

your affecte Son,

M. G. L.

---

¹ Tierney addressed the House on the subject of Lewis' "Monody on the Death of Sir John Moore" on May 9, 1809. The *terminus a quo* is June 10, when the theater closed.

² Canceled by a later hand.     ³ Or "Ministers."

Barnes. Sunday.[1]

My dear Mother,

You will be surprized to hear of the confusion in my Household. When I arrived at Barnes, I found *both* the Servants gone to Town, the House locked up, and (for fear my Host should betray their excursion) the Devils had taken the Key with them, and the locks were so good, that the Blacksmith tried to pick them in vain. But what angered me most was, that poor Jessy had been locked up in the cold for above thirty hours: they had put food by her to be sure; but if She eat it (as was natural) all in the first hour, She must have fasted for the last 29. You are also to understand, that they have both, but separately, played me this trick before; I then assured them, the First, who committed this fault again, should go as an example to the other; So they thought, they should nick me, by both being in fault at the same time; but on the contrary, I nicked *them*, and told them, they should both march off together. The case, was so flagrant, that when I said this to Cartier, He could find nothing to answer but—"Ma foi, Monsieur, il faut l'avouer, nous le méritons bien." However, Tears and compassion "for the weaker vessel" have made me accept M^rs Betty's solemn *oath* (for nothing less would I hear of) that She never will commit this fault again; but as Cartier has no excuse on earth, He must go positively. Therefore, pray, make some enquiries for another Man Servant for me—the wages, 30 Guineas: Board-wages, fourteen Shillings, and a Guinea, *when travelling*, only. He must be able to shave and keep accounts, not mind living always in the Country, nor walking a good deal, nor sitting up late. These are the only material points, besides the common ones of, honesty, sobriety &c. Send no letters after three o'clock on Wednesday. Poor Jessy seems quite humbled and low-spirited by her late involuntary retirement from Society.

Your affec^te Son,
M. G. Lewis

Betty is very anxious, that M^rs Blake should not know her misconduct, for She says, "She is the only Friend She has in the world." I have promised not to peach; therefore, mention nothing about it to the people of Foley Place. Perhaps, Godfrey the Baker may know of Somebody. I could wish, that M^r Ingall would enquire some day at Gen. Brownrigg's (but *not as from me*) what is become of a Servant called Southern; or to whom Miss B. gave his character?

[1] This undated letter must follow that of May ? 1809, since Cartier was then still employed.

I read your note to Graham, thinking at first, that you had sent it for my inspection.[1]— I am getting well, though slowly; I hope to be in Town about Monday Sen'night, but not sooner. My new Servant is very anxious to please, if Nature had not unluckily denied him the requisites.

He is very stupid, and very forgetful; and so awkward, that when He comes into a room, He seems to communicate the principle of life to all the books, and chairs, and cups, and saucers, they all tumble about so. I gave him a glass jar of magnesia yesterday to put upon a shelf, under which stood a single China-bason: In this shelf there was a single hole. He put the jar into the [h]ole, upon which it fell so exactly into the Bason, that He broke both. If He wants to put anything out of his [h]ands, immediately the room appears to him to be chuck-full; there is not a single corner unoccupied, and He turns round and round and round in the most comical embarrassment possible: But if He has one thing to put down, and another to take up, He does *neither*, but performs instead *half* the motions of *Each*.—This morning I bade him get some water, for there was none in the Ewer; So He asked me, whether I wanted to drink or to wash, as He could get it either in the Tumbler, or the Bason accordingly: He looked quite surprized at my engenuity, when I assured him, that if He got it in the Ewer, I could fill either. I am sure, He was the very Man who had the Cat and Kitten, and when He cut a large hole in the door for the *Cat* to go through, He cut a *little* one for the *Kitten*. However, He is very humble and attentive, and now I cannot afford such a Servant as would exactly suit me.— I hope [Miss Lacey] is quite recovered.[2]

your affec<sup>te</sup> Son

M. G. Lewis.

[1] The last page of a letter. Since he cannot afford a better servant, Lewis must not yet have received his inheritance. His father died May 17, 1812.

[2] All between "hope" and "your" canceled by a later hand.

The Albany. July 17.[1]

Sir,

I request you to inform the Committee, that it is not my wish to retain the Private Box for the next Season. I remain, Sir,

Your most obed<sup>t</sup>

M. G. Lewis.

[outside address:] C. W. Ward Esq<sup>r</sup>/Drury Lane Theatre.

[1] Lewis bought quarters at the Albany in June 1809. I assign the letter to that year on the flimsy reasoning that he may have wished to economize. The letter is inserted in a copy of Lewis' *The Love of Gain* in the Dyce Collection, Victoria and Albert Museum (pressmark 5786).

The Albany. October 10. [1810][1]

My dear Mother,

Frederick will have told yo[u] that I am here and well. I came from Lord Grey's by Sea; but I thought it as wel[l] not to tell you of my intention to do so, as it might have made you anxious for my safety, seeing that the project was really not without its dangers. A voyage by Sea can never be quite a safe thing, while there are storms, Privateers, drunken Pilots, and careless Captains; and more-over I found, that the navigation of the Coast is very dangerous from the numerous quicksand[s] which border almost the whole length. My Crew happened to be remarkably careful, & well experienced; but still they frequently preferred dropping anchor to running the risque of passing particular places in the Dark. Besides this, for the first three days we were involved in so thick a fog, that we were obliged to keep a Horn sounding day and night to prevent other Ships coming upon us unexpectedly. We past a vessel like our own, which had been run down in this manner, and was lying with only her mast-head above water. Besides this, the passage up the River from Greenwich to Wapping was the most nervous hour that I ever past, owing to the mul- titude of Shipping, which we were obliged to thread like a labyrinth. How- ever, our people were very careful, & I reached London much pleased that I had undertaken the voyage; for besides that I had seen much that was new to me, I had arrived by Sea at the expense of three Guineas, which by land would have been thirty. I saw Frederick, and am glad to hear from you so good an account of him. I certainly would readily serve him, having known him so long; and as I look upon M^r Ingall as having *really* been a very serviceable Friend to you and to have your interest very much at heart, I consider him as having a claim upon me, if I had any power: But that is exactly what I have not. As to Gen: Brownrigg, He has now no [m]ore influence in military matters, than *you* have. While the Duke was in office, and while Brownrigg was his Secretary, He could easily be of use; But now He could only get a commission by asking it as a favour done to himself, and this is more than any one has a right to require of another. Besides, I have already asked and obtained so many favours of him in the military line, that I cannot with any decency ask more; and lastly He has not only a great many of his own separate Relations in the Army, but there are also of mine R^t Sewell, M. Blake, and two of his own Sons, for whom all his military Interest must be required. As to the present Commander in Chief, I do not know him even to speak to. I certainly *could* introduce Frederick to Brownrigg; but I cannot see, of what use it would be, and merely taking a person to show him to the General, could only be considered by the Latter as a superfluous intrusion, and He would ask me (and w[ith] justice), "what the Devil, I brought the Lad for to *Him?*"—The Princess Amelia cannot last long, that is certain: as I had rather be out of Town during the fortnight when the Theatres will be closed, I am waiting for this even in order to go to Oak-End, & am at present most *uncommonly* well; but I have a pain in my wounded leg, which I verily beleive to be the Gout. Maria is in Town, and in very good health. When I was going to embark, it occurred to me that I might be drowned by the way, and that I might as well have disposed of what little plate, furniture &c I possess, by will. I have now repaired that omission; and I now tell it [you, in order] that if by any accident I should make a sudden Exit (which I do not just now intend) you may take care to enquire for my Will; by which means you may find yourself Heiress to half a dozen Tea-spoons, three broken-legged Chairs, and

> —"a copper skillet,
> Which runs as fast as you can fill it."

—I was glad to hear from Frederick,[2]

1 The reference to the Princess Amelia (d. 1810) identifies the year.
2 The remainder is lacking.

The Albany. Wednesday Dec 12. 1810

Dear St Aubyn,[1]

I cannot tell you, how much I am obliged by your remembering my request. Pray, have the goodness to send the Dog to my Chambers at the Albany, as soon as it is judged proper for it to quit the Mother: But not sooner, as I should be sorry to have the Animal suffer through my impatience. If you have several Puppies, Ly A— would prefer a male to a Female; But if that is not to be managed, the Female will be extremely acceptable.

I was just going to write to tell you , that I am going to Oak-End & to hope, that you would meet me there; but the direction, which you have given me for Wiltshire, puts this out of the case. I shall probably go to Oatlands & Lord Tankerville's about the 22d; & I meant, if you had been at home, to have sent you word, that if you would drive over for me I would come to pass a day with you at the expiration of my visit. But I conclude, that you have made your arrangements to pass your Christmas from home. But I trust, as soon as you come to Town, you will call at the Albany, & give me an opportunity of thanking you in person.

As you are partial to the Play, I must tell you, that an excellent little Actress has appeared in Mrs Jordan's lines who promises to be a very great acquisition. She plays sentimental & comic parts equally well, dances very prettily, has a very pretty figure, (not a very pretty face, but nothing ugly) & a voice so distinct that She is heard in a whisper all over the House. Her name is Miss Booth—& besides this, there is a very droll Farce by Colman; & above all, there is a Melodrama in rehearsal from the pen of no less a personage than Mr Skeffington! Think, what a treasure! Shall you be able to remain in the Country, & lose the first night?—My Uncle, Mrs Blake &c are all well: I have just got Mr Yorke to make Harry a Lt

Ever yours
M. G. Lewis.

1 James, the heir and eldest natural son of Sir John St. Aubyn (1758–1839), fifth Baronet.

March 22. 1811

Dear S<sup>t</sup> Aubyn,

a thousand thanks for the Dog, which I am assured by Lady Abdy, is very handsome, and just the thing which She wished to have. Are you now come to Town to remain?—I have a Melodrama in rehearsal at Covent Garden; and M<sup>rs</sup> Blake, M<sup>r</sup> Sewell, & his daughters are to sup with me after the Play, on the *Fifth* night. I shall let you know, as soon as the night is fixed, and I hope, you will make a point of going with us to the play and supping afterwards at the Albany. Probably, it will be on the Friday of the week *after Easter-Week.*

yours truly
M. G. Lewis.

The Albany. April 23. 1811

Dear S<sup>t</sup> Aubyn,

I understand, you are at Woburn, but expected daily in Town. According to my promise I apprize you, that on the 3<sup>d</sup> of May (Friday Sen'night) You are expected to go to the play in M<sup>rs</sup> Blake's Box, to see my new Nonsense, and to sup with me afterwards. If you are in Town, on *Saturday next*, will you meet me at the Lyceum Theatre; I have got places there, for which you will ask, and you will see the First representation of Arnold's new opera. Write me an answer, as soon as you can.

yours truly
M. G. Lewis

Thursday [outside date: May 2?, 1811]

Dear S<sup>t</sup> Aubyn,

I am extremely sorry to say, that circumstances prevent M<sup>rs</sup> Blake and my Uncle's family from coming to Town tomorrow; So the Play and the Supper are both put off, which I regret much, as I should have had great pleasure in receiving you. There is also another thing, which vexes me very much, or rather which *would* have vexed me very much, if you had not made me somewhat easy by mentioning, that the Greyhound Puppy was a favourite in your family. After all the fuss which She made about having one, and the trouble which I took to procure it, Lady Abdy now does not like the Greyhound, and wishes to return him. As I thought that you would be *glad*, to have him back, and besides I was rather angry at such caprice (even though caprice is a pretty woman's daily bread) I told her, I beleived, that I should have little difficulty in persuading you to take it back. Therefore[,] pray, let me know, whether It shall be sent to your chambers, or where. I assure you, I am truly grateful to you for your kindness about the Dog, though the Lady herself is so insensible of the favour. She shall ask long enough, before I take any more trouble for her.—Pray, come and see me at the Albany.

> Sincerely your[s,]
> M. G. Lewis

The Albany. Wednesday May. 1811

Dear S$^t$ Aubyn,

The Duchess of Devonshire does not take the Greyhound; therefore as soon as you can do it with your own convenience, you had better send for him to Lady Abdy's in Hill St. I am quite out of patience at her caprice, for really I think the Animal singularly pretty of the kind.—I hope, you won your race, and that I shall see you soon.

> Yours truly
> M. G. Lewis.

Oct$^r$ 12. [outside date: 1811]

Dear S$^t$ Aubyn,

I hope, this will find you in Town, and that you will dine with me at seven on Tuesday. If your Brother John is in Town, bring him with you. Send me an answer to the Albany, as soon as you can.

> Yours truly
> M. G. Lewis

The Albany. Oct$^r$ 17. 1811

Dear S$^t$ Aubyn,

I go to Oatlands on Saturday, & stay there Sunday. If you are at home; and can either come over for me yourself, or can send a pair of Horses to bring my Chaise over, or if Woburn Farm is near enough to Oatlands to allow of my walking over (that, is within two miles) I should be happy to pass Monday with you, and return to Town on Tuesday; If this finds you at Woburn, send your answer to the Albany; If I hear nothing from you, I shall conclude, that you are absent, and shall hope, that you will soon make me a visit at the Albany.

> Yours truly
> M G Lewis

The Albany. Nov<sup>r</sup> 24. 1811

My dear S<sup>t</sup> Aubyn,

Our friendship must certainly be the most convenient thing for *me* and the most *in*convenient for *you*, that can be imagined; for about once a Month I find out something for *you* to do for me, and for *me* to teaze you about. My present business regards the Presidentship of the Antiquarian Society, for which Lord Aberdeen is a Candidate; and if you would use your influence with your Father to get his vote for my Friend, you would infinitely oblige me. Nobody can be more qualified than Lord A. to fill the President's Chair, as well by his amiable manners and excellent character, as by his natural talents and literary acquirements. These are considerations which I mean to have weight with S<sup>t</sup> John; with yourself, I flatter myself, that it will be needless to say more, than that Lord A— is one of the Men whom I most esteem, and whose success in every object I should feel most pleasure in promoting. I must also beg you to mention to S<sup>t</sup> John, that particular circumstanc[es] prevent Lord Aberdeen's canvassing himself any person whatever; otherwise He might conceive the not receiving a personal application to be a mark of inattention. Pray, execute this commission for me *with warmth*, and let me know your success.

Ever yours most truly
M. G. Lewis

[outside address:] James S<sup>t</sup> Aubyn Esq<sup>r</sup>/Lincoln's Inn

The Albany. March 31. [1812][1]

My dear Mother,

One of your notes became due last Feb<sup>y</sup> S<sup>r</sup> H. L. sent it to me, and said, that it *must* be payed immediately. So I have discharged it, and you are now to repay *me*. Let me know, at what periods it would be convenient to you. You mention May; Will it suit you to repay £20 in May, & 20 in June? I should not chuse the payments to be less than £20 at a time. You must not forget, that on July 9<sup>th</sup> your second note becomes due; and that it is not in S<sup>r</sup> H. L.'s *power* to give you any delay. Maria is quite well. My Father has been extremely ill ever since November; not actually in danger, but in what the Physician called "a very precarious state." However, He is now a little better, & I hope, his complaint has taken a favourable turn. I wrote to him on Friday to request him to see me. My Sister said, the letter was just what She wished it to be"; So that I suppose it to be one with which He *ought* to be satisfied; yet there was nothing in it, but what I have said to him and written to him twenty times before. Maria told him, that She had a letter for him from Me, which She thought would give him pleasure, when his strength would allow him to read it. He said, "Well! Wait a little; Don't give it me just now." He has not yet asked for it; So its fate is still undecided. Maria told him, that his illness had affected me extremely; on which He said (with kindness and interest)—

"Ah! He's a foolish Boy." From all this, I have some little hope, that his illness must have softened him a little towards me. At all events, I shall have done all that it was in my power to do. When I can ask Taylor again for an Opera-Box, I will not forget you. My acquaintance with M^rs Carpenter has been dropped for many years, and did not end agreably; Therefore if you meet her again, pray, do not mention my name to her on any account. I will get M^rs2 Ingall's letter franked. I send you Timour the Tartar. By the Printer's omission of *"the Usurper's"* Bride, in the *advertisement* there is a piece of fine nonsense.[3]

Your affectionate Son<br>M G Lewis

The cupboard is of no sort of use to me; therefore if it will suit you, pray, send for it.

[1] This and the next two letters and one fragment of a letter, all concerned with Mr. Lewis Sr.'s illness, belong to the period March 31–May 17, 1812. The order is conjectural.

[2] Or "M^r."

[3] The Advertisement reads "to effect her Husband's release a Wife assumes the character of his Bride." In Lewis' copy of *Timour*, in my possession, "his" is corrected, apparently in Lewis' hand, to "the Usurper's."

My dear Mother,

I send you an Opera Box order for next Saturday; the new Ballet is beautiful, and will please you much both from the Music, and the picturesque Grouping of the Dancers. Pray, only take *five* persons, and leave word at the door (as before) that another Gentleman is to be admitted, as I may want one admission for myself. I have much to say to you, but nothing pleasing except that the account of my Father yesterday was rather more favourable. I will call on you either tomorrow, or the first fine morning; for six o'clock is an hour too late on the one hand, and too early on the other.

your affect^e Son<br>M. G. L.

Wednesday

You had better take Taylor's *note* with you as well as the *order*; lest the missing order should be presented.

The Albany. Tuesday.

My dear Mother

I am sorry to say, that your confidence in a reconciliation having taken place is unfounded. My Sister told my Father on Sunday Sen'night, that She had a letter for him from me, and that it could not but give him pleasure. This was eight whole days ago, & He has never asked for the letter, nor mentioned my name. Either the sense of his own illness occupies his mind too much to admit of his thinking of anything else, & He has forgotten my letter; or else He is waiting till his health shall be restored, in order that in case it should not be exactly what He has required, He may have strength enough to reject any reconciliation. However[,] I went to S^r W. Farquhar on Sunday Evening, & He said, "that in my Father's state it was absolutely necessary, that He *should* see my letter; that He felt for me, and understood perfectly the hardship of my case; that He would let Monday pass over, as there was on that day to be a consultation of Physicians, and it was desireable, that it should take place without my Father's being exposed to any agitation; But that on Tuesday He would speak to him himself on the subject of my letter, and would speak (not merely as a Physician, or even a Friend) but as a Father, to advise him how a Father ought to act in his situation." That his state is so dangerous, my Father has not any idea; Perhaps, when He is aware of it, He may feel his heart soften towards me, and his danger may diminish M^rs R's influence over him. I fear, that He is very ill indeed. S^r Walter told me, that there was no *immediate* danger, & that nothing fatal had as yet taken place: He might go on in his present state for Months. But He said of his ultimate recovery He had very little hope. Even should He get over the present illness, He would be subject to a similar one on the first occasion of cold. The complaint is an Hectic; of which, they say, few people at his time of life recover. Lushington was with me to-day, and says, that D^r Baillie yesterday allowed him to be in danger: L— added, that He could see him grow weaker every 24 hours, & that unless some *very* favourable change should take place, He did not think, that He would last as many weeks as Sir Walter says Months. You may beleive, that I am deeply affected by his danger; but yet I feel quite differently, I am persuaded, from what I should have done ten years ago. The *recital* of his sufferings pains me cruelly; but at least his alienation from me has spared me the agony of *witnessing* his gradual decay day after day, which I really think would have been insupportable: Thus is every evil still attended with some good. At present, his illness makes me melancholy; His sufferings give me pain; I am sincerely anxious to hear of his being better. But it is now above nine years since I have had any intercourse with him, that carried with it any kindness; His loss will alter none of the habits of my life; I shall have but few remembrances of his affection; I shall not miss his place at the table, nor the morning welcome, nor the affectionate good-night. Often and often in my early days, when I quite doated upon him, I have thought, that my heart would break, if I were ever obliged to attend him on a death-bed. Nine years of constant harshness or indifference on his part have now made us Strangers to each other; But still I dread so much the thoughts of witnessing his sufferings, that I scarsely know, whether for my *own* happiness I ought to wish for a reconciliation *now*.—To have been on such terms with him while He lived, as would have given me opportunities of contributing to make him happy, would have been worth any price; But I have done no wrong, and need not his *forgiveness*; In a mercenary view a reconciliation may be desireable for me; but in what other? Good God! To have his affection restored to me, merely that I may instantly lose it again for ever, it seems shocking to me; and the kinder that his treatment of me might be *now*, the more bitter will be my regrets at losing him. But He will decide as suits best with his own feelings and pleasure; For me, I must be content with thinking, that I have left nothing undone to effect a reconciliation. I assure you, my dear Mother, it was a great consolation to me, when I read in your letter your testimony, that I had nothing to blame myself for in my[1]

[1] The remainder is lacking.

Thursday.[1]

My dear Mother

I have seen my Father, and lose no time in telling it you. But I have seen him in a sad time. He was better yesterday morning; In the Evening a visible alteration took place; now there is no likelihood of any favourable change happening again. He only said to Me, "God bless you" two or three times; *I* was *ordered* not to speak; I made it up in *crying*, as you may well beleive. My head aches shockingly. I write to you from Devonshire Place. God bless you, my dearest Mother. I have suffered cruelly this morning, and feel, that I must suffer still more.

I think, you might as well write a *few words* (but mind, *only a few* and those *not* as strong, as I am sure you will feel) to thank Dr Jackson for this reconciliation. Nothing could be *more kind*, or *more anxious*, than He has been on this occasion; and He is entitled to gratitude from all, who feel affection for Me. You might send your letter to him to Devonshire Place, if you think proper to write one; but do not inclose it to *me*, nor mention that I did more than say that to Dr J's good offices I hold myself indebted for my Father's blessing.

your affecte Son<br>M. G. L.

[1] Probably May 14, 1812, the last Thursday before Mr. Lewis' death. In the salutation, "Mother" is canceled by a later hand but is legible, and so "affecte Son" at the end.

Barnes. Tuesday.[1]

My dear Mother,

as you may possibly not have seen your Brother William, I may as well tell you, that I received this Morning a copy of the Will. No bequests (except Rings to the three Executors, Brownrigg, W. Sewell, & Lushington of £100 each, and a year's wages to Servants) are made except to Mrs R— and myself. He leaves her £500, and a release *for her Family* for sums lent by him (the sum not mentioned, but avowedly several thousands) and to Myself He bequeaths everything else *without exception*. My Sisters have not so much as a token of remembrance; Neither is there in lieu of it any expression of affection for them, nor any recommendation of them or any one else to my care and kindness. Sophia is expressly barred from her claim to the £5000 in the Codicil to his Will; It is supposed, that the same was done in Maria's marriage settlement: In that case, we conceive, that the whole becomes mine, or rather that my Estate is releived from that claim on it. What my circumstances will turn out, I have still no idea; But I confess, the *general* terms of my Father's bequest to "His beloved Son" has fortified my feelings beyond any sum that He *could* have left me; and, if He meant to strengthen the claims upon me of all who are dear to him, He could not have taken a more effectual mode. You may conceive, what inexpressible satisfaction I feel in reflecting, that there was *no person*, about whom I could guess him to *wish* me to feel an interest, whom I did not mention kindly to him during the few days that I was suffered to pass under his roof.

And now, my dear Mother, I will give you a commission, that will be perfectly to your taste. Mrs Sewell has formerly not acted by you, as She should have done; In consequence, when She was in England, I shunned her; She perceived it, and therefore probably hopes for no favour from me: She is not mentioned in my Father's will; her situation is (I beleive) most forlorn, & his loss must be a terrible blow to her. Pray, write a few lines to her, and tell her from me, that I am aware of my Father's affection for her, am sensible how heavily She must feel his loss, and that I hope to find, that He has left me in circumstances that will permit me (without injustice to those who have stronger claims on me) to continue whatever little kindness He may have been in the custom of showing her. You may add, that as soon as my circumstances are ascertained, She shall hear from you again as to what it may be, or may not be, in my power to do for her; and beg her to acknowledge the receipt of your letter. Poor Woman! She *must* be in great affliction at this event. I know not her address, and therefore you had better send your letter to Sr H. Lushington. But pray, write without loss of time to releive her anxiety. I am not quite well, but yet not ill; and rather in melancholy spirits than in a very agitated frame of mind. God bless you, my dear Mother.

your truly affecte Son
M. G. Lewis

1 Mr. Lewis' will was proved May 30, 1812.

16 Green St Grosvenor Square. May 27. 1812.
My dear St Aubyn
.....................................................
Matt Lewis, is *now* a man of business having a vast sight of *family* Matters on his hands. I trust, & *hope*, he will have no time to *write another Timour*

God forbid!—"No further seek his Merits to disclose, or draw His *frailties* from their dread abode." I shall be very glad to find that he has given up all such Stuff, for, "*Nonsense* is *Nonsense*, in prose, or in Verse."

Y<sup>r</sup> attached & Sincere friend
A Blake.[1]

[1] Anna Blake, Lewis' aunt.

Green Street 1st June 1812.

Dear S<sup>t</sup> Aubyn—
   Julius Ceasar on *Thurs*day. We are going. Now will you, or will you not take a scramble by *way* of dinner, and go with us?—Let me know in *due* time, that is, as soon as you can, as I wish to know about the *Tickett*. You will be shabby in the extreme if you do not go with me, after all you have said.—It is *not* Timour. *I* am sorry for it.—You may not.

Y<sup>rs</sup> most Sincerely
A Blake.

[In another hand: M<sup>rs</sup> Blake/25 Oct<sup>r</sup> 1812./Oak End Lodge]
Dear S<sup>t</sup> Aubyn

I do not think among *un*certainties M<sup>r</sup> Betty need rank his *Successes* in his next Appearance upon a London Stage I hear from every one that He is *vile*. He is not to be endured. I always hated the vain Puppy. He will not have the cheif thing that recommended him formerly to publick notice, namely *Novelty*, in his favor this Year, & therefore *I* fancy he will regret his Appearance There is a book some time ago published that I shou'd like very much to buy containing all the Prologues & Epilogues that ever were spoken on Drury Lane & Covent Garden. There is one that Garrick spoke on his return from France after being absent for a few Years, that I wou'd advise M<sup>r</sup> *Betty* to read It is excellent!—I hope you have read or seen Matt Matt Lewis's "Rich & Poor." Even *I* like it. He seems *perfectly* to *understand* what an *ill bred* Man & *fashionable Gentleman* is.

Believe me Dear S<sup>t</sup> Aubyn
Very truly Sincerely
Your Attached friend
A Blake.

Nov<sup>r</sup> 30, 1812.

Sir,

I must request you to insert the name of the Hon: William Fraser in the Free-List, as one of my two Nominations.

your most obed<sup>t</sup>
M. G. Lewis

W. Ward Esq<sup>r</sup>

[outside address:] W. Ward Esq<sup>r</sup>/Secretary to the Committee/ Drury Lane Theatre

Oak End Lodge 23<sup>d</sup> Feb<sup>y</sup> [postmarked 1815]

My dear S<sup>t</sup> Aubyn,

. . . . . . . . . . . . . . . . . . . . . . . . . . . . . . . . . . . . . . . . . . . . . . .

So, *Mother Goos'es Son* has become scarce! Every body makes the same complaint even to his own Brother in Law. He is only *at home,* when he *professes* to be at home. This is vast nonsense, and very like some of his former Tales. I wrote to him the other day, & I therein mentioned the universal complaint that reached my ears, of the *scarcity* of his appearance, and yet strange as it may be, we have very fine weather altho' this said most enlightened body, has *not appeared.* Well my dear S<sup>t</sup> Aubyn, one of these days (if he has not already) he will *feel* the whole of his happiness to be *but* ideal. He pos[sess]es Money it is true, but I am pretty certain, it does not, make him a *happy* Man. I thought once that if ever Matt Lewis was a *rich Man, I* should be better off than I was. I do not think so *now.* I expect from *you full as much* as I do from *him,* and I am sure I shall not be mistaken. He has a *new* friend for every Month in the year. How fond he was of you when he was last down here! pressing me to *insist* on your coming or to pretent I shou'd be affronted & now he has forgot you.

. . . . . . . . . . . . . . . . . . . . . . . . . . . . . . . . . . . . . . . . . . . . . . .

Yours dear S<sup>t</sup> Aubyn ever Affectionately
A Blake.

The Albany. April 22. 1815

Dear S<sup>t</sup> Aubyn,

My Sister tells me, that the other night you made great complaints of me: I have been, and am likely to be, so rarely in Town, except for a single night that I have never been lucky enough to be at home when you called; But I beg you to observe, that I have been *twice* this year to Lincoln's Inn to look for you; once indeed I had no card; but the second time I left one, though I suppose, that by some accident you did not see it. I hope, this will exculpate me fully from the charge of intentional neglect, which I assure you, I do not deserve.

Yours truly
M G Lewis

Florence. October 1st 1816.

My dear Mother,

I am here quite well, and have hitherto been very much amused with my expedition. I have crost the Alps and the Apennines without breaking down; have seen the Cathedral of Milan, the Chartreuse-Church of Pavia, and the Gulph of Genoa; Have talked for half an hour to Maria Louisa, and have made a low bow to the Venus of Medicis and wished her joy of her safe arrival from Paris. In many things indeed I am disappointed; Except Holland, Upper Lombardy is the flattest ugliest Country, that I ever visited; No Trees but stiff straight Poplars, and in Summer the Rivers are nothing but great Channels of Stones. The weather till within these few days has been abominable; the Fruit is not fit to be eaten; and the Singers at the Opera bawl in a manner, that would get them hissed off the Stage in England. I am, therefore, not only glad to have seen all that I have seen, but delighted to think, that there never can be occasion for my seeing it again. But the Pictures and Statues exceed all praise!—The gentleman, who takes charge of this, is just come from Naples, where He left Maria and all her Children well. I hope sincerely, that the same is the case with yourself. Remember me to Sophia, Mrs Blake, and my two Uncles, and beleive me

your affecte Son

M G L.

Pray, make my compts to Mrs Ingall and Miss [Lacey].1

1 Canceled by a later hand.

Florence. Octr 11th 1816.1

Dear Sir,

The circular notes have reached me, and I thank you much for them. Upon enquiry at Donat Son's, I find, that He will give me a letter upon Rome, and only make me pay the single Commissin upon such sums, as I may draw for; But as I intend returning through the Tyrol, and know not how long I may be induced to stop there and in Switzerland on my way to Paris, it is always useful to have such a power ready by me, should I have any occasion for it. You will observe, that I refused to take the £300 at Geneva, and only took £50; But if I had taken it, I should have paid £12 and ½ per Cent! the consequence was that I was obliged to abandon that credit altogether, and get £100 at Genoa from Lord Ponsonby's Banker— the Meusi2 of Brussells, to whom you addrest me, is (I am aware) a Member of the States General, and (I beleive) even President of one of the Chambers; But He has left off business. The Letter upon Maunoir was given me by his eldest Son; in which open letter He directed Maunoir to let me have £300, only deducting his own (Maunoir's) Commission; But in a private letter to Maunoir, giving him advice of the one given to Myself, He directed him to deduct a commission also for Himself, Meus; which letter Maunoir sent me, to show that in charging a double Commission, He had only obeyed Meus's instructions. All this I immediately wrote to *Meus and Zanna* myself; and I hope, that you will not suffer the business to fall to the ground. I was the more displeased on this occasion, because the Father's respectable situation, and the obliging manners of his younger Son (whom I saw) had made me quite unprepared for such conduct, and thrown me compleatly off my gaurd. As to Maunoir, luckily I saw that there was something wrong from the very beginning, which induced me to look more narrowly into his charges and then at length out came the whole business. But at Geneva, the People are all Rogues from the first to the last, and nothing can equal their rascallity except their impenetrable stupidity.

I beleive, that I told you of M<sup>r</sup> Scott's refusal to sell his share of Hordley according to the valuation of our joint-Agent upon that Estate; I am by no means inclined to give a fancy price for it, and unless He alters his mind, that matter is at an end.[3] But as He *possibly* (although not probably, as He is by no means without a full share of *positiveness*) may alter his mind between this and next October, I will thank you to bear the matter in your memory; and let me know, as soon as your own concerns allow you to make the arrangement, which we talked about in London. The fact is, that the present management of the Estate cannot *possibly* continue after my return to Jamaica. Half of the Negroes on Cornwall[4] are my property; It is my *duty* to make them as happy as it is in my power; and they have a right to enjoy as many advantages from me, as are enjoyed by my Negroes upon Cornwall. Upon M<sup>r</sup> Scott's refusal to sell his share, I offered to go on jointly, provided I might have the power of increasing the various indulgences of the Negroes, as I had increased them at Cornwall and introducing such laws respecting them as I chose to do, and that without controul; As to the cultivation of the Soil &c, *that* He might order, as He pleased. He refused this proposal, and was pleased to deprecate my coming upon the Estate with such intentions, as utter ruin &c &c. With ideas so different, we never can go on together; and as He refuses to sell at a reasonable price (even supposing, that I could procure the money either from You, or from Miles in case of your continued inability) there remains nothing to be done, but to divide the Estate; a measure, which will be a heavy loss to both of us, as we shall be obliged to pay for the building of a second set of works. However, there is no remedy, for I *must* have my own negroes under my own controul. The point, therefore, now is, how to make the division with the *least* loss. Would it be trespassing very much upon your time and goodness to request you to see M<sup>r</sup> Scott respecting this division, and endeavouring by discussion to hit upon some means of getting the business completed as *oeconomically* as possible? Miles is at too great a distance; and besides, He is too much occupied (as I understand) in building a Palace to give himself much trouble about me. Besides, this is rather the business of an intelligent friendly Person, than of a mere Merchant, and you have already been so obliging to me, that if you undertake the discussion, I am sure, that you will do your best for me. It will require much thought, but we have time enough; as *nothing* must be *fixed*, till my arrival in Jamaica, which will not be till the end of next year: But the division may all be arranged previously. All that I insist upon is, that the Negroes shall be *halved exactly*, with no more in one portion, than in another. I do not wish to have a single Negroe more than belongs to my own Half; But I will not give up a finger, no, not so much as an hair of any one, who *ought* to belong to me. I also wish the business to be arranged by the end [of] next year[;] as I am determined to visit Hordley early in February . . . of . . .[5] for the pur[pose of] assimilating the management of my own share of it . . .[6] that already [est]ablished at Cornwall. If you are good enough to take any trouble on this subject (and all that you need take is, the discussing on my behalf M[r] Scott's various plans for the division) pray, write a line to beg him to call on you on the subject, whenever He may happen to come to London; He is to be heard of at M[rs] Pinnock's in Devonshire Place.— Have the goodness to enquire about my Stock-Dividends, if they have not been paid to you; and apply them, as we settled. M[r] Fraser of Cornhill and Field, the Broker, of Wamford Court, manage my Stock for me.—I forget, whether I requested you to tell Lord Holland, that I am ready to pay my share towards such Bulls, as He and You and our Agents may judge adviseable to send out; If H. Beckford had joined us, the risque and expense would have been less, and the advantage equal. As to number, that you must settle among you; But (nonsense as Lord H. may think it) they should be *Black*, without *one* white hair if possible.[7] Tell him also, that I have directed Lumley to send him a copy of my Cornwall Regulations: He will think many of them romantic and trifling; but He must recollect the meridian for which they were calculated; and those, which probably will appear to him the most childish and ridiculous, were exactly those allowed upon the Island to be the best adapted to the Great Children, with whom I had to deal. I shall make a copy of this letter, and send it by a private hand for fear of accidents. Pray, direct to me at my Banker's at Rome (Tolonia's).

yours truly,<br>M G Lewis

[outside address:] John Plummer, Esq[r]/32 Fenchurch S[t]/London/Angle-terre.

[1] Postmarked Oct. 31, 1816. Inscribed on the outside in another hand: "M. G. Lewis, Oct. 11. 1816/Ans[d] 5th Nov."

[2] The spelling is uncertain.

[3] The Scott here referred to is probably the Daniel Scott mentioned by Walter Scott in several letters of 1804–1805 to George Ellis. See particularly *Letters of Sir Walter Scott, 1831–1832*, ed. Grierson, 1937 [XII], 246, 247.

[4] A slip for "Hordley."      [5] The reading may be "February or of March."

[6] Illegible. There is space for about ten letters.

[7] Lewis' *Journal* for Feb. 27, 1816, reads: "The only horned cattle said to be fit for Jamaica work, are those which have a great deal of black in them. The white are terribly tormented by the insects, and they are weak and sluggish in proportion to their quantity of white." This attempt to improve the breed of cattle on the island failed (see *Journal* for Jan. 30, 1818).

Oak End Lodge 20th Novr 1816

My dear St Aubyn

. . . . . . . . . . . . . . . . . . . . . . . . . . . . . . . . . . . . . . . . . . . . . . . . . . . . . . . . . .

Your "*friend*" Mr Lewis, is in *Italy*. He returned from the West Indies & I am sorry to say, so much *dis*improved (a word of my own) that I think I may say, with perfect justice & truth, that, his friends in general wish He were among his *Black* Slaves again as being the only Creatures fit to bear with his Nonsense and Vanity. He returned, the most altered Man I ever knew and so very disagreeable that there was no bearing with him. *You* may wish to find him out, because you have not seen him of late, I who have, never propose asking *where* he is, lest, I *shou'd* find him out.

. . . . . . . . . . . . . . . . . . . . . . . . . . . . . . . . . . . . . . . . . . . . . . . . . . . . . . . . . .

Your Affectionate & Attached Friend
A Blake.

Rome. Jany 1st 1817.

My dear Mother,

I write a few lines just to wish you health and happiness through the new year, and to say that I am still alive and tolerably well. My eyes only are in a bad state, and plague me a good deal; I hope to get some advice for them soon, but at present there is nobody here, whom I dare trust with them. I am still greatly amused with Italy, and wonderfully so with Rome. But the People are insupportable, and I shun them like wildfire. I heard from Maria the other day, who is in low spirits[,] having sent her Boy Stephen to Sea; She is going to be confined again in March! There really is no end of it!—I beleive, I told you, that I was presented to Maria Louisa at Parma; I have since Kissed the Pope's hand (not his Toe) and now have nothing more to do at Rome. I shall probably go to Naples soon, but my stay there is very uncertain.—If I can find a good opportunity I shall run over to Greece; and you must not be surprized to see my next letter dated from Athens.—Make my compts to Mr I— and Miss L—[1]

and beleive me
Your affecte Son
M. G. L.

[1] "Miss L—" is canceled by a later hand.

Naples. March 13. 1817.

My dear Mother,

I have deferred writing to you from day to day, expecting to be able to tell you, that Maria was safely brought to bed; But I beleive, She puts it off out of consideration for *me*, in order that She may not lose my company, as long as I remain at Naples. However, I shall leave it the day after tomorrow; and I make no doubt, that She will be brought to bed in the Evening of the same day, in order to make the restraint which She has been putting upon herself for my sake the more striking, and her attention to me the more pointedly marked. I have now been here for nine weeks, and never thought it possible for me to be so much delighted with any place out of England. The climate is delicious, and the beauty of the Scenery beggars all description. As to winter, I am told, that it is *gone*; but I should never have found out that it was *come*, only that the day before yesterday, there fell three flakes and a half of snow; and *that* past for Winter. I look upon Maria as the most fortunate person in the world, since She cannot live in England at present, that her lot is cast to live at Naples. For my own part, I am determined, that if Jamaica should fail, or anything happen to make England odious to me, I shall ship myself off for Naples, and fix myself there immoveably. Rome did not agree with me; and in particular my eyes troubled me a good deal: But at Naples I have been (for me) singularly well, and I shall quit the place with the greatest regret; especially as its [distance] from England (and still more from [Jamaica]) is so great, that I cannot possibly return to visit it without a very great exertion. This is the extreme point of my travels; So that from this moment you may consider me as being upon my way home. I wrote to Theepwash on the 11th of December, and directed him to send letters to Naples under cover to Sr H. Lushington; However, they are not arrived, and now I have no chance of getting them before my arrival in Paris, which will not be for several Months. However, Maria has assured me of your being in good health, and that is the material point. Farewell, my dear Mother; Remember me most kindly to Sophia, my Uncles, and Mrs Blake; and beleive me

Your affecte Son,
M. G. L.

Oak End Lodge Sunday ye 11th Janry [postmarked 1818]
My dear St Aubyn

. . . . . . . . . . . . . . . . . . . . . . . . . . . . . . . . . . . . . . . . . . . . . . . . . . . . . . . . . . . . . . . .

Matt Lewis is *in Jamaica* again. It appears to be his Heaven!

. . . . . . . . . . . . . . . . . . . . . . . . . . . . . . . . . . . . . . . . . . . . . . . . . . . . . . . . . . . . . .

Very truly Your Affectionate friend
A Blake

Jamaica. March 31. 1818.

My dear Mother,

You see, I am still alive; and I am also still *well*, which is strange enough, for I have been doing everything that makes other People die outright here; However, it has done me no harm, and I begin to beleive (like Macbeth) that so long as I stay in Jamaica, *"I bear a charmed life."* I have been climbing over Mountains with knocked up Horses; fording Rivers which an Irishman would call "impassable"; been benighted without Moon or Stars in a road bordered by precipices & Swamps; crossing Bridges, whose supporters had rotted and tumbled into the Ravine beneath; Sitting at Midnight in violent perspiration for an hour at a Gate with Dew falling and Wind blowing on me (which is your only true receipt for getting a Jamaica fever) carried away Horses Carriage and all by a Mountain Torrent; Driving along the Sea, whose roaring frightened my young Horses, one of whom tumbled into the Waves, while the off-wheel flew up into the air; & thus the Chaise balanced backwards & forwards till luckily the Postillion pulled up the Horse again, or we should all have gone over into the Sea and been drowned to a certainty; and last and worst of all, when after a tremendous journey of two hundred Miles through the worst Roads possible I reached my new Estate of Hordley (which I had never visited, and was pictured to me as a perfect Paradise) I found it an absolute Hell; the Negroes were almost frantic from the ill-usage of no less than eight petty Tyrants; the attorney was sick in bed (as the Negroes said, through fright of me) the Rain fell in pail-fulls day after day; the Wind roared and howled incessantly; Down came the Mountain Torrents; the River became impassible, broke down the Dam-Head, and stopped all the Sugar-works for two days & nights. All the Whites abused th[e] Blacks; All the Blacks abused the Whites; & I beleive, they all spoke true. However, I bestirred myself with all my might & main, soothed, threatened, ordered, stormed, swore, & banged the doors till the whole House shook as if it was going to tumble about our ears; and by dint of all this, assisted by degrading the Black Governor, ordering away one of the White Book-keepers (upon which another Ran away of his own accord) gratifying the Negroes in proper points, scolding them upon others, making them dance, & giving them money & other little indulgences, I managed to get them all into good temper; and when I went away, they ran by the Carriage for five or six miles to see me as long as they could, and when they were obliged to return, they loaded me with prayers to come back again, and many of them went away crying. However, I have done all in my power to secure the poor Creatures ag[a]inst further ill-usage; and if my endeavours are marred by others, the crime must rest on *their* heads, not mine. God bless you, my dear Mother.

Ever your affec^te Son
M G Lewis

My compt to M^r I & . . . .[1]

---

[1] "M^r" may be "M^rs"; the final name is canceled by a later hand—"Miss Lacey"?

Oak End Lodge 17th July 1818.

My dear St Aubyn

It is indeed our poor friend Matt Lewis whose death you read of and of whom you have been kind enough to make your inquiries. He died of an Inflamation in the Stomach and of perseverence in doctoring himself in his own fashion. He was reading but the instant before he breathed his last. He has left many to regret his oddities among which I am sure I ever shall remain altho' during the last Twelvemonth we were not the best friends but I know full well how to attribute all his faults. Peace be to his Ashes!—

Matthew has died very rich. He has provided very liberally for his beloved Mother who mourns his loss beyond the expression of words. She really does suffer as one wou'd imagin, she who loved a Son as Mother never loved more fondly, wou'd do.—To his two Sisters he leaves his Estates & personal Property. Thus then closes the short career of one with whom we were ever pleased to pass an idle hour but who for ever more is lost to us!—'Tis sad my dear St Aubyn to reflect that such things are, and still more so, that it may be our own fate any one moment that ensues.— God bless! us all, & send that die when we may we may die in Charity with the whole World!—

. . . . . . . . . . . . . . . . . . . . . . . . . . . . . . . . . . . . . . . . . . . . . . . . . . . . . . . . .

Believe me Dear St Aubyn most truly Your Affectionate friend

A Blake.

[outside address:] James St Aubyn Esqr/Henworthey/Launceston/Cornwall.

Jany 24th 1819.[1]

My dear Sir,

It will be a great pleasure to all the family, if you will kindly fulfill your original intention, of inserting some little memorial of my dear Brother in the Quarterly [R]eview. Any thing from your pen, will indeed my dear Sir, be highly valued by us all; but more especially by myself!— There has appeared in "The Courier," & The Sunday paper called the ["]Weekly dispatch," a most scurrilous attack on the memory of my ex- cellent Brother.—It affects to treat only of his Literary character but in a most insidious manner accuses him of "vice, profligacy &c." and in one sentence (evidently off his guard) the author of this vile production thus actually seperates the two characters—"The Monk was an eloquent evil; But the Man who compounded it, knew in his own soul that he was mixing poison for the generation." In another part he says that "while he could *evade the law,* he cared not what mischief he produced to his fellow creatures.—Sir Henry Lushington saw the[se] paragraphs I have alluded to, in Galliani's pa[ris] paper as an extract from the Courier. He was com- pletely shocked & exasperated by it!—I have heard my Brother say that when a child he imbibed his first taste for romance, from the terrible stories of an old Nurse who used to gain much of his attention, when he was visiti[ng] at the house of a relative of our's, Stanstead Hall [,] a very fine *old* Mansion, the large Hall of which he has exactly described in the Monk under the name of the Hall in Lindenberg Castle, where The Bleeding Nun terrifies the assembled Domestics.—I must relate to you an anecdote of my Paternal Grandfather which is really worthy introduction, as a trait of character, in a Farce!—This old Gentleman was *a character*, good-hearted, passionate, excessively proud, & still more vain, and with a great partiality for his own opinion. An old Maiden Sister who much resembled him, one day differ[ed] with him as to the situation of a House on the Bath road, & both maintained his opinion with determined pertinacity. When the old Lady left the room, D$^r$ Cyril Jackson said to my Grand Father, "I thought, Sir, you never had been in the vicinity of Bath."—"I never have."—"Then pray Sir may I ask how you can be so certain as to the situation of the House; for I really think Miss Lewis is right."—"So she may be Sir—but I assure you, if that old woman should once get it into her head that she could by any possible means be in the right there would be no peace in the family. I therefore make [i]t a point to contradict her on *all* occasions!—Is not that rather a curious trait de caractère?—This old Gentleman had another absurdity—he was very proud of his family, and literally talked of representing the County of Radnor, because He was the elder branch, altho he had not a foot of Land in the County, but he firmly persuaded himself that M$^r$ Lewis of Radnor would make it a point to give up his seat in Parliament from deference to the *elder branch*. The head of the clan, is I know in Scotland always sure of a certain degree of respect, let his situation in other respects be what it may, but I believe that spirit in Wales died with "the Bard."—But my curious[2] old Grandfather was even more *vain* than than he was proud; for my Mother declares that he *died* from an illness produced by mortification & jealousy of my maternal Grandfather Sir Thomas Sewell, who as Master of the Rolls, and a Privy Counsellor was styled R$^t$ Hon$^{ble}$ whereas M$^r$ Lewis, who as Member of Council in Jamaica had been *there* styled honourable, could not endure to dwindle into nobody by the side of his Son's father in law! So you see at least, He *died Game!*—Now, dear Sir, if you should receive this letter in a serious & sensible mood, I ought to *apologise* for all this nonsensical chit-chat, but if you should be in a humor to enjoy the ludicrous positions in which human nature sometimes delights to shew herself, then I shall require no apology for having created a smile on your countenance.—I wish I could remember any traits of my dear Brother's character to impart to you. I think that the most prominent of his good qualities was *Mercy*. This was the *moral* of his *Monk*, and He exemplified it himself in his conduct to that good for nothing young Man Kelly, whose whole story indee[d] would tend greatly to illustrate my dear Brother's character. I will make a Friend write it, and also the copy of a Letter which He wrote to my Father on "the Monk" & they shall be forwarded to you as soon as I can get at the papers from which they must be copied. I am myself in so precarious a state of health that I must not write too much with my own hand. I am so worn with illness that you would not *know* me!—I thank you for the kind expressions you use concerning my little translation but you have mistaken me. It was published two years ago, so that all I wished was that you would ask for it at a circulating Library in your *"Northern Athens"*, as the more copies are disposed of, the sooner M^r Allman of Princes S^t Hanover Square will give £25, which he promised to give me when he had sold the first Edition. The title is "The Hero; or the adventures of a Night." I dare say you are acquainted with the original "La Nuit Anglaise," a very witty french work.³—A Friend of mine was told in a Bookseller's shop a day or two back, on his taking up The Castl[e] Spectre, "Ah! Sir, we want very much some Memoirs of that Gentleman, and wonder very much no one has offered any thing of that nature to the market. It is jus[t] at this season a *desideratum* in the Bookselling world."—In case you should not have seen it, I inclose in this, a copy of the most infamous attack on my late Brother's memory, & an answer which was inserted in the same Paper. I hear however that it originated in "the Courier" & has been copie[d] from *that* paper into Galliani's Paris paper [,] where Sir Henry Lushington saw it. It *ought* to be answered in the Courier also!—I am indeed hurt at any *injustice* done to my Brother's memory! I was his favourite Sister [;] he *owned* it; not as he said "that you are more amiable, or more sensible, or that you love me any *better* than Maria does, for you are *not* so.—But I do love you the best, because you love me more *as I like to be loved*. Your Sister loves me with reason & good sense. *You* love me with devotedness, & docility, which never waits for reason & good sense."—He once wrote me the following little Billet, when he had been affronted at what he considered as want of confidence in him.—"Dear Sophia, Do not let what I have said, distress you any longer. I spoke harshly, as I could not bear in you what seemed like want of confidence; but remember this, that I at present Love you better than any human being in the world; and that I shall *always* love you better than any being in the world *but one*."

Y^r affec^te Brother<br>M. G. Lewis.

It is but natural that I should feel anxious for every tribute being paid to the memory of so kind & affectionate a Brother, who has so kindly remembered his Sisters in his last moments.—The first opportunity in which I can speak to Sir H. Torrens, I will not forget your Son. I should be proud indeed to be of any *use* to you or your's.—*My* Son, by the bye, is just the character to profit by an Edinburgh education, and I shall hope that you will have an opportunity of making an acquaintance with him next Autumn. —I wish there was a chance of your being in Lon[don] this Spring! If it *should* so happen, if even for only a short time, I should be most truly gratef[ul] if you would find your way to N^o 13, Lower Seymour S^t Portman

Sq$^{re}$—and to desir[e] my regards to M$^{rs}$ Scott, or Lady Scott?—I hear news & rumours of news of your prosperity in which Believe me, no one can rejoice with you more truly than

Y$^r$ ob$^d$ Ser$^t$
Sophia E. Shedden

We have some MS of my Brother's worthy of publication. Is there not a method of bargaining with a Bookseller, to sell the Copyright for only a term of years? the family keeping possession of the original MS? Just before my Brother went to Jamaica, he offered the Journal of his former voyage thither to Murray for £2000. but had received no answer.

¹ To Walter Scott. In the MS the date follows the signature.

² "Curious" is not certain.

³ Paris, 1799, attributed to Louis François Marie Bellin de La Liborlière. See Alan D. McKillop, " 'The Hero; or, the Adventures of a Night,' " *MLN*, LIII (June 1938), 414–415.

Oak End Lodge 23$^d$ April 1819.

My dear S$^t$ Aubyn

. . . . . . . . . . . . . . . . . . . . . . . . . . . . . . . . . . . . . . . . . . . . . . . . . . . . . . . . . . . .

I have written to M$^{rs}$ Lewis who I am sure you will like whenever you see for she is Goodness—but as to the disposal of Matthews effects, M$^r$ Sewell is the person to apply to, He being his Exôr & Trustee, and I make no doubt, He will be able to obtain some such thing as You allude to, but, Matthew left the whole of his Library to William Lamb Lord Melbourne's eldest Son! ! ! which said M$^r$ Lamb cares so little for the Compliment paid Him that he is actually going to *sell it*, tho' the books are allowed by every one to be a most valuable Collection & valued at £3000.

. . . . . . . . . . . . . . . . . . . . . . . . . . . . . . . . . . . . . . . . . . . . . . . . . . . . . . . . . . . .

Y$^r$ attached affectionate friend
A Blake.

[To James St. Aubyn from Mrs. Lewis]

M$^{rs}$ Lewis's Complim$^{ts}$ to M$^r$ S$^t$ Aubyn, she feels great regret, that after the kindness of his former calls, she has not yet been able to ask the favor of seeing him: she hopes he excuses her, in consideration of the additional infliction in her family. M$^{rs}$ Lewis has seen very little company during the melancholy recollections to which she has been a prey within the last ten Months; but as she will be in Town in a very few days, she hopes that in consideration of his being the valued associate of those dear to her, she may be allowed to rank him as an acquaintance of her own, and to receive him rather as a friend, than on a first visit: She is not yet quite in spirits to offer him a party; but wishes to have the pleasure, of once meeting if only for half an hour, that she may thank him personally for his late attention, and she hopes lay the foundation for future intimacy. Mrs Lewis must be in Town on Thursday ye 29th to meet a young Lady from the Country, who forms part of her family, and another friend or two; if Mr St Aubyn can put up with so dull a party, Mrs L will be much flatterd if he will take an early tea with her about eight o'clock. Mrs Lewis will at the same time take the liberty of introducing the young Lady she has just mentiond, as she believes Mr St Aubyn is musical; and as she is intended for the profession, should any public exhibition of her talents take place, Mrs Lewis may one day perhaps venture to solicit his support of her, which would indeed be a real kindness. she comes to Town accompanied by her Master (with whose Mother she is boarding) in order to be heard by one of those whose names are establishd, that she may judge if it will be worth her while to pursue the study: her present Master is not without talent but by living in the Country is unknown; though highly approved of by some good judges; and at some future day, Mrs L will venture to ask in confidence, Mr St Aubyn's opinion of his teaching.

Richmond April ye 23d [1819]

Mrs L requests the favor of an answer either by the bearer or to Foley Place.


[To James St. Aubyn from Mrs. Lewis]

Dr. Sr

Both Miss Lacey and I feel very sensibly your obliging attention; and I should have been earlier in thanking you for your two Letters, had I not waited to shew them to Miss L, of whose arrival from the Country I was in daily expectation. Her answer was as I expected very grateful to you and Mr Willet; but having compassd the end she had in view, of shewing she might be trusted with parts above mediocrity, she is now content to wait the effect it may produce in the minds of managers. When I spoke to you the case was different. From what I understand she has proved herself to have a great deal of talent; yet I begin to cease wondering that she wants an engagement; she seems so entirely absorb'd in her part, that she forgets the little attentions necessary in dress &c; and I can perceive plainly, that if she dresses *without a glass, won't accept of a dresser* when she does not find one *at the Theatre,* she will increase any prejudice from little defects of voice, or want of proper Stage features, which otherwise might easily be removed, or passd over by the force of her good acting. The temptation to her playing at the Haymarket, was the prospect (and the assurance) of being supported by a regular Company; whereas nothing could be further from the truth, so that on the whole, though she has surprized people, and met with a great deal of applause, I cannot think she has done herself any good. I feel very angry with her for a careless girl; for I believe she acknowledges she was so dissatisfied with the Company (all but one or two) that she paid no attention to her appearance, and even left out half her part: One thing is very clear—that she is destined to be great or nothing; and that she must give herself a little more time & trouble in order to shew she can look as well on the Stage, as I know she can do off. I ought to apologize for teazing you with all this, but I am cruelly disappointed when people, intimate with managers, tell me "they are in raptures with her, and that having something peculiar to herself, she would not be an hour without an engagement," but from the circumstances I describe. 'Tis very provoking.

. . . . . . . . . . . . . . . . . . . . . . . . . . . . . . . . . . . . . . . . . . . . . . . . . . . . . . . . . . . . . . . . . . . .

> Yours very truly
> F M Lewis.

Foley Place
Jan^ry y^e 6^th [1820?]
I believe if Miss L should play again, it must not be to shew she can *act* well; but that she can *look* well. I really could tell you something quite ludicrous about it: she acknowledges that she rather thinks she went on *with snuff of the candle upon her face*. I think we may declare her *not fit for the profession*.


Oak End Lodge 7 Feby. [postmarked 1822]

Yes, my dear S^t Aubyn, we have lost our good old friend M^rs Lewis! a friend, whom I have known from my earliest infancy, & one whom I was taught to love. Her goodness of heart was rarely equalled, for I protest she lived, but to oblige. God will bless her, I am sure He will, for she deserved to be blessed.—

M^r Sewell felt the loss, as you may suppose He did with extreme sorrow of heart but with that resignation which marks his Conduct in all his losses.

M^rs Lewis died without having kept her Bed one day. She only *drooped*, as she called it, but thought so little of dying that she proposed to her Brother My going up as the following Week to stay with her for some time. Unhappily for me she died the *next Day*. Poor M^rs Lewis! long very long shall I remember your many excellencies & long very long shall I live before I ever meet with one who will ever love me as she did.

. . . . . . . . . . . . . . . . . . . . . . . . . . . . . . . . . . . . . . . . . . . . . . . . . . . . . . . . . . . . . . . . .

My spirits are, as you may imagin low, for indeed the remembrance of M^rs Lewis always distresses me.

. . . . . . . . . . . . . . . . . . . . . . . . . . . . . . . . . . . . . . . . . . . . . . . . . . . . . . . . . . . . . . . . . .

> Your Affectionate friend
> A Blake.

M^rs L. left all she had to Miss Lacy.

LEWIS' PRINCIPAL WORKS
WORKS CITED
NOTES
INDEX

| | |
|---|---|
| Add. MS.: | manuscript in the British Museum |
| AR: | *Analytical Review* |
| BM: | British Museum |
| Cr R: | *Critical Review* |
| DNB: | *Dictionary of National Biography* |
| Eu M: | *European Magazine* |
| F: | Forster Collection, Victoria and Albert Museum, South Kensington |
| GM: | *Gentleman's Magazine* |
| HCL: | Harvard College Library |
| HEHL: | Henry E. Huntington Library |
| HLQ: | *Huntington Library Quarterly* |
| J: | *Journal of a West India Proprietor* (London, 1834) |
| JEGP: | *Journal of English and Germanic Philology* |
| LA: | Larpent Collection, Henry E. Huntington Library |
| Life: | *The Life and Correspondence of M. G. Lewis*, by Mrs. Cornwall Baron-Wilson (London, 1839) |
| MLN: | *Modern Language Notes* |
| MMi: | *Monthly Mirror* |
| Mo M: | *Monthly Magazine* |
| MP: | *Modern Philology* |
| MR: | *Monthly Review* |
| N&Q: | *Notes and Queries* |
| NYPL: | New York Public Library |
| PBSA: | *Papers of the Bibliographical Society of America* |
| PEBS: | *Papers of the Edinburgh Bibliographical Society* |
| PQ: | *Philological Quarterly* |
| SB: | *Studies in Bibliography: Papers of the Bibliographical Society of the University of Virginia* |
| TLS: | London *Times Literary Supplement* |
| W: | Walpole Bequest, National Library of Scotland |

# LEWIS' PRINCIPAL WORKS

Titles are followed by dates of first editions. Theaters and dates of first stage performances are given in parentheses. Of many spurious works, only those cited in the text or notes are listed.

*The Monk: A Romance,* 1796.
*Village Virtues: A Dramatic Satire. In Two Parts,* 1796.
*The Minister: A Tragedy, in Five Acts,* 1797.
*The Castle Spectre: A Drama, in Five Acts,* 1798 (Drury Lane, Dec. 14, 1797).
*The Love of Gain: A Poem,* 1799.
*The Twins; or, Is It He, or His Brother? A Farce in Two Acts,* unpublished (Drury Lane, Apr. 8, 1799). HEHL MS LA 1245.
*The East Indian: A Comedy, in Five Acts,* 1800 (Drury Lane, Apr. 22, 1799).
*Rolla; or, The Peruvian Hero. A Tragedy, in Five Acts,* 1799.
*Tales of Wonder,* 1801.
*Adelmorn, the Outlaw: A Romantic Drama, in Three Acts,* 1801 (Drury Lane, May 4, 1801).
*Alfonso, King of Castile: A Tragedy, in Five Acts,* 1801 (Covent Garden, Jan. 15, 1802).
*The Captive: A Scene in a Private Mad-House,* not separately published (Covent Garden, Mar. 22, 1803).
*The Harper's Daughter; or, Love and Ambition. A Tragedy, in Five Acts,* unpublished, but see pp. 91, 307n86 (Covent Garden, May 4, 1803). HEHL MS LA 1377.
*The Bravo of Venice: A Romance,* 1805.
*Rugantino; or, The Bravo of Venice. A Grand Romantic Melo-Drama, in Two Acts,* 1805 (Covent Garden, Oct 18, 1805).
*Adelgitha; or, The Fruits of a Single Error. A Tragedy, in Five Acts,* 1806 (Drury Lane, Apr. 30, 1807).
*Feudal Tyrants; or, The Counts of Carlsheim and Sargans. A Romance,* 1806.
*The Wood Daemon; or, The Clock has Struck. A Grand Romantic Melo-Drama, in Two Acts,* unpublished (Drury Lane, Apr. 1, 1807).
*He Loves and He Rides Away: A Favourite Ballad,* 1808.
*Twelve Ballads, the Words and Music by M. G. Lewis,* 1808.
*Romantic Tales,* 1808.
*Venoni; or, The Novice of St. Mark's. A Drama, in Three Acts,* 1809 (Drury Lane, Dec. 1, 1808).

*Monody on the Death of Sir John Moore,* 1809 (recited at Drury Lane, Feb. 14, 1809).

[*Temper, or*] *The Domestic Tyrant: A Farce, in Two Acts,* unpublished (Lyceum by Drury Lane company, May 1, 1809). HEHL MS LA 1575.

*Timour the Tartar: A Grand Romantic Melo-Drama, in Two Acts,* 1811 (Covent Garden, Apr. 29, 1811).

*One O'Clock! or, The Knight and the Wood Daemon. A Grand Musical Romance, in Three Acts,* 1811 (Lyceum, Aug. 1, 1811).

*Rich and Poor: A Comic Opera, in Three Acts,* 1812 (Lyceum, July 22, 1812).

*Poems,* 1812.

*Journal of a West India Proprietor,* 1834.

## Spurious Works

*The Bleeding Nun of the Castle of Lindenberg; or, The History of Raymond & Agnes.* "By the author of the Castle Spectre," London, n.d. [dated by BM Catalogue 1823].

*The Castle of Lindenberg; or, The History of Raymond & Agnes, a Romance. By Matthew Gregory Lewis.* London, n.d. [1799?].

*The History of Raymond & Agnes; or, The Castle of Lindenberg, a Romance, by Matthew Gregory Lewis.* London, 1812.

*Raymond and Agnes, an Interesting Drama, in Two Acts. By M. G. Lewis.* Dick's Standard Plays, No. 268. New and complete edition. [London], n.d. [BM Catalogue: 1883].

*Raymond and Agnes; or, The Bleeding Nun. By M. G. Lewis.* Romanticist and Novelist's Library, IV. London, 1841.

*Raymond & Agnes; or, The Bleeding Nun of the Castle of Lindenberg. By the Late M. G. Lewis, Esq. Author of the Castle Spectre.* London, n.d. [watermarks: 1824].

*Raymond and Agnes; or, The Travellers Benighted; An Interesting Drama in Two Acts, by Matthew Gregory Lewis.* Cumberland's British Theatre, No. 298. London, n.d.

*Raymond and Agnes; The Travellers Benighted, or The Bleeding Nun of Lindenberg, an Interesting Drama in Two Acts, by Matthew Gregory Lewis.* . . . Cumberland's British Theatre, XXXVIII. London, n.d.

*Raymond and Agnes; The Travellers Benighted, or The Bleeding Nun of Lindenberg, an Interesting Drama in Two Acts, by Matthew Gregory Lewis.* . . . French's Standard Drama, CXCI. New York, n.d.

*Tales of Terror and Wonder, Collected by Matthew Gregory Lewis.* Introduction by Henry Morley. London, 1887.

*Tales in Verse of Terror and Wonder,* ed. Lloyd E. Smith. Little Blue Book No. 739, ed. E. Haldeman-Julius. Girard, Kansas, 1925.

# WORKS CITED

## Manuscripts

"Trustees Minute Book" and "Albany Register of Freeholders," two MS volumes at the Albany, Piccadilly.

Hardwick, Windham, and Liverpool Papers in the War Office correspondence at the British Museum: Add. MSS. 37877 (foll. 155–60, 172–3), 37882 (foll. 160–1), 37889 (fol. 154), 38213 (foll. 7–10), 38217 (fol. 119), 38309 (fol. 69), 38416 (fol. 125); and a MS note in *The Old Hag...*, 1801 (11602.dd.5.[1]).

Part of a letter from Lewis to Goethe at the Goethe- und Schiller-Archiv in Weimar.

Two MS notes, in a copy of Lewis' *Alfonso* (17477.36.47.25\*), and in a MS copy of "Quadrupeds . . . a Burlesque Entertainment" (LTR 17473.7.15\*) at the Harvard College Library.

MS copies of Lewis' dramas in the Larpent Collection: 1187, 1232, 1245, 1337, 1459, 1514, 1518, 1561, 1597, 1670, 1686, 1690, 1726; and two MS notes in John Payne Collier's copy of the *Biographia Dramatica* (R 13729) at the Henry E. Huntington Library.

Letter by Lewis to John Plummer, dated Oct. 11, 1816, at the Institute of Jamaica (B.W.I.).

Holograph of Lewis' poem "Love at Sale" at the University of Kansas Library.

Autograph letter (MA 1432) by Walter Scott to Lewis, dated May 29, 1798, at the Pierpont Morgan Library, a gift of Mr. DeCoursey Fales to the library.

Fourteen letters by and concerning Lewis in the Walpole Bequest: Vol. I, foll. 15, 17–19, 23–4, 26–7, 30–1; Vol. IX, foll. 8, 10; and verses on Lewis (MS. 3220, fol. 5) at the National Library of Scotland.

Copy of part of a letter dated July 12, 1805, by Robert Southey to C. W. W. Wynn at the National Library of Wales.

Copy of a letter by Lewis, dated Apr. 22 [1797], owned by Dean Julian Park, University of Buffalo.

"Petition of Appeal" in Chancery (Lushington vs. Sewell, June 21, 1829; C. 36, Bundle 29) at the Public Record Office, London.

Copies of the wills of Lewis' father and of Lewis, and of a codicil to Lewis' will at Somerset House, London.

Lewis MSS in the Forster Collection (F 375–8; pressmark 48.E.23, Nos. 1–120); in the Dyce Collection, two MS notes in Lewis' *Monk* (D.5780) and his *Romantic Tales* (D.5797) at the Victoria and Albert Museum.

MS poem and a note thereon in a copy of Lewis' *Tales of Wonder* (London, 1801) at the Yale University Library.

Autograph letters by Lewis, his mother, his aunt Anna Blake, James St. Aubyn, William Parnell Hayes, and Thomas Sheridan, and a MS note by Lewis in a copy of *Timour the Tartar*, in my possession.


## Books and Articles

*The Academy. A Record of Literature, Learning, Science, and Art.* I (1869).

Adolphus, John: *Memoirs of John Bannister, Comedian.* London, n.d. [preface dated 1838].

Airlie, Mabell, Countess of: *In Whig Society, 1775–1818; Compiled from the . . . Correspondence of Elizabeth, Viscountess Melbourne, and Emily Lamb, Countess Cowper.* . . . London, etc., 1921.

*Almagro & Claude; or Monastic Murder; Exemplified in the Dreadful Doom of an Unfortunate Nun.* London, n.d. Printed for Tegg and Castleman. . . . [The frontispiece, entitled "Almagro & Claude," is dated 1803].

*The Analytical Review.* XXIV (Oct. 1796), XXV (Apr. 1797), XXVIII (Aug. 1798).

*The Athenaeum.* No. 3808 (Oct. 20, 1900).

*Autograph Prices Current.* Ed. A. J. Herbert. Vol. VI. London, n.d.

Baker, David Erskine: *Biographia Dramatica* . . . Continued . . . by Isaac Reed . . . and Stephen Jones. 3 vols. London, 1812.

Baker, Ernest A.: *The History of the English Novel.* 10 vols. London, 1942.

Barker, G. F. Russell and Alan H. Stenning: *The Record of Old Westminsters: A Biographical List of All Those Who Are Known To Have Been Educated at Westminster School from the Earliest Times to 1927.* 2 vols. London, 1928.

Baron-Wilson, Margaret [Mrs. Cornwall Baron-Wilson]: *The Life and Correspondence of M. G. Lewis . . . with Many Pieces in Prose and Verse Never Before Published.* 2 vols. London, 1839.

————— *Our Actresses; or, Glances at Stage Favourites, Past and Present.* 2 vols. London, 1844.

Bayne, Thomas: "Scotch Words and English Commentators," *N&Q*, 9th Series, XI (Jan. 3, 1903), 1–2.

Beers, Henry A.: *A History of English Romanticism in the Eighteenth Century.* New York, 1926.

[Berry, Miss]: *Extracts of the Journals and Correspondence of Miss Berry from the Year 1783 to 1852.* Ed. Lady Theresa Lewis. 3 vols. London, 1865.

Birkenhead, Sheila: *Peace in Piccadilly: The Story of Albany.* New York, 1958.

Birkhead, Edith: *The Tale of Terror: A Study of the Gothic Romance.* London, 1921.

*Blackwell's,* No. 531. A bookseller's catalogue. Oxford, England, 1948.

*The Bleeding Nun of the Castle of Lindenberg; or, The History of Raymond & Agnes.* "By the author of the Castle Spectre." London, n.d. [dated by BM Catalogue 1823].

Boaden, James: *Aurelio and Miranda: A drama. In five acts.* London, 1799.

————— *Memoirs of the Life of John Philip Kemble, Esq. Including a History of the Stage, from the Time of Garrick to the Present Period.* 2 vols. London, 1825.

[Bowles, William Lisle]: *A Wiltshire Parson and His Friends: The Correspondence of Wiliam Lisle Bowles Together with Four Hitherto Unidentified Reviews by Coleridge.* Ed. Garland Greever. London, 1926.

[Brougham, Henry]: *The Life and Times of Henry Lord Brougham, Written by Himself.* 2nd edition. 3 vols. Edinburgh and London, 1871.

[Broughton, Lord (John Cam Hobhouse)]: *Recollections of a Long Life; by Lord Broughton.* . . . Ed. Lady Dorchester. 2 vols. London, 1909.

Burckhardt, C. H. A.: *Das Repertoire des Weimarischen Theaters unter Goethes Leitung 1791–1817.* Hamburg and Leipzig, 1891. [Not consulted. See p. 292n41].

[Bury, Lady Charlotte]: *The Diary of a Lady-in-Waiting by Lady Charlotte Bury, Being the Diary Illustrative of the Times of George the Fourth.* . . . Ed. A. Francis Steuart. London and New York, 1908.

Buyers, Geoffrey: "The Influence of Schiller's Drama and Fiction upon English Literature in the Period 1780–1830," *Englische Studien,* XLVIII (Apr. 1915), 349–393.

[Byron, Lord]: *The Works of Lord Byron. Letters and Journals.* Ed. Rowland E. Prothero. 6 vols. London, 1904–1924.

————— *The Works of Lord Byron. Poetry.* Ed. Ernest Hartley Coleridge. 7 vols. London, 1905–1924.

Cahusac, Louis de: *Zoroastre, opéra.* . . . Paris, 1756.

[Carlyle, Thomas]: *Early Letters of Thomas Carlyle.* Ed. Charles Eliot Norton. 2 vols. London and New York, 1886.

Carré, Jean-Marie: *Goethe en Angleterre: Étude de littérature comparée.* Paris [1920].

*A Catalogue of all Graduates . . . in the University of Oxford, between . . . 1659 . . . and 1850. . . .* Oxford, 1851.

[Cavendish, Lady Harriet]: *Hary-O: The Letters of Lady Harriet Cavendish, 1796–1809.* Ed. Sir George Leveson Gower and Iris Palmer. London [1940].

[Chateaubriand, François-René de]: *Mémoires d'Outre-Tombe.* Ed. Maurice Levaillant. 2nd edition. 4 vols. Paris [1947].

Child, Francis James: *The English and Scottish Popular Ballads.* 5 vols. Boston [1882–1898].

Church, Elizabeth: "A Bibliographical Myth," *MP,* XIX (Feb. 1922), 307–314.

[Coleridge, Samuel Taylor]: *Collected Letters of Samuel Taylor Coleridge.* Ed. Earl Leslie Griggs. 4 vols. Oxford, 1956–1959.

————— *The Complete Works of Samuel Taylor Coleridge.* Ed. W. G. T. Shedd. 7 vols. New York, 1884.

Colman, George, the younger: *Random Records.* 2 vols. London, 1830.

Conant, Martha Pike: *The Oriental Tale in England in the Eighteenth Century.* New York, 1908.

Constable, Thomas: *Archibald Constable and His Literary Correspondents: A Memorial by His Son Thomas Constable.* 3 vols. Edinburgh, 1873.

*The Courier.* Nos. 8022 (June 23, 1818), 8133 (Oct. 31, 1818).

*The Court Magazine, Containing Original Papers, by Distinguished Writers.* . . . Vol. IV (Jan.–June, 1834). London.

Coykendall, Frederick: "A Note on 'The Monk,'" *The Colophon, a Quarterly for Bookmen.* N.S. I (Summer 1935), 87–96.

*Critical Review.* XIX (1797), XXII (1798), XXVII (1799), XXX (1800), XXXIV (1802), 3rd Series, XI (1807).

Cundall, Frank: *Historic Jamaica.* London, 1915.

Dalzel, Andrew: *History of the University of Edinburgh from Its Foundation . . . with a Memoir of the Author* [by C. Innes]. Edinburgh, 1862.

[Dermody, Thomas]: *More Wonders! An Heroic Epistle to M. G. Lewis, Esq. M.P.* . . . by Mauritius Moonshine. . . . London, 1801.

————— *Poems, Moral and Descriptive.* London, 1800.

[Devonshire, Georgiana, Duchess of]: *The Two Duchesses . . . Family Correspondence of and Relating to Georgiana, Duchess of Devonshire, Elizabeth, Duchess of Devonshire* [and others] . . . *1777–1859.* Ed. Vere Foster. 2nd edition. London, 1898.

[Dudley, John William Ward, First Earl of]: *Letters to 'Ivy' from the First Earl of Dudley.* Ed. S. H. Romilly. London, 1905.

Duran, Don Agustin: *Romancero General, ó Colleccion de Romances Castellanos,* Vols. X and XVI of *Biblioteca Autores Españoles.* Madrid, 1849–51.

Dutton, Thomas: *The Literary Census: A Satirical Poem . . . Including . . . Strictures on the Pursuits of Literature.* . . . London, 1798.

*Edinburgh Review.* I (1803), LIX (1834).

Emerson, Oliver Farrar: "The Early Literary Life of Sir Walter Scott," *JEGP,* XXIII (1924), 28–62, 241–269, 389–417.

————— " 'Monk' Lewis and the *Tales of Terror,*" MLN, XXXVIII (Mar. 1923), 154–159.

Estève, Edmond: "Le 'Théâtre Monacal' sous la Révolution; Ses Précédents et Ses Suites," in *Études de Littérature Préromantique,* pp. 83–137. Paris, 1923.

*European Magazine.* XXXI (1797), XXXIII (1798), XXXV (1799), XXXVI (1799), XXXIX (1801), XLI (1802), XLVIII (1805), LI (1807), LV (1809), LIX (1811).

Evans, Bertrand: *Gothic Drama from Walpole to Shelley.* Berkeley and Los Angeles, 1947.

Ewen, Frederic: *The Prestige of Schiller in England, 1788–1859.* New York, 1932.

Fairchild, Hoxie N.: "Byron and Monk Lewis," *TLS,* May 11, 1946, p. 223.

Farley, Frank Edgar: *Scandinavian Influences in the English Romantic Movement.* Harvard Studies and Notes in Philology and Literature, IX. Boston, 1903.

[Ferrier, Susan]: *Memoir and Correspondence of Susan Ferrier 1782–1854.* . . . Ed. John A. Doyle. London, 1898.

Foster, Joseph: *Alumni Oxonienses: The Members of the University of Oxford 1715–1886.* . . . Oxford, 1888.

A Friend of Accuracy: "M. G. Lewis," *N&Q,* N.S. IV (Sept. 1957), 389.

A Friend to Genius: "An Apology for the Monk," *MMi,* III (Apr. 1797), 210–215.

*General Evening Post.* Mar. 31–Apr. 2, Apr. 30–May 3, 1807; Dec. 1–3, 1808; June 23–25, 1818.

Genest, John: *Some Account of the English Stage from the Restoration in 1660 to 1830.* 10 vols. Bath, 1832.

*Gentleman's Magazine.* LXIII (1793), LXIV (1794), LIX (Sup. for 1789), LXIX (1799), LXX (1800), LXXI (1801), LXXIX (1809), LXXXI (1811), LXXXVIII (1818).

*The Genuine Rejected Addresses, Presented to the Committee of Management for Drury-Lane Theatre.* . . . London, 1812.

Gerard, Frances: *A Grand Duchess: The Life of Anna Amalia Duchess of Saxe-Weimar-Eisenach and the Classical Circle of Weimar.* 2 vols. New York, 1902.

[Glenbervie, Sylvester Douglas, Lord]: *The Diaries of Sylvester Douglas (Lord Glenbervie).* Ed. Francis Bickley. 2 vols. London and New York, 1928.

[Goldsmith, Oliver]: *The Grumbler, an Adaptation by Oliver Goldsmith.* Introduction and notes by Alice I. Perry Wood. Cambridge, Mass., 1931.

"Gothic Horror," *Parade: A Pageant of Personalities and Events* (Sydney), Nov. 1958, pp. 38–39.

[Gower, Lord Granville Leveson]: *Lord Granville Leveson Gower (First Earl Granville), Private Correspondence, 1781 to 1821.* Ed. Castalia Countess Granville. 2 vols. London, 1916.

*The Greville Memoirs, 1814–1860.* Ed. Lytton Strachey and Roger Fulford. London, 1938.

[Grillparzer, Franz]: *Grillparzers Werke.* Ed. August Sauer. Vol. I. Wien and Leipzig, 1909.

Grose, Francis: *The Antiquities of England and Wales.* . . . 2nd edition. 8 vols. 1783.

Grosette, H[enry] W[illiam]: *Raymond and Agnes! or, The Bleeding Nun of Lindenberg. An Interesting Melo-Drama, in Two Acts.* . . . Duncombe's Edition. London, n.d.

Günther, Carl: *Heinrich Zschokkes Jugend- und Bildungsjahre (bis 1798).* . . . Aarau, 1918.

Guthke, Karl S.: "C. M. Wieland and M. G. Lewis," *Neophilologus,* XL (July 1956), 231–233.

———— *Englische Vorromantik und Deutscher Sturm und Drang: M. G. Lewis' Stellung in der Geschichte der Deutsch-Englischen Literaturbeziehungen.* Palaestra, Band 223. Göttingen, 1958.

———— "Die Erste Nachwirkung von Herders Volksliedern in England: Unveröffentliche Dokumente zu den 'Tales of Wonder,' " *Archiv,* CXCIII (Apr. 1957), 273–284.

———— "Die Herkunft des Weltliterarischen Typus der 'Femme Fatale' aus der Deutschen Volkssage," *Germanisch-Romanische Monatsschrift,* N.F. VI (July 1956), 294–296.

———— "Some Bibliographical Errors Concerning the Romantic Age," *PBSA,* LI (2nd quarter, 1957), 159–162.

———— "Some Notes on the Significance of the Weimar Court Stage in Anglo-German Literary Relations," *HLQ,* XX (May 1957), 281–283.

———— "Some Unidentified Early English Translations from Herder's *Volkslieder,*" *MLN,* LXXIII (Jan. 1958), 52–56.

———— "Some Unpublished Letters of M. G. Lewis," *N&Q,* N.S. IV (May 1957), 217–219.

[Hamilton, Anthony]: *Oeuvres du Comte Hamilton*. 2 vols. Ed. J. B. J. Champagnac. Paris, 1825.

[Hanmer, Sir Thomas]: *The Correspondence of Sir Thomas Hanmer, Bart., Speaker of the House of Commons. With a Memoir of His Life. . . .* Ed. Sir Henry Bunbury. London, 1838.

[Hazlitt, William]: *The Collected Works of William Hazlitt.* Ed. A. R. Waller and Arnold Glover. 12 vols. London and New York, 1902.

Herford, C. H.: *The Age of Wordsworth.* London, 1925.

Herzfeld, Georg: "Die Eigentliche Quelle von Lewis' 'Monk,'" *Archiv,* N.S. XI (Dec. 1903), 316–323.

———— "Eine Neue Quelle für Lewis' 'Monk,'" *Archiv,* N.S. IV (June 1900), 310–312.

———— "Noch Einmal die Quelle des 'Monk,'" *Archiv,* N.S. XV (Oct. 1905), 70–73.

Hofmann, Otto: *Studien zum Englischen Schauerroman.* Halle, 1915.

[Holland, Elizabeth, Lady]: *Elizabeth, Lady Holland to Her Son 1821–1845.* Ed. the Earl of Ilchester. London, 1946.

———— *The Journal of Elizabeth, Lady Holland (1791–1811).* Ed. the Earl of Ilchester. 2 vols. London, New York, etc., 1908.

[Holland, Henry Richard Vassall, Third Lord]: *Further Memoirs of the Whig Party 1807–1821, with Some Miscellaneous Reminiscences. . . .* Ed. Lord Stavordale. New York, 1905.

"The Horrors of Camouflage," *TLS,* May 6, 1960, p. 291.

Ilchester, the Earl of: *Chronicles of Holland House 1820–1900.* New York, 1938.

———— *The Home of the Hollands, 1605–1820.* London [1937].

*Impartial Strictures on a Poem Called 'The Pursuits of Literature' and Particularly a Vindication of the Romance of 'The Monk.'* London, 1798.

Jekyll, Walter: *Jamaican Song and Story: Annancy Stories, Digging Sings, Ring Tunes, and Dancing Tunes. . . .* London, 1907.

Jerrold, Clare: *The Story of Dorothy Jordan.* London, 1914.

Johnston, George P.: "The First Book Printed by James Ballantyne: Being An Apology for Tales of Terror; with Notes on Tales of Wonder and Tales of Terror," *PEBS,* 1890–1895, I (Part 4, Oct. 1894). Edinburgh, 1896.

———— "Note to a Paper Entitled The First Book Printed by James Ballantyne," *PEBS,* 1904–1913, IX (Part 2, Aug. 1912), 90.

*Journals of the House of Commons.* Vols. LII, LIV (1803).

*Journals of the House of Lords.* Vol. XXXVI (1783).

[Kelly, Sir Fitzroy]: "Sir Fitzroy Kelly," *DNB.*

———— "Sir Fitzroy Kelly," *Encyclopaedia Britannica.* 11th edition. New York, 1910.

Kelly, Isabella: *The Baron's Daughter.* London, 1802.

———— *A Collection of Poems and Fables.* London, 1794.

———— *A Modern Incident in Domestic Life. . . .* 2 vols. Brentford, 1803.

Kelly, Michael: *Reminiscences of Michael Kelly.* New York, 1826.

Killen, Alice M.: *Le Roman Terrifiant ou Roman Noir de Walpole à Anne Radcliffe. . . .* Paris, 1923.

Knight, William, ed.: *Letters of the Wordsworth Family from 1787 to 1855.* 3 vols. Boston and London, 1907.

Koeppel, Emil: "Matthew Gregory Lewis's Gedicht 'The Tailor's Wife' und

Bulwer's 'Wife of Miletus,'" in *Germanistische Abhandlungen*, pp. 135–142. Ed. Hermann Paul. Strassburg, 1902.

A Lady of Rank: *The Murdered Queen! or, Caroline of Brunswick*. London, 1838.

*Lady's Monthly Museum*. N.S. V (1808).

Lawrence-Archer, J. H.: *Monumental Inscriptions of the British West Indies*. London, 1875.

Lewis, Matthew Gregory: *The Castle Spectre*. Oxberry edition. London, 1818.

———— *The Isle of Devils. A Historical Tale, Funnded* [*sic*] *on an Anecdote in the Annals of Portugal. (From an Unpublished Manuscript.)* . . . Kingtson [*sic*], Jamaica, 1827.

———— *M. G. Lewis. Journal of a West India Proprietor, 1815–17*. Ed. Mona Wilson. Boston and New York, 1929.

———— *The Monk*. Original text, variant readings, and "A Note on the Text" by Louis F. Peck. Introduction by John Berryman. New York, 1952; Evergreen Edition, New York, 1959.

———— *The Monk*. Bestseller Library, London, 1960.

———— *The Monk: A Romance*. [Anonymous introduction.] 3 vols. London, 1906.

———— *One O'Clock! or, The Knight and the Wood Daemon; A Dramatic Romance*. Oxberry's New English Drama, XIX. London, 1824.

———— *Rosario or the Female Monk, a Romance, by Monk Lewis*. Ed. Max Maury. [U. S. A.], n.d.

———— *Timour the Tartar: A Grand Romantic Melo-Drama, in Two Acts*. . . . Cumberland's British Theatre, XXIX. London, n.d. [BM Catalogue: "1829, etc."].

Lockhart, John Gibson: *Memoirs of the Life of Sir Walter Scott*. 5 vols. Boston and New York, 1902.

*The London Chronicle*. Vol. LXXIII (1793).

Lovelace, Ralph Milbanke, Earl of: *Astarte: A Fragment of Truth Concerning George Gordon Byron, Sixth Lord Byron*. New edition. Ed. Mary Countess of Lovelace. New York, 1921.

[Lushington, Sir Stephen]: "Sir Stephen Lushington," *DNB*.

McKillop, Alen D.: " 'The Hero; or, The Adventures of a Night,' " *MLN*, LIII (June 1938), 414–415.

MacMillan, Dougald: *Catalogue of the Larpent Plays in the Huntington Library*. San Marino, Calif., 1939.

[Macready, William Charles]: *Macready's Reminiscences, and Selections from His Diaries and Letters*. Ed. Sir Frederick Pollock. New York, 1875.

Madden, R[ichard] R[obert]: *A Twelvemonth's Residence in the West Indies*. Philadelphia, 1835.

Margraf, Ernst: *Einfluss der Deutschen Litteratur auf die Englische am Ende des Achtzehnten und im Ersten Drittel des Neunzehnten Jahrhunderts*. Leipzig, 1901.

Marshall, Roderick: *Italy in English Literature, 1755–1815; Origins of the Romantic Interest in Italy*. New York, 1934.

Marsollier des Vivetières, Benoît Joseph: *Camille, ou le Souterrain, Comédie en Trois Actes, en Prose, Mêlée de Musique*. . . . Paris, 1791.

[Mathias, Thomas J.]: *The Pursuits of Literature. A Satirical Poem in Four Dialogues.* 3rd edition, London, 1797; 5th edition, London, 1798.

Medwin, Thomas: *Conversations of Lord Byron: Noted During a Residence with His Lordship at Pisa, in the Years 1821 and 1822.* 2nd edition. London, 1824.

[Melbourne, William Lamb, second Viscount]: *Lord Melbourne's Papers.* Ed. Lloyd C. Sanders, with a preface by The Earl Cowper. London and New York, 1889.

Melville, Lewis: *An Injured Queen; Caroline of Brunswick.* 2 vols. London, 1912.

Mercier, Louis Sebastien: *L'Habitant de la Guadeloupe, Comédie en Trois Actes.* . . . Paris, 1785.

Milner, H. M.: *Alonzo and Imogine; or, The Spectre Bride!* Lacy edition. London, n.d.

[Mitford, Mary Russell]: *Letters of Mary Russell Mitford.* 2nd Series. Ed. Henry Chorley. 2 vols. London, 1872.

———— *The Life of Mary Russell Mitford . . . Related in a Selection from Her Letters.* . . . Ed. A[lfred] G[uy] L'Estrange. 3 vols. London, 1870.

Möbius, H.: *Die Englischen Rosenkreuzerromane und Ihre Vorläufer.* . . . Hamburg, 1911.

*Monthly Magazine and British Register.* III (1797), IV (1797).

*Monthly Mirror.* II–V (1796–1798), VIII (1799), XI–XIV (1801–1802), XIX (1805), XX (1805), N.S. I (1807), IV (1808), V (1809).

*Monthly Review.* 2nd Series, XXI (1796), XXIII (1797), XXVI (1798), XXX (1799), L (1806), LIII (1807), LXI (1810).

[Moore, Thomas]: *Memoirs, Journal, and Correspondence of Thomas Moore.* Ed. Lord John Russell. 8 vols. London and Boston, 1853–56.

Moorman, Mary: *William Wordsworth: A Biography. The Early Years, 1770–1803.* Oxford, 1957.

*Morning Chronicle.* Mar. 26, 1803; Dec. 2, 12, 1808; May 2, 1809; Apr. 30, May 1, 3, Aug. 1, 3, 1811; June 24, 1818.

*Morning Herald.* June 21, 1796; Mar. 17, Dec. 26, 1797; Jan. 13, Feb. 5, 1798; Mar. 5, May 8, 1801; Jan. 16, 23, 1802.

Moss, Walter: "M. G. Lewis and Mme de Staël," *English Studies,* XXXIV (1953), 109–112.

Naubert, Christiane Benedicte Eugenie: *Elizabeth, Erbin von Toggenburg, oder Geschichte der Frauen in der Schweiz. Neue Ausgabe.* Leipzig, 1799.

Nicoll, Allardyce: *A History of English Drama, 1660–1900.* 4 vols. Cambridge, Eng., 1952–55.

An Octogenarian: *Sheridan and His Times.* 2 vols. London, 1859.

Oliphant, Margaret: *The Literary History of England in the End of the Eighteenth Century and Beginning of the Nineteenth Century.* 3 vols. New York, 1882.

Parreaux, André: *The Publication of The Monk: A Literary Event, 1796–1798.* Paris, 1960.

J. Pearson & Co.: undated bookseller's catalogue, No. 7, in Vol. II of Catalogue of Autographs [HCL: B 3850.5].

Peck, Louis F.: "Act III of Lewis's *Venoni*," *MLN,* LVIII (Apr. 1943), 265–268.

———— "An Adaptation of Kleist's *Die Familie Schroffenstein*," *JEGP*, XLIX (Jan. 1945), 9–11.

———— "An Early Tribute to Schiller in England," *Anglo-German and American-German Crosscurrents*, II (1961), in preparation.

———— "M. G. Lewis and the Larpent *Catalogue*," *HLQ*, V (Apr. 1942), 382–384.

———— "*The Monk* and *Le Diable Amoureux*," *MLN*, LXVIII (June 1953), 406–408.

———— "*The Monk* and Musäus' 'Die Entführung,'" *PQ*, XXXII (July 1953), 346–348.

———— "Southey and *Tales of Wonder*," *MLN*, L (Dec. 1935), 513–514.

Phlegon of Tralles: *Phlegontis Tralliani Opuscula*. . . . Ed. Georg. Frid. Franzius. Halae Magdeburgicae, 1775.

Planché, James Robinson: *Recollections and Reflections . . . A Professional Autobiography*. . . . New and rev. edition. London, 1901.

[Polidori, John William]: *The Diary of Dr. John William Polidori; 1816: Relating to Byron, Shelley, etc.* Ed. William Michael Rossetti. London, 1911.

Poyer, John: *The History of Barbados, from the First Discovery of the Island . . . till . . . 1801.* London, 1808.

Praz, Mario: *The Romantic Agony.* Tr. Angus Davidson. 2nd edition. London, New York, Toronto, 1951.

*The Quarterly Review.* Vol. XXII (1820).

Quinlan, Maurice J.: *Victorian Prelude: A History of English Manners, 1700–1830.* New York, 1941.

Radcliffe, Ann: *The Mysteries of Udolpho.* 4 vols. London, 1794.

Ragatz, Lowell Joseph: *A Guide for the Study of British Caribbean History, 1763–1834, Including the Abolition and Emancipation Movements.* Washington, 1932.

[Raikes, Thomas]: *A Portion of the Journal Kept by Thomas Raikes, Esq., from 1831 to 1847: Comprising Reminiscences of Social and Political Life in London and Paris During That Period.* 4 vols. London, 1856–57.

Railo, Eino: *The Haunted Castle, a Study of the Elements of English Romanticism.* London and New York, 1927.

Rea, Thomas: *Schiller's Dramas and Poems in England.* London, 1906.

*The Registers of Marriages of St. Mary le Bone, Middlesex, 1796–1801, Part VI, Publications of the Harleian Society*, LIV, London, 1924; and *1801–1806, Part VII*, London, 1925. Ed. Bruce Bannerman.

Rentsch, Max: *Matthew Gregory Lewis. Mit Besonderer Berücksichtigung Seines Romans "Ambrosio, or The Monk."* Leipzig, 1902.

Ritter, Otto: "Die Angebliche Quelle von M. G. Lewis' 'Monk,'" *Archiv*, N.S. XIII (Sept. 1904), 56–65.

———— "Studien zu M. G. Lewis' Roman 'Ambrosio, or The Monk,'" *Archiv*, N.S. XI (Sept. 1903), 106–121.

———— "Zu Archiv CXIII, 63 (Lewis' Monk)," *Archiv*, N.S. XIV (Mar. 1905), 167.

Roberts, W. Adolphe: *Jamaica: The Portrait of an Island.* New York, 1955.

Robertson, J. G.: "Goethe and Byron," *Publications of the English Goethe Society*, N.S. II (1925), 1–129.

[Rogers, Samuel]: *Recollections of the Table-Talk of Samuel Rogers. To Which Is Added Porsoniana.* London, 1856.

Sargeaunt, John: *Annals of Westminster School.* London, 1898.

*The Satirist or Monthly Meteor.* III (1808), IV (1809), VIII (1811), IX (1811), XI (1812).

Scarborough, Dorothy: *The Supernatural in Modern English Fiction.* New York and London, 1917.

[Schiller, Friedrich]: *Cabal and Love, a Tragedy. Translated from the German of Frederick Schiller. . . .* London and Leipsic, 1796.

———— *Kabale und Liebe: Ein Bürgerliches Trauerspiel von Friedrich Schiller.* Ed. William Addison Hervey. 2nd edition. New York, 1929.

[Schlegel, August Wilhelm von]: *August Wilhelm von Schlegels Sämmtliche Werke.* Ed. Eduard Böcking. 12 vols. 1846–47.

Schneider, Rudolf: *Der Mönch in der Englischen Dichtung bis auf Lewis's 'Monk,' 1795.* Palaestra, Band 155. Leipzig, 1928.

*Scots Magazine.* XXX, Appendix (1768), LXIV (1802).

Scott, D. F. S.: *Some English Correspondents of Goethe.* London, 1949.

[Scott, Sir Walter]: *The Correspondence of Sir Walter Scott and Charles Robert Maturin: with a Few Other Allied Letters.* Ed. Fannie E. Ratchford and William H. McCarthy, Jr. Austin, Texas, 1937.

———— *The Journal of Sir Walter Scott, the Text Revised from a Photostat in the National Library of Scotland.* Ed. John Guthrie Tait and W. M. Parker. Edinburgh and London, 1950.

———— *The Letters of Sir Walter Scott, 1787–1807.* Ed. H. J. C. Grierson and others. London, 1932.

———— *Minstrelsy of the Scottish Border, Consisting of Historical and Romantic Ballads Collected in the Southern Counties of Scotland with a Few of Modern Date Founded upon Local Tradition.* Edited, with a New Glossary, by Thomas Henderson. New York, n.d.

———— *The Poetical Works of Sir Walter Scott; with the Author's Introductions and Notes.* Ed. J. Logie Robertson. London, etc., 1916.

———— *The Private Letter-Books of Sir Walter Scott: Selections from the Abbotsford Manuscripts. . . .* London, 1930.

*The Scourge, or Monthly Expositor of Imposture and Folly.* Vol. IV (1812).

[Seward, Anna]: *Letters of Anna Seward: Written between the Years 1784 and 1807.* 6 vols. Edinburgh, 1811.

Sewell, Mrs. G.: *Poems.* Surrey, 1803.

[Sharpe, Charles Kirkpatrick]: *Letters from and to Charles Kirkpatrick Sharpe, Esq.* Ed. Alexander Allardyce. 2 vols. Edinburgh and London, 1888.

[Shelley, Frances Lady]: *The Diary of Frances Lady Shelley, 1787–1817.* Ed. Richard Edgcumbe. New York, 1913.

Shelley, Mary W.: *Frankenstein, or The Modern Prometheus.* Everyman Library. London, Toronto, New York, 1930.

[Shelley, Percy Bysshe]: *The Complete Works of Percy Bysshe Shelley.* Ed. Roger Ingpen and Walter E. Peck. 10 vols. London and New York, 1926–30.

Sherson, Erroll: *London's Lost Theatres of the Nineteenth Century, with Notes on Plays and Players Seen There. . . .* London, 1925.

Sichel, Walter: *Sheridan; from New and Original Material; Including a*

*Manuscript Diary by Georgiana Duchess of Devonshire*. 2 vols. Boston and New York, 1909.

Σ.Σ.: "Monk Lewis," *N&Q*, 2nd Series, X (Nov. 17, 1860), 396–397.

Sketchwell, Sir Barnaby: *London Characters; or Fashions and Customs of the Present Century*. 2 vols. London, 1809.

Smiles, Samuel: *A Publisher and His Friends: Memoir and Correspondence of the Late John Murray*. . . . 2 vols. London, 1891.

[Smith, Horace, and James Smith]: *Rejected Addresses: or, The New Theatrum Poetarum*. 18th edition. London, 1833.

[Soame, Henry Francis Robert]: *Epistle in Rhyme, to M. G. Lewis, Esq. M. P.* . . . . London, 1798.

*The Sorcerer: A Tale. From the German of Veit Weber*. London, 1795.

[Southey, Robert]: *The Life and Correspondence of the Late Robert Southey*. Ed. Charles Cuthbert Southey. 6 vols. London, 1850.

———— *Poems of Robert Southey*. Ed. Maurice H. Fitzgerald. London, New York, etc., 1909.

———— *The Poetical Works of Robert Southey, Collected by Himself*. 10 vols. London, 1838.

———— *Selections from the Letters of Robert Southey*. . . . Ed. John Wood Warter. 4 vols. London, 1856.

[Stanley, Maria Josepha Lady]: *The Early Married Life of Maria Josepha Lady Stanley*. Ed. Jane H. Adeane. London, 1899.

Stendhal [Marie Henri Beyle]: *Rome, Naples, et Florence*. Ed. Calmann-Lévy. Paris, n.d.

Stephen, Leslie: "Matthew Gregory Lewis," *DNB*.

[Stewart, John]: *An Account of Jamaica and Its Inhabitants*. "By a Gentleman Long Resident in the West Indies." London, 1808.

Stockley, V.: *German Literature as Known in England, 1750–1830*. London, 1929.

Summers, Montague: "Byron's 'Lovely Rosa,' " in *Essays in Petto*, pp. 57–73. London [1928].

———— *A Gothic Bibliography*. London [1940].

———— *The Gothic Quest: A History of the Gothic Novel*. London [1938].

*The Sun*. May 5, 1801.

[Taylor, George Watson]: *The Old Hag in a Red Cloak. A Romance. Inscribed to the Author of the Grim White Woman*. London, 1801.

[Taylor, William]: *A Memoir of the Life and Writings of the Late William Taylor of Norwich*. . . . Ed. J. W. Robberds. 2 vols. London, 1843.

[Thrale, Hester Lynch]: *Thraliana: The Diary of Mrs. Hester Lynch Thrale (Later Mrs. Piozzi) 1776–1809*. Ed. Katharine C. Balderston, 2nd ed. 2 vols. Oxford, 1951.

Thürnau, C.: *Die Geister in der Englischen Literatur des 18. Jahrhunderts*. . . . Palaestra, Band LV. Berlin, 1906.

Ticknor, George: *History of Spanish Literature*. 4th American edition. 3 vols. Boston, 1872.

———— *Life, Letters, and Journals of George Ticknor*. Ed. George Stillman Hillard. 10th edition. Boston, 1880.

*The Times* (London). June 24, 1818.

*The Times Literary Supplement* (London). May 11, 1946; May 6, 1960.

Todd, William B.: "The Early Editions and Issues of *The Monk*, with a Bibliography," *Studies in Bibliography: Papers of the Bibliographical Society of the University of Virginia*, II (1949–1950), 3–24.

Trelawny, Edward John: *The Last Days of Shelley and Byron: Being the Complete Text of Trelawny's "Recollections"* . . . *with Additions from Contemporary Sources*. Ed. J. E. Morpurgo. Westminster, 1952.

"Trollope on 'The Monk,' " *Nineteenth-Century Fiction*, IV (Sept. 1949), 167.

Varma, Devendra P.: *The Gothic Flame: Being a History of the Gothic Novel in England*. . . . London, 1957.

Waller, John: bookseller's catalogue, No. 117 (London, 1878), in Vol. III of Catalogue of Autographs [HCL: B 3850.5].

Watt, William W.: *Shilling Shockers of the Gothic School; A Study of Chapbook Gothic Romances*. Cambridge, Mass., 1932.

White, Newman Ivey: *The Unextinguished Hearth: Shelley and His Contemporary Critics*. Durham, 1938.

Wilberforce, Robert Isaac, and Samuel Wilberforce: *The Life of William Wilberforce*. 5 vols. London, 1838.

[Wilberforce, William]: *The Correspondence of William Wilberforce*. Ed. Robert Isaac Wilberforce and Samuel Wilberforce. 2 vols. London, 1840.

Williams, Cynric R.: *A Tour through the Island of Jamaica, from the Western to the Eastern End, in the Year 1823*. London, 1826.

Willoughby, L. A.: "Schiller's 'Kabale und Liebe' in English Translation," *Publications of the English Goethe Society*, N.S. I (1924), 44–66.

Young, M. J.: *Memoirs of Mrs. Crouch*. London, 1806.

# NOTES

## CHAPTER 1. EARLY YEARS

1. See Joseph Foster, *Alumni Oxoniensis* (Oxford, 1888), III, 847; Frank Cundall, *Historic Jamaica* (London, 1915); J. H. Lawrence-Archer, *Monumental Inscriptions of the British West Indies* (London, 1875).

2. G. F. Russell Barker and Alan H. Stenning, *The Record of Old Westminsters* (London, 1928), II, 576; *A Catalogue of All Graduates . . . of Oxford* (Oxford, 1851), p. 409.

3. Add. MS. 37877, foll. 155–160. All "Add. MSS." cited are in the British Museum.

4. Add. MSS. 37882, foll. 160–161; 37877, foll. 172–173.

5. Add. MS. 37877, foll. 172–173, 155–160.

6. Add. MSS. 37877, foll. 155–160, 172–173; 37882, foll. 160–161.

7. [Mrs. Cornwall Baron-Wilson], *The Life and Correspondence of M. G. Lewis . . .* (London, 1839), II, 83–84. This work is hereafter cited as *Life*.

8. *Journal of a West India Proprietor* (London, 1834), p. 116.

9. Add. MSS. 38213, foll. 7–10; 38217, fol. 119.

10. Cundall, p. 353.

11. *Life*, I, 8.

12. Though known as Maria, the older sister was probably named Frances Maria, like her mother. She is called Fanny Maria in the *DNB* article on Sir Stephen Lushington and in *The Registers of Marriages of St. Mary le Bone, Middlesex, 1796–1801*, Part VI, ed. W. Bruce Bannerman, Publications of the Harleian Society, LIV (London, 1924), 67. Matthew's brother was probably named for William Wildman, second Viscount Barrington (1717–1793), a former Secretary at War, responsible for both of Mr. Lewis' appointments, as we learn from Add. MS. 37882, foll. 160–161. According to Frank Algar, Esq., of Ilford, Essex, who kindly sent me the information, the Baptismal Register of St. Marylebone, London, gives the following dates of birth: Fanny Maria, October 5, 1776; Barrington, March 29, 1778; Sophia Elizabeth, February 10, 1780.

13. Forster Collection (F. 357–358: pressmark 48.E.23), No. 1, Victoria and Albert Museum. Subsequent citations of Lewis MSS in the Forster Collection appear in the text as F followed by page numbers.

14. *Saducismus Triumphatus: or, Full and Plain Evidence Concerning Witches and Apparitions*, 1666. The *Life* adds, "it may easily be supposed

that . . . [Lewis] often contemplated with . . . horror . . . the copper-plate of the 'devil beating his drum' over . . . 'Mr. Mompesson's house' " (I, 28). Anything easily supposed is ultimately reported as fact; thus, "Young Lewis gloated with a pleasing horror over Glanvil's pages and the wonderful copper-plates which embellished them . . ." (Henry A. Beers, *A History of English Romanticism in the Eighteenth Century*, New York, 1926, p. 408).

15. Walpole Bequest, National Library of Scotland, Vol. IX, fol. 10. In *The Private Letter-Books of Sir Walter Scott*, ed, Wilfred Partington (London, 1930), pp. 228–229, the hall is incorrectly named. It was Stanstead or Stansted, Montfichet, Essex. The seat of Thomas Heath, father of Catherine Heath, mother of Frances Sewell, it belonged to Lewis' maternal, not, as usually stated, to his paternal relatives.

16. *Life*, I, 29.

17. W, IX, fol. 10.

18. *Random Records* (London, 1830), I, 33–44.

19. Matthew entered Westminster on June 19, 1783. The month is incorrectly given as July in Barker and Stenning, II, 576.

20. *Life*, I, 42. The performance of *King John* may have been that of 1790, held during the Christmas holidays. Since the prologue was spoken by a boy who had left Westminster at the end of the previous term, other members of the cast also may have graduated. See John Sargeaunt, *Annals of Westminster School* (London, 1898), p. 213. This would have been true of Matthew, who entered Oxford in the spring of 1790.

21. *Life*, I, 45.

22. *Life*, I, 269.

23. Samuel Harrison (1760–1812), later the distinguished tenor?

24. *Journals of the House of Lords*, XXXVI (1783), 668–670.

25. Copy of a letter of July 27, 1782, by Charles Jenkinson, Secretary at War, later first Earl of Liverpool, Add. MS. 38309, fol. 69.

26. *Journals of the House of Lords*, XXXVI (1783), 634, 659, 668–670.

27. See Foster, III, 847.

28. *Random Records*, I, 265. Colman entered Christ Church eleven years before Lewis.

29. This is clear from Sophia Shedden's letter of Jan. 24, 1819, to Walter Scott, W, IX, fol. 10. Jackson later officiated at the marriages of Maria and Sophia. See *Registers of Marriages . . . 1796–1801*, Part VI (London, 1924), p. 67, and *Registers of Marriages . . . 1801–1806*, Part VII (London, 1925), p. 73.

30. *A Catalogue of All Graduates*, p. 409.

31. *The Monk*, London, 1796, I, 172–173 [ch. 3].

32. *Life*, II, 241–270. The original is in the Forster Collection, Nos. 109–116. A comparison of the text published in the *Life* with Lewis' MS in the Forster Collection shows numerous misreading and deliberate verbal changes, none of much consequence. The author of the *Life* apparently worked from a copy, since a note appears at the end of the MS: "This scrap seems part of the burlesque/ romance allready in the hands of M: [i.e.,

M$^{rs}$] C. B. Wilson/ I have just found it." The asterisks on p. 264 of the *Life* indicate omission of the following passage, which, however, was apparently canceled in the MS by Lewis himself: "Nay, I even went so far, that with tears in my eyes, I the other day offered to give him my hand that moment, provided He would only promise to insist upon no more of an Husband's priviledges than to touch my cheek, and that favour to be permitted but once in two Months: no soon [*sic*] had I pronounced these words than I reproached myself for having consented to such an indelicacy; yet as I had promised, resolved to sacrifice my own feelings, and would not recall the condescension and alluring proposition I had held out to my Lover. Would you beleive it, Honorina? the Monster refused the conditions; Nay, even dared to avow his licentious desires, and declared marriage was never intended to be united to Platonism and that He could not be contented with such slender fare."

33. At some time Lewis acquired a copy of Marsollier's drama (Paris, 1791), since one is included in Vol. VIII of an interesting collection of eighty-nine miscellaneous dramatic pieces in French, bound in sixteen volumes, each volume bearing Lewis' bookplate, in the library of the University of Kansas. I am indebted to Dean George Waggoner, College of Liberal Arts, University of Kansas, for calling the collection to my attention and to that library for permission to examine it. In connection with these dramas it may be pertinent to note that Sir William Hotham, visiting Lausanne, wrote to Lady Charlotte Bury: "Almost every day gives birth to some new 'petite pièce de théâtre,' chiefly stolen from the old Italian and English plays. I made a large collection of them for Lewis, by his desire; so that you may hope to see some of them done into English." See *The Diary of a Lady-in-Waiting by Lady Charlotte Bury*, ed. A. Francis Steuart (London and New York, 1908), II, 22. The letter is undated in the *Diary* but is placed between letters dated July 1815 and Dec. 3.

34. *Life*, I, 66–67.

35. Eino Railo, *The Haunted Castle* (London and New York, 1927), pp. 84, 87.

36. For a short account of Weimar at the time, see Frances Gerard, *A Grand Duchess: The Life of Anna Amalia, Duchess of Saxe-Weimar-Eisenach and the Classical Circle of Weimar* (New York, 1902), Vol. II.

37. See J. E. Morpurgo, ed., *The Last Days of Shelley and Byron: Being the Complete Text of Trelawney's 'Recollections'* . . . *with Additions from Contemporary Sources* (Westminster, 1952), pp. 130–131.

38. Andrew Dalzel, *History of the University of Edinburgh from its Foundation*. . . . *with a Memoir of the Author* [by C. Innes] (Edinburgh, 1862), I, 104. This mention of Lewis was first noted by Karl S. Guthke, "C. M. Wieland and M. G. Lewis," *Neophilologus*, 1956, pp. 231–233, 233n1.

39. From a microfilm of the MS in the Goethe-Archiv at Weimar kindly sent to me by Karl S. Guthke. The letter is dated April 21, 1799. It was published by D. F. S. Scott, *Some English Correspondents of Goethe* (London, 1949), pp. 1–2.

40. See Guthke, "C. M. Wieland and M. G. Lewis," pp. 232–233. Lewis' translation has not been found.

41. For possible traces of influence of the Weimar stage on Lewis' works, see Karl S. Guthke, "Some Notes on the Significance of the Weimar Court Stage in Anglo-German Literary Relations," *HLQ*, XX (May 1957), 281–283. For information concerning plays performed on the Weimar court stage during Lewis' visit, Guthke refers to C. H. A. Burckhardt, *Das Repertoire des Weimarischen Theaters unter Goethes Leitung 1791–1817* (Hamburg and Leipzig, 1891).

42. *The London Chronicle*, LXXIII (April 25–27, 1793), 403.

43. *Ibid.*, p. 404.

44. The passage in the MS is crossed out by a later hand but is easily read. It occurs between "possible" and "It is true," *Life*, I, 126.

45. His letter of Nov. 22, 1794, from the Hague says, "I expect to be . . . in Devonshire-place, within three weeks at latest." *Life*, I, 138.

46. The preface, dated May 24, 1801, to *Adelmorn* (London, 1801), p. ii, states: "This drama was written about six years ago."

47. Among undated letters in the Windham Papers (Add. MS. 37889, fol. 154), but the reference to twenty-three years' service indicates 1795.

48. *Adelmorn*, p. ix.


## CHAPTER 2. THE MONK

1. Forster Collection, No. 37, Victoria and Albert Museum.

2. *Extracts of the Journals and Correspondence of Miss Berry from the Years 1783 to 1852*, ed. Lady Theresa Lewis (London, 1865), II, 384n.

3. *Life*, I, 66–67, 70.

4. Without attempting completeness, I list chronologically works concerned with sources of *The Monk*, ranging from the mere mention of possibilities to serious studies. Of the early investigations, Ritter's "Studien" (1903) is the most detailed. Killen's book takes account of all work preceding it. The Herzfeld-Ritter controversy is best summarized by Railo, pp. 345–346n97. *Cr R*, XIX (Feb. 1797), 194–200; *Eu M*, XXXI (Feb. 1797), 112; *MR*, 2nd Series, XXIII (Aug. 1797), 451; A. W. von Schlegel's review of *The Monk* in the *Jenaische Allgemeine Literatur-Zeitung* (1798) reprinted in *August Wilhelm von Schlegels Sämmtliche Werke*, 12 vols., ed. Eduard Böcking (Leipzig, 1846–1847), XI, 269–274; M. G. Lewis, *Ambrosio, or The Monk: A Romance*, 4th ed., "With Considerable Additions and Alterations" (London, 1798), *passim*; prefatory remarks to *The Castle Spectre, a Drama*, in Oxberry's New English Drama (London, 1818), IV, [i]; James Boaden, *Memoirs of the Life of John Philip Kemble* (London, 1825), II, 227–228n; Georg Herzfeld, "Eine Neue Quelle für Lewis' 'Monk,'" *Archiv*, N.S. IV (June 1900), 310–312; Ernst Margraf, *Einfluss der Deutschen Litteratur auf die Englische am Ende des Achtzehnten und im Ersten Drittel des Neunzehnten Jahrhunderts* (Leipzig, 1901), pp. 10–11; Max Rentsch, *Matthew Gregory Lewis. Mit Besonderer Berücksichtigung seines Romans "Ambrosio, or The Monk"* (Leipzig 1902), pp. 128–135; Otto Ritter, "Studien zu M. G. Lewis' Roman 'Ambrosio, or The Monk,'" *Archiv*, N.S. XI (Sept. 1903), 106–

121; Georg Herzfeld, "Die Eigentliche Quelle von Lewis' 'Monk,'" *Archiv*, N.S. XI (Dec. 1903), 316–323; Otto Ritter, "Die Angebliche Quelle von M. G. Lewis' 'Monk,'" *Archiv*, N.S. XIII (Sept. 1904), 56–65; Georg Herzfeld, "Noch Einmal die Quelle des 'Monk,'" *Archiv*, N.S. XV (Oct. 1905), 70–73; Otto Ritter, "Zu Archiv CXIII, 63 (Lewis' *Monk*)," *Archiv*, N.S. XIV (Mar. 1905), 167; August Sauer, introduction to *Die Ahnfrau* in *Grillparzers Werke*, ed. August Sauer (Wein and Leipzig, 1909), I, L–LXV; H. Möbius, *Die Englische Rosenkreuzerromane und ihre Vorläufer* (Hamburg, 1911), p. 23n1; Otto Hofmann, *Studien zum englischen Schauerroman* (diss. Leipzig: Halle, 1915), *passim*; Edmond Estève, "Le Théâtre 'Monacal' sous la Révolution; Ses Précédents et Ses Suites," *Études de Littérature Préromantique* (Paris, 1923), pp. 83–137 (first published in *Revue d'Histoire Littéraire de la France*, 24th année, No. 2, Paris, Apr.–June 1917, pp. 177–222); Dorothy Scarborough, *The Supernatural in Modern English Fiction* (New York and London, 1917), pp. 16–17, 33; Jean-Marie Carré, *Goethe en Angleterre* (Paris, 1920), pp. 35–36; Edith Birkhead, *The Tale of Terror: A Study of the Gothic Romance* (London, 1921), pp. 68–69; Alice M. Killen, *Le Roman Terrifiant ou Roman Noir* (Paris, 1923), pp. 48–54, 214–217; Eino Railo, *The Haunted Castle* (London and New York, 1927), pp. 91–92, 345–346n97; Rudolf Schneider, *Der Mönch in der englischen Dichtung bis auf Lewis's 'Monk,' 1795* (Leipzig, 1928), pp. 171–175; Ernest A. Baker, *The History of the English Novel*, V (*The Novel of Sentiment and the Gothic Romance*), 2nd printing (London, 1942—first pub. 1929), 205–208; Frederic Ewen, *The Prestige of Schiller in England 1788–1859* (New York, 1932), pp. 40–42; Montague Summers, *The Gothic Quest* (London [1938]), pp. 223–228; Mario Praz, *The Romantic Agony*, tr. Angus Davidson, 2nd ed. (London, New York, Toronto, 1951), p. 169n54; Louis F. Peck, "*The Monk and Le Diable Amoureux*," *MLN*, LXVIII (June 1953), 406–408; Louis F. Peck, "*The Monk* and Musäus' 'Die Entführung,'" *PQ*, XXXII (July 1953), 346–348; Karl S. Guthke, "Die Herkunft des Weltliterarischen Typus der 'Femme Fatale' aus der Deutschen Volkssage," *Germanisch-Romanische Monatsschrift*, N. F. VI (July 1956), 294–296; Devendra P. Varma, *The Gothic Flame: Being a History of the Gothic Novel in England. . . .* (London, 1957), pp. 148–153; Karl S. Guthke, *Englische Vorromantik und Deutscher Sturm und Drang: M. G. Lewis' Stellung in der Geschichte der Deutsch-Englischen Literaturbeziehungen*, Palaestra, Band 223 (Göttingen, 1958), *passim*. This last-named work is by far the most comprehensive study of German influences upon Lewis. Except to call attention to some of Guthke's points, I have allowed my own account of Lewis' treatment of his German texts to remain as it was before the appearance of Guthke's work. The reader should consult the latter, however, for this aspect of Lewis' writings. For an indication of the gradual recognition of Lewis' importance for English-German literary relationships, see, for instance, Walter Moss, "M. G. Lewis and Mme de Stael," *ES*, XXXIV (1953), 109–112.

5. Scarborough, p. 17.

6. Peck, "*The Monk* and *Le Diable Amoureux*," pp. 406–408.

7. *Adelmorn, the Outlaw* (London, 1801), pp. [vii], ix.

8. *Ambrosio, or The Monk*, 4th ed. (London, 1798), II, 122.

9. Peck, "*The Monk* and Musäus' 'Die Entführung,' " pp. 346–348.

10. However, see Guthke, *Englische Vorromantik*, pp. 176–183.

11. 1787–98. An anonymous English translation, *The Sorcerer: A Tale. From the German of Veit Weber*, appeared in London in 1795 after *The Monk* was written.

12. *MR*, 2nd Series, XXIII (Aug. 1797), 451.

13. Estève, pp. 83–137.

14. William B. Todd, "The Early Editions and Issues of *The Monk*, with a Bibliography," *SB*, II (1949–50), 3–24, especially pp. 7, 8, 21. Since the appearance of Todd's article, two copies of the 1796 *Monk* with integral title leaves have been found.

15. II, 98. The present chapter, particularly where it treats the controversy raised by *The Monk*, inevitably duplicates much in André Parreaux's recent study *The Publication of The Monk: A Literary Event, 1796–1798* (Paris, 1960). I have allowed my own account to remain as it was before the appearance of this work, but refer the reader to Parreaux for additional details.

16. XXIV (Oct. 1796), 403–404.

17. XXXI (Feb. 1797), 111.

18. XIX (Feb. 1797), 194–200. The author is identified and the review reprinted in *A Wiltshire Parson and His Friends: The Correspondence of William Lisle Bowles*, ed. Garland Greever (London, 1926), pp. 165, 191–200. In his *Biographia Literaria*, ch. 18, Coleridge included *The Monk* among examples of "compositions universally . . . beloved and admired."

19. *The Pursuits of Literature*, 3rd ed. (London, 1797), p. 95nb. The fourth part, attacking Lewis, was first published on July 19, 1797, according to Todd, p. 13n28.

20. For Mathias' contribution to Italian studies in England, see Roderick Marshall, *Italy in English Literature, 1755–1815: Origins of the Romantic Interest in Italy* (New York, 1934), pp. 307–309.

21. *Pursuits*, p. 194.

22. For an account of these conservative tendencies, see Maurice J. Quinlan, *Victorian Prelude* (New York, 1941), and, especially for the reviews of the time, Newman Ivey White, *The Unextinguished Hearth: Shelley and His Contemporary Critics* (Durham, N.C., 1938), ch. 1.

23. 2nd Series XXIII, 451.

24. IV, 121.

25. LXIV (July 1802), 547.

26. III (Apr. 1797), 210.

27. From a copy kindly sent me by Dean Julian Park, University of Buffalo, of the letter in his possession.

28. London, 1798, p. 42.

29. *Literary Census*, p. 77.

30. *Ibid.*, pp. 73–74.

31. London. Though always called anonymous, the poem is included among other verses indicated as the work of Henry F. R. Soame, Esq. (1768–

1803), in *The Correspondence of Sir Thomas Hanmer* . . . , ed. Henry Bunbury (London, 1838), pp. 493–498. *Cr R*, XXX (Oct. 1800), 226, also attributes it to Soame.

32. *Thraliana: The Diary of Mrs. Hester Lynch Thrale (Later Mrs. Piozzi) 1776–1809*, ed. Katharine C. Balderston, 2nd ed. (Oxford, 1951), entry for Oct. 11, 1796, II, 969n5.

33. Letter of Dec. 27, 1796, to Mrs. Sneyd, *Letters of Anna Seward* (Edinburgh, 1811), IV, 292–293.

34. Robert Isaac Wilberforce and Samuel Wilberforce, *The Life of William Wilberforce* (London, 1838), II, 183–184.

35. *The Diary of Frances Lady Shelley 1787–1817*, ed. Richard Edgcumbe (New York, 1913), p. 7.

36. Preface to *Adelmorn* (London, 1801), p. v.

37. *MMi*, III (Apr. 1797), 249–250. The reviews attribute the piece only to Farley, whom I take to be the Charles Farley mentioned by Allardyce Nicoll, *A History of English Drama 1660–1900* (Cambridge, Eng., 1952–55), IV, 310.

38. *Morning Herald*, Mar. 17, 1797, p. [3]; John Genest, *Some Account of the English Stage, from the Restoration in 1660 to 1830* (Bath, 1832), VII, 312–313.

39. *The Satirist or Monthly Meteor*, IX (Nov. 1, 1811), 405, attributes it to "a Mr. Grosett," presumably Henry William Grosett or Grosette.

40. Such are *Raymond and Agnes; The Travellers Benighted, or, The Bleeding Nun of Lindenberg, an Interesting Drama in Two Acts* . . . , Cumberland's British Theatre, Vol. XXXVIII (London, n.d.), dated by the BM Catalogue "1829, etc."; with the same title, No. 191 of French's Standard Drama (New York, n.d.); *Raymond and Agnes; or The travellers benighted, an Interesting Drama in Two Acts. By Matthew Gregory Lewis*, No. 298, Cumberland's British Theatre; *Raymond and Agnes, an Interesting Drama in Two Acts. By M. G. Lewis*, No. 268, Dicks' Standard Plays, New and Complete Edition (dated by the BM Catalogue 1883). The HEHL MS LA 1597 is entitled "Raymond and Agnes or The Bleeding Nun. A Melo Drama in 2 acts" and bears the inscription "Theatre Royal, Norwich 22d Novr 1809" and an application for license dated "Theatre Colchester Novr 20th 1809." The *Catalogue of the Larpent Plays* (by Dougald MacMillan, San Marino, Calif., 1939) tentatively assigns this melodrama to Lewis and reports, p. 265, numerous differences between it and the published *Raymond and Agnes; The Travellers Benighted, or, The Bleeding Nun of Lindenberg*, "by Matthew Gregory Lewis" (London, n.d.). I have compared the MS with the same work and also with H. W. Grosette's *Raymond and Agnes! or, The Bleeding Nun of Lindenberg*, Duncombe's Edition (London, n.d.). Grosette is slightly closer to the MS than is the printed version attributed to Lewis. The Larpent Collection contains also a MS (LA 1690) inscribed "The Travellers benighted a Melo Drama in 2 Acts T R. H. Market September 26th 1811," which is closely related to LA 1597. It is reasonably certain that none of these productions is by Lewis. I have not seen the anonymous pantomine *Don Raymond; or, The Castle of Lindenburgh*, licensed for Covent Garden March 11, 1797 (LA 71, listed by Nicoll, III,

325). Presumably this is the ballet named in the following publication listed by Nicoll (III, 341): *Airs, Glees and Chorusses in a New Grand Ballet Pantomime of Action called Raymond and Agnes; or, The Castle of Lindenbergh*, 1797, performed Mar. 16, 1797, at Covent Garden, according to Nicoll. For French dramatic adaptations of *The Monk*, see Estève, pp. 121–122n4, and Summers, *Gothic Quest*, pp. 230–232.

41. W, I, fol. 15. The letter, undated, was written before Dec. 29, 1798.

42. J. P. Collier's copy of the *Biographia Dramatica* at the HEHL (R 13729) has the following MS note on *Aurelio and Miranda* (II, 44, entry 417): "And in the first instance it was called *the Monk*, then *Aurelio & last Aurelio & Miranda*." Michael Kelly supplied the music. See *Reminiscences of Michael Kelly* (New York, 1826), p. 295.

43. MS of the Prologue, LA 1232, HEHL.

44. W, I, fol. 17. Dated Jan. 6, 1799, not in Lewis' hand. For the cast, see *Eu M*, XXXV (Jan. 1799), 41.

45. James Boaden, *Memoirs of the Life of John Philip Kemble* (London, 1825), II, 229.

46. M. J. Young, *Memoirs of Mrs. Crouch* (London, 1806), II, 304.

47. *Ibid.*

48. Genest, VII, 410.

49. Letter of Mar. 2, 1842, in *The Life of Mary Russell Mitford . . . Related in a Selection from Her Letters to Her Friends*, ed. A. G. L'Estrange (London, 1870), III, 139–140.

50. *Ibid.*, III, 139n.

51. Nicoll, III, 318, 398.

52. Playbill in the HCL Theatre Collection for May 6, 1801.

53. Lacy edition (London, n.d.), p. 21n.

54. For other dramatic treatments of Alonzo and Imogine, see Nicoll, IV, 303, 304, 357. For an amusing account of a performance at Birmingham of a pantomime based on Lewis' ballad, see *Macready's Reminiscences, and Selections from His Diaries and Letters*, ed. Frederick Pollock (New York, 1875), pp. 18–19.

55. London, n.d. The edition I have seen appears from the preface to be the second. The NYPL Catalogue dates it 1799.

56. London, 1812.

57. As is pointed out in William W. Watt's entertaining study, *Shilling Shockers of the Gothic School: A Study of Chapbook Gothic Romances* (Cambridge, Mass., 1932), pp. 19–20. I have examined a copy of *Almagro and Claude* at the Kansas University Library. At the BM I have examined *The Bleeding Nun of the Castle of Lindenberg; or, The History of Raymond & Agnes. By the Author of the Castle Spectre* (London: printed by and for Hodgson & Co., n.d.; watermark 1822; dated by the BM Catalogue 1823); *Raymond & Agnes; or, The Bleeding Nun of the Castle of Lindenberg. By the late M. G. Lewis, Esq. Author of the Castle Spectre* (London: printed and sold by Dean and Munday, n.d.; dated "1820?" by the BM Catalogue, but a colored folding plate and all gatherings are watermarked 1824). *Ray-*

*mond and Agnes; or, The Bleeding Nun. By M. G. Lewis* was included in Vol. IV of the Romanticist and Novelist's Library (London, 1841).

58. *Morning Herald*, Feb. 5, 1798, p. [3]. The notice is signed "Oxford-street, Jan. 2d, *Joseph Bell.*"

59. LXXXVIII (N.S. 11), Aug. 1818, part 2, p. 183.

60. *Life*, I, 153–154. According to Thomas Medwin, Byron told him that Lewis "was forced to suppress" the book. See *Conversations of Lord Byron: Noted During a Residence with His Lordship at Pisa, in the Years 1821 and 1822*, 2nd ed. (London, 1824), p. 233.

61. *Rosario or the Female Monk, a Romance, by Monk Lewis*, ed. Max Maury (n.p. [U.S.A.], n.d.), introduction, p. 6.

62. *Pursuits*, 5th ed. (London, 1798), pp. 293–194.

63. *Epistle in Rhyme*, p. [2]n.

64. Textual differences among the first five London editions are recorded in *The Monk*. Original text, variant readings, and "A Note on the Text" by Louis F. Peck; introduction by John Berryman (New York, 1952; Evergreen Edition, 1959).

65. Todd points out (p. 20) that Bell's notation added to the announcement of the fourth edition appeared in *The East Indian* (1800) and the price of a guinea for a copy of the first edition in *Adelmorn* (1801).

66. *Adelmorn* (London, 1801), pp. v, vi.

67. *The Correspondence of Sir Walter Scott and Charles Robert Maturin*, ed. Fannie E. Ratchford and William H. McCarthy, Jr. (Austin, Texas, 1937), p. 14. The letter is dated Feb. 15.

68. *The Works of Lord Byron, Letters and Journals*, ed. Rowland E. Prothero (London and New York, 1922), II, 368.

69. Medwin, p. 229.

70. Letter of Sept. 25, 1817, to James Johnstone, *Early Letters of Thomas Carlyle*, ed. Charles Eliot Norton (London and New York, 1886), I, 121.

71. *The Collected Works of William Hazlitt*, ed. A. R. Waller and Arnold Glover (London, 1902–04), VIII, 127.

72. "Trollope on 'The Monk,'" *Nineteenth-Century Fiction*, IV (Sept. 1949), 167.

73. *The Literary History of England* (London, 1882), III, 163, 166.

74. Montague Summers, *A Gothic Bibliography* (London [1940]), pp. 419–422. The account in this work (pp. 419–420) of early London editions and issues of *The Monk*, following Frederick Coykendall, "A Note on 'The Monk,'" *The Colophon*, N.S. I (Summer 1935), 87–96, is invalidated by Todd's study. The latest edition of *The Monk* which I have seen, the paperback Bestseller Library issue (London, 1960), describes the book, on a gaudy front cover, as "the original horror novel—spinechilling and suspenseful," on the back as "a mass of murder, outrage, *diablerie* and indecency." The text is shortened and freely altered, with no indication of the fact. Thus, two editorial traditions with respect to *The Monk* are preserved. For a comment, see "The Horrors of Camouflage," *TLS*, May 6, 1960, p. 291.

75. See Killen, pp. 223–229, and Summers, *Gothic Bibliography*, pp.

423–424. The most recent translation I have seen is in French by Léon de Wailly (Paris: José Corti, 1958).

76. Medwin, p. 229.

77. Montague Summers, "Byron's 'Lovely Rosa,'" in *Essays in Petto* (London [1928]), pp. 66–67.

78. Chapter 5.

## CHAPTER 3.    SOCIETY

1. "Essay on Imitations of the Ancient Ballad," in *Minstrelsy of the Scottish Border*, ed. Thomas Henderson (New York, n.d.), p. 551.

2. *Journals of the House of Commons*, Reprinted by Order of the House of Commons (1803), LII, 86–87, 324–325, 403; *Journals of the House of Commons; from Nov. the 20th, 1798 . . . to Aug. the 27th, 1799 . . .*, LIV, 208–209.

3. *Eu M*, XLI (Mar. 1802), 216.

4. Letter of Sept. 14, 1809, to Lady Abercorn, *The Letters of Sir Walter Scott, 1808–1811*, ed. H. J. C. Grierson (London, 1932), p. 240.

5. See a letter of May 3, 1810, from the Princess to Lady Abercorn in Lewis Melville, *An Injured Queen: Caroline of Brunswick* (London, 1912), I, 192–193.

6. *Adelmorn, the Outlaw* (London, 1801), p. 101.

7. Giles Stephen Holland Fox-Strangways, sixth Earl of Ilchester, *Chronicles of Holland House 1820–1900* (New York, 1938), p. 55.

8. *The Diary of a Lady-in-Waiting by Charlotte Bury*, II, 325.

9. Letter of Nov. 19, 1802, in *Memoirs, Journal, and Correspondence of Thomas Moore*, ed. Lord John Russell (London and Boston, 1853–6), VIII, 45.

10. MS note by Scott on Byron's *Detached Thoughts*. See *The Works of Lord Byron. Letters and Journals*, II, 317.

11. *A Portion of the Journal Kept by Thomas Raikes, Esq., from 1831 to 1847* (London, 1856–57), III, 192. The text of the verses is reproduced from a MS copy in the Forster Collection, not from Raikes.

12. The Earl of Ilchester, *The Home of the Hollands 1605–1820* (London [1937]), p. 158.

13. *Lord Granville Leveson Gower (First Earl Granville), Private Correspondence, 1781 to 1821*, ed. Castalia Countess Granville (London, 1916), II, 397–398.

14. *The Diaries of Sylvester Douglas (Lord Glenbervie)*, ed. Francis Bickley (London, 1928), II, 126. Entry for Feb. 11, 1811.

15. Letter of Nov. 19, 1802, *Memoirs of Moore*, VIII, 45. He speaks of his newspaper also in a letter to Lady Melbourne of Oct. 1802, *In Whig Society 1775–1818*, ed. Mabell, Countess of Airlie (London, 1921), pp. 65, 67.

16. Letter of 1802 to Lady Melbourne, *In Whig Society*, pp. 65–66.

17. LXXI (Apr. 1801), 352.

18. London, 1808, p. [v].

19. I, 191, 194.

20. *Diary of a Lady-in-Waiting*, I, 152–153.

21. *Diary of a Lady-in-Waiting*, II, 336.

22. *Lord Melbourne's Papers*, ed. Lloyd C. Sanders (London and New York, 1889), p. 16. The letter, undated, is placed between letters of Jan. 14 and Feb. 8, 1800.

23. *The Journal of Elizabeth, Lady Holland 1791–1811*, ed. the Earl of Ilchester (London and New York, 1908), II, 87. Entry for May 30, 1800.

24. *Diary of a Lady-in-Waiting*, II, 306–307.

25. *The Love of Gain* (London, 1799), p. 27n.

26. *Lord Melbourne's Papers*, p. 9.

27. Letter of Feb. 8, 1800, to Lady Melbourne, *ibid.*, p. 18.

28. Letter of Mar. 5, 1799, W, I, fol. 19.

29. *Lord Melbourne's Papers*, p. 7.

30. *Ibid.*, p. 16.

31. *Ibid.*

32. *Journal of Lady Holland*, I, 167.

33. *Gower's Correspondence*, II, 397.

34. Hobhouse's diary for Aug. 7, 1817, in *Recollections of a Long Life; by Lord Broughton (John Cam Hobhouse); with Additional Extracts from His Private Diaries*, ed. Lady Dorchester, 2 vols. (London, 1909), II, 76.

35. *Journal of Lady Holland*, II, 60.

36. *Chronicles of Holland House*, p. 119.

37. The letter, in my possession, is undated. According to the *DNB*, William Parnell assumed the name Parnell-Hayes in 1796.

38. Ilchester, *Home of the Hollands*, p. 158.

39. Byron, *Letters and Journals*, II, 317.

40. *The Journal of Sir Walter Scott*, ed. John Guthrie Tait and W. M. Parker (Edinburgh and London, 1950), p. 6.

41. [Horace and James Smith], *Rejected Addresses: or The New Theatrum Poetarum*, 18th ed. (London, 1833), pp. 96–97.

42. *The Satirist or Monthly Meteor*, III (Nov. 1, 1808), 348–349.

43. *N&Q*, 2nd Series, X (Nov. 17, 1860), 396.

44. I recall the kindness of Miss M. A. Mather of Barnes, who remembered Lewis' cottage and pointed out to me one afternoon the spot where it used to stand.

45. Forster Collection, No. 72. The passage, omitted in the *Life*, precedes "I am very glad" (I, 354).

46. *Life*, I, 333.

47. *N&Q*, 2nd Series, X (Nov. 17, 1860), 396–397.

48. *Diary of a Lady-in-Waiting*, I, vi.

49. "Essay on Imitations," p. 553.

50. Oliver Farrar Emerson, "The Early Literary Life of Sir Walter Scott," *JEGP*, XXIII (1924), 43.

51. Byron, *Letters and Journals*, II, 317–318.

52. Letter of Apr. 1, 1801, in *Memoirs of Moore*, I, 113.

53. Letter of Nov. 19, 1802, in *Memoirs of Moore*, VIII, 43–44.

54. Letter of Nov. 23, 1814, to E. T. Dalton, in *Memoirs of Moore*, II, 56.

55. Letter of Mar. 5, 1799, to Scott, W, I, fol. 19. The date is apparently not in Lewis' hand.

56. Letter of June 9, 1803, to C. W. W. Wynn, in *The Life and Correspondence of the Late Robert Southey*, ed. Charles Cuthbert Southey (London, 1850), II, 211.

57. *The Poetical Works of Robert Southey*, collected by himself, 10 vols. (London, 1838), V, xiii.

58. Letter of July 10, 1805, to Peter Elmsley, *The Athenaeum*, No. 3808 (Oct. 20, 1900), 512.

59. Professor Kenneth Curry, the University of Tennessee, kindly sent me this quotation from a MS letter dated July 12, 1805, in the National Library of Wales, and also called my attention to the *Athenaeum* letter cited above.

60. Lines 265–282.

61. *The Complete Works of Percy Bysshe Shelley*, ed. Roger Ingpen and Walter E. Peck (London and New York, 1926–30), VI (1929), 147n.

62. Byron, *Letters and Journals*, II, 356–357.

63. Byron, *Letters and Journals*, II, 379–380.

64. Quotations from letters of Mar. 9 and 10, 1801, from John Wordsworth to Mary Hutchinson and Dorothy Wordsworth, in Mary Moorman, *William Wordsworth: A Biography. The Early Years 1770–1803* (Oxford, 1957), p. 507.

65. *Journal of Lady Holland*, I, 184. Entry for May, 1798.

66. *Gower's Correspondence*, II, 309.

67. Erroll Sherson, *London's Lost Theatres* (London [1925]), p. 282.

68. Undated letter in my possession, on paper watermarked 1802. In the first sentence, the readings "intense" and "then" are uncertain.

69. *Diary of a Lady-in-Waiting*, II, 235–237.

70. *Memoir and Correspondence of Susan Ferrier 1782–1854*, ed. John A. Doyle (London, 1898), pp. 93, 94n3, 136n1.

71. *Letters from and to Charles Kirkpatrick Sharpe, Esq.*, ed. Alexander Allardyce (Edinburgh and London, 1888), I, 33.

72. See Sharpe's undated letter "to a Lady," *ibid.*, II, 519. For an opinion of the *Life* by another contemporary, see three letters, of Feb. 23, Mar. 4 and 19, 1842, from Mary Russell Mitford to Miss Anderdon in *Letters of Mary Russell Mitford*, 2nd Series, ed. Henry Chorley (London, 1872), I, 195, 198–199, 200.

73. *Extracts of the Journals and Correspondence of Miss Berry from the Year 1783 to 1852*, ed. Lady Theresa Lewis (London, 1865), II, 502.

74. *Letters to 'Ivy' from the First Earl of Dudley*, ed. S. H. Romilly (London, 1905), pp. 129–130. The letter is dated Apr. 2, and by the editor 1811.

75. *Chateaubriand: Mémoires d'Outre-Tombe*, ed. Maurice Levaillant, 2nd ed. (Paris, 1947), I, 506–507.

76. *Life, Letters, and Journals of George Ticknor*, ed. George Stillman Hillard, 10th ed. (Boston, 1880), I, 67. Entry for June 27, 1815.

77. *Life of Ticknor*, I, 191.

78. Barrington died on January 13, 1800, according to *GM*, LXX (Feb. 1800), 184.

79. Medwin, *Conversations of Lord Byron*, pp. 235–236.

80. Add. MS. 38213, fol. 7.

81. Letter of July 25, 1781, Add. MS. 38216, foll. 303–304.

82. Letter of Mar. 28, 1782, Add. MS. 38218, foll. 67–68.

83. *GM*, LXIII (Oct. 1793), 966.

84. *GM*, LXIV (Mar. 1794), 286.

85. John Poyer, *The History of Barbados, from the First Discovery of the Island* (London, 1808), p. 611. For comments on Ricketts and his administration in Barbados, see pp. 632, 639, 650–651. For an estimate of Poyer's work by an authority on Jamaican history, see Lowell Joseph Ragatz, *A Guide for the Study of British Caribbean History, 1763–1834, Including the Abolition and Emancipation Movements* (Washington, 1932), p. 183.

86. Copy of a letter of Sept. 22, 1796, from Lord Liverpool to Mr. Lewis, Sr., Add. MS. 38310, fol. 166.

87. Copy of the will at Somerset House. Ricketts died on Apr. 8, 1800. See *GM*, LXX (Apr. 1800), 397.

88. He retired in August. See his memorandum to Windham accompanying a letter of Apr. 2, 1803, Add. MS. 37882, foll. 160–161.

89. Byron, *Letters and Journals*, II, 317.

90. II, 83–86. HEHL pressmark 143568 (2 v). The reference to the Argyll-rooms suggests that Lady Charlotte Campbell was the author.

91. *GM*, Supplement for 1789 (LIX, 1208), lists among marriages that of "Jas. Kelly, esq., son of Col. K. of the Madras establishment, to Miss Isabella Fordyce, daughter of Capt. Wm. F." Month and day are not given, but the marriage is listed before those of Dec. 10. According to the *DNB* also, Isabella Kelly was the daughter of "Capt. Fordyce," but her husband's name there appears as Capt. Robert Hawke Kelly (article on Sir Fitzroy Kelly).

92. Mrs. Isabella Kelly, *A Collection of Poems and Fables* (London, 1794), p. iv. The book contains two fables (pp. 54–72) narrating in veiled language her domestic difficulties. Frank Algar, Esq., of Ilford, Essex, informs me that in a second edition (1807) she refers to her father and to her husband as dead.

93. Fitzroy's birth date is given as Oct. 1796, in the *Encyclopaedia Britannica*, 11th ed. (article on Sir Fitzroy Kelly).

94. I, 273–274.

95. See his letter in the *Life*, I, 275–276, dated only Mar. 15. The year is 1803, since by evidence of content it is the letter next preceding that of Mar. 18, 1803, in F 43 and misdated 1804 in the *Life* (I, 278).

96. London, 1802, p. [iii].

97. *Life*, I, 275. The date of the letter is Mar. 15, 1803. See note 95 above.

98. Letter of Mar. 18, 1803, misdated 1804 in the *Life*, I, 278.

99. *A Modern Incident in Domestic Life* (London, 1803), I, 54–55.

100. Letter of Jan. 24, 1819, W, IX, fol. 10.

101. *Life*, II, 103.

102. The letter, which I have failed to trace, is quoted in an undated bookseller's catalogue (No. 7) of J. Pearson & Co., 46 Pall Mall, Item 244, p. 20, HCL pressmark B 3850.5.

103. Summers, *The Gothic Quest* (London [1938]), pp. 263–267; 305n160, 165, 166.

104. The anecdote as related by Summers (*Gothic Quest*, pp. 263–264) is an embroidering of this passage in Medwin (*Conversations*, p. 235).

105. Since it is clear from Lewis' codicil of Jan. 16, 1813 (undated in the *Life*, II, 382–386), that Kelly was not then twenty-one (*Life*, II, 384), he could not have been older than ten in 1802. Lewis' works and personality are just eccentric enough always to invite colorful writing, a tendency encouraged, at least in merely popular accounts, by the feeling that facts do not matter in the treatment of an historically minor figure. A recent example, pointed out to me by Mr. Ralph W. McComb, Librarian of the Pennsylvania State University, of this tendency is an anonymous article entitled "Gothic Horror" in *Parade: A Pageant of Personalities and Events* (Sydney), for Nov. 1958, where we learn that the "handsome" Lewis was reared in luxury, was denounced in Parliament as a debaucher of youth, bought a villa which was furnished with the luxury of a prince, where dukes and duchesses jostled with ballet girls, gamblers, and wits around the giant punchbowl at lavish champagne suppers, and so on (pp. 38–39).

106. The note, in Dyce's hand, appears on an end page of the Paris 1807 edition, Dyce Collection, Victoria and Albert Museum.

107. *Elizabeth, Lady Holland to Her Son 1821–1845*, ed. the Earl of Ilchester (London, 1946), p. 225. Planché describes two boys with whom he shared the room, "both as handsome as they were clever. They amused themselves with writing plays, and enacting the principal parts in them, displaying considerable histrionic ability. . . . They left school before me. The eldest I never saw again; he went to America, and died there." James Robinson Planché, *Recollections and Reflections . . . A Professional Autobiography*, rev. ed. (London, 1901), p. 11. While Planché does not say that the two boys were brothers, it is tempting to believe that the elder was William Martin Kelly. To deal with another supposed child of Lewis', the obituary in the *Gentleman's Magazine* ends with the statement, "He was never married, but has left one daughter" (LXXXVIII, Aug. 1818, 184). Noting the similarity of initials and literary interests, Professor Todd has suggested that this was the Mary G. Lewis who published a poem "Zelinda" (1823) and some novels: see William B. Todd, "The Early Editions and

Issues of *The Monk*, with a Bibliography," *SB*, II (1949–50), 15n35. Frank Algar, Esq., citing papers of the Royal Literary Fund (File No. 507), informs me that the author of "Zelinda" was Mary Gogo Lewis, daughter of a Mrs. Lewis who in 1826 was a prisoner in the Marshalsea for debt. Is it possible that the writer for the *Gentleman's Magazine* supposed Lewis to be the father of Miss Lacey, his mother's protégée?

108. A MS volume, entitled "Trustees Minute Book," at the Albany records that at a meeting of June 2, 1809, consent was given Mr. W^m Thorogood to sell his chambers K No. 1 to Matt^w Lewis Esq^re. The "Albany Register of Freeholders," a similar volume, gives June 1809 as the date of the deed to Lewis (p. "S"). The chambers were subject to a fee farm rent of £35 per annum ("Petition of Appeal," p. 20). For permission to examine the Albany volumes and for other courtesies, I am indebted to Captain Charles H. Adams, Secretary to the Albany. Lewis bequeathed "my Chambers in Albany (for which I paid 600 Guineas) with all the furniture except such articles as I may particularly except from this donation" to Lord Le Despencer (see copy of codicil to Lewis' will, Somerset House).

109. I record my gratitude to the late Mrs. Percy D. Leake, occupant of the quarters in 1933, for these details and for a pleasant afternoon tea in Lewis' former abode.

110. *Rejected Addresses*, p. 18. It has been suggested that Byron, who later took quarters at the Albany, was first introduced to it by Lewis. See Sheila Birkenhead, *Peace in Piccadilly: The Story of Albany* (New York, 1958), p. 85.

## CHAPTER 4. DRAMAS

1. Allardyce Nicoll, A *History of English Drama 1660–1900* (Cambridge, Eng., 1952–55), III, 22–39.

2. *Morning Herald*, June 21, 1796, p. [1], announces: "This Day is published, in Quarto, Price Two Shillings. . . ."

3. I have seen only two copies, one in the Dyce Collection, Victoria and Albert Museum, one in the HEHL.

4. Forster Collection, No. 6, Victoria and Albert Museum.

5. *MMi*, II (Aug. 1796), 229.

6. *MR*, 2nd Series, XXI (Nov. 1796), 336; *Cr R*, XIX (Feb, 1797), 222.

7. I have examined, not the 1795 publication, but a reprint: *Cabal and Love, a Tragedy. Translated from the German of Frederick Schiller . . .* (London and Leipsic, 1796). The author seems to have been J. C. C. Timaeus. See *Kabale und Liebe; ein Bürgerliches Trauerspiel von Friedrich Schiller*, ed. William Addison Hervey, 2nd ed. (New York, 1929), p. 266 and n2. A partial translation of Schiller's drama had already been published in the *Speculator* for 1790. See L. A. Willoughby, "Schiller's 'Kabale und Liebe' in English Translation," *Publications of the English Goethe Society*, N.S. I (1924), 46.

8. *The Minister, a Tragedy. In Five Acts* (London, 1797). April 1797 is

given as the date of publication by AR, XXV (Apr. 1797), recto back cover, and by the Mo M, III (Apr. 1797), 308.

9. For further examples of Lewis' elaboration see Hervey, p. 267n2, and Karl S. Guthke, *Englische Vorromantik und Deutscher Sturm und Drang: M. G. Lewis' Stellung in der Geschichte der Deutsch-Englischen Literaturbeziehungen*, Palaestra, Band 223 (Göttingen, 1958), pp. 159–160.

10. XXII (Jan. 1798), 104.

11. Railo, *The Haunted Castle*, p. 104.

12. Willoughby, p. 59. For other opinions, see Thomas Rea, *Schiller's Dramas and Poems in England* (London, 1906), p. 37; Geoffrey Buyers, "The Influence of Schiller's Drama and Fiction upon English Literature in the Period 1780–1830," *Englische Studien*, XLVIII (Apr. 1915), 358; and Hervey, pp. 266–267.

13. *Life*, I, 73.

14. *Life*, I, 211–213.

15. Bertrand Evans, *Gothic Drama from Walpole to Shelley* (Berkeley and Los Angeles, 1947), p. 132.

16. For this incident Lewis acknowledged a borrowing from "a German play" (*The Castle Spectre*, London, 1798, p. 41), which Karl S. Guthke identifies as Gustav Hagemann's *Ludwig der Springer*, played on the Weimar court stage in the 1792–93 season. See Guthke, "Some Notes on the Significance of the Weimar Court Stage in Anglo-German Literary Relations," HLQ, XX (May 1957), 283.

17. *MMi*, IV (Dec. 1797), 356. Similar testimony appears in the *Eu M*, XXXIII (Jan. 1798), 42, and in *Sheridan and His Times*, "by an Octogenarian" (London, 1859), II, 243.

18. James Boaden, *Memoirs of the Life of John Philip Kemble, Esq.* (London, 1825), II, 206.

19. *Reminiscences of Michael Kelly* p. 286.

20. *Morning Herald*, Dec. 26, 1797, p. [2].

21. *MMi*, V (Feb. 1798), 107.

22. *Ibid.*, IV (Dec. 1797), 356.

23. AR, XXVIII (Aug. 1798), 179–191; MR, 2nd Series, XXVI (May 1798), 96.

24. "Of the Impropriety of Theatrical Representations . . . ," GM, LXIX (June 1799), 470.

25. *The Castle Spectre* (London, 1798), pp. 101–102.

26. See LA 1187. MSS in the Larpent Collection at the HEHL are cited thus throughout.

27. These passages are Act I, Sc. 2, pp. 12–13, "Did it? . . . hatred to mankind"; Act IV, Sc. 1, pp. 64–65, "the white-man's God . . . tortures in the next!"; Act IV, Sc. 1, pp. 69–70, "Yes, thou art sweet . . . He comes." Part of a comic speech by Father Philip was similarly marked and retained (Act III, Sc. 3, p. 53, "yet I don't like . . . a worthy soul!").

28. *The Journal of Elizabeth Lady Holland 1791–1811*, I, 167.

29. Wordsworth's letter of Dec. 13 (1797) to Joseph Cottle, in *Letters*

*of the Wordsworth Family from 1787 to 1855*, ed. William Knight (Boston and London, 1907), I, 112.

30. See Hazlitt's "My First Acquaintance with Poets," *The Collected Works of William Hazlitt*, ed. A. R. Waller and Arnold Glover (London and New York, 1902–06), XII (1904), 271.

31. Letter of Mar. 6, 1798, to James Tobin, in *Letters of the Wordsworth Family*, I, 114.

32. *Collected Letters of Samuel Taylor Coleridge*, I, 378–379. The letter is dated Jan. [23]. In 1948 there was advertised for sale a copy of the first edition of *The Castle Spectre* with the inscription, thought to be Coleridge's, "S. T. Coleridge, Jan. 20, 1798" on the title page (Blackwell's Catalogue 531, p. 12, Item 138), apparently the copy mentioned by Griggs, p. 378n2.

33. *MMi*, V (Mar. 1798), 181.

34. It was advertised in the *Morning Herald* at least as early as Jan. 13, 1798, p. [1].

35. From a photostat of fol. 15, W, I. The letter is approximately dated by a reference to *Aurelio and Miranda* (performed Dec. 29, 1798) as in rehearsal.

36. Photostat of fol. 17, W, I. The date, Jan. 6, 1799, is not in Lewis' hand.

37. Medwin, *Conversations of Lord Byron*, p. 233.

38. Walter Sichel, *Sheridan; from New and Original Material* (Boston and New York, 1909), II, 277.

39. Since this comment was written, Guthke's thorough analysis of Lewis' translation has appeared. See *Englische Vorromantik*, pp. 55–77.

40. *MMi*, XI (Feb. 1801), 111–112; *MR*, 2nd Series, XXX (Oct. 1799), 214.

41. Photostat of fol. 17, W, I.

42. *Life*, I, 217, and John Adolphus, *Memoirs of John Bannister, Comedian* (London, n.d.), II, 40.

43. LA 1245. I am informed that the play will soon be available in an edition by Karl S. Guthke.

44. *Life*, I, 217.

45. Guthke, who has anticipated me in publishing the fact of Lewis' debt to Régnard, thinks it unlikely that Lewis had read *Les Ménechmes* but instead saw performed at Weimar *Die Zwillingsbrüder*, Friedrich Ludwig Schröder's adaptation of the French comedy. As he observes, the question cannot be settled, since Schröder's play was not published and seems to be lost. See Guthke, "Some Notes," pp. 281–283.

46. Clare Jerrold, *The Story of Dorothy Jordan* (London, 1914), p. 223.

47. Photostat of fol. 19, W, I. The date, Mar. 5, 1799, is not in Lewis' hand.

48. *Life*, I, 218.

49. *L'Habitant de la Guadeloupe. Comédie en Trois Actes* . . . (Paris, 1785), in Vol. XVI of Lewis' collection of dramas at the University of Kansas. See Chapter 1 above, n33.

50. London, 1800, p. 55n.

51. *Rich and Poor* (London, 1812), p. 46.

52. Compare *The East Indian*, Act III, Sc. 2, with *Don Juan ou le Festin de Pierre*, Act III, Sc. 3; and *The East Indian*, Act V, Sc. 1, with *Die Corsen*, Act IV, Sc. 3. The similarity to the German play was noted in the *Monthly Mirror*, VIII (Dec. 1799), 354–356. Allardyce Nicoll believes that Kotzebue's *Die Indianer in England* (1789) suggested "part of the theme of Lewis' *The East Indian*" (III, 122). In the German play a wealthy native of India performs charitable deeds in England, but Lewis apparently took this character from *The Memoirs of Miss Sidney Bidulph*. As Guthke has pointed out, Lewis' *East Indian* has frequently but incorrectly been called a translation of Kotzebue's drama. See Guthke, "Some Bibliographical Errors Concerning the Romantic Age," *PBSA*, LI (second quarter, 1957), 161–162.

53. *Rich and Poor*, advertisement.

54. *Eu M*, XXXV (May 1799), 327.

55. VIII (Dec. 1799), 367. See also *Eu M*, XXXVI (Dec. 1799), 399.

56. The dates of all performances were Apr. 22, May 1, Dec. 7, 10, 12, 14, 1799 (HCL playbills).

57. *Morning Herald*, Mar. 5, 1801, p. [3].

58. *Eu M*, XXXIX (May 1801), 359.

59. See *Morning Herald*, May 5, 1801, p. [3], and the preface to *Adelmorn* (London, 1801), p. iii.

60. The significance of this scene for Gothic drama and Romantic poetry has been brilliantly set forth by Evans, pp. 146–150.

61. May 8, 1801, p. [3].

62. Boaden, *Memoirs of Kemble*, II, 297.

63. May 5, 1801, p. [4].

64. XI (June 1801), 410–411.

65. XXXIX (May 1801), 359.

66. Preface to *Adelmorn*, pp. ii–iii.

67. The letter cannot be dated exactly, but it must antedate Mar. 4, 1801, when *Adelmorn* was in rehearsal. *Alfonso* was rejected at Drury Lane in favor of *Adelmorn*. See *Alfonso*, 2nd ed. (London, 1802), p. xii.

68. *MMi*, XII (Nov. 1801), 338.

69. *Alfonso* (London, 1801), preface, p. iv.

70. *Adelmorn*, p. 75n.

71. Act II, Sc. 2, p. 31.

72. Boaden, *Memoirs of Kemble*, II, 310.

73. LA 1337 contains the final scene presumably as it was performed. The play in MS is some two hundred lines shorter than in the printed form. One of the passages lacking in the MS is Orsino's soliloquy on prayer (Act IV, Sc. 2, pp. 69–70: "Virgins there request . . . Man is happy").

74. P. vii, HCL copy, pressmark 17477.36.47.25*.

75. XIII (June 1802), 410.

76. I (Jan. 1803), 314–317. The review, anonymous, is attributed to Smith by Henry Brougham, *The Life and Times of Henry Lord Brougham, Written by Himself*, 3 vols., 2nd ed. (Edinburgh and London, 1871), I, 256. For two hostile reviews, see *Morning Herald*, Jan. 16, 1802, p. [3] and Jan. 23, 1802, p. [3].

77. XXXIV (Mar. 1802), 355.

78. Letter of Nov. 9, 1802, to Miss Ponsonby, in *Letters of Anna Seward* (Edinburgh, 1811), VI, 57–58.

79. London, 1802, p. xii.

80. *The Genuine Rejected Addresses* (London, 1812), p. 32. The author of the verses is G. F. Busby, Esq.

81. *Reminiscences*, pp. 138–139.

82. *Life*, I, 233–234.

83. *Morning Chronicle*, Mar. 26, 1803, p. [3].

84. *The Satirist or Monthly Meteor*, XI (Dec. 1, 1812), 554.

85. *DNB* article on Lewis.

86. *The Harper's Daughter: or, Love and Ambition. A Tragedy, in Five Acts* . . . "with considerable alterations, as performed at the Philadelphia and Baltimore theatres," was published in Philadelphia in 1813.

87. For the text of the prologue, see a forthcoming note by Louis F. Peck, "An Early Tribute to Schiller in England," *Anglo-German and American-German Crosscurrents*, II (1961).

88. *Rugantino; or, The Bravo of Venice. A Grand Romantic Melodrama, in Two Acts* (London, 1805), p. vi.

89. Nicoll (IV, 84n1) notes that Guilbert de Pixérécourt's *L'Homme à Trois Visages, ou le Proscrit de Venise* (Paris, 1801) provided four English plays: Elliston's *The Venetian Outlaw* (Drury Lane, 1805), Lewis' *Rugantino* (Covent Garden, 1805), Powell's *The Venetian Outlaw* (1805), and an anonymous *Rugantino* (Surrey, 1831). For the relation of Zschokke's story to Pixérécourt, see Summers, *Gothic Quest*, pp. 269–270.

90. Letter of Oct. 24, 1805, to Lady Georgiana Morpeth, in *Hary-O: The Letters of Lady Harriet Cavendish, 1796–1809*, ed. Sir George Leveson Gower and Iris Palmer (London [1940]), p. 123.

91. *Eu M*, XLVIII (Oct. 1805), 305. See also *MMi*, XX (Oct. 1805), 273–274.

92. *Eu M*, XLVIII (Oct. 1805), 305.

93. LA 1459.

94. *Rugantino* (London, 1805), p. 46.

95. *MMi*, N.S. I (May 1807), 353n.

96. *Ibid.*, Mar. 1807, p. 212.

97. *Ibid.*, Apr. 1807, p. 278.

98. *Ibid.*, Apr. 1807, pp. 279–280.

99. *The Wood Daemon; or, The Clock has Struck* as performed in 1807 was not published, but the licenser's MS copy is in the Larpent Collection. Some differences between the licenser's copy (LA 1514) and *One O'Clock; or The Knight and the Wood Daemon* (London, 1811) are that in

the MS Clotilda is aunt, not sister, to Una, and is a comic figure; Oswy is a peasant, not a minstrel; and Una loves Hardyknute for his wealth, not because of a magic spell.

100. *MMi*, N.S. I (Apr. 1807), 280.

101. Evans, pp. 150–154.

102. N.S. I (Apr. 1807), 279.

103. *General Evening Post*, Mar. 31–Apr. 2, 1807, p. [4].

104. *Eu M*, LI (Apr. 1807), 292.

105. *MMi*, N.S. I (May 1807), 353.

106. *MR*, 2nd Series, L (July 1806), 329.

107. See his letter of Nov. 19, 1802, to Thomas Moore, in *Memoirs, Journal, and Correspondence of Thomas Moore*, VIII, 46.

108. Roderick Marshall, *Italy in English Literature 1755–1815* (New York, 1934), p. 295.

109. For a treatment of this point in *Adelgitha*, see Evans, pp. 156–157.

110. *Adelgitha* is represented in the Larpent Collection (LA 1518) not by a MS but by a copy of the second edition (London, 1806) with MS cancellations and the usual application to the licenser dated Apr. 22, 1807, in MS on the half-title page. A four-page MS of prologue and epilogue, probably in Lewis' hand, dated Apr. 27, 1807, is inserted.

111. *General Evening Post*, Apr. 30–May 2, 1807, p. [2].

112. *MMi*, N.S. IV (Dec. 1808), 373.

113. *Ibid.*, p. 377.

114. LA 1561.

115. *MMi*, N.S. IV (Dec. 1808), 375.

116. *Morning Chronicle*, Dec. 2, 1808, p. [3].

117. *General Evening Post*, Dec. 1–3, 1808, p. [2].

118. *Venoni* (London, 1809), p. vi.

119. For an account of the licenser's MSS of the original and the revised Act III and their relation to the published form, see Louis F. Peck, "Act III of Lewis's *Venoni*," MLN, LVIII (Apr. 1943), 265–268.

120. Dec. 12, 1808, p. [2].

121. See Louis F. Peck, "M. G. Lewis and the Larpent *Catalogue*," *HLQ*, V (Apr. 1942), 383–384.

122. *Morning Chronicle*, May 2, 1809, p. [4].

123. Alice I. Perry Wood, *The Grumbler, an Adaptation by Oliver Goldsmith* (Cambridge, Mass., 1931), introduction.

124. IV (June 1, 1809), 619.

125. N.S. V (May 1809), 306.

126. *The Diary of a Lady-in-Waiting by Lady Charlotte Bury*, I, 7.

127. According to one editor of *Timour*, it retained its popularity at the provincial theaters even when deprived of its cavalry. See prefatory remarks by "D.—G.," p. [3], Cumberland's British Theatre, XXIX (London, n.d.)

128. Short additions to the dialogue make the published play (London

[1811]) some eighty or ninety lines longer than the licenser's copy (LA 1670). The printed stage directions follow the MS closely, but two considerable differences occur: on p. 52, after "beyond" the MS reads "The extremity of the Fortress is formed by a Bastion, advancing far into the water, which is completely seperated [sic] from the land by a parapet, with a Cheveaux de Frize. (Musick while the Scene appears)"; the MS lacks "The Tartars . . . and Oglou" (pp. 55–56). The MS assigns a sixteen-line comic song to Liska ("Oh Lud! Oh Lud! what joy 'twill be") in place of that published on p. 26 and inferior to the latter.

129. *Eu M*, LIX (May 1811), 378.

130. *Morning Chronicle*, Apr. 30, 1811, p. [2].

131. *Eu M*, LIX (May 1811), 377, 378.

132. May 3, 1811, p. [3].

133. May 1, 1811, p. [3]; Aug. 3, 1811, p. [3]. There are others.

134. The author is unknown; the date of production is July 18, 1811. See Nicoll, IV, 523. A MS copy in the HCL (LTR 17473.7.15*) attributes it to Joseph Ebsworth.

135. *GM*, LXXXI (July 1811), 83.

136. *GM*, LXXXI (Aug. 1811), 186. Nicoll (IV, 283) gives the date of performance as July 26, 1811, and assigns the piece to Colman.

137. Nicoll, IV, 299. Performed June 10, 1811.

138. VIII (June 1, 1811), 486.

139. Byron, *Letters and Journals*, II, 157n.

140. Kelly, *Reminiscences*, p. 286.

141. Letter from Lady Stanley to Mrs. E. Stanley, dated 1812, *The Early Married Life of Maria Josepha Lady Stanley*, ed. Jane H. Adeane (London, 1899), p. 333. The letter is placed between others dated Feb. 26 and May 23, 1812.

142. In Volume I of Lewis' collection of French dramas at the University of Kansas, imprinted Paris, 1756. The opera was first performed in 1749.

143. The text of the licenser's copy (LA 1686) is almost identical with that of the printed drama (London [1811]), with two exceptions: the MS omits Hardyknute's song in Act II, Sc. 3, p. 57; and instead of the ballad in Act II, Sc. 1, p. 39, the MS contains one beginning "That my Heart, 'till it vibrates no longer."

144. Prefatory remarks by "P.P." to *One O'Clock! or, The Knight and the Wood Daemon. A Dramatic Romance*, p. iv, in Oxberry's New English Drama, XIX (London, 1824).

145. *Morning Chronicle*, Aug. 1, p. [3], and Aug. 2, p. [3], 1811.

146. The licenser's copy of *Rich and Poor* (LA 1726) in the Larpent Collection is titled "The East Indian An Opera in three Acts." It follows quite closely the text printed in 1812. Spaces are left for the three songs occurring in *Rich and Poor* (London, 1812) at p. 42 (Act II, Sc. 2, "Ah! who would . . ."), p. 65 (III, 2, "Hush! Forbear . . ."), and p. 80 (III, 3, "Now mercy bids . . ."). The Larpent Collection contains also a printed copy of *Rich and Poor* lacking title page but with one in MS inserted, read-

ing "Zorayda or Scenes in Fashionable Life, a Musical Burletta altered from a favorite Comedy—Intended for representation at the Olympic Theatre . . . 1821" (LA 2259). According to the *Catalogue of the Larpent Plays*, p. 371, this was produced at the Olympic on Nov. 19, 1821.

147. Hoxie N. Fairchild has suggested that another farewell to Spain by Byron (*Don Juan*, Canto II, stanzas 18–20) owes something to Lewis' "The Exile" in *The Monk*. See "Byron and Monk Lewis," *TLS*, May 11, 1946, p. 223.

148. *The Satirist or Monthly Meteor*, XI (Aug. 1, 1812), 172–173.

149. IV (Aug. 1, 1812), 170. See also IV (Oct. 1, 1812), 293–303.

150. *The Castle Spectre* (London, 1798), pp. 100–101; *Alfonso*, 2nd ed. (London, 1802), pp. xiv–xv; *Adelgitha* (London, 1806), p. 127.

151. For Lewis and the Gothic drama, see Evans, ch. 8.

152. Evans, p. 143.

153. *Adelmorn* (London, 1801), p. ix. In some copies the words "and the translation of a play of Kotzebue's" do not appear in the postscript.

154. C. H. Herford, *The Age of Wordsworth* (London, 1925), p. 94.


## CHAPTER 5.    PROSE AND VERSE

1. W, I, fol. 18. Of the eleven letters from Lewis to Scott in that collection, four were published in part by Scott in Note D of his appendix to "Essay on Imitations of the Ancient Ballad," *Minstrelsy of the Scottish Border*, Part III. Of these four, one was more fully reproduced in *The Private Letter-Books of Sir Walter Scott*, ed. Wilfred Partington (London, 1930), pp. 217–218. Complete texts of ten of the letters have recently been published by Karl S. Guthke, "Die erste Nachwirkung von Herders Volksliedern in England: Unveröffentliche Dokumente zu den 'Tales of Wonder,' " *Archiv*, CXCIII (Apr. 1957), 273–284.

2. *Journal of Lady Holland*, I, 224–225.

3. *The Love of Gain* (London, 1799), p. [iii]. I have not seen a second edition, but a third is dated 1799.

4. *Journal of Lady Holland*, I, 225.

5. XXVII (Oct. 1799), 231. See also AR, N.S. I (May 1799), 522–524; MR, 2nd Series, XXX (Sept. 1799), 22–25.

6. John Gibson Lockhart, *Memoirs of the Life of Sir Walter Scott* (Boston and New York, 1902), I, 270.

7. I am indebted to Professor Alan D. McKillop of Rice Institute for bringing this letter to my attention. It was acquired by the Pierpont Morgan Library in 1952, after my inquiries there. The Cranstoun mentioned in the letter was George Cranstoun, Scottish law student, later Lord Corehouse, who died in 1850. The ballad of the knight and the Elfin Queen is presumably "Tam Lin."

8. For the text of this letter I follow Guthke, "Die Erste Nachwirkung," pp. 275–276; for the remaining letters in the Walpole Bequest, I have used photostats obtained before the recent publication of the letters.

9. The letter is misdated 1799, but not in Lewis' hand. Obviously it precedes the one next quoted, which is dated Dec. 15, 1798, by Lewis.

10. This letter, omitted in the *Archiv* article cited above (n.1) is dated "Wellwyn—99" by Lewis and "6 Jan^y 1799" in another hand.

11. In 1831 Scott wrote that he had never seen the published form of his translation of *Goetz*. He suffered some embarrassment from the fact that it had been published, unaccountably, as by "William" Scott, though both Lewis and Bell had addressed him in correspondence as "Walter." See *Letters of Sir Walter Scott, 1831–1832*, ed. H. J. C. Grierson (London, 1937), [XII], 10 (and n.), 16–17.

12. *The Letters of Sir Walter Scott, 1787–1807* (London, 1932), p. 96.

13. The letter is dated 1800 in MS, not in Lewis' hand. This may be correct, if some copies of *Tales of Wonder* appeared in that year (see n. 25 below); otherwise the letter is probably to be dated 1801.

14. For a description of *An Apology for Tales of Terror* (Kelso, 1799), and an account of its confusion with other books, see George P. Johnston, "The First Book Printed by James Ballantyne: Being An Apology for Tales of Terror; with Notes on Tales of Wonder and Tales of Terror," *PEBS, 1890–1895*, I [Part 4], Oct. 1894 (Edinburgh, 1896). The bibliographical elucidation in this article was restated and supplemented by Elizabeth Church, "A Bibliographical Myth," *MP*, XIX (Feb. 1922), 307–314, whose article was followed by Oliver Farrar Emerson's " 'Monk' Lewis and the *Tales of Terror*," *MLN*, XXVIII (Mar. 1923), 154–159. See further, Emerson, "The Early Literary Life of Sir Walter Scott," *JEGP*, XXIII (1924), 28–62, 241–269, 389–417. Johnston followed his article with "Note to a Paper Entitled The First Book Printed by James Ballantyne," *PEBS, 1904–1913*, IX (Part 2, Aug. 1912), 90.

15. Lockhart, I, 270.

16. "Essay on Imitations," *Minstrelsy of the Scottish Border*, p. 554.

17. Letter to Miss Christian Rutherford, in Lockhart, I, 255.

18. Introductory note to "Glenfinlas," in *The Poetical Works of Sir Walter Scott*, ed. J. Logie Robertson (London and New York, 1916), p. 685.

19. Letter of Oct. 22, 1824, in Thomas Constable, *Archibald Constable and his Literary Correspondents* (Edinburgh, 1873), III, 300.

20. *The Works of Lord Byron. Letters and Journals*, II, 317.

21. Note to "Frederick and Alice" in *Poetical Works of Scott*, p. 653.

22. For a study important for correcting Lockhart's sometimes inaccurate account of the dates of composition of these poems and their relation to Lewis, see Emerson, "Early Literary Life of Scott," especially pp. 34–50.

23. Appendix to "Essay on Imitations," Note D, in *Minstrelsy*, p. 565.

24. Introductory note to "Glenfinlas," in *Poetical Works of Scott*, p. 685.

25. Emerson (" 'Monk' Lewis," pp. 154–155) pointed out that the *British Critic* for December 1800 carries a notice of *"Tales of Wonder . . . 1800,"* and that Anna Seward on January 5, 1801, mentions having received a copy of the *Tales*; he therefore believed the work was printed in 1800 and

suggested that issue in 1800 was intended and that some copies were so dated, but that, delays bringing the work so near 1801, the latter date was used for most copies.

26. Introductory note to "Glenfinlas," p. 685.

27. See Anna Seward's letter of Jan. 5, 1801, to Thomas Park, in *Letters of Anna Seward* (Edinburgh, 1811), V, 342, and Scott's introductory note to "Glenfinlas," p. 685.

28. Pp. 14–15. Though *More Wonders* is usually described as anonymous, an obituary notice of Thomas Dermody (1774–1802) in *MMi*, XIV (Aug. 1802), 75–80, ascribes it to him (pp. 78–79). If it is his, Dermody changed his sentiments, or at least his tactics, toward Lewis. His *Poems, Moral, and Descriptive* (London, 1800), p. 102, contains a highly laudatory sonnet "To the Author of the Monk, &c. &c.", in which Lewis is hailed as second only to Ariosto in fancy.

29. *The Poetical Works of Robert Southey*, VI, 4.

30. In a note to "The Gay Gold Ring" Lewis wrote "I once read in some Grecian author, whose name I have forgotten, the story which suggested to me the outline of the foregoing ballad" (*Tales of Wonder*, London, 1801, I, 99). He had in mind a narrative which can be found in *Phlegontis Tralliani Opuscula*, ed. Io. Georg. Frid. Franzius (Halae Magdeburgicae, 1775), a fact pointed out by C. Thürnau, *Die Geister in der englischen Literatur des 18. Jahrhunderts: ein Beitrag zur Geschichte der Romantik*, Palaestra, LV (Berlin, 1906), pp. 105–106. Though Lewis may easily have read Goethe's *Die Braut von Korinth*, which uses the same theme, "The Gay Gold Ring" shows no debt to Goethe's poem. Nevertheless, Lewis has been accused of borrowing from Goethe and of deliberately hiding the fact by citing a "Greek Author," an imaginary source suggested to him by "Korinth" in Goethe's title. See Railo, *The Haunted Castle*, p. 351.

31. For English translations of this poem prior to Lewis', and for scholarly treatment of all the Scandinavian poems represented in *Tales of Wonder*, see Frank Edgar Farley, *Scandinavian Influences in the English Romantic Movement*, Harvard Studies and Notes in Philology and Literature, IX (Boston, 1903).

32. Though the Brown MS versions of "Clerk Colvin" and "Willy's Lady" were preserved by a transcript, that of "King Henry" was lost; but some idea of Lewis' editing is gained by comparing his "Courteous King Jamie" with that of the Jamieson-Brown MS version and with "King Henrie" ("corrected by a recited fragment") in Scott's *Minstrelsy*. See Francis James Child, *The English and Scottish Popular Ballads* (Boston [1882–98]), I, 297–299, 372, and Scott's *Minstrelsy*, pp. 467–470.

33. For comment on glossary mistakes in *Tales of Wonder*, see Thomas Bayne, "Scotch Words and English Commentators," *N&Q*, 9th Series, XI (Jan. 3, 1903), 1–2. The writer mistakenly attributes to Lewis *Tales of Terror and Wonder*, the title created by Henry Morley.

34. "Essay on Imitations," p. 560.

35. Letter of May 30, 1799, to William Taylor, in *A Memoir of the Life and Writings of the Late William Taylor of Norwich*, ed. J. W. Robberds (London, 1843), I, 281.

36. Letter of May 11, 1798, in *Selections from the Letters of Robert*

*Southey*, ed. John Wood Warter (London, 1856), I, 54. I am obliged to Professor Kenneth Curry of the University of Tennessee for calling my attention to this passage.

37. "St. Patrick's Purgatory" appeared anonymously in the *Morning Post*, whence Lewis probably took it. In reprinting it in his collected poetry in 1838, Southey recalled that Lewis had "found it among the wefts and strays of the Press. He never knew that it was mine; but after his death I bestowed some pains in recomposing it, because he had thought it worth preserving." See *Poetical Works of Southey* (1838), VI, 40. "Bishop Bruno," "Lord William," "The Pious Painter," and "Cornelius Agrippa's Bloody Book" were also available in the *Morning Post*. See the introductory notes to these ballads in *Poems of Robert Southey*, ed. Maurice H. Fitzgerald (London and New York, 1909).

38. See L. F. Peck, "Southey and *Tales of Wonder*," MLN L (Dec. 1935), 513–514.

39. *Cr R*, XXXIV (Jan. 1802), 112, a review of the second edition, apparently by Coleridge.

40. London, 1801. The author explains in prefatory remarks (p. 3) that the verses were not designed for publication but found their way in a form containing many errors into a collection of poems called *The School for Satire*. A copy in the British Museum contains a MS note: "A privately Printed tract, satirical upon *Monk* Lewis. I find it reprinted in *Pieces of Poetry, with Two Dramas*. 2 vols. *Priv: Printed*. Chiswick. 1830. bearing internal Evidence of being the Works of *Geo. Watson Taylor*." The note, dated June 16, 1857, is signed "A.G.," presumably Alexander Gardine, whose name is stamped on the verso of the title page. On the other hand, Byron notes a poem in *The Statesman*, "supposed to be written by Mr. Jekyll," containing the line "For every one knows little Matt's an M.P." See *The Works of Lord Byron. Poetry*, ed. E. H. Coleridge (London and New York, 1901), I, 319n1.

41. A MS of the poem is inserted in a copy of *Tales of Wonder* (1801) at the Yale University Library. On an end page of Vol. I, a MS note signed "Stuart M. Samuel/May 1896" reads "The two parodies of Lewis' 'Wonder Tales' inserted in this volume are apparently by Sir Walter Scott & Robert Southey, contributors to the series." But the volume contains only one inserted poem, from which I quote with the permission of the library.

42. By Johnston's article cited above, n. 14.

43. *Life*, II, 43–45, 356.

44. A three-volume edition printed for R. Sammer, bookseller, Vienna, 1805, contains all the ballads which appeared in the first edition; and to fill out the third volume, seventeen other poems from various sources, including several by Wordsworth from *Lyrical Ballads*—an early borrowing, perhaps hitherto unnoticed, from that collection.

45. Not having seen Zschokke's prose work or his dramatic version, I rely for the plot on Carl Günther's summary in *Heinrich Zschokkes Jungend- und Bildungsjahre. . .* (Aarau, 1918), pp. 103–105. On the date of publication of the prose work, see Günther, p. 238n250. For a thorough treatment of Lewis' translation of Zschokke, correcting accounts by earlier scholars, see Guthke, *Englische Vorromantik*, ch. 12.

46. A review in *MMi*, XIX (Mar. 1805), 177, gives 1804 as the date of publication, as do several later accounts such as Summers' *Gothic Bibliography* (1940), p. 96. I have never seen a copy with the title page so dated and am inclined to believe that the date of Lewis' dedication (p. iii), Oct. 27, 1804, is the source of an error.

47. Lewis' source was pointed out by Georg Herzfeld, "Die Eigentliche Quelle von Lewis' 'Monk,'" *Archiv*, CXI (N.S. XI, Dec. 1903), 316–323. The length of the work and perhaps the difficulty of obtaining both the German and the English texts appear to have discouraged examination of *Feudal Tyrants* as a translation. It was described in the *Life* as "rather an English work copied from the German, than a translation of any portion of German literature" (II, 44); by Herzfeld as "nichts als eine ziemlich freie Uebersetzung" ("Eigentliche Quelle," p. 319); by Railo as "a fairly faithful translation" (*Haunted Castle*, p. 122); by V. Stockley as "a romance from the German," "really rather an English tale imitated from the German than an actual translation," and "a free imitation of a German work" (*German Literature as Known in England, 1750–1830*, pp. 219, 220, 297); Summers gave a synopsis of the story without reference to the German text (*Gothic Quest*, pp. 277–278). For the latter I have used *Elisabeth, Erbin von Toggenburg. . .*, Neue Ausgabe (Leipzig, 1799). Karl S. Guthke has recently scrutinized Lewis' translation of Naubert in great detail. See his *Englische Vorromantik*, pp. 184–196.

48. *Feudal Tyrants* (London, 1806), I, 1n.

49. For instance: "Gott weiss, welches die Quellen unüberwindbarer Macht sind, welche man in unsern Tagen immer bey den geistlichen Fürsten findet. Feige Herzen, schwache Arme, sorglose Unthätigkeit, welche Gegner für ritterliche Stärke und Heldenmuth!—Ohne Zweifel schlingt eine unsichtbare Ketter alle Söhne der Kirche insgeheim zasammen, und wird das Mittel, sei immer den Weltlichen überlegen zu erhalten so oft sie auch von ihnen besiegt werden" (p. 50); "Was ist schlauen Mönchen unmöglich?— der Schreiber dieser Blätter redet wider seinen Stand, aber er wiederholt es nochmals, was ist schlauer Bosheit, im Gewand der Heiligkeit, unmöglich?" (p. 516).

50. 2nd Series, LIII (Aug. 1807), 437–438.

51. 3rd Series, XI (July 1807), 273–278.

52. Guthke reports that *Les Orphelines de Werdenberg* (Paris, 1809), sometimes believed to have no connection with Lewis, is in fact a rather close translation of *Feudal Tyrants*, as the title page professes. As evidence of Lewis' popularity in France, the same writer points out that *La Soirée d'Eté*, two parts (Paris, 1801), "par l'auteur du Moine, traduit de l'anglais sur la 2e édition" is, on the other hand, not derived from anything by Lewis. See Guthke, "Some Bibilographical Errors Concerning the Romantic Age," *PBSA*, LI (2nd quarter, 1957), 159–160, and *Englische Vorromantik*, pp. 196–197.

53. I, 244. For some ballads not elsewhere published, see *Life*, I, ch. 9.

54. The letter is dated Jan. [23], 1798 in *Collected Letters of Samuel Taylor Coleridge*, I, 379.

55. Prefatory remarks by "P.P.," p. vi, Oxberry's New English Drama, XIX (London, 1824).

56. Adolphus, *Memoirs of John Bannister* (London, 1838), II, 52.

57. *Reminiscences of Michael Kelly*, p. 300.

58. *Ibid.*, p. 306.

59. A Drury Lane playbill of Apr. 19, 1813, in the HCL Theatre Collection announces a new ballad, "Beauty in Tears," composed by Parry, "the words adapted by M. G. Lewis, Esq." The bill for Apr. 20, however, gives it as "written and arranged" by Parry, while Lewis is named as adapter of the words of "a Simple Original COSSACK AIR," and so in later bills.

60. *Life*, I, 31, 246.

61. London. Printed and sold by Rt. Birchall, No. 133, New Bond Street. The only copy I have seen—BM pressmark H. 1797. pp. (12)—though displaying Lewis' note dated May 22, 1808, is watermarked 1822 and so must be a later issue.

62. A BM copy (pressmark H. 1416/3.), the only one I have seen, is undated, on paper watermarked 1804. The BM Catalogue gives "1809?" Since it was entered in the copyright register at Stationers' Hall on July 26, 1808, I assume that it was published in the latter half of 1808.

63. Drury Lane playbills in the HCL Theatre Collection for May 30, 1800, and May 22, 1802. One for Feb. 12, 1806, reads "Mr. BRAHAM will introduce a NEW AIR. Written for the Occasion [benefit night for the widow of the comedian Thomas King] by G. M. [*sic*] Lewis, Esq."; another, for June 6, 1817, "a new Hunting Song composed by . . . [J. Smith], called 'Now blushing Aurora peeps over the Plains,' the Words by LEE LEWIS, Esq.," possibly an error for M. G. Lewis. Charles Lee *Lewes* died in 1803.

64. *Romantic Tales* (London, 1808), I, vii–viii.

65. The Spanish versions of all six are available in Don Agustin Duran, *Romancero General, ó Coleccion de Romances Castellanos*, Vols. X and XVI of *Biblioteca Autores Españoles* (Madrid, 1849–51). In that work they are not listed by title but are numbered as follows: *Zayde and Zayda* 53, *Durandarte and Belerma* 387, *Admiral Guarino* 402, *King Rodrigo's Fall* 602, *The Loss of Alhama* 1064, *Alatar* 1109. For collections of Spanish ballads prior to Duran's which Lewis might have used, see George Ticknor, *History of Spanish Literature* (Boston, 1872), III, Appendix B, pp. 472–482.

66. Guthke has anticipated me in pointing out this fact. See "Some Unidentified Early English Translations from Herder's *Volkslieder*," *MLN*, LXXIII (Jan. 1958), 52–56.

67. In his preface to *Romantic Tales* Lewis quotes a description of the castle from "Wallis's 'History of the Antiquities of Northumberland' " and refers the reader to "Grose's Antiquities of England and Wales." Since the description by Wallis is quoted in Grose, Lewis may have used only the latter. See Francis Grose, *The Antiquities of England and Wales*, 2nd ed. (London, 1783), IV, 87.

68. A Drury Lane playbill in the HCL Theatre Collection for May 23, 1809, announces: "Mr. RAYMOND, will recite an interesting traditionary tale, entitled 'BILL JONES; or, the Ship Spectre.' "

69. See Scott's letter of Aug. 10, 1802, to Lady Anne Hamilton, in *Letters of Scott, 1787–1807*, p. 151.

70. *Romantic Tales*, I, viii–ix.

71. *Romantic Tales*, I, 20–21.

72. These remarks on *Mistrust* are drawn from Louis F. Peck, "An Adaptation of Kleist's *Die Familie Schroffenstein*," *JEGP*, XLIV (Jan. 1945), 9–11.

73. Appendix to Vol. XXX (1768), pp. 673–676.

74. N.S. V (Sept. 1808), 121–127. This small discovery was not the reward of laborious search. I found the article in the *Scots Magazine* and the *Lady's Monthly Museum* after noting that both are cited in the NED, to which I had turned in idle curiosity to see when the word *anaconda* entered the language.

75. See Guthke, "Some Notes," p. 282.

76. Lewis' source was identified by Martha Pike Conant, *The Oriental Tale in England in the Eighteenth Century* (New York, 1908), p. 71.

77. A copy of *Romantic Tales* in the Dyce Collection, Victoria and Albert Museum, contains a note in Alexander Dyce's hand: "Bell (the bookseller in Oxford Street and the publisher of Lewis's *Monk*) told me that he had in his keeping for many years the manuscript of *The Four Facardins* (see vol. ii), Lewis having originally intended that it should be published by him."

78. Lewis' only considerable addition is an introductory paragraph. He omits one passage apparently by an oversight. Compare *Romantic Tales*, II, 123–124, 208, with *Oeuvres du Comte Hamilton*, ed. J. B. J. Champagnac (Paris, 1825), II, 220, 266–269.

79. For instance, compare, in Wieland's satiric novel *Don Rosalvo von Rosalva* (Book I, ch. 10), the "feurige Kugel" which descends from the heavens, bursts, and reveals a beautiful fairy in a chariot of carbuncles drawn by serpents, with a similar phenomenon in Lewis' continuation (*Romantic Tales*, III, 23–27). Instead of a fairy, Lewis presents a hideous hag of the sort Wieland was fond of depicting. For a number of other resemblances, compare *Romantic Tales*, III, 25–27, with *Don Rosalvo*, Book II, ch. 2. Lewis' scene in which the court attendants dance against their will to the magic guitar suggests Wieland's monks and nuns similarly enchanted by the fairy horn in *Oberon* (*Romantic Tales*, III, 84–86: *Oberon*, Canto II, stanzas 37–38). Incidentally, Lewis translated Wieland's poem "Hann und Gulpenhé" as "The Taylor's Wife," published in the *Life* (II, 325–338), as was pointed out by Emil Koeppel, "Matthew Gregory Lewis's Gedicht 'The Tailor's Wife' und Bulwer's 'Wife of Miletus,'" *Germanistische Abhandlungen*, ed. Hermann Paul (Strassburg, 1902), pp. 135–142. See also Guthke, *Englische Vorromantik*, ch. 3.

80. LXXIX (Feb. 1809), 141.

81. *Romantic Tales by M. G. Lewis. Containing My Uncle's Garret Window; The Anaconda; and Amorassan* was published by William Smith (London, 1838). Lewis' translation and continuation of Hamilton's story, together with a continuation by "Monsieur de Levis," appeared as *The Four Facardins. A Fairy Tale by Count Anthony Hamilton* for the Lutetian Society (London, 1899), in an edition limited to 680 copies.

82. See Louis F. Peck. "M. G. Lewis and the Larpent *Catalogue*,"

*HLQ*, V (Apr. 1942), 383. For a derogatory review of the performance, see *MMi*, N.S. V (Feb. 1809), 118.

83. *Eu M*, LV (Feb. 1809), 144.

84. 2nd Series, LXI (Feb. 1810), 207.

85. *Monody on the Death of Sir John Moore* (London, 1809), p. viii. The *Life* states that only fifty copies were printed (I, 377).

86. In a letter to Miss Clavering, undated but assigned to 1812 in *Letters from and to Charles Kirkpatrick Sharpe*, II, 42.

87. Letter of Oct. 6, 1812, to Walter Scott, *ibid.*, II, 26. Of the first poem in the book, "Love at Sale," there is in the University of Kansas Library a holograph with Lewis' signature, addressed to "William Lock Jun^r Esq^r/Manchester Square." I am obliged to Professor Joseph Rubinstein, University of Kansas, for this information and for a photostat of the MS. "Pleasure and Desire" was sung in *Rich and Poor* (1812) to music by J. Arnold. For a parody by William Tierney of "Address to Youth," see *Journal of Lady Holland*, II, 74–75, entry for Apr. 27, 1800.

## CHAPTER 6. JAMAICA

1. Forster Collection, No. 91.

2. The will as written in 1800 provided £13,300 for Sophia; but a suitable arrangement having been made for her at her marriage, the provision was revoked in a codicil of January 17, 1804. The will was proved May 30, 1812. A copy is at Somerset House.

3. Letter of May 27, 1812, to James St. Aubyn, in my possession. James was the heir and eldest natural son of Sir John St. Aubyn (1758–1839), fifth Baronet, for whom see *DNB*.

4. The will is reproduced in part in the *Life*, II, 373–381. A complete copy is in Somerset House.

5. See a copy of the codicil in Somerset House. An inaccurate, undated transcript, now in the Forster Collection, was published with further errors in the *Life*, II, 382–388. Ten children of Maria's were living when Lewis died, five of Sophia's. See a "Petition of Appeal" in Chancery (Lushington *vs.* Sewell, June 24, 1829; C. 36, Bundle 29), at the Public Record Office, London, consisting of twenty-eight MS pages containing information about Lewis' Jamaica property and the Lushington and Sewell families.

6. This change was made before Nov. 1, 1815, the date of additional provisions published without date in the *Life*, II, 387–388.

7. Letter of Aug. 1812, in *Letters from and to Charles Kirkpatrick Sharpe, Esq.*, II, 10.

8. *Life*, II, 107–118, and *M. G. Lewis. Journal of a West India Proprietor, 1815–17*, ed. Mona Wilson (Boston and New York, 1929), p. 6.

9. The letter, in my possession, is dated Feb. 23, postmarked 1815.

10. *Further Memoirs of the Whig Party . . . by Henry Richard Vassall, Third Lord Holland*, ed. Lord Stavordale (New York, 1905), pp. 379–380.

11. Medwin, *Conversations of Lord Byron*, p. 236.

12. *Poems* (London, 1812), p. 34.

13. *Journal of a West India Proprietor* (London, 1834), p. 100. Subsequent citations to this work appear in the text as J followed by page numbers.

14. *Memoirs, Journal, and Correspondence of Thomas Moore*, VIII, 48.

15. Add. MS. 38,416, fol. 125.

16. "Petition of Appeal," p. 19.

17. *Ibid.*, pp. 19–20.

18. [John Stewart], *An Account of Jamaica and Its Inhabitants, by a Gentleman Long Resident in the West Indies* (London, 1808), pp. 126–143. For an estimate of Stewart's book by a modern student of Jamaican history, see Ragatz, *A Guide for the Study of British Caribbean History, 1763–1834*, p. 234.

19. Letter to Thomas Moore of Nov. 4, 1815, in *The Works of Lord Byron. Letters and Journals*, III, 244.

20. Letter of Nov. 7, 1815, *Life*, II, 122.

21. Letter of Jan. 10, 1816, *Life*, II, 126.

22. *Life*, II, 152–155.

23. See Lewis' letter of Oct. 16, 1817, to William Wilberforce in *Correspondence of William Wilberforce*, II, 384.

24. For a collection and an account of Annancy stories, see Walter Jekyll, *Jamaican Song and Story: Annancy Stories, Digging Sings, Ring Tunes, and Dancing Tunes* (London, 1907), published for the Folk-Lore Society, Vol. LV.

25. *Life of William Wilberforce* (London, 1838), IV, 292. Cynric R. Williams' *Tour through the Island of Jamaica* . . . (London, 1826) relates that Lewis arrived in Jamaica with exaggerated ideas of the cruelty inflicted upon the negroes and having found the opposite to be true, gave his revised impressions to Wilberforce, who "treated all he said with contempt or indifference" (pp. 76–77). But Williams' book is a proslavery account and hostile to Wilberforce. Ragatz (p. 237) finds it filled with "wild exaggerations and misstatements from cover to cover."

26. Letter of Nov. 20, 1816, to James St. Aubyn, in my possession.

27. Letter of Nov. 7, 1815, *Life*, II, 123.

28. Of Lewis' lost journal Charles Greville wrote in his memoirs on July 18, 1833: "I have read his Italian journal, which is entertaining but not so much so as the other [the Jamaica journal published in 1834], the subject being so much more hackneyed" (II, 398). Some five years later (Jan. 5, 1838) he wrote: "I am sadly annoyed to-day having got into a scrape about Lewis's Italian Journal. I sold the copyright to Bentley for £100, and now Lushington writes me word he will not have it published. If Bentley makes any difficulty I don't know what will happen." His footnote to this records that Bentley gave up the MS. See *The Greville Memoirs, 1814–1860*, ed. Lytton Strachey and Roger Fulford (London, 1938), II, 398, and IV, 11.

29. Shelley's *Journal* for Aug. 18, 1816, in *Complete Works of Shelley*, VI, 147.

30. Hobhouse's diary for July 2, 1811, in *Recollections of a Long Life*, I, 35.

31. Mary Shelley's introduction to the 1831 edition of *Frankenstein*, reprinted in the Everyman Library edition (London and New York, 1930), pp. viii–ix.

32. *The Diary of Dr. John William Polidori, 1816, Relating to Byron, Shelley, etc.*, ed. William Michael Rossetti (London, 1911), p. 125.

33. In addition to the five in Shelley's *Journal*, Medwin (*Conversations*, pp. 230–233) records two as repeated by Byron; two more are recounted in *Recollections of the Table-Talk of Samuel Rogers. To Which Is Added Porsoniana* (London, 1856), pp. 164–170. Another appears in the anonymous *Murdered Queen! Or, Caroline of Brunswick*, by a "Lady of Rank" (London, 1838), pp. 28–36. This work also contains (pp. 132–149) a story which the author professes to have taken from the MS of "Lord Byron's 'Guzman.' A Legend of Horror."

34. Shelley's *Journal* for Aug. 18, 1816, in *Complete Works of Shelley*, VI (1929), 147.

35. Letter of Apr. 4, 1817, in Byron, *Letters and Journals*, IV, 97.

36. J. G. Robertson, "Goethe and Byron," *Publications of the English Goethe Society*, N.S. II (1925), 10–11.

37. Letter of June 7, 1820, in Byron, *Letters and Journals*, V, 37. See also a letter of Apr. 4, 1817, to Samuel Rogers, *ibid.*, IV, 97.

38. Letter of Apr. 4, 1817, to Samuel Rogers, *ibid.*, IV, 97.

39. *Life*, II, 162.

40. Letter of Oct. 11, 1816, to John Plummer.

41. *Autograph Prices Current*, ed. A. J. Herbert (London, n.d.), VI, 100, records a letter, which I have not succeeded in tracing, from Lewis to Byron "giving an interesting description of the Simplon, etc., and containing some original verses, 13 lines . . . , Como, Sept. 1, 1816."

42. Letter of Jan. 2, 1821, in Byron, *Letters and Journals*, V, 213.

43. *The Two Duchesses . . . Family Correspondence of and relating to Georgiana, Duchess of Devonshire . . .*, ed. Vere Foster, 2nd ed. (London, 1898), p. 425.

44. His letter of Mar. 13, from Naples, says "I have now been here for nine weeks" (F 105).

45. See especially Lewis' letters of Feb. 24, 1805 (F 64), and one undated (F 66).

46. *Greville Memoirs*, II, 386–387.

47. Copy of codicil in Somerset House.

48. *Rome, Naples, et Florence*, ed. Calmann-Lévy (Paris, n.d.), p. 261. The passage is dated March 22.

49. Byron, *Letters and Journals*, IV, 142.

50. Byron's letter of July 15, 1817, to John Murray, *ibid.*, IV, 150.

51. Byron's letter of July 10, 1817, to Moore, *ibid.*, IV, 150, and Hobhouse's diary for July 31, 1817, *Recollections* II, 74.

52. *Detached Thoughts*, in Byron, *Letters and Journals*, V, 418.

53. Hobhouse's diary for Aug. 9, 1817, in *Recollections*, II, 76.

54. Byron's preface to *Marino Faliero*, in *The Works of Lord Byron. Poetry*, IV, 337.

55. Hobhouse's diary for Aug. 9, 1817, in *Recollections*, II, 77. The canto then consisted of 130 stanzas, the remainder being written after Lewis' departure.

56. Hobhouse's diary for Aug. 9, 1817, *Recollections*, II, 76–77.

57. Letter of Apr. 17, 1818, Mrs. Leigh to Lady Byron. Ralph Milbanke, Earl of Lovelace, *Astarte: A Fragment of Truth Concerning George Gordon Byron* . . . (New York, 1921), p. 349n2.

58. *The Academy. A Record of Literature, Learning, Science, and Art*, I, (Oct. 9, 1869), 1.

59. Lewis' *Journal*, ed. Mona Wilson, p. 13. For an interesting note on Tita, see pp. 345–346n18.

60. Letter of Aug. 9–10, 1821, to Mary Wollstonecraft Shelley, in *Complete Works of Shelley*, X, 305.

61. *Life*, II, 230, quoting "Miss F," a fellow passenger.

62. *Detached Thoughts*, in Byron, *Letters and Journals*, V, 418.

63. He anticipates this route in the letter of Oct. 11, 1816, to Plummer.

64. The letter is quoted in an undated bookseller's catalogue (No. 7) of J. Pearson & Co., 46 Pall Mall, Item 244, p. 20, in Vol. II of Catalogue of Autographs, HCL pressmark B 3850.5.

65. Letter of Oct. 11, 1816, to Plummer. The "Petition of Appeal" states that articles of agreement for Lewis' purchase were executed on or about Oct. 31, 1817, and that John Plummer and William Wilson, succeeding Thomas Plummer, were employed by Lewis as Messrs. Plummer and Co. as consignees of the produce of his Jamaica property.

66. "Petition of Appeal," pp. 19–20.

67. *Correspondence of Wilberforce*, II, 382. The reference must be to the Hordley purchase. In addition to the Cornwall and Hordley estates, Lewis owned at the time of his death two pieces of uncultivated land near Hector's River comprising about six hundred acres ("Petition of Appeal," p. 20).

68. *Life*, II, 190.

69. The letter is quoted in a bookseller's catalogue (No. 117) dated 1878, of John Waller, 2 Artesian Road, London, Item 120, p. 6, in Vol. III of Catalogue of Autographs, HCL pressmark B 3850.5. The letter as quoted is undated and could have been written before Lewis' first voyage to Jamaica. In the *Life* it is assigned to his second departure (II, 191).

70. According to a fellow passenger's account (*Life*, II, 202–203) and *The Court Magazine*, IV, (Feb. 1834), 80.

71. See also the letter of Mar. 31, 1818, to his mother (F 107–108).

72. R. R. Madden, *A Twelvemonth's Residence in the West Indies* (Philadelphia, 1835), II, 24, 27. For an estimate of this work and its author, see Ragatz, p. 229.

73. Madden, II, 25.

74. *Ibid.*, II, 31.

75. *Life*, II, 273.

76. Letter of Jan. 24, 1819, Sophia Shedden to Walter Scott, W, IX, fol. 10. The letter was published in part in *The Private Letter-Books of Sir Walter Scott: Selections from the Abbotsford Manuscripts*, ed. Wilfred Partington (London, 1930), pp. 228–230. John Murray wrote to Byron on July 7, 1818: "You will have read with surprise and regret an account of the death of your friend Monk Lewis on his return from a second voyage to the West Indies. He sent me his MS. notes upon the place to read, and very curious indeed they were, and I hope they will not be lost." Samuel Smiles, *A Publisher and His Friends: Memoir and Correspondence of the Late John Murray* (London, 1891), I, 395–396.

77. W, IX, fol. 10.

78. *Greville Memoirs*, II, 384.

79. *Ibid.*, II, 392–393, 398.

80. *Table Talk*, Mar. 20, 1834, in *The Complete Works of Samuel Taylor Coleridge*, ed. W. G. T. Shedd (New York, 1884), VI, 507.

81. With a new title page reading "new edition."

82. By Mona Wilson. See n. 8 above.

83. W. Adolphe Roberts, *Jamaica: The Portrait of an Island* (New York, 1955), p. 192.

84. LIX (Apr. 1834), 75.

85. *Table Talk*, VI, 507.

86. The Kingston edition (1827) is distinguished by two typographical errors on the title page: "Funnded" for "Founded" and "Kingtson" for "Kingston." The London publication (1812) appeared in an edition limited to 250 copies and a "Large Paper Edition" limited to 20 copies.

87. The letter, in my possession, has for outside address "T. Hill Esq^re," and the following note in another hand: "This is the last letter M^r Lewis ever wrote he died about 10 days after at Sea, this was written the Morn^g he sailed May 1818. T. Hill." In the second sentence the word following "am" is blotted and illegible; the spelling "Blackeston" is not certain; "necessity" is supplied, a hole occurring between "the" and "of"; after "Wife" a half line is torn and illegible. The last paragraph is written above the inside address. I am indebted to Professor Philip A. Shelley of Pennsylvania State University for calling my attention to this letter when it was offered for sale.

88. II, 198–205, 229–235, 368–372.

89. IV (Feb. 1834), 80–81.

90. Letter of July 17, 1818, to James St. Aubyn, in my possession.

91. Entry for June 30, 1818, *Recollections*, II, 100.

92. The *Sir Godfrey Webster* arrived at Deal and "sailed for the River" on June 22, 1818. See the *Courier*, No. 8022 (June 23, 1818), p. [3], under "Naval Intelligence." The captain's name is there given as Bayes; in the *Life* as Boyes.

93. Michael Kelly, *Reminiscences* (New York, 1826), p. 287.

94. *The Diary of a Lady-in-Waiting by Lady Charlotte Bury*, II, 240.

95. Kelly, *Reminiscences*, pp. 286–287.

96. The notice with slight differences in wording appeared in the

*Morning Chronicle* and the *Times,* June 24, and the *General Evening Post,*
June 23–25.

97. LXXXVIII (Aug. 1818), 183–184.

98. *The Courier* (London), No. 8133, p. [4].

99. Sophia's letter to Walter Scott, Jan. 24, 1819, W, IX, fol. 10. I
have consulted the *Courier* but neither of the other two periodicals. According to Sophia, an answer was inserted in one of them, but in which her
letter does not make clear.

100. An undated letter from Sophia to Walter Scott (W, IX, fol. 8)
which follows the letter last quoted mentions as about to be published
Scott's review of *Tales of the Dead.* This work is treated in an article in the
*Quarterly Review,* XXII (Jan. 1820), 348–380, without mention of Lewis.
The article is apparently not by Scott, since it contains complimentary
references to him and disagrees with one of his opinions.

101. The letter of July 17, 1818, cited above.

102. *Further Memoirs of the Whig Party,* ed. Lord Stavordale (New
York, 1905), p. 379.

103. Diary for Aug. 7, 1817, Hobhouse, II, 76.

104. Letter of July 17, 1818, cited above. I have improved Mrs. Blake's
punctuation of this passage.

# INDEX